D0895440

# CHRISTIANS AND JEWS IN GERMANY

Religion, Politics, and Ideology in
the Second Reich, 1870–1914

TAL, Uriel. **Christians and Jews in Germany; religion, politics, and ideology in the Second Reich, 1870–1914; tr. by N. J. Jacobs. Cornell, 1975. 359p il bibl 74-21612. 19.50. ISBN 0-8014-0879-2**

This book of impeccable scholarship is ground-breaking in its field. It presents a comprehensive analysis of the relationships between Jews and Gentiles in Germany during the years 1870–1914. Tal traces the growth of anti-Semitism as an important political force during the Second Reich, with special emphasis on its Christian religious roots. He does so while presenting his subject in the context of social and political phenomena current at the time. Tal also discusses the position of the Jews in German society and their reaction to anti-Semitism. The book is based on exhaustive research in German and Israeli archives. Tal, who is one of the leading scholars in this field, demonstrates in this book his considerable erudition in history, philosophy, and theology. The book contains a very valuable bibliographical essay and an index. It is highly recommended to all serious scholars in the field of German and Jewish history.

# CHRISTIANS AND JEWS IN GERMANY

Religion, Politics, and Ideology in
the Second Reich, 1870-1914

by URIEL TAL

translated by
Noah Jonathan Jacobs

CORNELL UNIVERSITY PRESS

ITHACA AND LONDON

This work is an authorized translation of the Hebrew original, (1914–1870) "יהדות ונצרות ב'רייך השני [Christians and Jews in the 'Second Reich' (1870–1914)], © The Magnes Press, The Hebrew University, Jerusalem, 1969.

This translation has been brought to publication with the aid of the Leo Baeck Institute. Cornell University Press also gratefully acknowledges a grant from the Andrew J. Mellon Foundation that aided in bringing this book to publication.

First published 1975 by Cornell University Press.
Published in the United Kingdom by Cornell University Press Ltd.,
2–4 Brook Street, London W1Y 1AA.

International Standard Book Number 0-8014-0879-2
Library of Congress Catalog Card Number 74-21612
Printed in the United States of America by Vail-Ballou Press, Inc.

TO MIRIK

# Contents

Foreword                                                          9
    by Shmuel Ettinger
Introduction                                                     15
Abbreviations                                                    25

**1** | The German Intellectuals and the Dynamics of Jewish
        Integration and Identity                                31
        The Intellectuals in the Second Reich      31
        Changing Attitudes of the Intellectuals      34
        Conflicting Opinions regarding Jewish Integration and
            Identity      63
        Conclusion      78

**2** | The *Kulturkampf* and the Status of the Jews
        in Germany                                              81
        *Kulturkampf*—Idea and Reality      81
        Catholic Attitudes toward Judaism and the Jews      85
        Changing Attitudes of the Jews      96
        The *Kulturkampf* and the Legal Status of the Jewish
            Communities      110
        Conclusion      118

**3** | The Christian State and the Jewish Citizen              121
        The Christian State—Watchword of Conservatism      121
        Internal Politics and Conservative Protestants      123
        Conservatism and Modernism      143
        Conclusion      156

**4** | Protestantism and Judaism in Liberal Perspective    160

Liberals among the Protestants and Jews    160
Negation of the "Christian State"    167
The Common Denominator    176
Conflict within Unity    191
Conclusion    220

**5** | Christian and Anti-Christian Anti-Semitism    223

Clarification of Terms    223
Christian Anti-Semitism    235
Anti-Christian Anti-Semitism    259
Conclusion    279

Conclusion                                                        290
Appendix: Facsimiles of Documents                                307
Bibliographical Essay                                            325
Index                                                            349

# Foreword

There has been no dearth of theories to explain the phenomenon of modern anti-Semitism in general and of German anti-Semitism in particular. Some writers stress the economic and social dislocations that accompanied Germany's rapid industrial expansion in the second half of the nineteenth century; others emphasize the peculiar social structure that had been imposed on the country by a victorious Prussia which left the political power in the hands of the hereditary aristocracy and Junkers, who exploited the craving of the middle classes for state protection. Still others discovered the chief cause of anti-Semitism in the basic ideological change that occurred when the country abandoned its rationalist humanistic outlook and traditional Christian principles in exchange for radical attitudes based on Social Darwinism and racial theories. All these factors doubtless played a considerable part in shaping political life and social ideologies in the later days of the German Empire. It seems, however, that the manifold problems connected with the growing power and influence of modern anti-Semitism are far more complex than the present-day literature on the subject would have us believe.

The distinction of this book lies in its essentially different assessment of the position of the Jews in the social and cultural life of Germany. The author does not subscribe to the view that German anti-Semitism was created by Nazi propaganda, that it arose with the "destruction of German political life," or that it was merely a chapter in the conflict between the state and the various classes that comprise society. Such interpretations tend to select one factor as an *unum necessarium* to serve as a comprehensive explanation of a complex phenomenon. This book analyzes the position of the Jews—a people with an ancient history, religion, and culture generally rejected by traditional European conceptions but preserved in their group consciousness—within German society at a time when it was passing through a difficult period of consolidation. The Jews are here regarded not merely as the object of historical events and changing conditions but as an active and influential element in its own right and one that played an important part in the general development of the country both by what it did and by what it failed to do. A broad and confident knowledge of the basic principles that underlie the complex social and intellectual developments in Germany and among the Jews enables Dr. Tal to examine the subtle forces behind the discordant doctrines that characterize this period of German history. An important segment of German society of that time, the political Left, is not treated by the author. This omission, however, does not impair the unity of the book or detract from its comprehensiveness and permits him to concentrate on some of the fundamental problems in the sphere of "the history of ideas."

The author does not restrict his discussion to a clarification of the historical roots of German anti-Semitism but deals with the whole complexity of the relations between Jews and Christians during the period of the Second Reich and their far-reaching consequences. One important conclusion that can be drawn from this comprehensive analysis is that the bulk of German society was either unwilling or unable to accept the existence of Jews as a distinct entity with a group consciousness of its own. Despite their different attitudes and conflicting ideologies, this was the prevailing view among the Liberal Progressives as among the extreme conservatives (and even among the Social Democrats). This attitude toward the Jews followed from the basic principle that did not recognize the right of heterogeneous elements to exist as distinctive minorities within the larger society. The price exacted for inclusion in the German nation was the effacement of all distinctive traits and the consequent loss of self-identity. The author, to be sure, is not unaware of the vast difference between those who looked forward to the eventual absorption and integration of the Jews and those who completely rejected the Jews for political, theological, or racial reasons on the grounds that the Jews were a source of "shallow rationalism" or "pernicious Manchesterism" in Germany, which was a "Christian country," and that there was an unbridgeable gulf between what they called the Semitic and the Aryan "essence." It is clear, however, that the genuine liberal attitude was not confined to any one group or party and that it was found among devout Catholics as among radical freethinkers. Dr. Tal's researches confirm the historical fact, also evident in other countries and in other periods, that precisely those who remain faithful to Christian tradition can find a definite place for Jews as a separate group within the nation whereas the extreme liberals, although prepared to admit into their society individuals of Jewish origin, deny that Judaism can have any meaningful existence within the framework of modern society and hence demand of members of the minority group that they sever all ties with their historic and religious heritage.

The abundant source material on which the author bases his study presents a dismal picture of a deep-rooted fear and hatred of Jews and Judaism among all classes of the population. The "Jewish question" was not one of marginal or secondary importance; it reflected the peculiar problems of that period. Another highly instructive conclusion derived from Dr. Tal's study is that the efforts of the Jews were ineffectual and at no time succeeded in breaking down the barrier of distrust and ill-will between them and the dominant majority—despite the Kantian constructions of Hermann Cohen, the sociopsychological principles of Moritz Lazarus and Heymann Steinthal, or the many expressions of patriotic sentiment on the part of the Jewish community as revealed in the publications and private documents of Jewish individuals and organizations. The deep gulf that separated Jews from non-Jews was undeniable. The Jews for the most part moved in Jewish circles, and they were of the opinion that their existence as a separate group within German society was legitimately derived from the universally accepted rational principles of a *Rechtstaat* based on individual rights and on the clear-cut separation of the political sphere from the sphere of faith and belief. But there were many Germans, perhaps the preponderant part of the population, who were unwilling to tolerate the Jews in their midst, and this must be borne in mind if we are to understand German anti-Semitism after the downfall of the Second Reich. From the highly instructive concluding chapter, "Christian and Anti-Christian Anti-Semitism," we learn that these two phenomena, particularly the latter, were not yet deeply rooted in German life at this period. After the outspoken anti-Semitic parties had made slight gains at the beginning of the 1890's their political power and public influence continued to decline until the beginning of the century. One of the chief contributions of this book toward the understanding of the nature of anti-Semitism consists in the distinction it makes between a politically well-organized and an intellectually rationalized tacit anti-Semitism. However, despite the rapid decline of these outspoken anti-Semitic parties their work had not been in vain. A number of their arguments and slogans were incorporated in the party platforms and publications of other parties and also adopted by more influential and "respectable" civic and social groups, thus serving to exacerbate chronic anti-Jewish feeling among the general public and the educated classes, who were not unreceptive to anti-Semitic propaganda. Because of the decline of these political parties, insufficient attention has been paid to anti-Semitism as an effective ideological weapon in the social life of Germany at the turn of the century.

The effectiveness of anti-Semitic propaganda was to a large extent due to the intensity of the political struggle between the opposing camps in Germany during the period of the Second Reich, and also to the political course adopted by the Left after the revocation of the antisocialist law in 1890. All the "Christian" traditional and "patriotic" elements in society were animated by a mythical belief in Germany's historic mission, and one of the strongest emotions they shared was an intense hatred of the Jew and the complete rejection of Judaism. Those who rejected this attitude—namely, the Social Democrats and the small liberal groups of freethinkers, who were called by the journalists of that day "the corps of Jewish defenders" (*Judenschutztruppe*)—were reviled as "internal enemies," infected by an "alien spirit." In order not to incur the odium of being "alien" and to enlist the support of the middle class, which was essential for gaining a parliamentary majority, the Social Democrats kept the Jewish question from becoming a central issue in the political struggle, though rejecting unequivocally open anti-Semitism; as a result the diffusion of anti-Semitic ideology and slogans of this period took place with little opposition, interrupted only by the feeble dissent of some Jewish defense organizations.

In this respect Germany differed from France and Russia, where the "Jewish question" had become the subject of an open political struggle. There was no lack of anti-Semitic publications in France during the last two decades of the century, including those that advocated racial doctrines. But at the height of the Dreyfus Affair the country's relation to Jews became one of the central issues in the deadly conflict between the royalist-clerical forces and the republican-radical forces. The struggle had torn France in two, but after the defeat of the extreme conservatives, anti-Semitism as an acceptable political and social ideology was abandoned and relegated to an insignificant place in the social and intellectual life of the country. The very fact that the political Left had rejected anti-Semitism in an open conflict committed many prominent persons, both in civil life and in government circles, to be strongly opposed to anti-Semitism.

In Russia the policy of the autocratic czarist regime to increase its popularity among the conservative and backward elements in the country by representing the Jews as the principal internal enemy was actively opposed by the Russian Liberation Movement, which included all the opposition parties, the liberals, and the revolutionaries. The question of the status of the Russian Jews and their rights became one of the principal issues in the political life of the country. With the overthrow of the czarist regime and its autocratic political structure in the Revolution in 1917 the proponents of anti-Semitic ideology suffered a crushing defeat.

In the Germany of the Second Reich such a development did not take place. How internal political divisions and social tensions affected the course of modern German history, how the Germans succumbed to the insidious political ideology of anti-Semitism after World War I, and how even educated Germans with religious affiliations and intellectual backgrounds were ensnared by its sophistries—the roots of all this are presented by the author in his illuminating study of this period in the history of the Jews and in the history of Europe.

SHMUEL ETTINGER

*Jerusalem*

# Introduction

Jewish history goes beyond the study of the Jewish people and their peculiar problems; it is also an integral part of the history of the nation in whose midst Jews dwell. The daily social intercourse between Jews and non-Jews, the legal status of the Jews, the degree of freedom granted them to determine their own way of life as individuals and as a group, the part they play in the economic and intellectual life of the country, their allegiance to their adopted country and the feeling of alienation in being excluded from its dominant culture, their attempts to integrate into an egalitarian society that permits them to preserve their identity as a separate Jewish community or into a society that insists on complete assimilation as the price of integration—these are problems of vital concern not only to Jews but to the nations in which they live.

During the periods in which the Christian nations of the world were struggling to achieve self-identity the condition of the Jews served as a touchstone of Christian attitudes and beliefs. The existence of the Jews, their very presence, acted as a kind of ferment that contributed to the growth of national consciousness. This position of the Jews among the nations imposed upon this particularistic people a universal mission, which is one of the paradoxes of Jewish history.

Before the advent of the modern period the separate existence of the Jews among the Christian nations was interpreted as an obstinate refusal on the part of the Jews to acknowledge Jesus as the Messiah. Despite the attempts of the church to wean them from their infidelity the Jews remained impenitent and obdurate. This disconcerted the Christian and tended to weaken his assurance in the merits of his own cause. If the Jews refused to acknowledge the truths of the new dispensation and the message of salvation that was primarily intended for them, perhaps the fault lay in the redemptive message itself and in the historical culture that produced it. This new wave of skepticism within the Christian world was directed against the Catholic social structure, which was based on an ecclesiastical authority entrusted with the keys of salvation in this world, and also against the Protestant social structure, which rested on the inner authority of the individual as a member of society and as a citizen of the country.

The church was plagued for centuries by this corroding skepticism that threatened to undermine its spiritual and political authority. One of the ways adopted by historical Christianity in its efforts to dispel this unsettling doubt was to attack the very source of skepticism—Judaism and the Jews. The conversion of the Jews seemed to recommend itself as an ideal solution to remove the source of doubt and uncertainty. A more feasible solution was for the church to humiliate the incredulous Jews, whose abject state would then bear witness, *testes veritatis nostrae,* to the indefeasible claims of the triumphant religion of Christianity.

With the rise of nationalism during the period of the Enlightenment and with the rapid development of industrial society this theological argument had apparently lost its cogency. From the historical sources at our disposal, however, we learn that the process of modernization, contrary to the beliefs of some contemporary historians, did not do away with the theological animus against Jews but merely presented it in new forms more in keeping with the modern spirit. The relations between Christianity and Judaism underwent profound changes with respect to content, but the historical structure of these relations, wherein the Christian saw his own image reflected, remained constant.

The period discussed in this study constitutes a new stage in this historical continuity, a stage in which the theological significance in the reciprocal relations between Christians and Jews was transferred to a secular sphere. The Jews now attempted to create a new place for themselves within the Christian environment on the assumption that with the spread of rational enlightenment, humanistic education, and equal civil rights, on the one hand, and with the development of modern industry and the rise of the new social classes, such as the intelligentsia and the liberal professions, on the other hand, a society would be created that would set no store on a man's social, ethnic, or religious origins but would judge him solely on the basis of those universal aspects that command the assent of men of all races and creeds. In this new society a man would not be asked whence he came but whither he was going. He would be judged by his achievements and not by the class to which he belonged, by his fruits and not by his roots. His religious affiliation would be regarded as a private matter, and there would be no need for him to deny it since, having been purified of all irrational elements, religion would no longer constitute a barrier between men. In the public domain, membership in a religious organization, including Judaism, would be valued only for its contribution in advancing man's ethical development and social welfare. In this age of endless moral progress there would be no need for the Jew to change his religion since the enlightened world, in which man's moral regeneration would have been achieved through the free exercise of human reason, would appreciate the ethical and historical significance of Judaism, including its contribution to the growth of Christianity. No importance would be attached to the church dogma according to which man's salvation would not be completed until the Jews acknowledged the kingdom of Jesus the Messiah and accepted the benefits of Christianity. A man's nationality would be determined not on the basis of his biological or ethnic origin but on a freely acknowledged allegiance to the country of his choice and a conscious identification with its language and culture.

The distinctive mark of this age was its strong assurance in the integrity of human reason. To attain freedom man need but follow the contours of his own rational mind, and this would deliver him from his irrational prejudices and from his dependence on his environment. In the realm of pure critical reason his autonomous ethical principles would liberate his mind from its dependence on the object of cognition; in the sphere of history man would attain freedom, and the Jew equality, by the application of the same rational principles. The millennium of truth seemed nigh.

This jubilant expansion of the rationalistic spirit dominated the religious and cultural life of German Jewry and determined its communal activities. Within this framework the German Jews, like most of the Jews in the West, pursued a double aim—to integrate completely into their environment as full-fledged Germans and at the same time preserve their separate Jewish existence. In the age of emancipation the Jews had rejected the nationality element in Judaism, had ceased to observe the traditional way of life with its laws and commandments, and for the most part disassociated themselves from Jewish society. After the French Revolution and the rise of nationalism they proclaimed themselves not only loyal citizens of the countries of their birth but also nationals of the European countries of their adoption. Nevertheless, they did not forsake their independent existence as Jews—unless they changed their religion, and sometimes not even after they had taken this step.

The struggle for separate Jewish existence was part of the larger problem of whether it was possible to be a Jew without acknowledging the nationality component in Judaism or without observing the Law and the Commandments within the framework of established religious institutions. Throughout this period, especially in the days of the controversy generated by Adolf von Harnack's views on the source of Jesus' teaching, this question was discussed as part of the general subject known as ''the essence of Judaism.'' At that time Judaism was defined as a community that was distinguished by its religion—a definition that did not include the element of Jewish national identity, particularly in its political sense, although it did not necessarily obligate a Jew to accept the halachic way of life. The disinclination of German Jewry to relinquish its separate Jewish existence was discussed by Professor Gershom G. Scholem in his lecture ''Germans and Jews,'' delivered at the Fifth Convention of the World Jewish Congress in Brussels (1966), wherein he stated that many German Jews from all classes of society were prepared to give up their Jewish nationality (*Volkstum*) but nevertheless desired in some way to preserve their Judaism ''as a heritage, as a religion.'' This kind of Judaism was defined by Professor Scholem as a mixture of rational religion and an emotional experience, regarded by many as a feeble faith that was poor in form and in content, but was nevertheless an important element in helping many Germans to define their status as Germans and as Jews.

The relations between Jews and Christians in Germany, and to a large extent throughout the countries of the West, were largely determined by this striving of the Jews to achieve both integration and identity. This double aspiration embodied two universal principles which dominated the modern era—equality and freedom. In their efforts to integrate into the surrounding society the Jews fought for the principle of equality, equality with respect to rights and obligations, with respect to economic and professional opportunities, and equality before the law as rational creatures, created in the image of God, and as citizens of a European nation. At the same time, in their desire to exist as a separate entity the Jews also defended the principle of freedom which, like the principle of equality, had its roots in rationalism. Man is by nature a rational creature and hence free to shape empirical reality in accordance with his ethical convictions based on his autonomous judgment, at the same time remaining faithful to himself, his culture, and religious heritage.

How the Jews struggled to achieve complete integration into German society during the period of the Second Reich and still retain their separate identity as Jews, how these efforts were received by the non-Jewish population of that period, and how they affected the relations between Jews and Christians are the questions we propose to investigate in the following pages.

The different chapters in this book are devoted to the various spheres of contact between Christians and Jews during the period from 1870 to 1914, each chapter retaining its special emphasis and restricted interest without losing sight of the general view. The first chapter is devoted chiefly to the period of the Prussian wars several years prior to the creation of the empire, that is, from 1860 onward. The second chapter deals with the *Kulturkampf* in the seventies and the beginning of the eighties. The third chapter discusses the development of Conservative Protestant ideology and political influence in relation to Jews and Judaism, with special emphasis on the last two decades of the century. A large part of the fourth chapter is taken up with the polemics concerning "the essence of Christianity and Judaism" following Harnack's public lectures during the year 1899–1900. The fifth and last chapter discusses the similarities and differences between Christian anti-Semitism and anti-Christian anti-Semitism and thus serves to connect the beginning of the period studied in this book, when the term "anti-Semitism" was first coined, with the end of this period, that is, with the generation that preceded the Third Reich.

From the geographical and ecological point of view our discussion is confined to the German states under the hegemony of the kingdom of Prussia. In his proclamation at the founding of the empire after the victory of Germany over France, delivered in the Hall of Mirrors at Versailles on January 18, 1871, Wilhelm I, the king of Prussia, defined this empire as "the restoration of the German Reich." He thus emphasized one of the factors which was to influence the course of the entire period—the historic consciousness of those generations for whom the German Empire was a continuation of the Carolingian dynasty, which was founded in 800 A.D. when Charlemagne proclaimed the *Romanum gubernans Imperium*. The Reich was thus to be looked upon as a renewal of

the early German nationalism of Luther's day, that is, the period beginning in 1517 when Luther nailed his historic Ninety-five Theses on the
door of the castle church in Wittenberg or beginning in the year 1520
when Melanchthon and the humanists supported the schism with Rome.

Embedded in the historic consciousness of the German Empire is the
concept "Reich," and hence the term "Second Reich" is frequently
employed in this study to designate the German Empire. This name has
become common in historiography only recently, but many historians
continue to use the term "German Empire" or "Wilhelmian period."
We prefer to use "Second Reich" since, considering the deep influence
the state as an institution and the empire as an idea had on German history,
the term "Reich" is common to all three regimes, including the Third
Reich. The designation "Second Reich" would then indicate the historical connection between the First Reich, as the Holy Roman Empire of the
German nation was called, and the Second Reich, which is the subject of
our study, and then between these and the Third Reich, the period from
1933 to the end of World War II. In adopting the term "Second Reich"
we are following the current usage of scholars, such as Salo W. Baron in
his epochal work on modern nationalism and religion.

Our preoccupation with the German scene requires further study of the
history of the relations between Christians and Jews in other countries,
such as the Austro-Hungarian Empire and France, countries that had experienced during that same period anti-Semitic, extreme nationalistic, or
fascist tendencies.

In this study we have attempted to follow the principles of historiography known today as "intellectual history" or "the social history
of ideas" and, to some extent, *Kulturgeschichte,* which are primarily
concerned with the historical study of the reciprocal relations between
belief and action, opinions and their consequences, speculation and experimentation, theory and practice. This historiographical approach was
called by Moritz Steinschneider "the study of the history of civilization,"
which he explained in a series of lectures as early as the year 1859, sum-
marizing and adapting them in the years 1895–1901 and finally publishing them in the *Jewish Quarterly Review* in 1903–1904. Civilization for
Steinschneider was the bright focal point of history, for culture was the
sphere in which spirit is transformed into empirical patterns. The concept
"culture," like the German concept *"Bildung,"* was understood by him

to include the development of the human spirit through man's cultural achievements whereby form is imprinted on matter.

With these views of Steinschneider in mind we shall discuss the relation between Jews and Christians as a chapter in the cultural, social, and religious history of these two groups. Insofar as ideas appear in our study they are treated not as abstract concepts but from the standpoint of their social roots, impact, and consequences. Similarly, the history of ideas is not discussed as abstract speculative history, but as history in which ideas are incorporated in a living context.

Also in the presentation of the representative views of the various schools of thought we have sought to explain not so much their genesis, their pure intellectual content, or a priori presuppositions as the ways in which speculative thought is actualized in history itself. In the spirit of the phenomenological school of F. J. J. Buytendijk, and particularly of Helmut Plessner, the history of the various schools of thought and social movements is studied as phenomenological history, that is, as the history of attitudes as reflected in human existence. Since such an existence is conceived in phenomenological form, that is, as an empirical phenomenon with an ontological meaning, it can manifest itself as a social group, an economic need, a political interest, a religious movement, an intellectual system, or as man himself and the relation between his thoughts and his deeds. The structure of these historical phenomena is not accidental. It consists of the subject who, consciously or unconsciously, creates the relationship to society, to the world, or to himself; and of the critical self-awareness of the subject. This critical consciousness is made possible by man's anthropological situation, which expresses itself in the historical process, a situation which Plessner calls "excentric"; that is, man is included within historical reality and is also conscious of this inclusion, being part of empirical reality and at the same time consciously confronted with it.

The practical consequences of this methodology for our study have to do with the selection and critical evaluation of historical sources. The primary consequence is the realization that in investigating the spiritual aspects of social phenomena, world views, and the history of ideas it is not possible to limit oneself to the intellectual systems of prominent thinkers. In this study we have therefore concentrated more on sources derived from a more popular sphere of thought, in the manner of the "middle-brow writers," as they were called by the late Richard Hofstadter. Thus, in our study of the reaction against rationalism and neo-Kantian criticism we collected many documents that reveal the attitudes not only of prominent philosophers, but of students, the educated public, and, especially, members of the liberal professions who were not specialists but who had a genuine interest in social and intellectual problems. This obliged us to investigate more common sources, such as private correspondence, family archives, small-town newspapers, records of spontaneous meetings held in the homes of private citizens and in nonprofessional circles. Also in our discussion of the systems of leading thinkers we did not attempt only to analyze the intellectual content of their ideas but rather to indicate their influence in affecting the intellectual, educational, and even political climate among the different classes of society.

This study is to a large extent based on original sources found in many archives, literary remains, periodicals, and in the vast polemical literature of the period we are studying. I am greatly indebted to the late Professor Israel Halpern for encouraging me to delve into such source material.

This book could not have been written were it not for the scholarly assistance I received from Professor Shmuel Ettinger.

For help in gaining access to original sources I wish to thank Rachel Blumenthal, deceased, and also the following institutions: General Archives for Jewish History in Jerusalem (now named The Central Archives for the Jewish People) and its staff of workers; the Jewish National and University Library in Jerusalem; Library of the Yad Vashem Institute in Jerusalem; Kommision für Zeitgeschichte bei der katholischen Akademie, Forschungsstelle, Bonn; Institut für Politische Wissenschaft der Johann Wolfgang Goethe Universität, Frankfurt a/M; Stadts-und Universitätsbibliothek, Frankfurt a/M; Universitätsbibliothek, Heidelberg; Bundesarchiv, Koblenz; Kloster Loccum; Stadtsbibliothek, Mainz; Staatsarchiv, Marburg; Evangelische Arbeitsgemeinschaft für kirchliche Zeitgeschichte, München; Institutum Judaicum Delitzschianum, Münster; Zentralbibliothek, Zürich; Bibliothèque Nationale, Paris; New York Public Library; and the Hebrew Union College Library in Cincinnati.

Acknowledgment is also due the Magnes Press, and the Yad Vashem Institute, for their aid in the publication of the original Hebrew version. The publication of the English-language version would not have been possible without the assistance of the Leo Baeck Institute in Jerusalem and New York. I wish to express my appreciation to its respective directors, as well as to the staff of Cornell University Press.

Finally, I owe a special debt of gratitude to Noah J. Jacobs for his skillful translation of the Hebrew text and the German sources. His wide knowledge and linguistic sensitivity have produced an accurate and creative translation.

To all the above-named individuals and institutions the author is deeply indebted, but he alone remains responsible for any errors or defects in the volume that is now presented to the English reader.

URIEL TAL

*Tel-Aviv*

# Abbreviations

*Archives, Legacies, and Collections of Sources*

B.A.K.    Bundesarchiv, Koblenz
B.N.P.    Bibliothèque Nationale, Paris
G.A.J.    General Archives for Jewish History, Jerusalem (now named the Central Archives for the Jewish People)
      A.F.   Archiv Dr. Ismar Freund
      G.A.   Gesamtarchiv der Juden
      H.M., Pl.,  Collection of Rabbi S. R. Hirsch
      M.   Institutions and organizations
      T.D.   National, local, and community organizations
S.A.M.    Staatsarchiv, Marburg
S.U.F.    Stadts-und Universitätsbibliothek, Frankfurt a/M
U.B.H.    Universitätsbibliothek, Heidelberg
Z.B.Z.    Zentralbibliothek, Zürich

F.A.    Family archives
This category includes sources found in family archives and legacies. Many of these sources were preserved by the late historian Eleonore Sterling. Additional sources, such as letters, diaries, sermons, and reminiscences, were placed at my disposal by the late Professor Karl Thieme. The numbers of the files in the notes are given in accordance with the volume of source material now in preparation.

*Periodicals (sources and studies)*

A.C.    Antisemitische Correspondenz, ed. Theodor Fritsch, Leipzig, 1885 ff. (Deutsch Soziale Blätter der D.S.P., ed. Liebermann von Sonnenberg, 1894 ff.).
A.E.L.K.Z.    Allgemeine Evangelisch-Lutherische Kirchenzeitung, ed. Dr. C. Ernst Luthardt, Leipzig, 1871 ff.

| | |
|---|---|
| A.G. | Der Alte Glaube, Evangelisch-Lutherisches Gemeindeblatt für die gebildeten Stände, mit literarischem Beilag; Freiherr Ernst Roeder von Diersburg, Leipzig, 1900 ff. |
| A.J. | Antisemitisches Jahrbuch, ed. W. Giese, Berlin, 1897 ff. |
| A.K. | Antisemiten-Katechismus, ed. Theodor Fritsch (25th ed.) Leipzig, 1893 ff. (Handbuch der Judenfrage, 31st ed., 1932). |
| A.M. | Antisemitisches Monatsblatt für die Mitglieder und Freunde der DSRP, Gotha, Berlin, 1897 ff. |
| A.S. | Antisemitenspiegel, die Antisemiten im Lichte des Christenthums, des Rechtes und der Moral, Danzig 1890, 1892, 1900; Antisemitenspiegel, die Antisemiten im Lichte des Christenthums, des Rechtes und der Wissenschaft, Frankfurt a/M, 1911. |
| A.S.W.S.P. | Archiv für Sozialwissenschaften und Sozialpolitik, Tübingen, 1925 (Vol. 54). |
| A.Z.d.J. | Allgemeine Zeitung des Judenthums, Leipzig, Berlin, 1870 ff. |
| C.A.J.L. | Central-Anzeiger für jüdische Literatur, Blätter für neuere und ältere Literatur des Judenthums, ed. M. N. Bruell, ergänzt von M. Steinschneider, Frankfurt a/M, 1890 ff. |
| Ch.W. | Die Christliche Welt, ein Evangelisch-Lutherisches Gemeindeblatt für die Gebildeten, Leipzig (Magdeburg), 1887 ff. |
| D.E.K.Z. | Deutsche Evangelische Kirchenzeitung, Wochenschrift zur Pflege evangelisches Gemeindelebens und zur Förderung kirchlicher Selbständigkeit, ed. Adolph Stöcker, Hof und Domprediger in Berlin, Berlin, 1887 ff. |
| D.I. | Der Israelit, Centralorgan für das orthodoxe Judenthum, Mainz, Frankfurt a/M, 1860 ff. |
| D.L.B. | Deutsches Literaturblatt, ed. Wilhelm Herbst, Gotha, 1878 ff. |
| D.N. | Die Nation, Wochenschrift für Politik, Volkswirtschaft und Literatur, ed. Theodor Barth, Berlin, 1882 ff. |
| D.P.B. | Deutsches Protestantenblatt (Norddeutsches P.B.), 1878 ff. |
| F.I.F. | Frankfurter Israelitisches Familienblatt, 1905 ff. |
| H. | Hammer, Blätter für deutschen Sinn, ed. Theodor Fritsch, Leipzig, 1901 ff. |
| H.S. | Historische Studien, Berlin, 1940 ff. |
| H.T.R. | Harvard Theological Review, 1966. |
| H.Z. | Historische Zeitschrift, München, 1889 (Vol. 61). |
| I.D.R. | Im Deutschen Reich, Zeitschrift des Central-Vereins deutscher Staatsbürger jüdischen Glaubens, Berlin, 1895 ff. |
| I.W. | Israelitische Wochenschrift für die religiösen und sozialen Interessen des Judenthums, ed. Treuenfels/Rahmer, Breslau/ |

|          |                                                                                                                                                          |
|----------|----------------------------------------------------------------------------------------------------------------------------------------------------------|
|          | Magdeburg, 1870 ff (Supplement: Das Jüdische Literaturblatt, 1873 ff; Supplement: Jüdisches Familienblatt zur Unterhaltung und Belehrung für die Israelitische Jugend, 1886 ff). |
| J.J.G.L. | Jahrbuch für jüdische Geschichte und Literatur, Berlin, 1898 ff.                                                                                          |
| J.P.     | Die Jüdische Presse, Organ für die Gesamtinteressen des Judenthums, Berlin, 1870 ff.                                                                      |
| J.S.S.   | Jewish Social Studies, New York, 1940 ff.                                                                                                                 |
| J.Z.W.L. | Jüdische Zeitschrift für Wissenschaft und Leben, Breslau, 1862 ff.                                                                                        |
| K.K.     | Der Kulturkämpfer, Zeitschrift für öffentliche Angelegenheiten, ed. Otto Glagau, Berlin, 1880 ff.                                                         |
| K.Z.     | Neue Preussische Kreuz-Zeitung, Berlin, 1878 ff.                                                                                                          |
| L.B.Y.   | Yearbook of the Leo Baeck Institute, London, 1956 ff.                                                                                                     |
| M.G.J.V. | Mitteilungen der Gesellschaft für jüdische Volkskunde, Hamburg, 1898 ff.                                                                                  |
| M.G.K.   | Monatsschrift für die gesamte Kultur, unter ständiger Mitarbeit von Eduard v. Hartmann, Theodor Lipps, Otto Pfleiderer, Ferdinand Toennies, ed. Graf von Hoensbroech, Berlin, 1903 ff. |
| M.G.W.J. | Monatsschrift für Geschichte und Wissenschaft des Judenthums, Breslau, 1851 ff.                                                                           |
| M.W.J.   | Magazin für die Wissenschaft des Judenthums, Berlin, 1876 ff.                                                                                             |
| M.V.A.A. | Mittheilungen aus dem Verein zur Abwehr des Antisemitismus, Berlin, 1891 ff.                                                                              |
| N.E.K.Z. | Neue Evangelische Kirchenzeitung, auf Veranstaltung des deutschen Zweiges des Evangelischen Bundes, ed. H. Messner, Leipzig, 1871 ff.                     |
| N.L.K.Z. | Neue Lutherische Kirchenzeitung, ed. Pastor Greve, Breslau, 1900 ff.                                                                                      |
| O.W.     | Ost und West, Monatsschrift für modernes Judenthum, Berlin, 1901 ff.                                                                                      |
| P.J.     | Preussische Jahrbücher, Berlin, 1864 ff.                                                                                                                  |
| P.M.     | Protestantische Monatshefte, Neue Folge der Protestantischen Kirchenzeitung, ed. Julius Websky, Berlin, 1897 ff.                                          |
| P.V.     | Politische Vierteljahresschrift, Zeitschrift der Deutschen Vereinigung für Politische Wissenschaft, Köln, Opladen, 1960 ff.                               |
| S.A.H.   | Saat auf Hoffnung, Zeitschrift des Evangelisch-Lutherischen Zentralvereins für Mission unter Israel, ed. Gustaf H. Dalmann, with the aid of Franz Delitzsch, Leipzig, 1863 ff. |
| T.L.B.   | Theologisches Literaturblatt, ed. C. E. Luthardt, Leipzig, 1880 ff.                                                                                       |
| V.K.     | Die Volkskirche, Zeitstimmen aus der Lutherischen Kirche in Deutschland, ed. K. Knoke, Hannover, 1877 ff.                                                 |

Z.K.W.K.L.    Zeitschrift für Kirchliche Wissenschaft und Kirchliches Leben, ed. C. E. Luthardt, Leipzig, 1880 ff.

Z.R.G.G.    Zeitschrift für Religions- und Geistesgeschichte, Köln, 1956 ff.

Z.V.P.S.W.    Zeitschrift für Völkerpsychologie und Sprachwissenschaft, ed. M. Lazarus and H. Steinthal, Berlin, 1860 ff.

Z.T.K.    Zeitschrift für Theologie und Kirche, ed. J. Gottschick, Freiburg, 1890 ff.

# CHRISTIANS AND JEWS IN GERMANY

Religion, Politics, and Ideology in
the Second Reich, 1870–1914

# 1 | The German Intellectuals and the Dynamics of Jewish Integration and Identity

The Intellectuals in the Second Reich

Of all the German social classes the intellectuals, especially the liberal intellectuals, were the most sympathetic to the Jews. The designation "intellectuals" refers to the members of the educated class and the liberal professions, particularly those engaged in creating social values and, to a certain extent, in transmitting these values to the youth of the country and to the general public. This intellectual class differed from other social groups which performed a similar function, such as the creators of popular folklore and other forms of indigenous culture, in that they applied critical rational criteria to their creations within a relatively open society. Our analysis will be confined to the attitudes of the liberal intellectuals who supported the Second Reich and Bismarck's policies. This group included those who were in general agreement with the regime, but also those who criticized and even opposed it; those liberal intellectuals who kept aloof from political activity, "the unpolitical Germans" as they were called by Thomas Mann, are treated here only insofar as they can be shown to have exerted some influence on the society around them.[1]

This intellectual class in Germany, whose influence extended far beyond its numerical representation in the general population, was the class on which the Jews pinned their hopes for achieving full integration, and it was also the one from which they suffered their deepest disappoint-

1. For the distinction between the active and passive attitude of the intellectuals to politics, see Fritz Stern, "The Political Consequences of the Unpolitical German," *History,* No. 3, 1960, p. 104 ff; Ralf Dahrendorf, "Demokratie und Sozialstruktur in Deutschland," *Gesellschaft und Freiheit,* München, 1961, p. 260 ff; U. Tal, "The Intellectual Elite in Germany and Its Attitude to the Jews in the Bismarckian Period," in the collection *Elite and Leadership Groups* (Hebrew), Jerusalem, 1966, p. 98 ff. On the attitude of Liberal Protestant intellectuals to the Jews, see further, Chap. 4, p. 160 ff.

ment. Even at the beginning of the period we are discussing, the liberal intellectuals were known to believe ''that the desire of the Jews to be German was to all intents and purposes unrealistic as long as Judaism was not absorbed in its German-Christian environment by complete assimilation and dissolution by means of miscegenation.'' [2] However, in seeking a practical solution to the problem of Jewish integration, the liberal intellectuals were faced with two incompatible tasks. The first was to enable the Jews, as a foreign body, to integrate fully into German society and culture without discrediting the movement, for the most part led by the intellectuals, for the national unification of Germany or, in the language of the period, for the unity of the German spirit. In this matter the liberal intellectuals adopted the view of the early advocates of the emancipation in Germany, in the days of Frederick the Great and Wilhelm von Humboldt, according to which the price to be paid by the Jews for admission into German society was the repudiation of their Jewish identity. The second task of the intellectuals was to defend the right of autonomous self-determination which they regarded as the indefeasible right of all men and all citizens, including Jews, by virtue of natural law. Ever since the beginning of the nineteenth century this principle of self-determination served as the basis for the emancipation of the German peasant, tenant farmer, and artisan, of men of learning, scientists, clergy, and teachers, of the Protestants in their struggle against the Catholic church and the ultramontane regime of the Hapsburgs, and of the Jews over against the dominant Christian society. Hence, this dilemma was not regarded by the intellectuals as exclusively Jewish, but rather as a reflection of their own existential problems and, primarily, as the crucial problem of the freedom of the individual in modern society with respect to his duties as a citizen.

In the circles we are discussing this question raised doubts in the minds of the intellectuals as to how they could support the existing regime and

2. *Über die Anreden an die neu aufzunehmenden Christen,* Leipzig, 1880, p. 2. This pamphlet, published anonymously, was written by non-Orthodox Jewish teachers, concerning whom see G.A.J. G.A.M. 8/2 ''Verein israelitischer Lehrer Mitteldeutschlands.'' One of the young intellectuals referred to in the original source is Friedrich Paulsen, as we learn from a personal letter in F.A., No. 14, but the words that are here attributed to Paulsen are much stronger than those in his original talk to the students in Berlin at the end of 1870 in which he said that ''the Jews who wish to preserve their separate tradition inspire respect in an enlightened man, but they cannot expect to be regarded by Christians as ''Volksgenossen gleicher Stammeseigentümlichkeiten'' (op. cit., F.A., No. 14), and see Paulsen's view in his most important work, *System der Ethik,* 6th ed., Vol. II, Berlin, 1902, pp. 258, 561.

the national renascence movement and still preserve their freedom, how they could subscribe to the policies of the ruling authorities without violating their intellectual integrity, or engage in political activity without compromising their rational and ethical principles. That a considerable number of intellectuals were aware of this dilemma is reflected in an interesting document of the 1860's which speaks of "the inability to escape from the predicament in which the educated man finds himself when he . . . wishes to perform his national and civic duty and when he [wishes] at the same time to fulfill his obligations in the autonomous world of the spirit . . . without resorting to the dangerous conception that identifies spirit with the state or the erroneous [conception] that identifies idea with reality." [3]

The German intellectuals were thus presented with a perplexing alternative. From the very outset they had been in the vanguard of the movement that supported the industrial revolution, the national renascence, freedom of rational inquiry, and cosmopolitanism. Since the authorities in the larger German states were not averse to these progressive changes, the intellectuals found themselves in a position of being revolutionaries and at the same time supporters of the regime. This predicament was reflected in the circumstance that the organization of most institutions of research and higher learning was controlled by the regime (or under its comprehensive supervision), a condition that continued, even after the establishment of the German Empire, to exert considerable influence on the development of the German intellectual classes, as we shall have occasion to note later in our discussion.

It was in this connection that the question of Jewish integration into German society arose for the intellectuals. The degree of success with

3. This document is perhaps one of the most important in this discussion; it was put at my disposal by the late Professor Karl Thieme (in file 2/b). It was difficult to identify the author's signature, but in my opinion the text was written by Professor Rudolf von Gneist. The fear of a new Hegelian interpretation as expressed in this excerpt recurs in Gneist's writings similarly and at times almost identically formulated, and is also found in his last years and in a period when he spoke out openly against political anti-Semitism. Thieme agreed with my supposition, but had some reservations; in his opinion the German intellectuals, including the liberals among them, did not succeed in freeing themselves from Hegel's influence in all matters pertaining to the absolute identification between idea and reality, between spirit and state. Thieme's death prevented further clarification. See the important discussion in Hans Paul Bahrdt, *Reflexionen über die gesellschaftlichen Voraussetzungen des Antisemitismus in Deutschland, Entscheidungsjahr 1932,* ed. by W. E. Mosse, Tübingen, 1966, p. 146 ff.

which the Jews could accomplish such integration and still retain their separate identity as Jews was one of the criteria whereby the intellectuals could measure their own success in their efforts to combine what the political scientist Johann Caspar Bluntschli called "freedom with responsibility, independence with relationship [to the regime], voluntary self-determination while accepting the burden of active citizenship for the sake of freedom." [4]

In the light of these considerations the question we shall be concerned with is the attitude of the liberal intellectuals toward the ways in which the Jews are to be integrated into the life of German society, the place this attitude occupies in the overall view of the liberal intellectual to political authority in general and, in particular, to the question of his freedom and independence in fulfilling his civil obligations as a citizen of the state.

## Changing Attitudes of the Intellectuals

In the early stages of the Prussian-Danish War many circles among the liberal intellectuals still maintained an attitude of reserve toward Bismarck's policies. The leaders of these circles, who were also prominent in the political life of the country—university professors such as Rudolf von Gneist, Rudolf von Bennigsen, Heinrich von Sybel, as well as writers and artists, especially in the large cities—criticized Bismarck's policies from two points of view. In the sphere of internal politics they were opposed to the persecution of the Progressive Liberals and of the radical Left; they also condemned the Press Regulation (Presseverordnung) of June 1, 1863, which empowered official censors to suppress social or political criticism, even when made with what Karl Twesten called "constructive intentions." Twesten goes on to say that "even such a patriot was persecuted and condemned as a criminal . . . for the monarchical regime today is built on the denial of individual freedom." [5] Criticism was also directed against Bismarck's famous state-

4. From the collection *Kulturkampf*, Berlin, 1887, p. 14 (hereafter *Kulturkampf*); Bluntschli's words were spoken in the spring of 1871, following the proclamation of the establishment of the German Empire at Versailles.

[5] The collection of Mss. for the history of liberalism, in the official archives of Koblenz, B.A.K., KL.E(3); see there the attitude of the intellectuals toward Bismarck throughout the period: "Urteile bedeutender Persönlichkeiten über Bismarck als Antwort auf eine Umfrage der Gegenwart," B.A.K., KL.E(159).

ment concerning his policy of "blood and iron," which Theodor Fontane characterized as "a heritage of Teutonic madness from the days of Friedrich Ludwig Jahn. . . . From a spiritual state (*Staat des Geistes*) Prussia has been turned into a police state (*Polizeistaat*)." [6]

In the sphere of foreign relations the criticism of the liberal intellectuals was directed against Bismarck's arbitrary policies. Except for isolated cases there was little opposition on the part of the liberal intellectuals to the Prussian-Danish War as such, the opposition being directed for the most part against Bismarck's reasons for waging it. The war itself was justified in the eyes of professors and students in the universities of Greater Prussia insofar as it was a war to liberate the territories of Sleswig, Holstein, and the smaller Duchy of Lauenburg from subjection to the Danish crown. This War of Liberation was being waged so that the population of these regions could be granted the right of self-determination in the matter of national identity and political citizenship. However, Bismarck's aim in this war, as the liberals were quick to point out, was to annex these territories to the Kingdom of Prussia by the use of force and by deceiving their inhabitants as well as the Austrian army, his ally in the war.

After the famous storming of the Düppel defenses in April 1864 and other successes of the Prussian armies, criticism of this kind decreased. As early as 1863, Professor Hermann Baumgarten, the distinguished historian, warned his countrymen of the danger of "moral deterioration" that faced Prussia should it continue to tolerate Bismarck's highhanded policies. But some eight or nine months thereafter, in speaking to the students of the Technische Hochschule in Karlsruhe, he declared that the annexation of the conquered territories was vital to Prussia's military power and to the future independence of Germany as a whole, and was therefore to be considered a sacred moral duty.

A similar change was to be seen in the attitude of the *Preussische Jahrbücher,* the organ of the liberal and the right-wing liberal intellectuals. At the beginning of the sixties this publication spoke of the danger of "Bismarck's despotic rule," but in the spring of 1864 its editors declared that the liberation of these territories from the Danish crown might indeed intensify the "national feeling" of the Prussians, but it need not entail an increase in the "national power" of the monarchy. This goal could be at-

6. Ibid., KL.E(3).

tained by annexation or, in Baumgarten's words, by "complete incorporation" of the conquered territories. Since such annexation was in the interests of the country, it was not only necessary but morally justifiable: "We believe that what serves the welfare of the nation and necessary for its progress is an ethical and lawful goal." [7] On closer examination this attitude proves to be ambiguous, and we must distinguish between its two meanings if we are to understand the role of the German intellectual class in the Bismarckian era, and particularly its complicated approach to the Jewish question.

One school of thought among those who supported the war and the annexation of the conquered territories was given definite expression by prominent persons, such as Heinrich von Treitschke, Wilhelm Wehrpfennig, and other contributors to the *Preussische Jahrbücher;* at the head of the movement were men like Johann Gustav Droysen, Hermann Baumgarten, as well as eminent educators, and economists such as Georg von Siemens. The objectives of this movement were summarized by Treitschke in the pages of the *Preussische Jahrbücher* in 1865 and also by David Friedrich Strauss in a series of popular lectures given in the same year; both concluded that the campaign against Denmark was of momentous consequence for the future of German unification and hence also for the future of Europe. This was the first time that Prussia's capacity for leadership was put to the historic test. Prussia's victory would not only demonstrate its power; it would also vindicate its hegemony over a united Germany. Similarly, its defeat would not only expose its weakness but also invalidate its claims to such hegemony. This led Treitschke to regard the war as an attempt to create "a secure habitation for the German spirit, perhaps to the end of days." [8]

It was the opinion of men like Treitschke, Strauss, Konstantin Rössler, as well as the publicist Moritz Busch, the jurist A. Mittelstadt, and the

7. ". . . und wir halten was zum Heil der Nation förderlich und notwendig ist auch für ein sittliches und gerechtes Ziel," P.J., Vol. 13, 1864, p. 666.

8. P.J., Vol. 15, 1865, p. 323; see also Friedrich C. Sell, *Die Tragödie des deutschen Liberalismus,* Stuttgart, 1953, p. 213; Treitschke's programmatic work, "Die Lösung der schleswig-holsteinischen Frage," republished in his collection of political essays *Zehn Jahre Deutscher Kämpfe; Schriften zur Tagespolitik,* Berlin, 1897, pp. 12, 21–23, 27–28. On the marked influence of Treitschke's attitude on the question of the annexation of Sleswig-Holstein and on the question of Prussian nationalism against the background of German unity, see Andreas Dorpalen, *Heinrich von Treitschke,* New Haven, 1957, p. 102 ff.

literary historian Erich Schmidt, that in view of these lofty aims Prussia would be abdicating its moral power if it were to defer the decision of the annexation of the conquered territories to the indigenous population itself. The people of Sleswig or Holstein by themselves, like all other people, were not capable of making political decisions of historical or metaphysical significance. The use of naked force to bring about annexation could of course be interpreted as an infringement of the rights of the individual in these conquered regions. But as compensation for any such violation the inhabitants of these territories would be given the opportunity to take part in the unification of Germany and hence also in a concrete development of the German spirit or, in the words of D. F. Strauss, in "the exaltation of the German soul."

The second school of thought found among the intellectuals who supported the war and Bismarck's policies was represented chiefly by the university professors Theodor Mommsen, Rudolf von Gneist, Eduard Zeller, and, at a later date, by the writer Karl Hillebrand, the physiologist Jacob Molleschott, as well as by groups of students, writers, critics, and journalists, especially in the large cities. Compulsory annexation by Prussia was characterized as "a brutal rape," and its justification, namely, that it afforded the inhabitants of the conquered territories an opportunity to take part in a German renascence of the spirit, was described by Hillebrand as "an insult to the fathers of humanism and liberalism in Germany, and an insult to the legacy of Wilhelm von Humboldt." [9]

These circles, as well as the majority of the Progressive Liberals, were in favor of annexing the conquered territories to Greater Prussia but, as we have stated, were opposed to the use of force to that end and declared that "the inhabitants of the territories should have the right to choose annexation to Prussia of their own free will." [10] Theodor Mommsen in his *Die Annexion Schleswig-Holsteins* in 1864, as well as Rudolf von Gneist in his two university lectures of that same year, declared that it was unlawful for Prussia to deny the people of Sleswig-Holstein the right of self-determination. At the same time, however, they pointed out that this right should not be divorced from the historic reality in which the inhabitants found themselves, a reality that demanded complete annexation. The only way to avoid this predicament, according to the view of von Gneist's students in their publication *Die Jugend*, was to adopt the for-

9. See n. 5.    10. Ibid.

mula "that one should desire what one's duty as a citizen dictates." [11]
Mommsen, and following him Bluntschli, asserted that one's duty is to
defend the natural right of self-determination and to adapt its limits and
contents to conform to the needs of the nation. The individual has a just
claim to self-determination, but the state reserves the right to define its
nature in actual practice (*Entscheidungsrecht*). Since the state cannot law-
fully impose its will on the individual, the only way the individual can
safeguard his autonomy and at the same time preserve the sovereignty of
the state is to consider the two wills, his own and that of the state, as one.

When we examine the attitude of the liberal intellectuals toward the
state and toward the political sphere in general, two views emerge—one
that acknowledges the power and authority of the state over the individual
citizen, and another that rejects this view and urges the individual citizen
to identify himself with the national state. The first or "authoritarian"
point of view insists on the sharp distinction between the public domain
of politics and the private life of the individual; the second or "identification" point of view, which negates external authority, sees no need for
having two separate authorities which, it believes, should become one
through the individual's internalization of the external state authority.

It would seem on first glance that these two views that characterized
the attitude of the intellectuals toward the political sphere were held by
different people and at different times; in reality, however, they were to
be found in the same people in whom they produced confused and ambivalent feelings. Thus, for example, from the correspondence between
Johann Gustav Droysen and Heinrich von Sybel, or from the various
works of Heinrich von Treitschke, we gain a vivid impression of the intense inner struggle of the individual to reconcile these divergent views.
Some intellectuals, to be sure, were aware of the ambiguous character of
their relationship to political authority. In analyzing these attitudes it is
important to keep in mind that even when the various views seem to be
clearly expressed they only rarely reflect the complex spiritual and intellectual reality as it existed at the time. This is also true of the views
expressed by the liberal intellectuals regarding the basic problems that
arose in the sixties and in the first half of the seventies with respect to the
legal status of Jews.

Until the annexation of Sleswig-Holstein and the enactment of the

11. Single issue, Berlin, 1865, p. 1; in F.A., No. 4/6.

Prussian laws of October 1, 1867, the Jews of these regions enjoyed a separate legal status, a status that was formally confirmed shortly before the German conquest, in Sleswig on February 8, 1854, and in Holstein on July 14, 1863. As in the other German states until the year 1876, special laws made religious affiliation obligatory for all Jews (*Parochialzwang*). The new regulations, especially in the duchy of Holstein, affected many areas of Jewish life. For example, Jewish parents were obliged to provide their children with a Jewish education. Boys at the age of fifteen (girls at the age of fourteen) were required to take a state examination (*Religions-prüfung*) as a prerequisite for being granted civil rights on coming of age. The regulation (par. 17) states that only those who successfully pass these examinations were eligible to teach in the university, to receive a marriage license, to be accepted as a member of a guild, and so on.[12]

From the middle of the sixties until the enactment of the Law of Separation in 1876 these special regulations for Jews, including compulsory religious affiliation, were not in force. In theory this represented a victory for the principles of the emancipation, and it was so regarded by the liberal intellectuals. Actually, however, distinguished representatives of the large Jewish communities under the leadership of prominent persons in Berlin and Leipzig were conducting official and unofficial negotiations in an effort to prevent the repeal of some of these special regulations. Ludwig Philippson, who at that time was the leading figure in these negotiations, wrote a letter to Moritz Kohner, an influential member of the Jewish community in Leipzig, in which he stated: "The small number of Jewish communities in Sleswig-Holstein will be a test case for our success or failure in the coming legal struggle . . . there is no self-interest involved in this case, and if we do not succeed here in our struggle to retain compulsory religious affiliation, it will indicate that the purpose of the emancipation will only have been to hasten our disintegration."[13]

The arguments advanced by Philippson against having parts of the special regulations for Jews repealed, arguments which were severely criticized by a number of prominent intellectuals, were the following: (1)

---

12. Jacob Nachod, Chairman of the Committee of D.I.G.B., *Entstehungsgeschichte und Rechtscharacter der Emanzipationsbestimmungen,* Leipzig, 1878, p. 1 ff.

13. Ibid. Useful information on a similar mood in the large Jewish communities may be found in F.A., Nos. 8, 9. For the historical background, especially from the political and social point of view, see the comprehensive and detailed study, Jacob Toury, *Die politischen Orientierungen der Juden in Deutschland, von Jena bis Weimar,* Tübingen, 1966, p. 110 ff (hereafter, J. Toury).

To abandon the principle of obligatory religious affiliation would lead to a disintegration of the Jewish community and its vital communal services; those who provide such services, including teachers, would be dismissed; and for the non-Orthodox community these restraints that hindered complete absorption by the non-Jewish environment would have been removed. (2) This threat to the continuity of Jewish life was contrary to liberal principles, for it represented an effective and far-reaching intervention of the state in the private life of the citizen and constituted a violation of his freedom of religion and conscience, both in theory and in practice. On the other hand, to leave some of the special religious regulations intact (such as those pertaining to the churches), especially the regulation concerning compulsory religious affiliation, would guarantee the continued existence of the Jewish communities and were therefore indispensable for the preservation of the Jewish religion. (3) State support of religious communities benefited the state itself since religion, including religious education, inculcated civic virtues and also served to counteract the pernicious influence that immoral doctrines, such as ethical relativism and pessimism, had upon the youth.[14]

This attitude of some of the Jewish leaders of large communities was well received in conservative Protestant circles, but was met with antagonism and even ridicule by the liberal intellectuals. In private archives preserved by some families in Berlin, Frankfurt, and Leipzig we find interesting reports of intimate meetings that took place in the autumn of 1865 in the homes of liberals who supported the cause of Jewish emancipation. This attitude toward the question of compulsory religious affiliation was invariably described by Jewish leaders as "petty bourgeois . . . anarchistic . . . the naive political thinking of small-town Lutheran pastors who want to impose religion on the population by force. . . . The Jews delude themselves in thinking that Jewish identity can be maintained by means of obsolete, reactionary regulations, such as compulsory religious affiliation. . . . Such an affiliation is meaningless for progressive Jews, and there is no justification for obstructing the process of complete assimilation among us. . . . Nor should religion be exploited for political ends, as is the case when the separate existence of a public Jewish organization is artificially preserved . . . especially since religion as such is now an anachronism." [15]

14. Ibid., F.A., Nos. 8, 9.    15. F.A., No. 4.

These reactions were heard at a time when the question was being discussed officially and unofficially, and even in intimate circles, and hence
may well serve to illustrate the two divergent attitudes of the intellectuals
discussed above. Some members of these circles, among them men intimately associated with Jews, were of the opinion that the Jews should
relinquish all attempts to preserve their separate identity: "Even if they
see in this a kind of coercion, [they must realize that] equality can be
purchased only at the price of concessions." [16] The second group which
subscribed to the principle of "identification" and which included lawyers, doctors, and political figures who came from the ranks of the Progressives demanded of their Jewish friends that they cease this "insipid
talk" (*geschmacklose Gequatsch*) about the prophetic and ethical mission
of modern Judaism. Now, with the rise of the kingdom of Prussia and its
growing power, the Jews should abandon all notions of a separate mission. There was only one mission that could still enlist the sympathies of
this group and that was proof against rational criticism, declared the revolutionary poet and art historian Gottfried Kinkel, and that was the historical and universal mission of the German nation. As long as the German
Jews failed to regard this as the final consummation of their own historical tradition, they would not achieve the equality they aspired to—"for it
is they who continue to separate their will from the will of the nation." [17]

After Austria had been defeated by Russia in August 1866, the intellectuals presented with greater force and clarity their attitude toward the
state and the nation, toward political power in general, and toward the
Jews. At the beginning of the military campaign, as in the years
1863–1864, there were still many liberal intellectuals who opposed Bismarck's policies; but, during the war, when the nation was gripped by the
fever of national enthusiasm, there was increased support for the regime's
foreign and domestic policies, especially among the Protestants. This
support, however, was even then not wholehearted, and conflicting views
continued to produce perplexity and dissension. Men like Rudolf von
Jhering, Johann Gustav Droysen, Heinrich von Sybel, and Rudolf von
Gneist were deeply impressed by the military and political successes of
Prussia, but they saw in the widespread veneration of power and military
prowess portents of Germany's overweening nationalism.

The attitude of the liberal intellectuals was determined by a number of

---

16. Ibid.    17. Ibid.

interrelated factors. They supported the Hohenzollerns against the Hapsburgs in the hope that this would strengthen German nationalism, but at
the same time they feared that the national state would become absolute
and despotic. It was felt in these circles that with the liberation from
Catholic or ultramontane influences they could look forward to the rapid
industrialization and modernization of a united Kleindeutschland (that is,
Germany without Austria), but they were apprehensive of the growing
power of the industrialists who, to safeguard their interests and consolidate their recent gains, were likely to ally themselves with the conservatives and agrarians. This compelled them to support the hegemony of the
Prussian monarchy, but not without misgivings of the increasing power of
the hereditary social classes, such as the Junkers, landowners, army officers, and civil servants.

This vacillating attitude had an inhibiting effect on the political activity
of many liberal intellectuals. Those who were impatient of delay, however, chafed at these restraints and turned to the state in the two senses
described above as "authoritarian" and "identification." In an important
article entitled "German Liberalism," published in 1866 in the *Preussische Jahrbücher* (Vol. 18), the historian Hermann Baumgarten clearly
set forth the basic principles of the "authoritarian" approach. Speaking
also for those who shared this approach—such as Hermann von Helmholtz, Rudolf von Jhering, Konstantin Rössler—the author deplored the
fact that the intellectuals were too engrossed in the world of ideals and
scientific analysis. Scientific research should be divorced from politics,
not only that scientific objectivity may be preserved but, even more important, that politics may be relieved of the burden of abstract idealism
and sterile analysis. The aim of science, Baumgarten asserted, is the discovery of truth. But where the theoretical and analytical enterprise of
science ends, the synthetic task of politics begins. This task in his day
was to achieve the national unity of Germany, to foster the pan-Germanic
spirit within the different states and among the various social classes that
lived separated from one another, to confer upon the state supreme authority over the citizen, and to educate the latter to place his duties as a
citizen above his own selfish desires.

In the "political correspondence" of the *Preussische Jahrbücher* of
February 1867 we find the view stated in no uncertain terms that if Germany should be confronted with the alternative of realizing the aims of
national unity or those of liberalism, it was the plain duty of the Germans

to choose the former. If this process of national unification should necessitate the rule of a military dictatorship under a despotic *Führer*, the Germans would still be bound to choose national unification and all that it entailed rather than freedom and the classical values of liberalism.[18]

A few years after the publication of this article the principal organ of Germany Jewry, the *Allgemeine Zeitung des Judenthums,* propounded an apparently similar thesis, although directed to a different end, urging German Jews to abandon liberalism should it prove incompatible with the preservation of Jewish uniqueness. In a programmatic article called "Liberalism and Judaism" the journal warned its readers of the dangers of egalitarianism implicit in the philosophy of liberalism. Liberalism was opposed to all particularistic movements, for it was inflamed with a democratic fervor to reduce all differences to uniformity and to abolish all distinctions among the different religions and social groups within the Reich. But Judaism, the article continued, was "a great historic-religious individuality . . . and since German liberalism is incapable of tolerating [the existence of] any individuality whatsoever, particularly in the political or economic sphere, however innocuous, we can only censure its error, deplore its inadequacies, and refuse to follow in its footsteps." [19]

In the summer of 1873 the liberal intellectuals reacted to these two articles, namely, to the declaration in the *Preussische Jahrbücher* of February 1867 which asserted that liberalism should be discarded if it conflicted with nationalism, and to the declaration in the *Allgemeine Zeitung des Judenthums* in 1872 which also asserted that liberalism should be discarded if it conflicted with the continued existence of the Jewish community as a separate and distinct religious entity. The immediate cause of this reaction on the part of the intellectuals was the famous declaration of February 8, 1873, by Rudolf Virchow, an eminent pathologist and one of the leaders of the Progressive Liberals, which stated that in view of the ultramontane danger a situation was likely to arise in which the Reich would be compelled to accept a temporary "dictatorship of ministers." [20]

In answer to this declaration the liberal intellectuals met in Berlin to discuss "the danger of despotism that faces us as a result of the violent

18. P.J., Vol. 19, 1867, p. 224 ff; excerpt from an important source quoted by Koppel S. Pinson, *Modern Germany—Its History and Civilization,* New York, 1955, p. 152.

19. A.Z.d.J., Vol. 36, 1872, No. 23, pp. 442–443; see there, issue No. 11, p. 199 ff.

20. *Stenographischer Bericht über die Verhandlungen des Preussischen Landtags-Abgeordnetenhaus,* Vol. I, p. 662; see further, Chap. 2.

form of the *Kulturkampf.''* According to the minutes of the meeting, which have in part been preserved (in the Thieme Collection, No. 14/b), the participants generally agreed that a common denominator was evident between the nationalistic, romantic, or even reactionary tendencies of many of the liberal statesmen and the aspirations of the leaders of the Jewish communities to establish Jewish separatism along historical, nonrational lines that were neither wholly religious nor wholly national. Professor Julius Winter, who was on friendly terms with the Jewish community, argued that both sides were advocating antiquated, romantic, and antiliberal ideas, although each group evoked a different national ideal to justify its position. Two Protestant medical scientists who took part in the meeting, both actively in favor of the social integration of Jews and who later were known as prominent opponents of political anti-Semitism, quoted another example from the *Allgemeine Zeitung des Judenthums* to illustrate what they called "a primitive and narrow-minded urge for separatism . . . on the part of the leaders of the Jewish communities . . . and an unwillingness to have the Jewish community identify itself completely with the German national will." This passage appeared in 1871 in an editorial which bore the caption "Germany and Austria." The same journal proclaimed that "Judaism is not only the religion of the individual Jew; it has also risen to a consciousness of its historical and universal mission; the Jewish community is also conscious of the fact that, despite the tendency to uniformity, it still occupies a unique position." [21] The new political boundaries between Austria and Germany, the article went on to say, did not apply to the Jews. Since the Jews occupied a special place within German culture, all German-speaking Jews, including the citizens of Austria and other foreign countries, would continue to maintain their common historical, cultural, and religious ties, just as they had done before the separation of Austria and Germany. Those who attended the meeting called this a separatist approach and argued that it bore witness to the fact that the Jewish leadership was still far from understanding the vast change that had taken place in German nationalism in those years. The victory of Prussia over Austria had imposed upon every enlightened German the sacred duty "to renounce all that is un-German."

Another note heard among the liberal intellectuals, even among those

21. A.Z.d.J., Vol. 35, 1871, p. 63 ff.

in favor of the legal and social emancipation of the Jews, was one that condemned "the arrogant self-exaltation of the spokesmen of organized Jewry." [22] This was in reference to another article in the *Allgemeine Zeitung des Judenthums* of that same year (1871) which bore the title, "How Are We to Regard the Matter," and which stated, among other things, that Prussia's national war against France was of no concern to German Jewry: "The political changes resulting from these wars in no way concern us. . . . We are interested in other problems of a loftier nature." The article went on to state that since the Jews did not constitute a political bloc, they could have no interest in these wars: "Of what benefit are these new political arrangements to us if they do not make us better, nobler, more upright, more God-fearing, more enlightened." [23] Sentiments such as these, the German intellectuals pointed out, testified to the petty bourgeois, conservative character and "ethical hypocrisy" of the leaders of the Jewish community, a character associated with the reactionary clergy and not with an enlightened modern community.

After Prussia's victory over France and the establishment of the German Empire, there was an upsurge of national feeling in intellectual circles and greater interest in the monarchy (*Staatsbewusstsein*). Among the intellectuals this renascence took on a complex character and was even imbued with a prophetic spirit by some of the theologians among them. Professor Adolf Hausrath of Heidelberg, one of the leading Protestant theologians, described Prussia's military victory as "a victory of German enlightenment over ultramontane spiritual enslavement . . . of the Protestant over the jesuitical spirit." [24] In 1871 the influential periodical *Neue Evangelische Kirchenzeitung* called on all Catholics to repent, for the consequences of the war had clearly demonstrated that "all the nations that reject the teachings of the New Testament are destined to disappear from the earth." [25]

This point of view seems to be far removed from that of the nontheological liberal elements among the intellectuals. A comparison of their phraseology and modes of thought, however, reveals that these two groups had a common interest which manifested itself in two particulars.

22. From F.A., Nos. 8, 9.
23. A.Z.d.J., Vol. 35, 1871, pp. 1–3; "It's none of our business what will develop from these battles for the political world . . . we are concerned with other, loftier questions."
24. K. H. Höfele, "Sendungsglauben und Epochenbewusstsein in Deutschland, 1870/1," Z.R.G.G., Vol. 15, 1963, p. 270.
25. Ibid.

They both detected deep spiritual forces at work in historical events, whether religious or secular. Prussia's victory over France, in particular, was interpreted as indisputable evidence that she was spiritually superior to that country and, indeed, to all the countries of the West and their democratic institutions. Second, both groups read a higher meaning into the empirical facts of history and interpreted Prussia's military successes in the three national wars in the sixties as de facto evidence of her political ascendancy and hegemony.

The spiritual significance attached to the establishment of the Empire was defined by the historian Ferdinand Gregorovius (1821–1891) in Hegelian and romantic terms when he spoke of Prussia's victory as having "the biblical greatness of the Day of Judgment." The same thought was expressed in a series of talks on "The Duties of the Educated," which reached the members of the university faculties in the form of a brochure, that is, the notion that the recent military successes were a de facto vindication of the victor's superiority and "of the German spirit as an ethical phenomenon that has been blessed with favor and justice from the very beginning of Creation." [26] The Darwinian version of this sentiment was formulated that same year by the eminent physiologist Jacob Molleschott. In explaining Darwin's principle of natural selection (according to the first edition of 1859) he pointed out that the Germans went beyond the English conception of the principle of the survival of the fittest as an empirical biological fact and sought to justify it on moral grounds. This construction, according to Molleschott, goes back to the Lutheran tradition which holds that man is capable of leading a blessed life nourished by faith, and this bears witness to the efficacy of grace and not works. What is true with respect to the struggle for existence in the case of the individual and the biological species, Molleschott added, also applies to the nation's struggle for survival, so that Prussia's victories are morally justified in the historical struggle for power and dominion.

In its national sentiments, as in other matters, the attitude of the intellectual class was ambiguous. Some of its most prominent members did not share the popular veneration for the state and its growing power. The

---

26. "Über die Pflichten der Gebildeten," in *Glaube und Bildung*, Berlin, Leipzig, pp. 1–2). The work appeared anonymously, but seems to have been written by Rudolf von Gneist, one of the leaders of the Liberal Protestants and National Liberalism. On several occasions during this period Gneist expressed himself in a similar vein, almost in the same words; see *Kulturkampf*, op. cit., note 4. The words of Ferdinand Gregorovius are cited by Höfele, op. cit., note 24, p. 267.

poet Georg Herwegh, who had fled to Switzerland because of his revolutionary activities, warned his countrymen on his return just before the establishment of the German Empire that the nation was imperiled by "Bismarck's despotic rule . . . and the power state [*Machtstaat*]." Jakob Burckhardt pointed to the danger of the rising masses with their egalitarian ethics, their rejection of traditional social values, and the consequent deterioration of the aesthetic and cultural life of Germany and the western world, which could only lead to the inevitable triumph of despotism. With the advent of revolutionary socialism in the second half of the forties and with the upsurge of nationalism and a strong centralized state at the beginning of the seventies, Burckhardt again warned his contemporaries of the two dangers that threatened man's freedom and the human spirit, the military state, and the political messianism of the educated class—the fanatics of state supremacy (*Staatsfanatiker*) and the zealous idealists, on the one hand, and the voluntary submission of the masses to the despotism of these political messiahs, on the other. Friedrich Nietzsche, wielding his mother tongue with unrivaled vigor, sought to arouse his generation to the evils of the time, to the sterility of contemporary culture, ethics, and religion and to the ominous rise of political and spiritual despotism. He warned against attempts to find simple solutions for the existential problems of those days by stretching them on the procrustean bed of racial and political anti-Semitism as formulated by Paul de Lagarde, Richard Wagner, and Professor Adolf Wahrmund.[27]

These views were well received by the intellectuals, but did not express the increasing misgivings that they felt as a class toward the regime and its policies. More characteristic of their attitude was the vacillation of the "noncommittal supporters," best exemplified by Friedrich Theodor Vischer, an advocate of extreme individualism who fought against what he described as "Prussian absolutism . . . which suppresses every vestige of originality in the citizen . . . and attributes individuality to the hereditary classes instead of to man, to the individual." On the other hand, Vischer was convinced that the exigencies of the conflict required the enlightened public to support Bismarck's efficient and highly

27. See the important work by Fritz Stern, *The Politics of Cultural Despair*, Berkeley, Los Angeles, 1961, p. 285. On the relation between Burckhardt's despair concerning the future of culture and his attitude to the Jewish question, see Hans Liebeschütz, "Das Judentum im Geschichtsbild Jakob Burckhardts," L.B.Y., Vol. IV, London, 1959, p. 61 ff. Also by the same author (hereafter, Liebeschütz), *Das Judentum im deutschen Geschichtsbild von Hegel bis Max Weber*, Tübingen, 1967, p. 157 ff.

centralized regime "if we are to achieve national unity which is the prerequisite for civil liberty." [28]

These attitudes reflected the dilemma in which the intellectuals found themselves. They were conscious of the heavy responsibility that rested upon them. Above all, they felt it to be their duty, in the Kantian sense, to take a definite stand on the basic issues of the day, and this was reinforced by the Protestant ethic of the moral command, a principle that was widely accepted by the intellectuals. This principle, however, as it passed from its theoretical formulation to the stubborn realm of politics could not be realized by the intellectual without compromising his freedom or identifying himself completely with the sovereign will. This dilemma was intensely felt by such men as Hugo Sommer, a prolific contributor to the *Preussische Jahrbücher,* the writer Theodor Fontane, the physicist Hermann von Helmholtz, the physiologist Emil Dubois-Reymond, and especially by the historical philosopher Wilhelm Dilthey early in his career.[29] On the one hand, the intellectual was constrained to identify himself with the state and with the political sphere as a whole once he decided to accept his political responsibilities. But as a spiritual heir of the Enlightenment his first allegiance was to the autonomy of human reason and its dictates, which are incompatible with the compromising entanglements of political action. On the other hand, to be remiss in his responsibilities to the state and to ignore its growing power, the intellectual felt, would also result in alienation and a loss of identity. His sense of responsibility, the characteristic trait of the adherents of the Enlightenment, urged him to forego his private broodings, throw in his lot with generic humanity, and devote his energies to the work of shaping reality. The times called for a reconciliation of the luminous goals of the Enlightenment with the imperious claims of the state in the interest of the common man.[30]

These ambiguous attitudes of the liberal intellectuals were concretely formulated in the years 1879–1880 in the course of the renewed discussions of the Jewish problem. During this period in Berlin and in other large cities there arose groups of intellectuals and liberal statesmen who wished to combat political anti-Semitism. For example, besides the well-

28. F.A., Nos. 8, 9.
29. A collection of interesting material is to be found in the booklet *Zur Selbstkritik des gebildeten Bürgerthums und dessen Einstellung in Staats-und Kulturangelegenheiten,* Berlin, 1878, pp. 2–7.
30. Ibid., p. 10.

known group of notables which issued a manifesto on November 12, 1880, against Adolf Stöcker and other anti-Semitic agitators, we find prominent liberal intellectuals: doctors, jurists, writers, historians, scientists, and, particularly, political figures from among the Progressive Liberals. Similar groups to combat political anti-Semitism were formed during the months preceding the elections to the Reichstag in 1881 and 1884, and then in 1891–1892 with the founding of the League to Combat Anti-Semitism (Verein zur Abwehr des Antisemitismus). Highly interesting evidence has been preserved in a number of family archives already mentioned in connection with the informal meetings that took place in the large cities between Jewish and Christian intellectuals, many of them related by intermarriage.

From these various representative sources a relatively clear picture emerges of the ambiguous attitude of the liberal intellectuals toward the political sphere in general as well as their views concerning the price the Jews were to pay to be admitted into the dominant society. In a letter written in the year 1880–1881 by Dr. Reichert, a member of the Academy of Sciences who also belonged to the group of notables mentioned above, the position of the intellectual is described as follows: "This testifies to the fact that our relation to our Jewish fellow-citizens teaches us more about our own relation to the liberal idea . . . [similar to] the way that the idea of agape in the New Testament is reflected in the attitude of the Church to the Jews." [31] The letter quotes excerpts containing the views of Max von Forckenberg, the mayor of Berlin and one of the leading opponents of anti-Semitism of that day, taken from discussions conducted by a number of notables before the manifesto was issued (or perhaps during the time it was being formulated). The dispute revolved around the key sentence in the manifesto. The published formulation stated that the anti-Semitic propaganda was ineffective because, among other things, "it primarily attacks those [among the Jews] who in all

31. F.A., No. 16. For basic relevant material, see: the "Erklärung," signed by seventy-five German intellectuals condemning the first popular political anti-Semitic manifestations of 1879–1880, issued Nov. 12, 1880, and reprinted in Walter Boehlich, *Der Berliner Antisemitismusstreit,* Frankfurt a/M, 1965, pp. 202–204 (hereafter, Boehlich). This comprehensive collection of sources also contains references to additional sources and studies relevant to this dispute, as well as an analytical survey by the editor. (2) *Die Verurtheilung der antisemitischen Bewegung durch die Wahlmänner aus den vier Berliner Landtags-Wahlkreisen, am 12.1.1881,* Berlin, 1881, pp. 3–15. (3) For similar proclamations condemning "blatant anti-Semitism," see Friedrich Müller, *Stöckers angeblich ethnisch-soziale Judenfrage,* Würzburg, 1881, p. 71 ff.

honesty and sincerity [and] by loyally participating in the life of the nation seek to get rid of their distinctiveness.'' The anti-Semites, the manifesto goes on to say, thus make it difficult for the liberals, both Jews and Christians, to attain their chief goal, namely, to do away with those differences which serve to separate Jews from non-Jews within the German nation.

In the original draft cited by Reichert and his colleagues (which may not have been the only version under consideration) we find instead of the phrase "by loyally participating in the life of the nation" the phrase "for the purpose of complete absorption into the nation." In the discussion concerning the methods to be used in combating anti-Semitism which subsequently took place in Berlin at the beginning of 1881 under the auspices of the Progressive party, it was pointed out that those who had supported the original draft the previous year urging that the Jews be completely absorbed into the nation were in fact supporting the view advocated by Theodor Mommsen in his famous debate in 1880 with Heinrich von Treitschke.[32] As an exponent of what we have called "identification," Mommsen called upon the Jews to integrate completely with their non-Jewish environment. This demand, which was primarily addressed to non-Orthodox Jews, in no way denied the Jews the right to retain their separate identity but, as the Progressives pointed out, was to be regarded as the completion (*Vollendung*) of Jewish uniqueness, being at once both realization and perfection. In defending this interpretation, which was likewise published on the eve of the Reichstag elections of 1881, the Liberal Progressives took their stand on the following excerpt from Mommsen's essay, "One Word More Concerning Our Judaism"

What we cannot save them from is the feeling of alienation and inequality that the Christian German experiences even today when he faces the German Jew. . . . But the blame for this, at least in part, rests upon the Jews. The word "Christianity" [*Christenheit*] in our day no longer has the same meaning it once had; nevertheless, it is the only designation we have to denote the international civili-

---

32. The dispute between Theodor Mommsen and Heinrich von Treitschke, and the public debate that followed the latter's article "Unsere Aussichten," P.J., November 1879. See Reuwen Michael, "Grätz contra Treitschke," *Bulletin,* Leo Baeck Institute, Tel-Aviv, 1961, Vol. IV, No. 16, p. 30 ff; Hans Liebeschütz, "Treitschke and Mommsen on Jewry and Judaism," L.B.Y. Year Book, Vol. VII, 1962, p. 153 ff; Liebeschütz, pp. 157 ff, 193 ff. The minutes of this political and ideological discussion, in which only Liberal-Progressive intellectuals and professional people took part, are to be found in the pamphlet *Vor der fünften Legislaturperiode,* Berlin, 1881.

zation of our day that unites millions and millions of the highly populated globe. To be excluded from this sphere and still live within the nation is indeed possible, but it is difficult and fraught with danger. He whose conscience, from the positive or negative point of view, does not permit him to withdraw from Judaism and accept Christianity, will act accordingly but must be prepared to bear the consequences. . . . It is a well-known fact, however, that most Jews do not change their religion, not because of scruples of conscience but mainly for altogether different feelings, feelings that I fully comprehend but cannot justify. Also the greater part of specifically Jewish organizations as they exist here in Berlin, for example, seem to me—except where they are clearly of a religious nature—to be absolutely harmful. I would never be associated with a welfare organization whose laws required it to render aid only to the inhabitants of Holstein; and with all the respect I have for the aims and activities of these societies, I see in their separate existence nothing more than the belated influence of the [pre-emancipation], of the days of "protected Jews". . . . . Admission into a large nation carries with it a price of its own; the people of Hanover and the people of Hessen, and we the people of Sleswig-Holstein are prepared to pay this price, and we feel that in doing so we are surrendering part of our independence. But we surrender it to our common fatherland. Also the Jews will not again be led by Moses to the Promised Land.[33]

Those who took part in the above discussions early in 1881 to consider ways of combating anti-Semitism stated further that it is in this spirit that we must understand Mommsen's argument, namely, that in the history of the nations the Jews have been regarded as a ferment and as a disintegrative force in the prenational period. Hoffmann, the rector of the University of Berlin, pointed out that Mommsen, as is evident from his *History of Rome* (Vol. III) and his essay "Contra Treitschke" (1880), interpreted this disruptive force in a positive sense, as a ferment indispensable to a people in a transitional stage from a tribal and particularistic social structure to a national, universal structure. At this historical stage of transition the ferment hastened the disintegration of the traditional particularistic units and neutralized the historical contradictions among the various tribes that hindered the process of national unification. The Jews constituted such a ferment, so that since the time when they lost their country they contributed greatly in eradicating differences and in advancing the

---

33. Boehlich, pp. 224–225. Fragments from this source are cited in Shmuel Ettinger's source book, *The Beginnings of Modern Anti-Semitism* (Hebrew), Akadamon, Jerusalem, 1964, and also by Dov Kulka, *Anti-Semitism in Europe 1848–1914,* Akadamon, Jerusalem, 1968.

cause of universalism, at the same time being able to adapt themselves to this universalism. This disintegrative Jewish force, Mommsen and his liberal supporters concluded, was therefore as necessary in the present period of the national consolidation of the German Empire as it was in the days of Caesar. Just as the Jews had served in the past as an element in the decomposition of the tribal units (*ein Element der Decomposition der Stämme*) and thus contributed to the consolidation of the Roman Empire, Mommsen wrote in 1880, so also must they serve in a similar capacity in a period of a renascent German nationalism, when the Reich was struggling to achieve inner unity and make one nation of the German states. This was a necessary task but also a painful one in two senses: it was difficult for the German national and tribal units (and this included the Jews) to relinquish their historical distinctiveness, and it was also difficult for those who were conscious of their national and monarchist responsibilities (and this again included the Jews) to eliminate intertribal friction, which was nevertheless the essential condition for the creation of German nationalism. Hence, far from deploring this historic cosmopolitan role of the Jews, Mommsen welcomed it as a providential means to facilitate the dissolution of indigenous particularistic groups and so promote the formation of universal national entities, and with this in mind he concluded: "I am inclined to believe that Providence knows better than Herr Stöcker why it was desirable to add a certain percentage of Israel in the smelting furnace to temper the German metal." [34]

These views of Mommsen and his liberal followers were widely discussed for a long time. The anti-Semites seized upon his characterization of the Jews as a disruptive element that contributed to the dissolution of national groups or particularistic tribes. This passage in his essay was taken out of its context and used as a propaganda slogan; it first appeared in the early publications of the anti-Semitic movement, such as *Die Deutsche Wacht,* Theodor Fritsch's popular anti-Semitic catechism, the teachings of Houston Stewart Chamberlain, and, finally, in the official ideology of the Nazis in the Third Reich. That Mommsen himself would never have countenanced such anti-Semitic propaganda, which he called

34. Ibid., pp. 217–218; and the source in the well-known historical work, Theodor Mommsen, *Römische Geschichte,* Berlin, 1875, Vol. III, p. 550 ff.: "Also in the ancient world Judaism was an effective ferment of cosmopolitanism and national decomposition, and as such a justifiable member in the Cesarian state whose politics was in reality nothing more than world-citizenship, whose *Volkstuemlichkeit* was at bottom nothing else than humanity."

"the monster of national feeling," nor lent his name to support its aims is but another illustration of the vagaries of history from which we can derive a twofold truth, namely, that in the course of history the meaning of ideas, concepts, or even words is not impartially determined, but defined by the needs of succeeding generations. On the other hand, the question arises whether it is purely accidental that precisely these words should lend themselves to an interpretation that is diametrically opposed to the one originally intended. Mommsen did not have in mind the integration of Jews within a pluralistic society which ensured the coexistence of various hereditary groups as part of one united nationality, but rather an integration within a uniform, homogeneous society, and this meant, as far as the Jews were concerned, extinction as the price for integration. In this demand we see one of the important aspects of the renewed German nationalism of those years.[35]

Among the first to recognize the inner logic of this point of view immediately after the publication of Mommsen's words was Heinrich Graetz. In a letter to Professor Jacob Bernays (December 15, 1880) he

35. The immediate reaction of the anti-Semites, in the journal, *Die Deutsche Wacht,* in an article called "Theodor Mommsen und sein Wort über unser Judenthum," moved the Executive Committee of the Gemeindebund in its meeting on Feb. 24, 1881, to institute legal proceedings against the Verlagsbuchhandlung Otto Hentze. This step was part of a broader policy pursued by a number of leaders of the Jewish communities beginning late in the seventies calling on the organized Jewish community to combat political and racial anti-Semitism by legal means. For this, see publications of the Gemeindebund, *Mittheilungen,* No. 9, July 1881, p. 31; and the report of B. Jacobsohn, *Der D.I.G.B.,* Leipzig, 1879, p. 29 ff ; also files in archives containing important records of the legal proceedings against political and racial anti-Semitism: G.A.J., G.A.M1/16 D.I.G.B. No. 15 "Strafanträge in Bekämpfung des Antisemitismus"; M1/13, D.I.G.B. No. 44 "Anträge in Bekämpfung des Antisemitismus." For examples of other reactions to Mommsen's attitude, see M. Güdemann, *Nationaljudenthum,* Leipzig, Wien, 1897, p. 27 ff. A typical historico-apologetical discussion by Hermann Vogelstein of Königsberg of Mommsen's general attitude to Judaism and to the Jews as expressed in Vol. III of his *History of Rome,* and also in Vol. V, is "Kein anderer Gott ist so von Haus aus der Gott nur der Seinen gewesen wie Jahwe, und keiner es so ohne Unterschied von Zeit und Ort geblieben" (No other God has from the very outset been the God of his people alone as Yahwe, and none has remained as such irrespective of time and place, *History of Rome,* Vol. V, p. 487). An anti-Semitic source is Paul de Lagarde, "Programm für die konservative Partei Preussens, 1884," in *Deutsche Schriften, Gesamtausgabe,* Göttingen, 1903, p. 366 ff: "It would no doubt be proper to get rid of those who even in the opinion of the eminent Th. Mommsen have always advanced decomposition." One of the political, ideological works of the early anti-Semitic parties is G. Stille, "Die Juden im Römischen Reich" in *Antisemitisches Jahrbuch,* Berlin, 1899, p. 1 ff. Of the extreme nationalistic circles, one of the many examples that give a contrary interpretation to Mommsen's words discussed above is Erich Lehnhardt, "Judenthum und Antisemitismus," P.J., Vol. 55, 1885, p. 670.

pointed out that Mommsen's proposed solution of the Jewish question entailed an exorbitant price: "He treats us Jews with great consideration, but at what price!—that we merge completely with Christianity." [36]

The early political and national consequences of this conception, insofar as it involved the attempt of Jews to assimilate "the German spirit" while retaining their separate identity, were evident as early as the sixties, during the period of the Prussian-German wars. The rise of a relatively extreme form of monarchist nationalism was now attended by a new development in the key concept of *Volk* and its various manifestations as the spirit, the soul, and the ethnic origin of a people (*Volksgeist, Volksseele, Volksstamm*). In contrast to earlier times we find that the concept of

36. This letter by Graetz has now been reprinted in Reuwen Michael's work (op. cit., note 32). Concerning the reservations of German Jewry to Graetz's violent criticism of Christianity and his nationalistic approach as expressed in his general historiography and in his essay on Treitschke, see *Schlesische Presse,* Vol. 7, Dec. 28, 1879 (now in the Boehlich collection, p. 25 ff, 45 ff); also the correspondence between the leaders of the Jewish communities and some of the Jewish historians: G.A.J., G.A. M1/24 D.I.G.B. Correspondenz, Historische Commission; and J. Meisel, "The Historical Commission for the History of the Jews in Germany" (Hebrew), *Zion,* Vol. 19, 1954, pp. 171–172. In his letter of Nov. 30, 1885, to Dr. Samuel Kristeller, one of the heads of the Gemeindebund, Professor H. Breslau points out the harm which in his opinion and in the opinion of many Jews in Germany had been caused by Graetz's attitude: "In his judgment personalities like Treitschke and Mommsen are in complete agreement. The latter ("One Word More about Our Judaism," Berlin, 1880, p. 6) relegates Graetz's 'talmudic style of historical writing' to a literary corner and puts it . . . on the same level as ultramontane historical falsification. I, for my part, was unfortunately not in a position to contradict these views and statements of Treitschke and Mommsen in good conscience, and had to confine myself to absolving the Jewish community of responsibility for this historical writing." In the letter the word *"Geschichtsfälschungen"* was erased, and in its place the author put the original word *"Tendenzschriften"* (tendentious writings); for an explanation of this correction see Breslau's postcard of Nov. 30, 1885, in the archives mentioned above; see Shmuel Ettinger, "Graetz's Historiographical Work" (Hebrew) in the collection *Historians and Historical Schools,* Jerusalem, 1962, p. 84 ff. Treitschke's criticisms of Graetz have been collected in an essay "Herr Grätz und sein Judenthum," which appeared in P.J. in December 1897 (Boehlich, p. 31 ff.) Breslau's public apology and his argument that the Jewish community was not responsible for Graetz's views was the answer to Treitschke's statement in this essay (Boehlich, p. 93) that part of German Jewry regarded Graetz's historiography as a "standard work," and in following Graetz "Jewish journalists" were encouraged to treat "Christianity and Germanism with malevolent derision" (in *Form gehässiger Witzelei gegen Christenthum und Germanenthum*). Graetz's position in the dispute is now amply documented in *Zvi Graetz: Paths of Jewish History, Essays, Diary, Letters,* trans. by J. Tolkes, ed. by Shmuel Ettinger, and with an autobiographical introduction by Reuwen Michael, Jerusalem, 1969; see Ettinger's introduction, p. 28 ff, also translated sources, pp. 226–228, 283.

*Volksgeist* in its Hegelian sense was much less in vogue during the period of the Second Reich and became more and more attached to the romantic notions found in the works of J. G. Fichte, J. G. Herder, L. Arnim, F. L. Jahn, and the legal historical school of F. K. von Savigny and G. F. Puchta. An ideology that emphasized natural origins with deep roots in a common biological past and with a common ethnic mentality that stems from ancient traditions was resurrected by the brothers Grimm—an ideology that excluded Jews as the members of a "foreign racial tribe."

This critical change in the direction of thought and feeling is clearly reflected in Treitschke's theoretical writings and public utterances. Until the sixties Treitschke understood the concepts *Volksgeist* and *Volkswesen* as metaphysical realities in the Hegelian sense and, hence, as the bearers of the spirit of universal reason as it moves toward its final goal: to the knowledge of itself, to its absolute realization, and ultimately to absolute freedom. At this stage he had still not adopted Fichte's romantic ideas. The concept of a primordial people (*Urvolk*) with its own national consciousness and with a national language to serve as a vehicle of its thoughts and as the depository of its ancient wisdom was for Treitschke a romantic notion without a metaphysical basis and hence without ontological certainty. But during the period in which he wrote the introduction to the "History of the Early 19th Century," which formed part of his comprehensive *German History,* a basic change took place in his attitude either because he was influenced by the nature of the material he was working with in connection with his historical investigations or by Prussia's national wars in the second half of the sixties. The change became apparent when he rejected the Hegelian identification of cognition and existence, of concept and reality—and it was this that enabled him to return to the irrational sources of romanticism. *Volksgeist* and *Volkswesen* became the vehicles for the realization of historical facts or ethnic characteristics and not for metaphysical-rational essences. Jahn's principle of German nationalism, the linguistic studies and folkloric researches of Jakob and Wilhelm Grimm, Fichte's notion of the primordial roots of nationalism were from then on endowed with ethical and didactic significance by Treitschke, the embodiment of autarkic truths untouched by changing regimes or personal decisions.

These views had a deep and lasting influence on the development of the Christian character of German nationalism by justifying the irrational and antiliberal interpretation of the principle of equality, which also served as a basis for Treitschke's anti-Semitic teachings.[37] Racial and political anti-Semitism derived its aggressive nationalist and monarchist tendencies from Treitschke; the National Liberals, the Free Conservatives, the students, and the youth, however, appropriated his demand for the total merging of the Jews and Judaism with the Christian Protestant environment. This demand became the indispensable condition for the formal emancipation of German Jewry, and in this both the supporters of Treitschke and his opponents were in agreement.

At first it seemed that Mommsen and the liberal circles were opposed to these exclusive ethnic and romantic attitudes. Moreover, in a polemical article of November 1880, Mommsen stated that the national renascence would create a situation in which "a war will be waged of all against all," after which German citizenship would be rooted not in natural law but in romantic and mythological principles, such as racial purity or the naive, irrational faith in the teachings of the New Testament. The day was not far distant, Mommsen continued, when the German citizen would be able only "to identify himself as qualified for ploughing," and hence modern anti-Semitism should be regarded as but another stage in the series of struggles in defense of the German nation and its culture, such as the *Kulturkampf* and the class war.[38]

Here we have a clear instance of the two conflicting attitudes within the intellectual class as supporters of the national movement with respect to the demand that the Jews surrender their separate status. Mommsen had urged the Jews to conduct themselves like any other German ethnic group, to abandon their parochial attachments, and to merge fully with the rest of the nation: "We are in this of one mind, that the German nation is based on the federation and, in a certain sense, the fusion (*Verschmelzen*) of the various German tribes." [39] In a similar vein his opponent, Treitschke, declared: "I live in the hope that the emancipation in the years to come will result in an inner fusion and in a united nation." [40] In the light of these views the position defended by Moritz Lazarus in this debate, that "Judaism is German just as Christianity is German," was unrealistic and opposed to the tendencies of the two schools of thought among the intellectuals as represented by Mommsen and Treitschke.

37. See H. Liebeschütz, "Treitschke and Mommsen on Jewry and Judaism, L.B.Y. Vol. VII, 1962, p. 153 ff, Liebeschütz, p. 157 ff, 193 ff.
38. Boehlich, p. 211.    39. Ibid., p. 212.    40. Ibid., p. 210.

A few years after these words had been written the editorial staff of the *Preussische Jahrbücher* provided some clarification of the political and social motives that prompted this ideological point of view. At the end of the seventies and during the eighties the circles close to this journal became increasingly critical of what they called the outmoded, inflexible, and unrealistic policy of the Progressive Liberals, the men of the *Freisinn-Fortschritt,* and of German Jewry as well. In this concerted attack against such Jews as Eduard Lasker, Ludwig Bamberger, and Paul Nathan, and against such leaders of the Progressives and of the *Nation,* as Theodor Barth, Eugen Richter, and Professor Albert Hänel, the *Preussische Jahrbücher* contended that the obstinate adherence of the Jews to the principles of classical liberalism, Manchesterism, and the obsolete ideals of Jewish emancipation was calculated to retard the growth of nationalism and monarchism in the empire, and thus indirectly encourage subversive social forces, including radicalism, skepticism, and pessimism. The criticism of the National Liberals and the *Preussische Jahrbücher,* as opposed to that of the *Freisinn-Fortschritt,* was directed against the comprehensive social legislation enacted by Bismarck and the Conservative coalition at the beginning of the eighties. The Manchester party, as the progressive circles were called, saw in this antiliberal legislation a clear case of interference on the part of the regime in the private life of the citizen and in the social and economic life of the country. The progressives feared the growing power of the Social Democrats no less than that of the National Liberals; but they feared even more the growing power of the state, and they opposed "the demand that the State itself should take over the organization of society and the economy, and not rely on the fact that social harmony will be created and maintained by its own powers." [41]

In dealing with the Jewish question the "Manchesterites," who were committed to the principle of classical liberalism, were obliged, as were the Jews themselves, to adjust to the new reality. In view of the growing industrialization of German society and the moral deterioration occasioned by the new materialism, the Manchester Progressives and the Jews saw as the only solution an unreserved acceptance of the policies of the national state and the cooperation of all elements within it in developing the latent primordial forces within the German people. The nature of

41. *Das deutsche Bildungswesen im letzten Wahlkampf,* Beilage, Berlin, 1906; from F.A., No. 4.

these forces was clearly set forth in a commemorative editorial in the
*Preussische Jahrbücher* on the death of Eduard Lasker: "The most important principle of the liberals, and the one that serves as a permanent
source for its justification . . . is nothing more than the legacy of Luther,
according to which the state, like faith, is prohibited from exercising
dominion over us by means of external compulsion, which is nourished
by a slavish phantasy, but [the authority of the state, like faith] should
flow from our innermost conscience, from our own autonomous will." [42]

Accordingly, the liberal intellectuals proposed that German Jewry
should curtail or eliminate its separate activity in the sphere of social
work and abandon its legal struggle against political anti-Semitism; and
there were some who recommended a maximum restriction of separate
Jewish education. Organized Jewish leadership might not be prepared to
make such drastic restrictions, but then it should not regard separate Jewish existence as an organic part of German nationalism. In circles friendly
to Jews in Berlin the question was asked how the Jews hoped to achieve
complete integration with the Germans when even a step so essential for
the future of the political and national German state as Jewish emancipation was described by the spokesmen of liberal Judaism not as the consummation of German liberalism but as the realization of the law of
Moses and the ethics of the prophets. Furthermore, German Jewry understood emancipation in a sense contrary to that in which the Christians understood it, namely, not as the removal of barriers that had hitherto
prevented Jews from completely assimilating to their environment, but
rather as an incentive to continue to cultivate Jewish uniqueness. In this
connection the German liberals cited the decisions of the Reform Jewish
synod of the year 1869, calling special attention to the following passage:
"The synod recognizes in the development and realization of these principles guarantees that will secure for Judaism and its adherents, in the

---

42. P.J., Vol. 53, 1884, pp. 203, 426, and former issues of P.J., e.g. Vol. 52, 1883, p.
92, severely criticize the Manchester party and its obsolete liberal policies. Shortly thereafter in 1885 this journal attacked the socialists, also from the standpoint of national monarchism. In its criticism of G. Adler's book on the history of the first socialist workers' movement, the journal stated: "The weapons for combating the theories of Manchester
individualism do not belong to these socialists, but to German philosophy. Practical
thoughts, not only deeds, come from Prussia's statesmen" (P.J., Vol. 56, 1885, p. 432).
To complete the subject discussed in this chapter, see the three important studies, Wilhelm
Mommsen, *Stein, Ranke, Bismarck, ein Beitrag zur politischen und sozialen Bewegung des
19. Jahrhundert,* München, 1954, p. 257 ff; Hajo Holborn, "Der deutsche Idealismus in
sozial-geschichtlicher Beleuchtung," *Historische Zeitschrift,* Vol. 174, 1952, p. 366 ff;
Friedrich C. Sell, *Die Tragödie des deutschen Liberalismus,* Stuttgart, 1953, p. 208 ff.

present and in the future, the vital conditions for Judaism's unrestricted existence and highest development.'' [43]

In letters that have been preserved in a number of family archives of members of enlightened circles in Berlin, Frankfurt, and Breslau and in the files and archives of the Deutsch-Israelitischer Gemeindebund, we find evidence that even the Jews themselves, especially those who did not take part in organized Jewish life, viewed with skepticism and even misgivings the attempts of the leaders of the Jewish Gemeindebund in Germany and of the local Jewish communities "to renew in an artificial manner . . . the feeling of solidarity among Jewish citizens in the area of social welfare and in the care of the sick and needy . . . as if distinctions could be made in man's social needs on the basis of religious affiliation, [distinctions] which are in fact purely accidental.'' [44]

43. F.A., No. 12. The quotation is taken from *"Verhandlungen und Resolutionen der ersten israelitischen Synode zu Leipzig, 29 Juni–4 Juli 1869,* Leipzig, 1870. Concerning Liberal Judaism, see further Chap. 4.

44. F.A., Nos. 14–15, reported by B. Jacobsohn, the secretary of the Gemeindebund in the period after the establishment of the empire, who speaks of the reservations of the German Jews in supporting a separate Jewish organization. The minutes and the correspondence between the heads of the Jewish communities in the seventies and eighties, corroborate the argument of the Christian intellectuals that many non-Orthodox Jews were unwilling to maintain separate Jewish organizations. An important argument that helped convince these circles that were removed from organized Jewish life to support Jewish organizations was that the influx of large numbers of Jews from Eastern Europe would increase anti-Semitic feeling. These fears prompted German Jewry to restrict this migration from the East, or at least to encourage it to continue farther west across the seas; in the seventies and eighties and at the beginning of the century these fears served as an incentive to organize Jewish life and support its institutions. This can be seen from a circular letter sent to the leaders of the Jewish communities in July 1872: "Even many decades ago this degrading activity which depicted Judaism in the eyes of our non-Jewish citizens as a danger of far-reaching significance has been recognized by many large communities" (G.A.J., G.A. M1/37). Further testimony to the meager interest shown by German Jewry for separate organizations is provided by teachers and local leaders in G.A.J., G.A. M7/1, "Protokolle des Vereins Israelitischer Kultusbeamten", and in the archives for the history of the Gemeindebund, G.A.J., G.A. M1/3, M1/4, M1/9. To balance the argument, cf. additional testimony from the Orthodox circles, *Die Jüdische Presse,* Vol. 2, 1871, No. 18, "Zur Gemeindebundfrage"; No. 38, 40, "Die Jüdische Gemeinde und der Gemeindebund"; *Der Israelit,* Vol. 18, 1877, No. 45–50, "Die Ursachen der Lebensunfähigkeit des D.I.G.B." The fears of the Jews that separatistic activities would widen the gulf between them and the Christian Germans led a considerable number of people in the community who were active in political affairs, even in Liberal Progressive circles, to abstain from engaging in a public political struggle against anti-Semitism. See reports of the Gemeindebund and, following the parliamentary discussions denouncing anti-Semitism, Nov. 20, 22, 1880, see *Mittheilungen,* No. 9, 1881, p. 20 ff. With the intensification of anti-Semitic feeling and the increasing number of intermarriages beginning in the nineties the non-Orthodox German Jews became more interested in promoting separate Jewish activities.

In a public statement issued by a number of intellectual groups denouncing the anti-Semitic bill presented to the Parliament in March 1881 another thesis of Mommsen's was repeated. In Mommsen's view Christianity was no longer regarded as a metaphysical or theological religion by the enlightened German but rather as a historical and humanistic component of German culture that must perforce be accepted by all who wished to integrate into this culture. In that case, added Professor A. Kirchhoff, a member of the Academy of Sciences and an outspoken foe of anti-Semitism, Mommsen's argument also applied to the German Jews—a view corroborated by Hermann Cohen (who was also cited by Treitschke). The leaders of the Jewish communities and of the Jewish organizations, however, were trying to impose on the Jewish community an artificial Jewish ideology devoid of authentic content.

The above allusion to the views of Hermann Cohen refers to his polemical essay "A Statement on the Jewish Question" (*Ein Bekenntniss in der Judenfrage*) written in 1880, with which he entered the public debate occasioned by Treitschke's article on the Jewish question, a debate that also involved him in a controversy with the spokesmen of the Jewish camp, such as Heinrich Graetz and Moritz Lazarus. Kirchhoff cites Cohen's statement to the effect that Christianity, and especially Lutheran Protestantism, was a spiritual composite of Western culture in general and of German culture in particular, in which connection Cohen observed that "with reference to the scientific concept of religion I am unable to discover any distinction between Jewish monotheism and Protestant Christianity." [45] But, contrary to the interpretation given to Cohen's words by Kirchhoff, who considers this approach as leading necessarily to the complete and final disappearance of Judaism, Cohen himself developed a more complex conception in which both elements, the ideal Jewish-Christian rapproachement and the principle of Jewish uniqueness, appear side by side. This relationship between Judaism and Christianity, particularly between Judaism and Lutheran Protestantism, at this stage in the development of Cohen's system will become clearer if we briefly review some of the basic elements in his general position.

Cohen's belief in Jewish-Christian coexistence was based on the Kantian idea that all religions, especially the monotheistic religions, have in common a basic principle. He followed Kant in holding that to assume

45. Boehlich, p. 127.

the existence of different kinds of religions is as unwarranted as to assume the existence of different kinds of moralities. The differences between religions can be explained, and even justified, in the light of the
different historical origins and literary forms of expression, but from the
standpoint of their essential nature there is only "one single religion that
is valid for all men and for all times." [46] This applies especially to
monotheism, Cohen continued, for monotheism expresses ethical autonomy in its absolute and hence universal form. It follows then that just
as there is only one pure ethical autonomy that is unconditioned and indivisible, there is also one pure monotheism that is unconditioned and indivisible. The element that Kantian ethics and monotheistic religion have in
common, Cohen added, is the absolute and autonomous structure of the
ethical categorical imperative; the difference between them lies in the authoritative sources that are invoked to support and justify it. In monotheism the ethical imperative has its source of authority in God, that is, in a
pure and absolute spirituality; in German idealism it has its source in the
Kantian legacy, which Cohen defined as sacred and inviolable and based
on a postulate that derives the moral law from the legislative power of
reason.[47] The introduction of Christian elements at this point, particularly
Luther's principle of internalizing the moral imperative, served as a kind
of bridge between the Jewish ethical teaching of an absolute divine source
and the absolute rational source of the Kantian moral imperative. This
bridge between religion and reason is created by Christianity by means of
the dogma of incarnation, which Cohen defined as "the Christological
form of humanizing the Divine," the historical link between Judaism on
the one hand and Hellenism and humanism on the other and, from the
dogmatic point of view, between God and man. This bridge created
religious forms that attenuated the distinction between God and man by
humanizing God and also historical-cultural forms humanizing religion.

In the light of these basic distinctions Cohen's answer to the question
of the continued separation of Judaism from German Christianity remains
ambiguous. On the one hand there was a realistic as well as a moral basis
for Judaism's continued existence as an inseparable part of German
Christianity, one that went back to sixteenth-century German history
which teaches us that "the Germans are a religious people and will
remain as such despite all cultural changes." This historical reality,

---

46. Ibid.      47. Ibid., p. 128.

Cohen added, also obliged the Jewish minority to retain its religious identity if it wished to become an inseparable part of the German people: "A nation that desires to strengthen the basis of its political existence must attend to its religious foundations. . . . Such a common effort will enable it to preserve the religious differences inherent in its historical tradition without detriment to the homogeneous national culture." [48] It is precisely the differences between the two religions that obligated the Jews to preserve their own. Despite the common origin and interests of the two religions and despite our "appreciation of the historical and cultural achievements of Christianity . . . we have no need to acknowledge the gospel of the Son of God, for we know that with all the need for humanizing morality there is also the need to preserve the original core of the God of the prophets, which no amount of humanization [*Vermenschlichung*] could eradicate: 'To whom then will ye liken me, or shall I be equal' (Isaiah 40:25). At the heart of God's faith, which is eternal and not merely cosmological, all Christians are children of Israel." [49]

At the same time, however, another aspect of Cohen's system enjoined the complete merging of Judaism with Lutheran Protestantism and also with Kantian autonomous ethics, the common element of both being biblical prophecy, the internalization and humanization of the moral imperative and the principle of ethical responsibility that enables man to make ethical decisions of his own free will, that is, consciously, since it is derived from the sovereign faculty of human reason, the common ground of religion and humanism, of pure monotheistic faith and pure rational judgment. From this basic element that Judaism and German Christianity have in common Cohen concluded that "our Jewish religion, in the form that it lives in our hearts today, is in fact already culturally and historically allied with Protestantism; for just as Protestantism has thrown off the yoke of ecclesiastical tradition, so have we [behaved] more or less openly and without pretense of simulation toward the Talmud; but in a much deeper sense, in all questions that relate to the spiritual questions of religion we think and feel in the Protestant spirit, so that this religious kinship is in fact the strongest and most effective means for a national inner fusion." [50]

Cohen's analysis fails to give us a clear answer to the dilemma between complete Jewish integration into the dominant Christian society of

48. Ibid., p. 130.    49. Ibid., p. 129.    50. Ibid., p. 148.

Germany and a separate Jewish existence within that society. In his controversy with Moritz Lazarus he claimed for Judaism an intermediate position in which it was to continue to exist for the time being as a separate religious and communal group conscious of its spiritual mission, a position which he defended as "the preservation of monotheism as a separate mission until a purer form of Christianity arises, but after the attainment [of this pure form] to be the common mission of all monotheists." [51]

## Conflicting Opinions regarding Jewish Integration and Identity

A characteristic feature of these discussions during the last quarter of the nineteenth century between the Jews and the German intellectuals who supported the cause of nationalism was the desire on the part of both sides to achieve a common goal: the complete assimilation of the Jews into the enlightened liberal society of Germany and its culture. A strong faith in the eventual success of this process was an important element in their united campaign against their combined foes: the racial and political anti-Semites, the clerical circles among the conservative Protestants and Catholics, and even the anarchists, communists, socialists, and what was called "the masses and the mass-cult," all of whom made common cause against the liberal intellectuals and the Jews.

In addition to inner differences that were to be found in all groups, these two groups placed a different construction on what was meant by "the full integration of German Jewry." The spokesmen of the Jewish communities interpreted integration as a process that would enable them to retain some kind of separate identity as Jews without jeopardizing their full membership in the German nation. The Christians, however, understood Jewish integration as a process that would deprive Jewish identity, except for the Orthodox element, of all meaning or justification.

Among the different interpretations given to the historical-ethnographical concept that was prevalent during the last third of the nineteenth century we find one that is directly opposed to the conception described above, that the two religions are united in a common work of redemption. This interpretation is expressed by the terms "composite mixture" (*mixtum compositum*) or "mixture" (*Mischung*), "intermix-

51. Ibid., p. 141.

ture'' (*Vermischung*), and ''mixed race'' (*Mischvolk*). As early as the beginning of the seventies Rudolf von Gneist had warned his countrymen of the danger inherent in the racial theories of German nationalism. In opposition to the racial theories and romantic ideology that based German national character on a common origin and purity of blood, Gneist asserted that the factors that formed the character of the nation—language, customs, legal systems, and religion—were produced by a heterogeneous historical mixture of races and not by a pure homogeneous race. Since the character of a civilized people is formed by a number of divergent historical influences, he added, there is not a single civilized nation in which any of these basic factors have been preserved in their original racial purity. The culture of a people is a *mixtum compositum,* and its ethnic composition the product of intermixture with people of different origins. Thus, we cannot speak of racial purity since all nations are of mixed blood—which may well have been the distinctive factor that proved favorable to their growth and vitality.[52]

In the last two decades of the century this idea was also expounded by prominent opponents of political anti-Semitism, such as the university professors Rudolf von Jhering and Albrecht Weber, as well as by a

52. Rudolf von Gneist, ''Über das Nationalitätsprinzip in der Staatsbildung,'' in Hirth's *Annalen des Deutschen Reichs,* 1872, p. 928 ff. Gneist's views are discussed by Hugo Preuss in his essay ''Nationalität und Staatsgedanken,'' *Die Nation,* Vol. 4, 1887, No. 18, p. 271. The idea that a people or nation is composed not of pure ethnic-racial but of mixed ethnic-historical elements was accepted by most historians, jurists, and writers on political and social affairs during the period of the German Empire; see H. Delbrück, *Regierung und Volkswille,* Berlin, 1914, p. 4; Fr. Meinecke, *Weltbürgerthum und Nationalstaat,* 1907 (7th ed., 1928), p. 1 ff; Erste Soziologentagung, Frankfurt, 1910, Diskussionsrede . . . M. Webers zu dem Vortrag von A. Plötz über ''Die Begriffe Rasse und Gesellschaft'' in M. Weber, *Gesammelte Aufsätze zur Soziologie und Sozialpolitik,* Tübingen, 1929, p. 456 ff. Felix von Luschan, on the occasion of the annual meeting of the German Anthopological Society in Ulm in 1892, related that he had prepared the first scientific study of the racial character of the Jews. He rejected the racial theories of Houston Stewart Chamberlain and approved of the scientific approach of the editors of the Jewish journal *Zeitschrift für Demographie und Statistik der Juden;* he defined the historical character of the Jews as a ''*Mischvolk''* who in the course of their long history had mixed with the people among whom they lived, and he saw no reason why the Jewish question of his day could not be solved by the complete absorption of the Jews into the dominant Christian German society. Because of this obvious solution Luschan wondered why the Jews kept emphasizing their unique position as a chosen people or their separate status as a pure ethnic body: ''I have never understood why so many Jews, and precisely most writers who deal with the Jewish question . . . are so persistent in emphasizing the uniqueness and the absolute racial purity of the 'chosen people' '' (Felix von Luschan, *Völker, Rassen, Sprachen,* Berlin, 1922, pp. 165–166).

number of scholars who subscribed to racial doctrines, such as Felix von Luschan and Werner Sombart. In these circles the view was current that it was both necessary and desirable that ethnic groups and different races should intermingle and that such a mixture will produce a stronger nation.[53] An apparently similar view was expressed by Jewish spokesmen such as Rabbi Manuel Joel, for example, who in the course of his debate with Treitschke in 1879–1880 declared: ''Could Herr von Treitschke testify to the whereabouts of his forefathers 1,800 years ago? Could the professor testify under oath that he is the direct descendant of the Germans who lived in the oak forests of Germany . . . and is modern nationality today composed solely of the members of this original group? Are not the English a great nation . . . and is this not precisely because they are mixed?'' [54]

Different conclusions, however, were drawn from these apparently similar conceptions. Prominent members of the leading Jewish organizations in the large Jewish communities, members of the German-Jewish Gemeindebund, the Union of Rabbis (Rabbiner-Verband) and the Jewish Teachers' Association (Verband der jüdischen Lehrervereine im Deutschen Reiche), as well as the Jewish spokesmen in their dispute with Treitschke, such as Manuel Joel, Moritz Lazarus, Ludwig Bamberger, and Harry Breslau, concluded from this principle of *mixtum compositum* that since civilized nations consist of people of different origins and religions, there could be no objection to including the Jews in this composite without necessarily doing away with Judaism in the process. When Harry Breslau in his debate with Treitschke declared that the greater part of German Jewry was prepared ''to be absorbed into the German nation,'' he did not have in mind wholesale conversion and the extinction of Judaism but rather a union of mutual interest and benefit between Judaism and Germanism and their reciprocal cultural influences.[55] Treitschke, on the other hand, interpreted the principle of integration as a complete ethnic-religious fusion in the sense of miscegenation and hence declared that ''the emancipation had a positive effect in that it deprived the Jews of all cause for justified complaints; but it also made miscegenation difficult, at all times the most effective means for the neutralization of tribal differences. The number of converts to Christianity was greatly reduced,

53. A. S. Danzig, 1892, p. 176 ff; W. Sombart, *Die Juden und das Wirtschaftsleben,* Leipzig (1911), 1918, p. 384 ff.
54. Boehlich, p. 20.      55. Ibid., p. 62.

but intermarriages between Christians and nonconverted Jews will continue to remain exceptional as long as our people will regard Christianity with reverence.'' [56]

Treitschke's opponents among the intellectual Progressive Liberals refrained from using such strong, unambiguous language, but on this central issue they were in agreement with their opponents among the nationalists and among the right-wing liberals. Even moderate Progressives like Professor Heinrich von Sybel, who some years before had spoken of Judaism's miraculous power to withstand its misfortunes, now urged the Jews to forego their separate identity and accept the principle as formulated by von Sybel, namely, "the conscious internalization of the normative authority that has been conferred upon German history," and earnestly suggested that they accede to the national will "whose central principle now is a consciousness of the unity of the spirit as the highest regulative principle of the German monarchist society.'' [57]

Behind all these discussions of the German intellectuals was the desire to come to grips with a widespread spiritual and social crisis, which was chiefly reflected in the skeptical attitude in many intellectual circles (especially among the students and the youth) regarding the effectiveness of education, intellect, humanism, and liberalism or, as the writer Theodor Fontane expressed it, regarding the ability of the German rational culture as a whole to provide an adequate answer to the spiritual and cultural problems that afflict society. Hoffmann, the rector of the University of Berlin, described this crisis as "a lack of faith on the part of a generation fascinated by the achievements of the natural sciences and Prussian politics in the authority of the spirit, of morality and reason.'' [58] There were, of course, intellectuals who did not isolate themselves completely from public life and who nevertheless sought to preserve their independent intellectual integrity; but they were becoming more and more conscious of their inability to provide answers that would serve as a guide for the youth of the country and for German society as a whole in the face of the rising masses in the industrial urban centers. An increasing awareness on the part of the intellectuals of their own impotence and the dangers it involved was reflected in their literary journals, such as the *Preussische*

---

56. Ibid., p. 79.
57. "Das Bewusstsein der Einheit des Geistes als oberstes Ordnungsprinzip der deutschen Staatsgesellschaft," F.A., No. 18/c.
58. In the minutes, op. cit., note 32, p. 20.

*Jahrbücher, Die Gegenwart, Deutsches Literaturblatt,* and, beginning in the early eighties, in *Die Nation* and the *Christliche Welt,* as well as in personal correspondence and in discussions, both public and private. It now became clear to these groups that were in the forefront of the nationalist and monarchist movement that they were powerless against the first manifestations of their own success. This is evident, for example, in a letter sent by Heinrich von Sybel to Hermann Baumgarten on January 27, 1871, in which we still find effusive expressions of mingled reverence and elation inspired by the establishment of the empire—"The substance of all our desires and aspirations of the last twenty years has now been realized in a supereminent and enduring form"—together with presentiments of failure and disenchantment that would follow the realization of these high hopes. At the beginning of the eighties these sentiments were interpreted to mean that only the "unity of the spirit" was capable of saving Germany from falling prey to cynicism, pessimism, or the revolutionary Left.

A similar solution, although more explicit and more extreme, was now proposed by Treitschke's political opponent. In a letter to Gustav Schmoller on August 7, 1874, Treitschke expressed the fear felt by the "entire spiritual aristocracy of Germany" in face of the rising lower social classes and the growing strength of the Left, which aroused in his words "fears for the ideal cultural possessions that are imperiled by the brutish movement of the lower masses." [59] This fear took possession of nationalists and extremists like Treitschke and Konstantin Rössler, of relative moderates, such as Eduard Zeller in the last years of his life, and some of the prominent writers on current political affairs, like Hugo Sommer and Julian Schmidt. Some Progressives connected with *Die Nation* expressed their misgivings as to the ability of traditional liberalism or rational-critical thought to withstand the pernicious effects of positivism, technical progress, public administration, and politics on modern man. These critics pointed out that the administrative, political, and economic spheres were depriving man of the fruit of his labors, a loss that was already being felt in all these areas. They were equally alarmed at the rise of materialism, nihilism, socialism, and the proletarianization of culture and social manners, as well as the harmful effects of political activity and chauvinism on the life of the individual—which had reached a point

59. Boehlich, p. 247; see K. H. Höfele's essay, op. cit., note 24; and F. Sell's book, chaps. x, xi, xii.

where, as Dr. Hoffmann declared: "Realistic events, such as Prussia's military victory over France, the proclamation of the establishment of the German Empire, and also primitive conceptions of heroism involving nothing more than brute force . . . have become a fearful and revolting substitute for civilized forms and planned order." [60]

This comprehensive indictment that the intellectuals drew up against the age itself and also against their own inability to cope with the new ideas of the educated classes reflected a complex spiritual phenomenon with a pronounced irrational aspect and with many inner contradictions. In the last third of the nineteenth century and at the beginning of the twentieth the educated classes [61] experienced a profound disillusionment in the heritage of rationalism and liberalism—a disillusionment, on the one hand, in the heritage of G. W. Leibniz, Christian Wolff, G. E. Lessing, and J. F. Herbart and, on the other hand, in rational critical thought in its revived form beginning in the sixties with the neo-Kantian school of Kuno Fischer, Eduard Zeller, Otto Liebmann, and Friedrich A. Lange and his criticism of materialism. At the same time, however, these disillusioned circles continued to adhere to the basic assumptions of the systems they were criticizing in order to counteract the dominant tendencies of the day: "The relativity of values . . . the illusion that values, beliefs, ideas and world-views are nothing but the product of mechanical, physio-

60. Op. cit., note 58.

61. In gathering source material for the purpose of analyzing the attitudes of the liberal intellectuals the author has not relied on the opinions and beliefs of prominent groups only, but rather on the sentiments expressed by the man on the street, teachers, students, writers, journalists, and members of the liberal professions, such as doctors and architects, who are not accustomed to deal with intellectual and social questions in their daily work. To arrive at a balanced and representative picture we have used biographical and pedagogical sources in addition to the formal, traditional sources: personal archives preserved by Jewish and Christian families who belonged to the intellectual class, correspondence, compositions of students in the secondary schools, excerpts from diaries. The source material that we have gathered over a period of several years, although not complete, is designed to give the reader a faithful picture of the prevailing mood of the period in the following regions: Pomerania, Posen, Silesia, the Rhineland, Hessen-Nassau, and, to a lesser extent, Hanover. Relatively much source material has been preserved by families in the large cities, Berlin, Leipzig, Frankfurt. Additional sources: K. H. Höfele, "Selbstverständnis und Zeitkritik des deutschen Bürgerthums vor dem ersten Weltkrieg," Z.R.G.G., Vol. VII, No. 1, 1956, p. 40 ff; Wolfgang Frhr. von Löhneysen, "Der Einfluss der Reichsgründung etc.," ibid., Vol. XII, No. 1, 1960, p. 18 ff; Harry Pross, *Die Zerstörung der deutschen Politik, Dokumente 1871–1933,* Frankfurt a/M, 1959, chaps. i, ii, vii; Ernst Weymar, "Die 'deutsche Sendung' als Leitgedanke im Geschichtsunterricht in den höheren Schulen," *Tribüne,* Vol. 5, No. 17, 1966, p. 1820 ff.

logical or chemical processes and . . . in this they followed the popularizers of the natural sciences, such as Karl Vogt, Louis Büchner, and even
the author of *The Riddle of the Universe,* Ernst Heinrich Haeckel. . . .
The youth were thus attracted to materialism or anthropocentrism in their
crude forms, relying on excerpts from Feuerbach and imagining that all
manifestations of the spirit are nothing but projections of material needs
or social interests.'' [62]

In this spirit teachers and political writers pointed out the dangerous
logical confusion that existed in the prevailing mode of thought. These
descriptions of chemical, anatomical, or economic influences on the formation and growth of culture in their society, whether they conformed to
rigid, scientific standards or whether they were misleading popular repre-
sentations, now became the chief criteria in evaluating the validity and
relevancy of a culture or an ethical system. Beliefs and ideas were taken
to be nothing more than the products of glandular secretion, blood circu-
lation, cerebral vibrations, or of social and economic needs, and of no
greater value or consequence than any other physiological or empirical
phenomenon. All this imbued young students with skepticism and intellectual arrogance, for they believed that they had discovered behind the
confused vistas of the empirical world values and principles which they
now recognized as illusions. These precocious passions enticed them into
appropriating imperfectly apprehended themes culled from the philosophical systems of Schopenhauer and Hartmann, a fashion which did not
escape the censure of their teachers and such eminent personalities as
Dilthey, Friedrich Paulsen, and Theodor Fontane. We can see this from
the titles of the compositions written by students in the upper classes of
the secondary schools in Prussia in the eighties and the beginning of the
nineties: ''The Enlightenment with Reference to the Natural Sciences'';
''World-views as Guides to Life''; [63] ''Eduard von Hartmann's Chief
Stages of Illusion.'' These students would repeat catch phrases, such as,
''The pursuit of fortune or happiness only leads to misfortune and sorrow. . . . The longing for the next world ends in the disillusionment of
this world. . . . The pursuit of progress leads to sorrow, penury and self-
destruction . . . existence is nothing but affliction. . . . Man's faith and
hopes will find their fulfillment with the inescapable destruction of the

62. From Professor Eduard Zeller's lecture on ''Die sittliche Bildung,'' 1873, as recorded by his students in F.A., No. 14, p. 1.
63. F.A., Nos. 4, 5, 9, 12.

world." [64] Liberal teachers and educators were at first perplexed by these gloomy views, but they soon realized that not only had they failed to give the youth convincing answers but that they themselves, including an increasing number of those who still recalled "the revolution of the professors in St. Paul's Church" in 1848, were beginning to lose their faith in the liberal and rational tradition.

A basic assumption of liberalism which is derived from the doctrine of pre-established harmony of Leibniz-Wolff is that external noninterference is sufficient to ensure the exercise of free will. Although the free will develops by virtue of a universal and supravolitional progression, it contains within itself in inchoate form and *in potentia* the full realization of freedom, happiness, and the *summum bonum* of the human species. This basic assumption was now defined by the old Liberals themselves as "an optimism that was alien to reality" (*wirklichkeitsfremder Optimismus*) and hence as an intellectual, rational paradigm of progressive inner perfection of man's rational nature, "whereas real human nature in its original state and without subsequent improvement is not compatible with this belief in progress." [65]

As a result of this subordinate position to which man's speculative powers were being relegated, people began to lose faith in the pedagogical and ethical teachings of Herbart and in the enlightened doctrines of Leibniz and Lessing. It could no longer be assumed that freedom, intellect, and personality proceed from potentiality to actuality by a process of autonomous thinking whose principal function is to raise the latent meanings implicit in thought (or, as Herbart expressed it, in the thinking rational soul) to the level of conceptualization which constitutes man's active consciousness. This in turn tended to weaken the belief that self-consciousness and intellectual contemplation, and their power to make cognition and knowledge possible, are effective in the world of external objects since, according to Herbart, this external world is made relevant to us only by internalizing our impressions and by thought thinking itself and its content.

64. Ibid.; see Hugo Sommer, "Die Ethik des Pessimismus," *Preussische Jahrbücher,* Vol. 43, 1879, p. 375 ff. A summary of Sommer's criticism of Hartmann's teaching is that atheism in his system "absolutizes the individual and anthropomorphizes the absolute," ibid., p. 358. Sommer, like many liberal intellectuals, believed that an answer to that relativism was Lotze's system, especially *Mikrokosmos, Ideen zur Naturgeschichte und Geschichte der Menschheit,* Leipzig, 1856–1864.

65. F.A., No. 4.

The problem that engaged the minds of the liberal intellectuals was, above all, concerned with the pedagogical and political relevancy of neo-Kantianism. The various interpretations of this problem at the end of the nineteenth and the beginning of the twentieth century prevalent among students, teachers, and the educated public in general present an instructive picture.[66] The problem arose with Kant's attempt to establish man's spiritual autonomy in two spheres: first, in the sphere of cognition, by liberating knowledge from its dependence on sense impressions of the cognized object; second, in the ethical sphere, by liberating moral decisions from their dependence on the practical consequences of the moral act. The central import of Kant's attempt was also felt by the intellectuals who followed him and they conceived it to be their "highest goal . . . that man as a creature of cognition should be able to confront sense impression actively and not passively, not as an absorber or sponge, but as a constructor and shaper and, hence, as a free agent." [67] The difficulty, however, which was clearly seen by Friedrich Paulsen, for example, at the end of the eighties, was how to attain this freedom without being alienated from reality. Kant's "Copernican revolution" had transferred the focal point of empirical cognition and moral judgment from external objects and the consequences of acts to the cognizing subject, to man himself. Kant was thus able to establish man's autonomy: instead of cognition regulating itself according "to the objects, things, acts and reality as a whole, all these are made to conform to human thought, will and judgments." [68] For Kant—and also for the neo-Kantians, Otto Liebmann, Eduard Zeller, and, later, Hermann Cohen and Paul Natorp—man's rational sovereignty had been established over against the world of objects and sense impressions, chance occurrences and passive feelings, as well as over against Hegel's absolute idealism in which "man is

66. In addition to the original sources mentioned above, n. 61, there are the following sources from periodicals: *Preussische Jahrbücher,* Vol. 36, 1875, pp. 283 ff, 422 ff, 469 ff; Vol. 37, 1876, pp. 177 ff, 217 ff; Vol. 38, 1876, pp. 513 ff, 650 ff; Vol. 42, 1878, p. 377 ff; Vol. 48, 1881, pp. 386 ff, 449 ff, 533 ff; Vol. 49, 1882, pp. 1 ff, 537 ff; Vol. 50, 1882, p. 102 ff; Vol. 53, 1884, p. 105 ff; Vol. 56, 1885, pp. 464 ff, 646 ff; *Deutsches Literaturblatt,* Vol. V, No. 37, 1882, p. 145 ff; *Die Gegenwart,* Vol. XVII, No. 1, 1880, p. 2 ff, No. 2, p. 17 ff; and *Die Nation,* Vol. IV, No. 18, 1887, p. 270 ff; Vol. V, No. 52, 1887, p. 729 ff; Vol. X, No. 17, 1892, p. 256 ff; No. 18, p. 272 ff.

67. F.A., No. 2.

68. From Friedrich Paulsen's lecture "Erkenntnis und Erziehung," according to the notes taken by some of his students, F.A., No. 2. The philosophical problem discussed is from Kant's *Critique of Pure Reason,* Introduction, 2d ed., Riga, 1787.

swallowed up in the evolving universal Absolute Spirit and when this Spirit attains its freedom, the freedom of the individual human spirit vanishes." [69]

To ensure the undisputed autonomy of human reason, however, Kant was constrained to confine its activities to the empirical world, to sever sense from understanding and body from spirit, without any discernible principle of interpenetration or transformation, and thus he introduced an uncompromising dualism at the heart of his system. When the time came to apply Kant's system to historical and social realities, it became evident that in the two spheres of empirical cognition and ethical judgment man's freedom can be exercised only by transferring empirical and ethical reality from the real world to the world of theoretical reason, so that not essences but their appearances become the object of cognition. These appearances, moreover, are isolated from reality, "imprisoned in abstract mental concepts, cleansed of all dross of corporeality, that is, of reality . . . which is too high a price to pay to liberate impressions from external objects." [70] This is also true of moral judgments where the desire to safeguard moral decisions from being influenced by practical consequences, subjective motives, and irrelevant distractions of an irrational, emotional, or social nature removes ethics from reality, and "drowns [human actions] in a sea of principles, intentionalities and rules of evaluation that have nothing to do with existential human problems and their realization." [71] An objectivity thus arrived at is devoid of objects, and it transports man to a world of the imagination which is the product of his thought alone, an objectivity that is "all spiritual, all tautological . . . which, instead of leading to a congruence of the object of cognition with cognition itself, leads to a self-cognition of reason that is devoid of objects . . . so that the world is not constructed into a meaningful form, but becomes a meaningless pale design." [72]

In the purely philosophical discussions the immanent, systematic, and theoretical aspects of these questions were treated, such as: the problem of schematism in Kant's system, the problem of how synthetic judgments a priori are possible, or the dilemma that arises when, on the one hand,

---

69. Op. cit., n. 67; and to complete the historical picture, see F. Sell, chap. xiii.
70. Ibid.
71. F.A., Nos. 4, 5, 9, 12; see Hugo Sommer, "Über das Wesen und die Bedeutung der menschlichen Freiheit," P.J., Vol. 48, 1881, No. 6, p. 535 ff.
72. F.A., No. 4.

we acknowledge the existence of the thing-in-itself which as such affects (*afficiert*) our cognition when we seek to cognize it in its particularity and, on the other hand, when we find that we must cut ourselves off from the thing-in-itself if we wish to safeguard the freedom of cognition and moral judgment and guarantee man's spiritual autonomy. The cultural, pedagogical, and ideological aspects of these questions, however, were discussed in educated circles in their historical context and from the practical standpoint of their relevancy to contemporary problems. In this respect the educated liberal circles were inclined to confuse the basic tendency of neo-Kantianism to safeguard the freedom of cognition and moral judgment with the disappointment of being "cut off from real existence . . . and deprived of explicit positive values." The feeling of emptiness experienced by this generation as a reaction to the "formal conception" of the Kantian theory of cognition and ethics was discussed at great length in the circles of the *Preussische Jahrbücher* during the eighties and nineties. The critic Julian Schmidt characterized this attitude as follows: "What Kant had in mind was not men's activity but their judgment . . . man's actions should be determined not by his thoughts but in accordance with laws . . . [this doctrine] evades the gravest ethical questions . . . we are presented here with an inadequate criterion for evaluating human actions." [73] Similarly, Hugo Sommer praised Hermann Lotze's philosophical system for its understanding of the weakness of the *Critique of Pure Reason* in its sharp separation between the sensible and the theoretical, a separation that leads to the grave misunderstanding that because the principle of self-determination liberates cognition and judgment from sense stimuli we are faced with moral lawlessness and the complete independence of the normative values associated with existence. The skepticism and disillusionment of that period was described by the teachers in the Prussian secondary schools in 1906 in philosophical terms: "It is true that the receptivity of the senses and the spontaneity of reason can, by means of the laws of cognition, confer unity on the multiplicity of phenomena, so that the fortuitous sense impressions may be reconstructed and subsumed under a rule of nature that could be recognized objectively"; however, since this synthetic and creative goal is attained by being cut off from reality as such in the attempt to preserve the uncorrupted autonomy of cognition and judgment, it follows that the world

73. P.J., Vol. 50, 1882, p. 511.

becomes the arena for man's self-glorification and the exercise of his sterile reason.[74]

At about the turn of the century the neo-Kantian school, led by Hermann Cohen, went over to logical idealism, which, as defined by Paul Natorp and other scholars, was an even more formal system than that of Kant or of the neo-Kantians of the sixties. The dilemma between sensible existence as such and the desire to safeguard cognition and judgment from being dependent on the senses reached its most acute stage in Cohen's system. In the first decade of this century we begin to have ample evidence of discussions, student compositions, and excerpts from the conversations of educated men, in which we meet with the recurrent criticism that in Cohen's system neo-Kantianism is carried to a point where sensation and the cognized object lose all their natural existential content or disappear completely. Cognition, moral judgment, and faith in the law of Moses and the prophets are all purged of every vestige of reality and innate original matter until every natural substance is reduced to its ultimate relations and swallowed up by being dissolved into qualitative differences by means of logical or mathematical operations that are divorced from reality. In Kant's system there is still room for receptivity and the existence of sensible matter not created by human consciousness; [75] in Cohen's system, however, existence is imprisoned in a self-contained logical network of interrelationships, as if the entire world of man "was created out of human consciousness alone, and brought to light in a purified mathematical form." [76]

It is not surprising then that many liberal intellectuals, including opponents of Treitschke and Adolf Stöcker, and thereafter also of political and racial anti-Semitism, should express their disappointment with "the clannish, provincial reaction of the Jews to this spiritual crisis, one that is likely to endanger the humanistic character of the German nation." [77] The principal arguments that were heard in the last two decades of the nineteenth-century will become clearer in the course of our analysis of the issues involved.

With the growing skepticism among the intellectuals toward the liberal-rationalistic heritage, a mood set in which quickly gained strength as the century proceeded, a mood that was clearly inimical to liberalism, hu-

74. F.A., No. 4.
75. As reported by Professor F. Paulsen's students, op. cit., n. 68.
76. Ibid.        77. F.A., No. 20.

manism, rationalism, and, hence, to the very foundations of the legal, social, and economic emancipation of the Jews. Jewish leaders, Jewish writers on political and current affairs, teachers, rabbis, and the Jewish educated class in general were aware of this growing danger; but, as the German liberals contended, instead of combating it as full-fledged German citizens with weapons taken from the arsenal of Germany's historical heritage, they met this crisis with tedious reproofs, exhorting the Jews to return to the faith of their fathers and to outmoded beliefs which could not be taken seriously by the great majority of enlightened Jews.[78] Thus, for example, Gustav Karpeles, who delivered a lecture in 1888 under the auspices of the Mendelssohn Society of Frankfurt in which he urged German Jews to look upon Moses Mendelssohn's legacy as an instrument for strengthening "our religious Jewish particularity," received a letter from his friend Heymann Steinthal a few years later informing him that his colleagues at the University of Berlin felt that it was high time that German Jewry should become interested in Mendelssohn from a national German point of view or from the standpoint of universal culture and not from a narrow, parochial Jewish point of view, and ask itself what Mendelssohn

78. Ibid. An instructive expression of the critical approach of the Liberal Progressives may be found in the debate that took place between these circles and some of the spokesmen of the Jewish community, including Professor Heymann Steinthal, following the proclamaon of the rabbis in 1893. In this proclamation seventy-three of the non-Orthodox rabbis again advanced the familiar apologetic argument that the Talmud and the oral law are binding only to the extent that they are able to withstand modern man's rational criticism. Moreover, the oral law at no time possessed the normative authority of the written law. Despite these words of clarification, some liberal circles, such as the editors of the widely read *Berliner Presse* of Feb. 18, 1893, took the position that the argument put forward by the German rabbis in their proclamation demonstrates that even modern Judaism had not yet liberated itself from the authority of the oral law, and that as long as the Jews continued to teach these traditions, it would be impossible for them to integrate completely into German society: "As long as the Talmud will continue to exist and be studied, as it is in Jewish schools, for example, . . . the tendentious exploitation of its contents will not cease." These words were answered by Professor Steinthal in the pages of the periodical devoted to the cause of combating anti-Semitism, M.V.A.A., Feb. 26, 1893, and subsequently in A.Z.d.J., Vol. 57, 1893, No. 9, p. 97 ff, wherein he declared that the proposed conditions for complete integration were unacceptable to German Jewry and that it would not abandon its historic tradition, including the oral law, in order to achieve equality in Germany. This debate, which compelled the spokesmen of the organized Jewish community to defend the halachic tradition in a more extreme form than they generally adopted, began in the eighties following the public debate and the legal battle around the Judenspiegel of Dr. Justus; see extensive documentation of the affair in the files of the archives: G.A.J. G.A. M1/20 D.I.G.B. No. 48, "Gutachten über den Schulchan Aruch"; G.A. M1/17, D.I.G.B. No. 45, "Antisemitica: Process Contra Justus," Münster, Westphalen.

had contributed to the sum total of German thought. If German Jews would show greater interest in Mendelssohn's exemplary writings in the field of aesthetics, such as his *Betrachtungen über die Quellen und die Verbindungen der schönen Künste und Wissenschaften,* Steinthal's Christian colleagues went on to say, they would not be reduced to defending such a narrow apologetic movement as the renewal of the Jewish faith with its doctrine of the chosen people. [79]

The German liberal intellectuals in the period we are discussing reproached the Jewish leaders, educators, writers on public affairs, and the Jewish intellectual class in general for having failed to come to grips with the basic problems of the generation, and to the extent that they had considered these problems it was only to use them as tools of propaganda to strengthen Jewish separatism, thus withdrawing organized Judaism from the momentous spiritual struggle in which the German nation now found itself. There were two aspects of this spiritual struggle which the intellectuals selected for special consideration:

If the individual German, in order to safeguard his absolute autonomous status, would continue to pursue the rational-critical ideal, that is, a cognition not dependent on a world of external objects and moral judgments not dependent on the consequences of acts, and if he failed to receive a satisfactory answer from the neo-Kantians, he would be driven to embrace an irrational, romantic philosophy and be tempted to turn the principle of objectivity, which was restricted by Kant to scientific experience, into an unlimited subjectivity "that will make cognition a purely subjective process, completely and exclusively I-bound, I-related, I-conditioned." An eclectic world view was developing, composed of a mixture of themes from the systems of Fichte and F. Schelling, romantic

79. F.A., No. 2; the private letters in which this information appears seem to contain some errors. Until now we have not come across any reference to the lecture allegedly given by Gustav Karpeles and his definition of "Besonderheit"; but in the same Mendelssohn Union in Frankfurt a lecture was given April 17, 1888, on the same subject by Adolf Bruell in which, among other things, he expressed sentiments similar to those attributed to Karpeles. In speaking of the aims of the Gemeindebund, Bruell stated: "In addition to the consciousness that we are Germans with all the duties and all the rights of Germans, the Gemeindebund desires to strengthen our religious and Jewish distinctiveness . . . and to do so for the common good," G.A.J. T.D. 171 b, Separatadbruck, Dr. A. Bruell's "Populär wissenschaftliche Monatblätter," p. 2. The allusion to "the chosen people" refers to Steinthal's essay, "Das auservählte Volk oder Juden und Deutsche," A.Z.d.j., 1890, No. 17, reprinted in H. Steinthal, *Über Juden und Judentum,* ed. by Gustav Karpeles, Berlin 1906, p. 12 ff.

German mythology, the historical jurisprudence of Savigny and G. F. Puchta, which opposed natural law as illusory and fictitious, and Nietzsche's glorification of the superman, his will to power and master morality. Some penetrating insights into the prevailing mood in the eighties of the last century among senior high school students is provided by the testimony of one of their teachers, Franz Albrecht, and may be summarized as follows: There was a growing tendency among the youth to adopt a mythical world view or a kind of mythical feeling about the world which abolishes the basic dualism between man as the conscious shaper of his world and the objects of the external world that confront him.[80] This cosmic conception includes all existence and makes no distinction between man and the rest of the world, animate or inanimate. Man no longer imposes laws on the world of phenomena, for he himself is now subject to the natural laws that govern the world. In this shift of sovereignty from the life of the spirit to the life of myth man surrenders his uniqueness as a rational creature created in the image of God; he is identified with the world of nature and relegated to a zoological category. The individual is now amenable to the extravagant claims of racial doctrines and nationalistic sentiments. In the words of Dr. Albrecht, "There is but a short distance between Fichte's *Urvolk* and Treitschke."

The second tendency in this spiritual struggle which many liberal intellectuals at the close of the century found distressing was likewise taken to be a reaction to the failure of the neo-Kantians to consider the transitional stages between autonomous cognition and self-subsistent reality, between autonomous moral judgments and human actions. This deprived the individual of his peculiar status as subject and reconciled him to the doctrines of positivism and empiricism which defined him as a passive creature whose character and fate are determined by natural laws of growth and not by the higher processes of thought. In short, man is causally dependent on physical processes, or even reducible to them, and is subject to external influences beyond his control and often beyond his knowledge. Whether these external forces are called natural selection and the struggle for existence or biological, sociological, or economic conditioning, the

80. Franz Albrecht, "Über die neue Prüfungsordnung vom 5.2.1887," F.A., No. 4. For the intellectual-historical sources of this world view beginning in the second half of the eighteenth century, see the informative essay by Jacob Talmon, "Herder and the German Mind," *The Unique and the Universal, Some Historical Reflections*, London, 1965, p. 91 ff.

result is that the individual consciously accepts a nonrational authority and at the same time feels exempted from personal responsibility.

These two tendencies described above reflected the liberal conception in general and the critical neo-Kantian position in particular, and in a discussion conducted by teachers in 1906 these tendencies were described as having produced, no doubt referring to the students, "a disastrous befuddlement of human nature" (*verhängnisvolle Verwirrung des menschlichen Wesens*).[81] At that time, around the turn of the century, many intellectuals thought they found a solution in what was called "the unity of the spirit," that is, the German spirit, and this provided them with social, political, and nationalistic answers to questions that were basically theoretical, spiritual, or even cognitive. However, the essential purpose of these answers, insofar as they touched on the status of the Jews, was to impress upon them the need to remove all traces of Jewish identity, especially when it assumed the form of religious affiliation, for it was thought that this would hasten the spiritual and national unity of Germany, which, in turn, would of necessity lead to political unification.


Conclusion

In this chapter we have attempted to investigate the attitude of the liberal intellectuals from the time of the establishment of the German Empire, and especially during the Bismarckian period, to the question as to how the Jews were to be integrated into their German surroundings, and the importance of this attitude in determining the overall relation of the intellectuals to the political realities of that day. Our investigation has led us to the following conclusions.

A considerable number of liberal intellectuals were opposed to the principle of excluding the Jews from German society after they had been granted formal equal rights and were in favor of having the Jews integrated into German culture and nationality, with the proviso, however, that they relinquish their separate status and identity. This attitude was summed up in a single sentence by Professor Rudolf von Gneist in a strong speech against political anti-Semitism in 1881: "When the Jews will give up their distinctiveness, we shall witness the final consumma-

81. *Das deutsche Bildungswesen im letzten Wahlkampf,* Berlin, 1906, pp. 14–15 (F.A., No. 4, p. 12), an anonymous pamphlet apparently written by a group of secondary school teachers belonging to the Liberal Secession party.

tion of the emancipation.'' [82] The surrender of Jewish distinctiveness as the necessary condition for full admission to German society was understood in two senses: as a duty incumbent upon Jews by virtue of an external authority vested in the sovereignty of the state; and as an inner duty freely assumed by the autonomous decision of the Jews themselves. The first approach insisted that the Jews should willingly forfeit their separate identity simply by obeying the law of the state, that is, by placing the political exigencies of German national unity above the communal (and intercommunal) needs of a separate Jewish existence. The second approach opposed external compulsion and the coercion of the individual will and looked forward to the disappearance of Jewish particularism as a result of the voluntary acquiescence of the individual will to relinquish its particularity in favor of the German national will, with which it now identified its own.

These attitudes were represented by different individuals and by various groups, but they were often found in the same person. This ambivalent attitude was reflected in common semantic usage: those who adhered to the authoritarian approach spoke of the individual as a ''subject'' (*Untertan*), and those who adhered to the principle of identification spoke of him as a ''citizen'' (*Staatsbürger, Mitbürger*). The former described the political regime of the Prussian monarchy, and subsequently that of the German Empire, as an ''authoritarian state'' (*Obrigkeitsstaat*) which existed by the grace of God and the use of ''force'' (*Gewalt*) to compel strict ''obedience'' (*Gehorsam*). The latter spoke of a parliamentary regime that depended on ''the united will of the state'' (*der einheitliche Staatswille*) invested with ''power'' (*Macht*) to obtain the consent of the citizen through his ''internalized consciousness of duty'' (*verinnerlichtes Pflichtbewusstsein*).

These attitudes of the liberal intellectuals came not so much from their preoccupation with the Jewish question as such as from their desire to gain a deeper understanding of themselves and a sense of identification in a conscious confrontation with the Jewish question. Both groups were faced with a similar problem. The intellectual was required to forego his individual critical attitude in the interests of national unity and state power, just as the Jew was required to surrender his separatist position in the interests of that same national unity. The intellectual was expected to

---

82. From the collection, *Kulturkampf,* Berlin, 1887, p. 15; see above, n. 4.

make a compromise between rational or purely ethical considerations and political or existential needs, and the Jew between the particularism of the Jewish community and the universal nationalism under which his particularistic communal existence was to be subsumed. Both the intellectual and the Jew sought to identify the individual will with that of the state and the nation, but were not prepared to risk losing their freedom in the process. They both measured the gulf, but could not find the strength to make the final bound, moving irresolutely between two worlds they could not reconcile—the German intellectual with his fidelity to the Kantian world of rationality and ethical freedom, on the one hand, and his allegiance to the political state, on the other; and the Jew with his deep need to preserve his umbilical attachment to Judaism, and his national duty as a German to sever it.[83]

83. These changes in the attitude of the intellectuals concerning the place of the Jews in non-Jewish society, in the national state, and in western Christian civilization represent a new stage in the history of this social class. To understand the extent of this change we must study the early stages in the development of the intellectual class, beginning in the last third of the eighteenth century, when rationalists and men of the Enlightenment began to form open and relatively neutral social cells. See Jacob Katz, *Tradition and Crisis, Jewish Society at the Close of the Middle Ages,* Glencoe, Ill., 1961, chap. xxiii, "The Rise of the Neutral Society," p. 284 ff, especially p. 291 ff; and J. Katz, *Die Entstehung der Judenassimilation in Deutschland und deren Ideologie,* Frankfurt a/M., 1935, "Die neutralisierte Gesellschaftsform," pp. 32 ff, 40, 62 ff. One of the changes that took place in the development of the intellectuals was the change in the interpretation of the concept "Jewish emancipation"; on the early history of this concept, see Jacob Katz, "The Term 'Jewish Emancipation': Its Origin and Historical Impact," in *Studies in Nineteenth-Century Jewish Intellectual History,* ed. A. Altmann, Cambridge, 1964, p. 1 ff; and Jacob Toury, "Emancipation and Assimilation: Concepts and Conditions" (Hebrew), *Yalkut Moreshet,* Merchaviah, 1964, Vol. II.2, p. 167 ff.

# 2 | The *Kulturkampf* and the Status of the Jews in Germany

*Kulturkampf*—Idea and Reality

In the 1880's and thereafter the concept *Kulturkampf* was used more extensively in a number of studies devoted to the history of that period; [1] after the turn of the century the term began to be used to denote the anticlerical political movement that sought to separate religious authority from civil government and to subordinate the church to state control. The term was used by liberal leaders in a broader sense to include the struggle to define the limits of religious authority with respect to society, science, and culture.[2] Historical studies continued to emphasize the fact that the separation of church and state was only one of the aims of the *Kulturkampf* in a broader struggle in which these two claimants for supremacy sought to restore their influence by propagating their ideas and consolidating their positions, pending a modus vivendi that would lead to a division of political power between them.[3] From this point of view the historians Friedrich Sell, Heinrich Bornkamm, Hajo Holborn, Fritz Stern, and others [4] declared that the purpose of the *Kulturkampf* in Germany

1. For early collections of source material in which the concept of *Kulturkampf* appears, see *Das Staatsarchiv, Sammlung der offiziellen Aktenstücke zur Geschichte der Gegenwart (1861–1887)*, Hamburg, 1919; N. Siegfried, *Aktenstücke betreffend den preussischen Kulturkampf*, Freiburg, 1882; Friedrich Schulte, *Geschichte des Kulturkampfes in Preussen, dargestellt in Aktenstücken*, Essen, 1882.
2. G. Franz, *Kulturkampf, Staat und Katholische Kirche in Mitteleuropa von der Säkularisation bis zum Abschluss des preussischen Kulturkampfes*, München, 1956, p. 5 (hereafter, G. Franz).
3. G. Franz, pp. 9 ff, 247 ff, 284 ff.
4. Friedrich Sell, "Motive, Methoden und Ideen des Bismarckschen Kulturkampfes," *Theologische Rundschau*, Vol. 9, 1937, p. 229 ff; H. Bornkamm, "Die Staatsidee im Kulturkampf," H.Z., Vol. 170 1950. p. 41 ff; H. Holborn, "Der deutsche Idealismus in sozialgeschichtlicher Bedeutung, H.Z., Vol. 174, 1952, p. 366 ff (hereafter, Holborn); F. Stern, "The Political Consequences of the Unpolitical German," *History*, Vol. III, New York, 1960, p. 106 ff.

was not only to safeguard the sovereignty of the state from being controlled by the church and religion, but it was also the struggle of particularistic social and religious forces to assert their independence, and even their right of existence, in the face of the egalitarian tendencies of the "cultural state" (Kulturstaat).[5]

It is this historiographical method of studying the Kulturkampf that we shall apply to a problem that has until now received scant attention—the relation of this historical phenomenon to the status of the Jews in Germany. A study of the original sources clearly reveals that each of the principal parties engaged in this struggle in the Second Reich—the Liberals, the Conservatives, and the Liberal Protestants, the ultramontane Catholics, and the Old Catholics (Alt-Katholiken)—regarded the position of the Jews during that period as a convenient standard of comparison in evaluating the political and moral character of this struggle. This circumstance brings us to the consideration of the subject of this chapter, the relations between the Kulturkampf and the Jews.[6]

The term Kulturkampf was coined by Rudolf Virchow, the eminent German pathologist and one of the founders of the Progressive party, in a speech which he delivered in the Prussian Lower Chamber on January 17, 1873.[7] In speaking of the character of this struggle several weeks later [8] he declared that its historical significance was more than political and that it was not confined to the efforts of Bismarck and the Liberals to curb the particularistic power of the ultramontane Catholics in the Second Reich. The Kulturkampf, he asserted, had a twofold aim: (1) to liberate religion from the domination of the church and secular life from the domination of religion; and (2) to urge the national state to recognize its duty to bring about such a liberation and to impose it on the nation as a whole. To achieve this end, however, it would be necessary to conduct a Kulturkampf, a struggle in behalf of secular culture, even if this meant establishing a "dictatorship of ministers." [9]

5. For the general historical background of Germany's growing power in the days of Bismarck and Wilhelm II, see also Fritz Stern, "The Maturing of the Nation-State," Chapters in Western Civilization, Vol. II, 3d ed., New York, 1952, p. 375 ff.

6. This subject has also been treated by the author in Zion, Vol. 29, Nov. 3–4, 1964, p. 208 ff.

7. Stenographischer Bericht über die Verhandlungen des preussischen Landtags-Abgeordnetenhauses, vom 17.1.1873, Vol. I, Berlin, pp. 629–635.

8. Ibid., p. 662.

9. Ibid.; see also Erich Schmidt-Volkmar, Der Kulturkampf in Deutschland (1871–1890), Göttingen, 1962, p. 80 (hereafter, Schmidt-Volkmar). This passage from Virchow is cited by Schmidt-Volkmar in connection with the parliamentary debate on the

The ambiguity of this position illustrated the dilemma that faced German liberalism from the very outset, as was pointed out by Eugen Richter, one of the leaders in Virchow's Progressive party. On the one hand, it advocated the principle of noninterference on the part of the state in the life of the individual, a principle of classical "Manchester" liberalism in which the Progressives saw the only guarantee of man's spiritual freedom in the spheres of economics, culture, education, and religion; on the other hand, in the actual process of securing this freedom for the individual, liberalism could not rely on the so-called naive belief of the rationalists and the men of the Enlightenment in a pre-established harmony with its bleak promises of universal felicity, and it soon realized that "it was not possible for the state to liberate itself from clerical domination without interfering in the course of events." [10] Such interference, Richter added, must obviously proceed from the power of the state.

During the period of the *Kulturkampf,* which began at the end of 1871 and ended officially in 1887 with the proclamations of Bismarck and Pope Leo XIII,[11] this historical dilemma that faced liberalism assumed an additional dimension. The liberal intellectuals began to realize more and more that human freedom was not an abstraction that existed *in vacuo,* but something that must be achieved within the limits of historical nationalism and within the framework of a historical state, in this instance the Protestant Prussian monarchy which was the symbol and focal point of the Reich's nationalism. The principle of historical nationalism and the historical state was a continuation of the Lutheran tradition according to which the church was not separate from the state but subordinate to its

resolution for state supervision of education which was characterized by the liberal spokesman of the Center, Mallinckrodt, as a measure that made for dictatorship in the field of education. The chairman of the Catholic parliamentary faction, Windhorst, saw this resolution as a turning point in the history of Prussia, for it would lead a secular regime to seek the source of its sovereign authority in the state and not in God; see ibid., pp. 80–81.

10. "Unterlagen zur Geschichte des Liberalismus," B.A.K. KL.E., No. (3–9).

11. The special legislation of the *Kulturkampf* terminated in 1876; political and diplomatic negotiations between Bismarck, the Vatican, the Center, and other bodies to put an end to this struggle began in 1878–1879. Beginning with the eighties persecution of the Catholics diminished considerably, a political and ideological campaign was inaugurated to annul the special laws of the *Kulturkampf,* and new amendments were introduced to reconcile contradictions between the authorities and the Catholics (*Milderungsgesetze*). In 1887, Bismarck, Pope Leo XIII, and Windhorst issued official declarations terminating this struggle: *Stenographische Berichte über die Verhandlungen des preussischen Abgeordneten- und Herrenhauses,* Vol. I, 1887, p. 1127 ff. See G. Franz, p. 275; Schmidt-Volkmar, p. 298 ff; A.Z.d.J., 1886, No. 22, p. 29. For the legal basis of the concluding stages of the *Kulturkampf,* see B.A.K., P. 135/10834.

sovereign power (*staatliche Kirchenhoheit*), so that the Lutheran church, which was one of the symbols of a resurgent German nationalism, was an integral part of the imperial regime.[12]

With the intensification of the *Kulturkampf* the efforts of the National Liberals were increasingly directed to transforming the Reich from a constitutional state (*Rechtsstaat*) based on universal rational principles to a cultural state (*Kulturstaat*) based on historical national principles. Those who formulated the ideology of the National Liberal party—for example, Rudolf von Gneist, who was the first to formulate the principle of the constitutional state as the basis for the Second Reich, Theodor Mommsen, Heinrich von Sybel, Alfred Dove, and others—saw the *Kulturkampf* as "a momentous turning point in which the German state . . . attained self-knowledge, that is, its full freedom." [13] By virtue of this freedom, the leaders of the National Liberals added, the national state gave concrete form to the historical principle of its sovereignty over the church and established itself as "our *Kulturstaat,* to strengthen which the *Kulturkampf* has been forced upon us." [14]

This conception of the relation between church and state that was current among the liberal parties in the seventies and eighties was directly opposed to that of the enlightened Jewish community in Germany at that time, including its national and regional leaders, its rabbis, educators, writers, and scientists who, for the most part, still adhered to the old conception of "Manchesterism," as classical liberalism was then called—a conception which, in the opinion of the *Preussische Jahrbücher,* was an antiquated and outmoded notion that retarded the growth of the German monarchy.[15] This notion of the Liberals was based on the conviction that a rational and ethical harmony operated *in potentia* in economics, politics, education, and in the daily affairs of men that was bound to achieve a rationally ordered society, and that this providential harmony that resolved all perplexities and conflicts would also reconcile the interests of

12. Holborn, p. 371 ff.

13. *Kulturkampf,* p. 2. See also Schmidt-Volkmar, p. 110.

14. *Kulturkampf,* pp. 6, 8, 9, 14. The interesting definition by Professor Philip Zorn, one of the leading Protestant theologians of that day was: "The *Kulturkampf* . . . is not a struggle of the imperial Prussian morality against Christianity, but a struggle for the basic Christian principle of freedom of conscience on which the state is founded," *P.J.,* Vol. 39, 1877, p. 198.

15. *P.J.,* Vol. 42, 1878, p. 377 ff; Vol. 52, 1883, p. 92; Vol. 53, 1884, p. 201 ff; Vol. 55, 1885, p. 667 ff; Vol. 64, 1889, p. 560 ff.

church and state, secure social equality for the Jews of Germany, and remove all the irrational obstacles in the path of complete integration into their German environment.

The contradiction between idea and reality, between aspiration and achievement, between the high hopes of the Emancipation of 1869 and the realities that followed a few years thereafter, became apparent to Jewish leaders with the changing attitude of the Catholics to Judaism and the Jews, as will become clear in the following pages.

## Catholic Attitudes toward Judaism and the Jews

The attitude of the Catholics toward the Jews during the period of the *Kulturkampf* was determined by the general problem of the emancipation as it affected modern man in all areas of life. The deliverance (*Erlösung*) of modern man from traditional Christian beliefs and the consequent dissolution (*Auflösung*) of authority and discipline, it was argued, had filled him with a dread of isolation and a loss of confidence in all schemes of social regeneration.[16] This problem had already engaged the minds of Catholic thinkers and influenced Catholic policy in Germany at the beginning of the nineteenth century. The rise of nationalism and secularism, the French Revolution and the defeat of Napoleon, the romantic renascence, the rise of liberalism and humanism in the days of Humboldt and Hardenberg—all obliged German Catholicism to find a way of reconciling the Roman ecclesiastical and political traditions that had come down from the days of the Peace of Westphalia in 1648 with the modern culture that was based on "the emancipation of conscience."

A further stage in this conception of the problem of the emancipation was reached at the beginning of the *Kulturkampf* when Rudolf Virchow proclaimed that the legal goal of this struggle was "the emancipation of the state."[17] This emancipation, however, Ludwig Windhorst and Hermann von Mallinckrodt maintained, was tantamount to secular supremacy which would only succeed in encouraging the growth of materialism,

16. For an analogous attitude of the Conservative Protestants, see F. S. Warneck, *Das Prinzip der politischen Gleichberechtigung und die modernen Emancipationsfragen,* Hamburg, 1881, p. 6 ff: "Modern emancipation will lead humanity back to "the chaotic condition of desolation and emptiness . . . depriving freedom of all its moral content" (p. 11). See N. Rotenstreich, *Judaism and the Rights of Jews* (Hebrew), Tel-Aviv, 1959, p. 63 ff.

17. *Stenographischer Bericht über die Verhandlungen des preussischen Landtags-Abgeordnetenhauses, vom". 17.1.1873,* Vol. I, p. 629 ff.

egotism, and self-interest to the detriment of the public welfare. The rule of secularism, added the spokesmen of the Center party, would of necessity lead to moral deterioration, irresponsibility, and a general indifference to public affairs, and this in turn would foster an excessive veneration for the state, which was the precise goal to which the leaders of the *Kulturkampf* aspired.[18] In this context the concept of emancipation, as interpreted by the Catholics after the Napoleonic wars and especially during the period of the *Kulturkampf,* acquired a double meaning. As the struggle to attain equal political rights, it received the support of the Catholic community, especially in the Protestant states of Germany and, with the increasing persecution of the Catholics during this period, the "ultramontanists" and the members of the Center party began to regard the struggle for political emancipation as their historical and ethical mission.

The emancipation from tradition, the gospel of progress, and the principle of social equality, a boundless hope in man's rational faculties—the distinctive marks of the modern spirit—were accompanied by an open hostility to the principle of authority as taught by the Catholic church that vitiated the ethical heritage of the individual, corrupted the integrity of family life, and undermined the foundations of the traditional ecclesiastical and political structure. From this point of view the emancipation should be regarded not as a movement that conferred equal rights on modern man or that liberated him from the irrational traditions of the past, but as a movement that alienated him from the origins of cognitive truth and from the religious springs of faith from which the believer derived the theological certitude of his redemption. The *Kulturkampf* was therefore interpreted as a divine punishment for flouting traditional authority, a sin that was exemplified in the political and social spheres by the emancipation of woman from the authority of her husband, the serf from the authority of his master, the believer from the authority of the church, and by modern man's exclusion from the historical process of salvation (*Heilsgeschichte*).[19]

18. The argument of the leaders of the Center that the concept "emancipation of the state" meant secular rule is based on the definition Virchow himself gave in his above-mentioned speech in the Prussian Lower House (above, n. 17) in which he stated that this "emancipation of the state," which in his opinion was the goal of the *Kulturkampf,* meant a secularization (*Verweltlichung*) of the state.

19. "Freiheit oder Autorität," pub. by Bonifacius Verein, Paderborn, 1878, p. 5 ff. For the source of the concept "Jewish emancipation" and its historical development, see Jacob Katz, "The Term 'Jewish Emancipation': Its Origin and Historical Impact" in *Studies in*

With the loss of authority in private and public life, the Catholic spokesmen declared, man was forced to rely on his own unassisted efforts and on the power of his rational faculties. But the brute facts of life refused to conform to the contours of his mind; his aggressive cognition failed to comprehend existence.[20] He then returned from his cerebral adventures to the authority of the state and entrusted it with his freedom in exchange for the healing balm of salvation. In the eyes of the Catholics, the *Kulturkampf* was nothing more than the violent reaction of the disillusioned liberals in their unwarranted faith in human reason which prompted them, after they had emancipated themselves from religious beliefs and ecclesiastical authority, to accord supreme value to national culture and the national state. Man as a citizen was thus deprived of his true freedom, namely, Christian grace that descends upon the believer when he accepts the yoke of ecclesiastical authority.

As a consequence of these contradictory meanings of the concept of emancipation the relation of the Catholics to the Jews during the period of the *Kulturkampf* often took on an ambiguous character. In the view of the liberals within the Center party the position of the Jews served as one of the criteria in evaluating the emancipation of the religious and national minorities in Germany, and this meant equal rights. In the view of the Catholic Conservatives, however, the first result of Jewish emancipation was "the incitement of the mob to storm the Moabite monastery," [21] that is, it served as a criterion for assessing the disruptive force of the eman-

---

*Nineteenth-Century Jewish Intellectual History,* ed. Alexander Altmann, Cambridge, Mass., 1964, pp. 1–25. See also the semantic-historical clarification of the concept of emancipation in Jacob Toury, "Emancipation and Assimilation: Concepts and Conditions" (Hebrew), *Yalkut Moreshet,* Vol. II, 1964, p. 167 ff.

20. See report, "Gegen die Ultramontanen Scribenten," and in it typical quotations from *Die Centrumsfraction auf dem ersten deutschen Reichstage,* by W. E. Freiherr von Ketteler, Bishop of Mainz, 1872, p. 10: "that the principal representative of the allegedly liberal Germanism is Judaism, that the German people now goes back to the Jews to learn the essence of German character," A.Z.d.J., Vol. 36, 1872, No. 13, p. 243; No. 14, p. 265.

21. *Liberalismus und Manchestertum,* Leipzig, 1882, Vol. 4, Preface, (hereafter, *Liberalism*). This collection of pamphlets was published anonymously, but from the content and style of the anti-Semitic diatribes in these pamphlets it can be assumed that they were written, and no doubt published, by the circles of the Bonifacius Verein in Westphalia. This notion that the Jews had incited the mob to storm the monastery of the Moabites on August 4, 1869, received the official seal of approval of a number of spokesmen of the Center party; see the writing of the Catholic conservative: P. Majunke, *Geschichte des Kulturkampfes in Preussen, etc.,* Paderborn, 1890, p. 25. Schmidt-Clausing, p. 91, in addition to the words of Majunke, also cites the arguments of other Catholics who blamed the Jews, and not Bismarck, for the *Kulturkampf.*

cipation in general, the principal consequence of which was to alienate modern man from the religious sources of tradition, discipline, and authority.[22]

The Catholic attitude toward the Jews during the period of the *Kulturkampf* was derived from this ambiguous conception of the emancipation in general and from Jewish emancipation in particular. At the beginning of the struggle this attitude was called by Catholics and Jews *judenfeindlich* or *judengegnerisch* (hostile or antagonistic to Jews), whereby many Catholics expressed the distinction between their attitude toward Jews and Judaism and that of the political and racial anti-Semitism of the anti-Semitic parties, the middle-class reform organizations, the farmers, and the national-racial (*völkisch*) movement. This kind of anti-Semitism was still called "non-Christian anti-Semitism" by the spokesmen of the conservative Catholics, a term they used in order to stress: (1) that their methods, from the political and economic point of view, were not those of the anti-Semitic parties; and (2) that their objection to Judaism stemmed from the historical Jewish position which obdurately rejected the principles of the Catholic faith and the belief in Jesus as the Savior and in the church as the kingdom of heaven on earth. The concept of anti-Semitism without the above-mentioned descriptive appellations, such as "anti-Jewish," was current among the Catholics especially at the end of the eighties and, to an even greater extent, during the second half of the nineties when the anti-Semitic agitation of the political parties declined.[23]

22. The sources of this ambivalent attitude of the Catholics during the period of the *Kulturkampf* go back to the days of reaction after the Revolution of 1848 and to the debate concerning the emancipation in the 1850's and 1860's. A comprehensive account of this debate, written from an anti-Jewish point of view, appeared in the 1854 issue of the widely read Catholic annual *Deutsche Volkshalle*. See especially copies 31–59 and *Stenographische Berichte über die Verhandlungen des Reichstages des Norddeutschen Bundes,* Vol. I, 1867, p. 258 ff.

23. The historical studies of the relations between Catholics and Jews in the days of the Second Reich are for the most part written in a spirit of racial anti-Semitism, under the influence of Austrian anti-Semitism and from the standpoint of the ideology of the Nazi period. Nevertheless, these studies are not without scientific value, especially as historical testimony of the writers themselves and the period in which they lived. For the terms *Judenfeindlich, Judengegnerisch,* see dissertation by Fritz Schmidt-Clausing, "Judengegnerische Strömungen im deutschen Katholizismus des 19. Jahrhunderts, eine religionspolitische Untersuchung," Jena, 1942 (hereafter, Schmidt-Clausing), especially the Introduction and p. 91 ff. This dissertation, which was placed at my disposal by the University of Jena, was written in the spirit of two well-known anti-Semitic scholars: J. A. Kofler, *Katholische*

The different attitudes of the Catholics toward the Jews had developed historically from the state of mind and feelings of a number of Catholic leaders in Germany and Austria around the middle of the nineteenth century, foremost among whom were Sebastian Brunner, a prominent member of the conservative clergy, Konrad Martin, the bishop of Paderborn, as well as some of the enlightened circles that had gathered around the Catholic periodical published in Munich, the *Historisch-politische Blätter*.[24] The opposition of the Catholics to Jewish equal rights, and their subsequent opposition to the social emancipation of the Jews, was a direct consequence of their repudiation of the rationalistic basis on which the emancipation rested. The leading figures among the conservative Catholics rejected the humanistic principle of the emancipation concerning the equal status of all men, asserting that the concrete realization of this conception in the social and political life of the country would be ruinous to all aspects of man's communal life and that behind this process of disintegration was Judaism as a religion, the Jews as a people, and the Jew as the symbol of fallen man's unregenerate nature.[25]

In the year 1848, more than twenty years before the appearance of August Rohling's early writings vilifying the "talmudic Jew," the Catholic theologians Sebastian Brunner and Konrad Martin had already pointed out the danger of "talmudic anti-Christianity" whose two principal points were the stubborn refusal of the Jews to acknowledge the truths of salvation and of the church that proclaimed them, and Jewish economic power, political guile, and moral corruption which were calculated to subvert Christian life. This danger that threatened the national state and

*Kirche und Judenthum*, München, 1928 (hereafter, Kofler), see especially chaps. iii–vi, p. 17 ff, and Josef Roth, *Die Katholische Kirche und die Judenfrage, Forschungen zur Judenfrage*, Vol. IV, *Sitzungsberichte der vierten Münchner Arbeitstagung des Reichsinstitut für Geschichte des neuen Deutschlands vom 4. bis 6. Juli 1939*, 2d ed., Hamburg, 1943, p. 162 ff. Further clarification of the different terms used by Catholic leaders to describe anti-Jewish attitudes in the light of the rise of racial anti-Semitism, occurs in a series of pamphlets published in the nineties by the League to Combat Anti-Semitism (Verein zur Abwehr des Antisemitismus): *Die Antisemiten und das Christentum* (No. 4), *Antisemitisches Christentum und Christlicher Antisemitismus* (No. 7); *Katholische Stimmen über die Judenfrage* (No. 14). See also a study written in the Nazi spirit, J. Müller, "Die Entwicklung des Rassenantisemitismus in den letzten Jahrzehnten des neunzehnten Jahrhunderts," H.S., Vol. 372, 1940, pp. 6 ff, 33 ff, 76 ff.

24. The influence of Ignaz Döllinger on the attitude of German Catholicism toward Judaism is not discussed in this chapter since we are not dealing here with the history of the national Old Catholics.

25. *Zur Judenfrage*, Leipzig, 1878, p. 2 ff. See below, n. 47.

its Christian culture would greatly increase, Brunner and Martin warned, if the Jews were granted equal rights and if their historical disabilities were removed.[26]

During the *Kulturkampf* in 1876, the second edition of Bishop Martin's book was published by the Catholic theologian Joseph Rebbert, one of the editors of the periodical *Leo,* as part of his own polemical booklet against the Jews which he called *Blicke ins talmudische Judenthum (Glimpses into Talmudic Judaism).*[27] This booklet contained the traditional arguments against the "immoral laws" laid down for Jews pertaining to their economic, social, and political association with pagans which, in the author's opinion, included Christians. These traditional arguments were now being employed as political propaganda against Bismarck and the Liberals who were accused by the ultramontane circles in Westphalia and by the political anti-Semites of being *"Kulturkämpfer* for the sake of the Jews."[28] At the request of the Jewish Gemeindebund the Prussian public prosecutor preferred charges against Rebbert and the publishers of his book and won the case,[29] whereupon an open letter was published to Dr. Moritz Kohner, at that time the general secretary of the Gemeindebund, stating among other things: "In the lawsuit against the Christians you won as Jews but lost as liberals since you demonstrated, although reluctantly, that religious freedom can be achieved only with the help of state power."[30]

During the years when the *Kulturkampf* had reached its high point and especially in the period of the reaction to this struggle, from 1878 until the end of the eighties, this anti-Jewish attitude was widespread among

---

26. Konrad Martin, "Blicke ins talmudische Judenthum," *Theologische Vierteljahresschrift,* Bonn, 1848. See Kofler, p. 42.

27. J. Rebbert, *Blicke ins talmudische Judenthum, nach Forschungen von Bischof Dr. K. Martin,* Paderborn, 1876.

28. Otto Glagau, *Liberalismus und Manchesterthum,* Berlin, Leipzig, 1878, pp. 1–2 (hereafter, Glagau). The name of this pamphlet is the same as that of the polemical collection mentioned above in n. 21, but there is no connection between the two works.

29. G.A.J. G.A.M 1/13, M 1/16. For similar legal action by the Gemeindebund against those responsible for the publication of the rabble-rousing work *Nicht Judenhatz: Aber Christenschutz,* Paderborn, 1876, see: Bernhard Jacobsohn, *Der Deutsch-Israelitische Gemeindebund,* Leipzig, 1879, p. 29.

30. *Der Domvikar Schröder und unsere jüdischen Mitbürger,* Leipzig, 1878, p. 5. From the content it is difficult to discover the intention of the anonymous authors in their proceedings against Professor Rebbert or against the curate Schröder; there is no doubt, however, that the work was written by Conservative Protestants who belonged to the Luthardt circle or even by Luthardt himself.

the Catholics, particularly in the Rhineland, in Westphalia, and even outside of Greater Prussia, especially in Bavaria. Rebbert defined this renewed anti-Jewish attitude as follows: "Our struggle against talmudic
Judaism is nothing but self-defense . . . for in these days of the *Kulturkampf*, Jewish emancipation is likely to infect Christians, so that [the
Jews] will bring about an emancipation of the Christian from his Christianity." [31]

In this process of consolidating anti-Jewish feeling among the conservative and "ultramontane" Catholics various social, political, and intellectual groups took part. As early as 1874 the theologian and popular
writer Alban Stolz stated that the Catholics should have learned a lesson
from the drastic May Laws, namely, the need to counteract the pernicious
influence of liberalism and Judaism on Christian life, on traditional social
institutions, and on the character of the Christian-German citizen.[32] In
1875 a series of anti-Semitic articles appeared in *Germania*, the organ of
the Center party in Berlin, attacking Jewish dominance in journalism, in
the economic and cultural life of the country, and especially in the policies of Bismarck and the Liberals.[33]

This period also witnessed a marked increase in the dissemination of
the polemical works of A. Rohling and J. Ecker against the Talmud and
the Schulchan Aruch, the authoritative code of Jewish laws and customs
compiled by the Talmudic scholar Joseph Caro in the sixteenth century.
The ostensibly scientific arguments in these anti-Semitic tracts against
what they described as the inhuman character of rabbinic Judaism, the
self-exaltation of Judaism over Christianity, and the corrupting influence
of Jews on the German nation, its national economy, culture, language,
and character, appealed to Catholics who at that time were being persecuted within the framework of the *Kulturkampf*. Writings in condemnation of the Talmud, the Schulchan Aruch, and the Jewish heritage in gen-

31. Glagau, p. 2. A similar warning of the dangerous consequences of Jewish emancipation, according to Christians in the period under discussion, is to be found in the important
work of the conservative Protestant bishop, H. Martensen, *Die christliche Ethik,* Karlsruhe,
Leipzig, 1886, 3d improved ed., par. 4, "eine Emancipation von dem Christenthum
selbst."

32. Anon., *Zur Notwehr gegen die Judenschaft,* Berlin, 1877, pp. 1–2 (hereafter,
Anon.). See popular publications of Stolz, "Armut und Geldsachen": "If only the Christians were clever enough and would say to everyone who would try to do business with
them in curt monosyllables: 'Get out, Jew, and stay out.' " Introduction in Kofler, p. 43.

33. P. Massing, *Vorgeschichte des politischen Antisemitismus,* Frankfurt a/M, 1959, p.
17 ff (original title: *Rehearsal for Destruction,* New York, 1949; hereafter, P. Massing).

eral were intended to disclose to the Catholic community the truth behind the *Kulturkampf,* namely, Jewish domination of the economic and political life of Germany in accordance with the Talmudic laws relating to Jewish dealings with pagans, "laws in the Jewish religion that are still valid today." [34]

Beginning with the second half of the seventies even the social-economic movement of the Catholics was drawn into this process of consolidating anti-Jewish feeling. At the head of this movement was Ludwig Erler, the heir to W. E. von Ketteler's office in Mainz, and Professor Georg Ratzinger, statesman, economist, and a member of the Bavarian parliament. Taking part in this movement were also the Dominican theologian Albert M. Weiss, the historian and jurist Simon Eichner, and Constantin Frantz. [35] The leaders of this anti-Jewish revival, despite their different methods, gave a more or less coherent account of what they called the historical image and character of the Jews. In the early days of Christianity, they explained, and even more after Christianity had spread throughout the pagan world, the Jews were regarded (as in the period of the *Kulturkampf* when liberalism was in the ascendancy) as shameless intrigants, swindlers, venal, unscrupulous exploiters who lived off their

34. *Über Kultur und Religion, eine Streitschrift gegen christliche Unduldsamkeit,* Magdeburg, 1876, Appendix 11 (hereafter, *Kultur*). See also detailed testimony in the files of G.A.J. G.A.M. 1/13, 1/16, 1/17, 1/20.

35. Above, n. 23; see also Beda Weber, Stadtpfarrer in Frankfurt a/M, Domkapitular in Limburg, *Cartons aus dem deutschen Kirchenleben,* Mainz, 1858, p. 237 ff. Beda Weber's book contains most of the arguments against Jews latei used in thc *Kulturkampf*. In addition to the accusations of Jewish control of the economy and culture and the harmful Jewish influence on the moral education of German youth and on public opinion in general, racial arguments were now added: Jewish avarice and usury (*Schacherjuden*), or even obnoxious esthetic traits, such as the odor of garlic that was characteristic of Jews, were not the product of historical conditions but of Jewish blood which could not be changed by external circumstances. See also Schmidt-Clausing, p. 83, and Georg Ratzinger, *Die Volkswirtschaft in ihren sittlichen Grundlagen, ethisch-soziale Studien über Cultur und Civilisation,* Freiburg, 1881, pp. 287 ff, 377 ff (hereafter, Ratzinger). In the second edition issued in 1895 the anti-Jewish animus was considerably more blatant; see ibid., pp. 342, 436, 543, and also Ludwig Erler, *Historisch-kritische Übersicht der nationalökonomischen und social politischen Literatur,* pub. by *Archiv für Kirchenrecht,* Mainz, 1879–1885, Vols. 41–44, 48, 50, 53 (hereafter, Erler). This series also seems to have appeared in the form of a collection in 1900 issued by the above-named Archiv; the collection itself, however, has not come to my personal attention. See also Franz Hettinger, *Aus Welt und Kirche,* Vol. II, 2d ed., Freiburg, 1888, pp. 40 ff, 118, 121, 325. Of the works of the Dominican Albert Maria Weiss, I found only late editions, see Kofler, p. 45 ff. We still lack comprehensive studies of blood libels which, especially after the Tissa-Eslar affair, increased in central and eastern Europe and in the Balkan countries.

hosts like parasites and who incited, seduced, and slandered all except their coreligionists. Many persecutions of the Christians were instigated by Jewish calumny. The testimony of Saint Justin, who was martyred in Rome in 165 A.D., and of Tertullian, one of the greatest of the early Christian apologists, concerning the deceitfulness of the Jews and their depravity were not isolated instances; they confirmed the testimony of the Apostle Paul who described the Jews as those "who both killed the Lord Jesus, and their own prophets, and have persecuted us; and they please not God, and are contrary to all men . . . for the wrath is come upon them to the uttermost." [36] The persecution of the Catholics by the Prussian authorities, just as the persecutions of the Christians in the days of the Roman Empire, was the insidious work of the crafty Jews.

To this historical characterization of Judaism and the Jews another factor was now added, namely, the economic role of the Jews. Until the seventies German historiography had concerned itself with the contribution of the Jews to the growth of European cities and to the development of the mercantile and industrial economy. Now, as a result of the *Kulturkampf* and also as a result of the financial crash of 1873, the emphasis was shifted to an analysis of the calamitous influence of the Jews in the sphere of economics. This tendency had been initiated in the days of W. E. von Ketteler in 1862 when an attack was launched against what he called the destructive and corrupting influence of capitalism, industrialism, and the Jews on the national economy, on the family, and on the public morality of Christian society, especially among the workers and the members of the lower middle class. The traditional values of discipline, modesty, family integrity, and ecclesiastical authority were being undermined by the financial power of Jews and by the modern economic system.[37] In 1872, with the political and economic rise of the Liberals, Ketteler declared that Jewish dominance had reached a point where even "German character" (*deutsches Wesen*) was being determined by Jews.[38]

The anti-Semitic movement in the Second Reich and the Catholic attitude toward the Jews were characterized by a contempt for Jews on the one hand and a fear of their power on the other. This is apparent, for ex-

36. The New Testament source is Epistle to I Thessalonians 2:15, 16.
37. W. E. Freiherr von Ketteler, *Freiheit, Autorität und Kirche, Erörterungen über die grossen Problem der Gegenwart,* Mainz, 1862, p. 125; see *Historisch-politische Blätter für das katholische Deutschland,* München, 1859, Vol. 43, No. 2, p. 82; see also *Die 15 Generalversammlung der deutschen Katholiken,* Frankfurt a/M, 1863, p. 2 ff.
38. Above, n. 20; see also Schmidt-Clausing, p. 120.

ample, in the interpretation given by Ludwig Erler and Professor Ratzinger to the religious crisis of the *Kulturkampf* and to the economic and social crisis of that period, which they attributed to rapid industrial expansion, reckless speculation, and the financial crash. These two spokesmen of the Catholic community described the place of the Jews in the economic and political development of the country as follows: from the moment the Jews appeared on the stage of history they betrayed the basic ethical and prophetic principles of monotheism; they were cunning and unscrupulous nomads who roamed from one culture to another and from one economic region to another, impoverishing, corrupting, and undermining every historic culture with which they came in contact. Wherever they came they brought with them the seeds of dissolution, insidiously subverting the Christian countries in which they lived. Now they were at work ruining the German economy and German civilization. An economic ethos of work and not simply profit and investments, a discipline of obedience out of love, faith, and humility, a sense of responsibility to one's work and family, the qualities of probity, devotion, and fidelity—all were repugnant to the destructive nature of the Jewish character.[39]

In this connection Hettinger, Erler, Ratzinger, and other Catholic spokesmen were fond of citing authorities from the history of the Catholic church, such as the Council of Elvira in the year 306 which forbade Christians to associate with Jews or marry them and councils which debarred Jews from holding public offices in the administration of justice involving passing sentence or imposing fines on Christians. This Catholic attitude toward Jews developed as a result of basic changes that took place in the political conceptions of the "ultramontanists" at the end of the seventies when the *Kulturkampf* legislation was concluded,[40] changes which consisted principally in: (1) the transition (except for the Old Catholics) from a favorable attitude toward the monarchy under the Austrian Catholic Hapsburgs to a strong feeling of national patriotism; (2) the transition from subservience to Rome in political and educational affairs

39. Erler and Ratzinger, above, n. 35. In Vol. 43, p. 361, of the series in which Erler's articles were published the editors appended a note to indicate their reservations with respect to the content; see also Kofler, chap. viii, p. 41 ff, *Zeitgenössischer katholischer Antisemitismus.*

40. Josef Roth in his work *Die katholische Kirche und die Judenfrage: Forschungen zur Judenfrage,* Vol. IV, 2d ed., Hamburg, 1943, p. 170, repeats these examples, which he took from Kofler, p. 32.

to a less dependent position in these spheres, especially beginning with the German Catholic conventions in Breslau in the year 1886; and (3) the transition from a diversified social structure with rival interests to a united (although not unified) structure of an all-Catholic political party.

This period then was one of transition from an attitude of reserve toward the renascent nationalism of the Reich and its centralizing tendencies to an attitude of participation in the affairs of the monarchy. German historiography has justly concluded that the principal political result of the *Kulturkampf* was the defeat of liberalism and the ascendancy of the Christian parties. After the conclusion of the *Kulturkampf* legislation, and to a greater degree after this struggle had come to an end in the second half of the eighties, the Center became a political and social bloc without whose support no coalition would have succeeded in governing the Second Reich.[41] The changes of this transitional period were gradually consolidated, beginning with Bismarck's meeting with the papal legate in Kissingen in 1878 and then when the leaders of the Center joined Bismarck's antiliberal customs policy the following year, reaching its high point in the year 1887 when the last reforms were passed returning the confiscated property of the Catholic clergy. The "ultramontane" Catholics were thus gradually integrated into the national political framework of the Reich. The ideological basis for this change was laid down in 1878 when, following the encyclical of Pope Leo XIII of that same year, the Center announced its determination to strengthen the social and moral foundations of the country. In the spirit of this encyclical the leaders of the Center also warned of the danger that threatened the Christian religion from the disintegrating influences of social democracy on the one hand and liberalism and materialism on the other. They thus accepted the policy of conciliation proposed by Leo XIII, adding aims of their own designed to give them greater political autonomy and a larger degree of independence from Rome. When Bismarck joined the conservative elements in the Reich in 1877–1888, the ground was prepared for complete Catholic integration into the national monarchy of the Second Reich. In this process of integration the "ultramontane" Catholics adopted an anti-Jewish attitude as an ideological framework that would enable the "Cath-

41. Wilhelm Mommsen, *Stein, Ranke, Bismarck, Ein Beitrag zur politisch und sozialen Bewegung des 19. Jahrhunderts*, München, 1954, p. 269. See also the works of Heinrich Bornkamm and H. Holborn, above n. 4.

olics who until now were supporters of the house of Hapsburg and who dreamed of a Greater Germany . . . to find a common language with the Protestant community and with the masses.'' [42]

### Changing Attitudes of the Jews

Even in the early stages of the *Kulturkampf* (1871–1875) the leaders of the Jewish community wavered between two extremes: identification with the aims of the war in theory, and disassociation from the violent course that the war took in practice; support for the liberal camp which had endorsed Bismarck's policies at the beginning of the struggle and, at the same time, a fear of the growing *étatist* tendencies within this camp in favor of a strong centralized state; faith in the policy of separation of church and state, but also the fear that this policy might lead to a separation of community and religion and thus undermine the principal basis on which Jewish life rested after complete emancipation. [43]

Most Jewish leaders, as well as members of the liberal professions and the educated Jewish class in general, supported Bismarck, who in their view had bestowed upon the German nation "the most precious of possessions . . . . power and freedom." [44] They were in favor of the initial laws passed in 1871–1872 by the kingdom of Prussia against the ultramontanists and applauded the law of July 4, 1872, that had proscribed the Jesuits and other Catholic orders. The appointment of Adelbert Falk as minister of religion and culture in the early part of 1872 was welcomed by the Jews of Prussia, for in this appointment they saw "an opening for a true liberal policy . . . that would guarantee freedom of conscience and religion for all citizens . . . in contrast to the clerical regime in the days of Müller." [45]

At the end of 1872 the governing body of the Jewish Gemeindebund

---

42. *Die Wahlaufrufe der Zentrumspartei,* pub. by D.S.R.P., Leipzig, 1893, pp. 1–2.

43. A.Z.d.J., Vol. 39, 1875, pp. 263 ff, 279 ff. To complete the picture, see the instructive historico-political analysis of J. Toury, p. 246 ff.

44. Letter of the Jewish Gemeindebund in Germany (D.I.G.B.) to Bismarck, April 14, 1872, on the state of the Jews in the Balkan and eastern countries G.A.J. G.A.M 1/35.

45. *Die Zentrumfraction und der Ultramontanismus . . . ,* pub. by the Committee of the D.I.G.B., Leipzig, 1876, p. 14 (hereafter, *Zentrum*). The criticism against Müller was concerned with his opposition to the appointment of Jews to responsible positions in the public schools. For the general political attitude in this matter, see A.Z.d.J., Vol. 35, 1871, pp. 211, 229, 249, 855; Vol. 36, 1872, pp. 264–265; Vol. 37, 1873, pp. 271–272.

published a series of public statements in favor of the law passed December 10, 1871, which contested the right of the ultramontane Catholic clergy to dismiss teachers and priests who belonged to national German movements, and teachers and liberal priests who refused to acknowledge the principle of papal infallibility.[46] These publications of the governing body of the Gemeindebund aroused bitter opposition in a number of rabbis of the non-Orthodox community, among them Manuel Joel, who maintained that the state had no legal or moral right to interfere in the internal affairs of religious societies (*Religionsgenossenschaften*) in the Reich and that there was no reason, a fortiori, why the principal Jewish organization in the Reich should support this antiliberal policy since "it presented a grave danger to the basic freedom of religion in the state to have the regime intervene and decide whether Dr. Wollmann should continue to serve as the director of the Catholic Teachers Seminary. . . . To us, as members of a religion of a minority group such a policy could be all the more dangerous." [47]

This critical approach, however, was acceptable to only a small minority of German Jews, and the general opinion, insofar as it was publicly expressed, was clearly in favor of the initial steps taken by the regime against the ultramontanists. The support of these measures grew stronger during the month of May 1873 when Bismarck and Falk adopted a more drastic policy in the conduct of the *Kulturkampf* by instituting a more rigorous secular supervision of the school system and the training of teachers and priests, a strict censorship of the members of the Catholic

46. *Zentrum*, p. 4.
47. *Zur Judenfrage*, p. 32. This collection of essays, letters, and other works was published by the conservative Protestant circles of the Mission and seems to have been edited by Luthardt. Since official Jewish circles were not accustomed to publish criticisms of this kind, this document assumes special significance. Theologians and political figures among the Conservative Protestants were interested in the publication of the criticism by the Jewish rabbis, for by the middle of the seventies they also had begun to resent increasing state intervention in religious affairs and in the inner workings of the ecclesiastical organization. I discovered the collection in the archives of the Lutheran Evangelical monastery in Loccum near Hanover in West Germany. The note in the text about Dr. Wollmann refers to an incident which at that time caused a great stir among the people, namely, the decision of the Prussian minister of culture and public worship to annul Bishop Kremenetz's dismissal of Dr. Wollmann, the director of the Seminary for Catholic Teachers in Braunsberg, because of his refusal to acknowledge the dogma of papal infallibility. The Catholic clergy interpreted this as an unjustified state intervention in the internal affairs of the church; the Liberals, however, regarded the decision of the minister as an important step in strengthening the authority of the state over the church.

clergy, teachers, writers, and even political figures known to be "ul-tramontanists," the establishment of a secular court for the adjudication of ecclesiastical matters, the supervision of the internal affairs of state and regional ecclesiastical organizations, and the prosecution and expulsion of Catholics suspected of disloyalty to the nationalist movement. All these were described by the leaders of the councils of the large communities as "measures in defense of liberalism, nationalism, and scientific progress, measures that have been forced upon us by the ultramontanists." [48]

In the first four years of the *Kulturkampf* the Jewish communities showed great interest in its progress; it was a serious topic of public debates and private discussions in the Jewish community; it was a familiar subject of humor and satire in regional and local newspapers and a phenomenon that was closely examined by the councils of the Jewish communities. The analysis of these diverse sources [49] enables us to understand the way in which the *Kulturkampf* was interpreted by German Jewry, which may be summarized as follows:

(1) The *Kulturkampf* was regarded as an intellectual movement as well as a political campaign directed against the "ultramontanists" who, as the German Jews thought, had repudiated the rational and universalistic principles of liberalism on which the emancipation, with its ideals of equality, progress, and a common human destiny, was based; and who also refused to recognize the imperial symbols of the new German nation, which was also the nation of the German Jews. Above all, the "ultramontanists" had rejected the concept of nationality as it was understood in those days by the Jews in Germany and as it was formulated by the schools of *Völkerpsychologie* under Moritz Lazarus and Heymann Steinthal, according to which nationality could be acquired only by an act of will and by a conscious identification with the deeds and the creative,

48. *Zur Judenfrage,* p. 34.

49. The sources in our possession, except for the current Jewish press, refer to the following cities: Berlin, Breslau, Cologne, Frankfurt a/M, Glogau, Halberstadt, Leipzig, Magdeburg, Münster, Posen, Stettin. For the legal-political background, see files of the state archives in Koblenz: B.A.K. P/135/3148; P/135/8225, Angriffe gegen das Dogma der Unfehlbarkeit; see also in the files of B.A.K., "Die Rückwirkung des Dogmas der Infallibilität auf das Verhältnis zwischen Staat und Kirche." For resemblances and differences in the legal-political status of Jews and Catholics in the *Kulturkampf,* see B.A.K. P/135/3258; P/135/11944; P/135/11948 (photographic reproductions of the last two files are to be found in the General Archives for Jewish History).

expressive forms of the nation—its mother tongue, which was the indispensable organ in the creation of reality and the receptacle of its deepest loyalties, and its aesthetic creations in which the soul of a people was given visible shape.[50] Since Jewish emancipation was dependent on the realization of these liberal, humanistic values that were repugnant to the deepest convictions of the ultramontanists, it was natural for the Jews in this struggle to look forward to a victory of the Liberals.

(2) German nationality, which many Jews had accepted as their own, included among its traditional values the principle of religious toleration, a principle that had been acknowledged in 1648 with the Peace of Westphalia, that is, long before the rise of liberalism and modern science. These historical foundations of toleration were strengthened and developed in the days of the enlightened rule of Frederick the Great and thereafter during the period of the emancipation until they bore fruit in the 1860's. In all these changing conceptions of the principles of toleration, progress, and emancipation, the Jews in Germany followed in the footsteps of the National Liberals, the Liberal and Conservative Protestants, that is, those elements which formed the backbone of the renascent German nationalism and which endeavored to develop the nationalism of the Reich on historical German foundations and not on "French" rationalism. Since this historical nationalism was to be based on irrational romantic ideas, the Lutheran Reformation had to be reassessed to take the place of the rationalistic Enlightenment and redefined as the source of human freedom and civil liberties in the national state. In a eulogy written at the death of Eduard Lasker the editors of the *Preussische Jahrbücher* now maintained that it was not classical rationalism or "Manchesterism" but "the legacy of Luther" that was the most important element in liberalism,[51] and added, in the spirit of late nineteenth-century liberal Protestantism, that the principal aim of this legacy was to transfer the source of religious and political authority from the church to the individual conscience, the source of human and civil freedom. But the principle

50. For this conception in the original see M. Lazarus, H. Steinthal, "Einleitende Gedanken über Völker-Psychologie," Z.V.P.S.W., Vol. 1, Berlin, 1860, p. 6 ff, p. 4 ff. Conscious acknowledgment of identification as the basis of national membership is formulated on p. 37 as follows: "Here is a case where cognition creates its own object, that is it is identical with it"; also see the public lecture given by M. Lazarus at the Hochschule für die Wissenschaft des Judenthums on Dec. 2, 1879, printed in the collection of speeches *Treu und Frei,* Leipzig, 1887, p. 53 ff.

51. P.J., Vol. 53, 1884, p. 203.

of internalizing the authority which, under the influence of Richard Rothe and later Adolf von Harnack, had been passed from Liberal Protestantism to the political regime of the Reich, seemed to the leaders of the Jewish community to be "an expression of the loss of liberal truths as a result of having absolute power conferred upon the state during the period of the *Kulturkampf* and under the inspiration of that struggle." [52]

The position taken by the leaders of the Jewish community thus suffered from an inner contradiction. As German nationalism became more imbued with Lutheran symbols, the Jewish leaders began to realize that emancipation could be attained only if civic equality were based on rationalistic and liberal principles; [53] at the same time, as the *Kulturkampf* proceeded, the German Jews themselves became increasingly critical of the secular, rationalistic principles of the Enlightenment and the French Revolution—and these, they feared, could have a disintegrating effect on the Jewish community which, after all, was distinguished by its separate religion, its members being Germans of the Mosaic persuasion. In the face of these fears the leading figures and the educators among the German Jews, including the circle close to the *Allgemeine Zeitung des Judenthums,* reacted as the Conservative Protestants and at times as the Liberal Protestants, by emphasizing the religious foundations of the Enlightenment and the emancipation and minimizing its rationalistic, secular elements. [54]

In the early years of the *Kulturkampf,* however, it became plain to the German Jews that their fate was bound up with that of rationalism and liberalism, and in their criticism of the "ultramontane" Catholics they concentrated to a considerable extent on what they considered to be the "ultramontane" opposition to the principles of tolerance, freedom, equality, and liberalism. Not only did the Catholics deny the basic rational elements of religious tolerance, Steinthal declared in 1873, but the "ul-

52. *Der Antisemitismus, Reden etc.,* pub. by the Committee of the D.I.G.B., Leipzig, Berlin, 1888, p. 6. The pamphlet contains speeches and reports by local and regional functionaries beginning with the eighties, in the days of Förster's anti-Semitic petition to the Prussian Lower House, until the year of publication. In most cases, as in this instance, the names of the speakers do not appear, and the speeches are given in the name of the Gemeindebund. But it seems that the words quoted here were spoken by Dr. Kristeller who was at the time one of the heads of the Gemeindebund and connected with the Progressive Liberals.

53. "Der Liberalismus und das Judenthum," A.Z.d.J., Vol. 36, 1872, pp. 441–442; see the arguments of the Conservative Protestants, "Unsere Hauptanklagen gegen den Liberalismus," *Kreuzzeitung,* 1878, Nos. 189, 193, 194, 195.

54. *Zur Judenfrage,* p. 38.

tramontanists'' were not disposed to regard the historical development of the principle of toleration as a genuine and integral part of German national character. In two lectures devoted to this subject that same year Rabbi Manuel Joel illustrated this attitude with the example of the papal bull Zelo Domus of the year 1648 in which the pope rejected the principle of tolerance as it was set forth in the Peace of Westphalia. In 1873, after the enactment of the severe May Laws against the ''ultramontanists,'' the leaders of the Jewish Gemeindebund suggested to the councils of the Jewish community, the organizations of Jewish teachers, and the rabbis in the various communities that in their explanations of the antiliberal and nonrational attitude of the Catholics they could avail themselves of another convincing example, namely, the encyclical of Pope Gregory XVI of August 15, 1832, in which the pope described the liberal principle of ''freedom of conscience that rests on the foundation of German humanism and hence also on the foundation of our emancipation'' as a ''hallucination'' (*deliramentum*).[55]

In this spirit public criticism was conducted, apparently in a systematic and organized manner, against the two principal documents around which the *Kulturkampf* revolved: the encyclical of Pius IX of July 8, 1864, which reiterated the opposition to the historical and rational principle of toleration, and the *Syllabus Errorum Nostri Temporis* (*Syllabus of the Principal Errors of Our Time*), which was attached to the condemnation of the principle of toleration. The leaders of the Jewish community—the rabbis in their sermons, the teachers in the classroom, and the journalists in the press—deplored what they called the uncivilized and antiliberal aspects of this *Syllabus Errorum*. Steinthal found this document obnoxious in two respects: [56] first, that the pope should have repeated the traditional invidious distinction between Israel before the appearance of Jesus (*populus Israel*) and the subsequent inferior seed of Israel (*gens Judaeorum*) until the Christian curse returned (*quia Judaeorum gens toto celo ab honore Jesu Christi Filii Dei aliena est,* etc.) [57]; second, that the

55. Ibid.

56. *Rechtsschutz und Antisemitenschutz* . . . , pub. by C. V., Berlin, 1894, pp. 1–4. Steinthal's speech, ''Über die päpstliche Unfehlbarkeit,'' was given in 1874 or perhaps in 1875.

57. *Rechtsschutz,* op. cit. It seems that Steinthal here confused two different documents of the Catholic church. The words quoted do not appear in the *Syllabus Errorum* but in the declaration of the regional Concilium that convened in Prague in 1860; see *Acta et Decreta Sacrorum Conciliorum Recentiorum, Collectio Lacensis,* V. Friburgi, 1879, p. 443. According to Schmidt-Clausing, p. 88 ff, this declaration was confirmed by Pope Pius IX. I found no evidence for this assumption; but if it is true it may account for Steinthal's error.

duty to obey this or any other syllabus should appear reasonable to intellectuals and enlightened people. Par. 15 of the *Syllabus,* in which a basic premise of modern culture was defined as an error, namely, that man is free to choose his religion in accordance with his rational and independent conscience, was often cited as an instance of Catholic intolerance. The spokesmen of the Jewish community also cited Par. 77 and 79 in which all criticism of the Catholic religion, its theoretical foundations or public utterances, was branded as an error: "We fear not only hostile anti-Jewish sentiments; we fear fanaticism, dogmatism, contempt for science and intelligence, and stultification through clerical rule (*Verdummung durch Pfaffen*)." [58]

(3) In the context of this polemic against the *Syllabus Errorum* in the years 1871–1873, Jewish economists and jurists and members of the Liberal Progressive party attempted to establish a connection between the theoretical elements of the *Syllabus Errorum* and the economic policy of the conservative wing of the Center party.[59] Jewish economists and jurists asserted that the "ultramontanists" adhered to an economic policy that was contrary to the ideal of *laissez faire,* free trade and free competition, especially among the large producers; that they favored the policy of protective tariff and sought to preserve the traditional, irrational character of the social classes and the system of production. The common element that this *Syllabus* and the papal encyclicals had in common with the economic policy of the ultramontanists was then the general "ultramontane" world view which converted religious, social, and economic traditions into dogmas; and dogmatism, as such, was in the eyes of the liberals an obstacle that hindered them from achieving their goals and hence also an obstacle that hindered the Jews from achieving equality.

This appraisal of the economic policy of German Catholicism, both in its theoretical and practical aspects, was not entirely objective. It is true that as early as the second half of the seventies the Center party had consistently supported Bismarck's protective tariff policy, and this was the first step in restricting the *Kulturkampf.*[60] The economic policy of the Catholics, however, was highly complicated and cannot be characterized

---

58. Above, n. 57. In the same vein, see A.Z.d.J., Vol. 35, 1871, p. 250.

59. L. Bamberger et al., *Staatssozialismus,* Leipzig, 1879, p. 1. See also criticism of the editorial staff of the *Preussische Jahrbücher* directed against the economic views of Bamberger, Barth, and other "Manchesterites" P.J., Vol. 53, 1884, p. 426.

60. Schmidt-Volkmar, p. 201 ff.

as antiliberal in all its aspects. The remarkable fact about the Center party, from the social-economic point of view, was that it consisted of political forces, social classes, and pressure groups with diverse and even conflicting interests, a workers' movement with a social-Christian ideology formulated by Ketteler, members of the lower middle class, impoverished urban groups (*die kleine Leute*) who had been cut off from their original class and rural culture and gone to the industrial urban areas into which they had not yet integrated, the rising and relatively stable middle class, members of the liberal professions and professional academicians, peasants, landowners, and members of the aristocracy. All these "were united in the period of the *Kulturkampf,* and hence destroyed the illusion of classical liberalism according to which enlightened society was composed of single enlightened individuals . . . [and destroyed] . . . the illusion of the socialists that the process of social organization is conditioned by material interests." [61]

These developments in the Center party were well known to Jewish liberals and their leaders and hence their arguments against the Catholics were essentially of an ideological and polemical character and primarily directed not against the conservative Catholic mentality, as it were, but against the success of the Center party in being able to combine diverse and even conflicting social and economic interests within one political party. The heads of the Gemeindebund interpreted "this clerical attitude . . . as a consequence of the *Kulturkampf* and contrary to the original aims of this struggle." [62] In addition to all this, the German Jews looked upon the *Kulturkampf* as a continuation of the struggle against their historical adversary, Catholicism, which they claimed had always been opposed to Judaism and the Jews—a subject that will be treated in the last section of this chapter.

At the same time, critical and even derogatory views of the *Kulturkampf* were to be heard among the German Jews during its early years. In most instances these criticisms did not reflect differences of opinion between different individuals or groups, but rather the contradictory attitudes that existed simultaneously in the minds of the leaders of the Jewish community. The dilemma in which the liberal movement as a whole found itself between the ideals of freedom and nonintervention by the

61. *Kulturkampf,* p. 16. These words were cited in the name of the liberal wing of the Center's leadership, without giving their names; see G. Franz, p. 247 ff.

62. *Zentrum,* p. 5.

state on the one hand and the imposition of these ideals on the citizen by the power of the state on the other accounts for the changing and inconsistent attitudes of the German Jews during this period.

The political campaign to consolidate critical opinion during the early stages of the *Kulturkampf* began with the public debate caused by the "Pulpit Paragraph" (*Kanzelparagraph*) passed by the Reichstag on March 10, 1871, forbidding sermons considered to be detrimental to the interests of the state.[63] Such a prohibition was to a certain extent already in force in Bavaria where its purpose was to restrain the liberal Catholic and Protestant clergy from preaching sermons that were critical of the conservative Bavarian government; now, however, even before the struggle had reached its full force, the law was directed not against the liberal but against the "ultramontanist" preachers in most of the states of the Reich. Although this measure was not unfavorable to the interests of German Jewry, for it was officially defined as a means of achieving the separation of church and state, there were a number of prominent figures such as Emil Lehmann, a leader of Reform Judaism and an official in the municipality of his native city of Dresden, who regarded this law as "a first step in granting the state complete power."[64]

The second stage in consolidating the critical attitude of German Jewry to the *Kulturkampf* was marked by the public debate in the years 1871–1874 between the spokesmen of the National Liberals, particularly Heinrich von Treitschke and the members of his circle on the staff of the *Preussische Jahrbücher,* and the spokesmen of the Center party, led by Ludwig Windhorst, the brothers August and Peter Reichensperger, and Hermann von Mallinckrodt. The beginning of this debate had its roots in the "Pulpit Paragraph" mentioned above, in defense of which the National Liberals advanced the following arguments:

(1) This measure for the purpose of effecting the separation between church and state did not apply to the entire church, as had been assumed by the Liberal Progressives, "Manchesterites," and Jews,[65] but only to the "ultramontanist" Catholic church; whereas the Protestant church,

63. Schmidt-Volkmar, p. 71.

64. A letter from Lehmann to Moritz Kohner of April 24, 1871, according to Jacobsohn, secretary of the D.I.G.B., in a eulogy on the death of Kohner, March 22, 1877, which was published by the Council of the Gemeindebund as a pamphlet, *Jüdische Religionsübung im deutschen Reich,* Leipzig, 1879, p. 9.

65. *Kulturkampf,* Introduction, p. vi.

ever since the time of the Reformation and especially after the "Union" of the Lutherans and Reformers at the beginning of the nineteenth century, was a historical and organic part of the state.

(2) This measure did not contradict the basic principles of freedom and liberalism. On the contrary, by prohibiting "ultramontane" sermons that were critical of the regime the Reich was helping the citizen to identify himself completely with the state and to accept, consciously and of his own free will, the yoke of its authority; such an acceptance on the part of the citizen, Konstantin Rössler maintained in the spirit of the Hegelian right, was the only way he could achieve freedom. From these arguments Rudolf von Bennigsen, one of the leading National Liberals and the head of the German Protestant Society (Deutscher Protestantenverein), concluded that the liberal citizen who was not prepared to subject himself to an ecclesiastical institution such as the "ultramontanist," for example, could attain freedom only within the historical framework of which he was an organic part, that is, the state. Just as the Christian derived his deep assurance of salvation by freely identifying himself with Jesus, the German experienced the feeling of belonging to a nationality by freely identifying himself with the state. Here, observed Rudolf von Bennigsen, were "the deep roots of the *Kulturkampf,* and not until the historic state, which has been the champion of freedom since the time of Luther's Reformation, asserts its sovereignty over religion and nationality shall we feel safe from the ultramontanists." [66]

(3) The Catholic argument that the source of political sovereignty did not reside in the state nor in the political sphere but in the realm of transcendental values was answered by Treitschke in his programmatic speech on the *Kulturkampf* in the Prussian Lower Chamber in May 1873 and in a series of critical articles in the *Preussische Jahrbücher* during the years 1872–1874. Treitschke contended that, in contradistinction to the "ultramontanists" who wished to introduce foreign influences into German culture, nationality, and politics, the National Liberals believed that the source of state power was to be found in the state itself, that is, in the spirit of a people or its *Volksgeist* which, in Treitschke's romantic interpretation of the Hegelian conception of the state, was defined as the historical essence of the nation which reaches its perfection, and hence its

66. Ibid.

full strength and freedom, in the state by virtue of the power that resides in the state and for the benefit of the state.[67]

A similar conclusion was reached by Eduard Lasker, although he started from an opposite premise. In the course of a parliamentary discussion in February 1872 concerning compulsory government supervision of the school system, Lasker spoke on what he called the principle of the ethical autarchy of the state. Lasker, like most liberals of the Left, repudiated the *étatist* goals of the extreme National Liberals. With respect to the antiultramontane legislation, however, Lasker insisted that the moral right of the state to enforce laws was not derived from a metaphysical system external to the state and that the source of the state's power resided in the state itself. Only within the framework of the state could man free himself from alien systems, that is, achieve full freedom.[68]

In countering these arguments, the spokesmen of the Center during the years 1871–1875 dwelled on the fact that the National Liberals had made the state all-powerful and that the laws enacted within the framework of the *Kulturkampf* not only failed to advance civilization but led to "an excessive concentration of state power . . . and to a deification of the state." [69] This was also the view represented by Ludwig Windhorst,

67. Henrich von Treitschke, *Die Maigesetze und ihre Folgen (10.XII.1873), Zehn Jahre deutscher Kämpfe: Schriften zur Tagespolitik,* Vol. II, Berlin, 1897, pp. 83–96. See also his speeches and writings in the years 1875–1876 in the Hendel edition, *Aufsätze, Reden und Briefe,* Vol. III, 1929, pp. 587 ff, 594 ff, Vol. IV, pp. 295 ff, 586 ff. Great care must be exercised in determining the relationship between Treitschke's views and Hegel's political theory, which has been done by Shlomo Avineri, "The Problem of War in Hegel's Thought," *Journal of the History of Ideas,* Vol. 22, 1961, No. 4, p. 464. We are not referring here to the difference in their conception, but to the romantic, mythical, and nondialectical interpretation of Hegelian concepts in Treitschke's historical and political views; see W. Bussmann, *Treitschke: Sein Werk und Geschichtsbild,* Göttigen, 1952, pp. 153 ff, 191 ff.

68. *Stenographische Berichte über die Verhandlungen des Abgeordnetenhauses vom 8.II.1872,* p. 677. See also, Schmidt-Volkmar, p. 80. A similar version, although with a mythical, irrational, and romantic tendency, is found later "that one must deduce the moral judgment concerning the state from nature and from the vital ends of the state and not from the individual," *Politik,* Vol. I, Berlin, 1897, p. 105.

69. Ludwig Windthorst, *Das sogennante Primat des Staates, Rede etc.,* Berlin, 1874, p. 1; *Stenographische Berichte des Abgeordnetenhauses, etc., 1872/3,* Vol. I, p. 472: "They do not want true freedom; they want the omnipotence of the state, which regulates every human activity from womb to tomb and controls it through the police. They want every individual to find his place within this system because they believe that the omnipotent state would no doubt always do the best that is possible. They deny the infallibility of the Pope and transfer this infallibility to the omnipotent state in every respect." The source is cited in F. Sell, pp. 254/255.

Peter Reichensperger, and others who contended that the materialistic philosophies expounded in popular form by liberals in the universities, in the schools, and in the press would inevitably lead to total secularization and create a spiritual vacuum of religious unbelief and a rebellion against all authority. This would drive the individual into the arms of the state and compel him to acknowledge its power and submit to its dictates; for neither the individual nor the community could exist without authority. In 1872, Peter Reichensperger foresaw that this development must lead to a power state (*Machtstaat*),[70] an omnipotent state that would not hesitate to crush every national, religious, or cultural minority in the Reich. Similarly, the liberal leader of the Center, Ludwig Windhorst, in his speech to the Prussian Diet on February 8, 1872, warned that a state without God ends in self-deification.[71]

This dispute that took place in the years 1871–1875 between the National Liberals and Progressives on the one hand and the Catholics on the other placed German Jewry in a dilemma. Many Jews regarded themselves as political and ideological allies of the liberals. At the same time, however, the attitude of some political leaders, such as Treitschke, Bennigsen, Lasker, Virchow, and others, despite the differences among them, embarrassed and at times antagonized the leaders of the Gemeindebund, Jewish students, rabbis, teachers, and the readers of the *Allgemeine Zeitung des Judenthums,* for they saw that the policy of the liberals in the conduct of the *Kulturkampf* would not liberate the state from church domination and, hence, far from achieving spiritual and cultural freedom, including the freedom to be different, would lead to a rigid standardization imposed from above by a highly centralized state.[72] They challenged the validity of Virchow's so-called scientific liberalism and denounced the popular scientific materialism taught by Ernst Haeckel and Louis Büchner which, supported by secular rationalism and religious apathy, threatened to crush the life of the spirit with its deadening uniformity. Martin Philippson warned that Virchow's demand for "the unifica-

70. *Kulturkampf,* Introduction, p. v.

71. In the above-mentioned Protocol, n. 70, pp. 472, 673.

72. *Kultur,* pp. 2, 6, 9. The work was published anonymously, but it is evident from its content and style that it was written by Rabbi Dr. Moritz Rahmer, one of the leaders of the Jewish community in Magdeburg, and editor of the journal *Israelitische Wochenschrift für die religiösen und sozialen Interessen des Judenthums;* see also: G.A.J. G.A. M 7/1.

tion of the spirit'' [73] presented a threat to both Judaism and Catholicism and, indeed, to every minority group that sought to preserve its distinctive character. The representatives of the rabbis and teachers of the large communities [74] pointed out in their dispute with national liberalism, as interpreted by Treitschke and Bennigsen, that such an interpretation of the *Kulturkampf* sought to identify the Reich with the Protestant state which was based on ''personality that strives for freedom, that is, for certitude of salvation as it is revealed in the gospels and not in rationalism . . . and in this redemptive task of the state the Reich and not the individual will become the source of authority and morality.'' [75]

The principal organ of German Jewry, the *Allgemeine Zeitung des Judenthums*, dealt with this issue without equivocation or evasion. As early as 1872 it expressed its opposition to egalitarianism (*Gleichmacherei*) and to leveling (*Nivellierung*),[76] principles to which secular national liberalism would subject the Jews and every other religious minority in the Reich. This paper was forthright in its condemnation of the growing secular influence in the country and characterized it as an attempt on the part of the German liberals to imitate the French in their misguided efforts to identify religion with the church, an error that had weakened both the political power of the church and the moral authority of religion, thus making it difficult for the Jewish community to insist on retaining its separate religious identity. This devotion to the principle of egalitarianism on the part of the German liberals, the *Allgemeine Zeitung* declared, was nothing but ''a fear of all strong individuality . . . and a distrust of all religious manifestations.'' [77] German Jewry, however, being essentially a religious community, had a mission to uphold individuality and freedom as supreme values. Judaism was not a church and hence need not incur the hostility of the liberals or the state; it occupied a

73. *Kultur,* p. 10. This pamphlet does not give the source of this phrase by Virchow, and it seems that the reference is to a lecture he delivered at the forty-fourth convention of German scientists and doctors in Rostock on Sept. 22, 1871. In this lecture entitled ''Über die Aufgaben der Naturwissenschaften in dem neuen nationalen Leben Deutschlands,'' Virchow complained about the lack of unity in the intellectual life of Germany by using the above expression ''die Einigung der Geister.'' For another reaction to Virchow's phrase, see periodical edited by Moritz Lazarus and Heymann Steinthal, Z. V.P.S.W., Vol. 8, 1875, p. iii; see also the reaction of the A.Z.d.J. to the parliamentary debate between Rudolf Virchow and Ludwig Windhorst, ''Eine Discussion im preussischen Abgeordnetenhause,'' 1883, No. 11, p. 170.

74. *Kultur,* p. 2 ff.    75. Ibid.    76. A.Z.d.J., Vol. 36, 1872, No. 23, p. 442.
77. Ibid.

unique position and could not be compared to any other existing church.[78] The principal element of this uniqueness was "a strong and vital individuality, an enduring historical-religious individuality." [79] If German liberalism was unable to tolerate an individuality such as this, an individuality that aspired only to cultural and religious identity and was in no way opposed to cultural and religious identity, "there is nothing we can do except express our disapproval, deplore its shortsightedness, and refrain from following in its footsteps." [80] In that same year the *Allgemeine Zeitung* protested that scientific liberalism and the scientific world view were undermining the spiritual life of the country and especially the particularism of the religious minorities, and unless resisted would lead to cultural and intellectual regimentation.[81]

These changing evaluations of liberalism on the part of many leaders of the Jewish community were clearly formulated and publicly expressed, especially with respect to the excesses of the *Kulturkampf* and the fear of an emerging police state.[82]

78. Ibid.

79. Ibid. Similarly, A.Z.d.J., Vol. 37, 1873, No. 7, p. 99, "dass der Character unserer Zeit in der Geltung der Individualität liegt." These views were summed up by Martin Philippson at the end of the nineteenth century as follows: "The Jewish community, which is dispersed throughout the whole world, is no doubt a cosmopolitan group in the best sense of the word, and hence serves as a living contradiction of the exaggerated and pathological development of the national principle in our time" ("Die über die ganze Erde zerstreute jüdische Gemeinschaft, zweifellos ein kosmopolitisches Element, im besten Sinne, und deshalb ein lebendiger Widerspruch gegen die übermässige krankhafte Entfaltung des Nationalprinzips in unserer Zeit"), J.J.G.L., Vol. 2, 1899, p. 6.

80. J.J.G.L., Vol. 2, 1899, p. 443; see also A.Z.d.J., Vol. 35, 1871, pp. 41 ff, 107 ff, 169 ff, 189 ff, 895 ff; Vol. 37, 1873, p. 199 ff; Vol. 38, 1874, p. 17 ff; Vol. 39, 1875, pp. 1 ff, 279 ff.

81. A.Z.d.J., Vol. 36, 1872, pp. 463 464.

82. *Kultur*, p. 14. This emphasis placed on the historical, political, and ethical uniqueness of the status of German Jewry was expressed by a small group of leaders, functionaries, and scholars of the Wissenschaft des Judenthums. The sources at the disposal of the historian in and outside of Israel in general do not reflect the attitudes, activities, and opinions of those Jewish groups—and these were by far the majority—that did not take part in organized Jewish life. There is reason to believe that in the days of the *Kulturkampf* most of the Jewish intellectuals, professional men, and members of the upper middle class were far removed from Jewish roots and Jewish social life. It is therefore doubtful that these circles shared this consciousness of Jewish uniqueness as it was expressed by the leaders of organized Judaism.

The *Kulturkampf* and the Legal Status of the Jewish Communities

Many changes took place in the legal and public status of the Jewish communities in the course of this struggle, especially with respect to the reform legislation of the years 1873–1876 in the kingdom of Greater Prussia and, to some extent, in the Reich as a whole. The purpose of these reforms was to define the juridical authority and the public status of ecclesiastical and communal organizations.

At the end of March 1873 the National Liberals and Minister of Education and Public Worship Adelbert Falk introduced a parliamentary motion to repeal some of the clauses in the basic Prussian law of November 30, 1850, including par. 15 which provided that "the Evangelical and the Roman Catholic church, and all other religious societies, shall regulate and conduct their affairs in an independent manner." [83] The law also stipulated that all religious organizations should continue to retain control of their funds and be entitled to levy taxes for the maintenance of internal institutions in the sphere of religion and public worship, culture, education, and social welfare. The motion to rescind par. 15 was introduced by the Liberals in order to weaken the authority of the Catholic clergy and to establish a supreme state authority within the country.[84] Bismarck and the National Liberals thereby hoped to buttress the claims of state sovereignty over against the church, religion, culture, and education.[85] The proposed law was passed by the Prussian Diet in May 1873 and became an effective legal weapon which intensified the struggle.

In the polemical pamphlet *Gegen Christliche Intoleranz* [86] (*Against Christian Intolerance*) the leaders of the Magdeburg community declared that the proposed law would obscure the distinctive character of the Jewish communities. The opponents of the law agreed that the law would diminish the power of the community leadership which, they claimed, was feeble enough as it was. Furthermore, to weaken the particularistic authority of the Jewish community would deprive its leadership of the

83. The different versions of this law and its legal, political, and ideological meaning as interpreted by the legislators are collected in the file G.A.J., Acta des Cultus-Ministeriums, Vol. II, 1847–1871, Judensachen von Berlin, Reference No. 256/III/2(b), Film-reel No. 1710; see also A.Z.d.J., Vol. 39, 1875, pp. 263 ff, 279 ff.

84. *Kulturkampf,* Introduction, p. ii.

85. Ibid. In the language of the source, "die staatlichen Hochheitsansprüche über Kirche, Cultur, Bildung und Schulwesen . . . zu stärken."

86. *Kultur,* pp. 12–14.

necessary power to collect taxes for the basic communal services and projects.

Two years later, when there was renewed discussion about deleting par. 15 from the law of 1850, the *Allgemeine Zeitung* published a strongly worded article criticizing these ''new steps in the sphere of ecclesiastical policy.'' [87] This criticism was directed against those measures advocated by the National Liberals in the course of the struggle which were designed, the article asserted, to weaken religion as a cohesive social force that was capable of uniting the various particularistic social and cultural groups in the Reich. The *Allgemeine Zeitung* referred to a number of paragraphs in the laws enacted during the period of the *Kulturkampf*, among them reforms in civil marriages, secular governmental supervision of religious education instead of church supervision, and the Law of Separation, which shall concern us later. The article expressed the fear that the adoption of this measure would destroy the legal status of the religious communities and reduce them to the level of private organizations.[88] Furthermore, the article continued, this measure, which would endanger the continued existence of the religious communities, was the result of muddled thinking on the part of the German liberals. While the struggle to curb the political power of the church might be necessary, the church must not be identified with religion nor must the status of religion be reduced.

Many leaders of the Jewish community failed to see that this par. 15 of the law of 1850 was an expression of pre-emancipation policy. On the contrary, in the light of the changes that took place during the years 1873–1876, this paragraph was interpreted as an expression of a tolerant and noncoercive attitude so that, in the words of the leaders of the Magdeburg community: ''Par. 15 serves as a legal authorization equally for all religions to preserve their physical existence and their spiritual uniqueness.'' [89] It was felt that to rescind this paragraph was to permit

---

87. A.Z.d.J., Vol. 39, 1875, p. 279.     88. Ibid.

89. *Kultur,* pp. 12–14. To complete the picture of the general legal background concerning the annulment of Par. 15 of the law of 1850, see the archive of A. Freund, G.A.J., XVIII, M.S.S., M/23, Gesetz betreffend die Abänderung der Artikeln 15, 18 der Verfassungsurkunde vom 31.I.1850, am 5.IV.1873 (18.VI.1878). Equal rights for all religions and particularistic groups in the Reich to be different and at the same time be an inseparable part of the German nation and the revived nationalism of the Second Reich was the official policy of the Gemeindebund in Germany, in the days of the *Kulturkampf,* see G.A.J. G.A., M 1/1; M1/3; M1/4; M1/7; M1/8; M1/9.

the principle of egalitarianism to gain the ascendancy over a religiously apathetic Jewish community and thus endanger its very existence.

After lengthy parliamentary discussions of the proposal to remove par. 15 from the law of 1850, both houses of the Prussian Diet on May 14, 1873, passed the fourth law in a series known as the May Laws, the so-called Law of Separation (*Austrittsgesetz*),[90] which became the principal legal and ideological weapon of the *Kulturkampf*. This law permitted the Protestants and the Catholics to withdraw from the church and also from the religious community (*Parochie*) to which they belonged, without thereby being automatically expelled from the Christian religion or from any particular sect within Christianity.

As in all the legal, political, and intellectual controversies discussed above, the leaders of the *Kulturkampf* hoped that this law would weaken Catholic power by permitting Liberal or National Catholics (*Altkatholiken; Reformkatholiken*) to withdraw from conservative ecclesiastical organizations, which were described as "dogmatic and ultramontanist," and establish new religious communities without being expelled from the Roman Catholic religion as a whole. The first version of the law, as passed by the Prussian Diet during the second week of May 1873, made a distinction between Jews and Christians. Catholics and Protestants were permitted to withdraw not only from their religious communities (*Parochien*) but also from their sect, their faith, or the church to which they belonged without being considered, from the standpoint of their legal status, as having withdrawn from Christianity. The withdrawal of a Jew from his congregation (*Synagogengemeinde*), however, was interpreted, according to the explanations appended to par. 8 of the law in its initial formulation, as a withdrawal from Judaism. In the eyes of the law a Jew who thus separated himself from the religious community was without a religion and regarded as an atheist or as one who was indifferent to religion. In the very first discussion of this law in the Prussian Diet on March 19, 1873, Eduard Lasker pointed out that the law in this form was discriminatory and prejudicial to those Jews who, because of religious

90. G.A.J. Acta Generalia etc. betreffend den Austritt aus der Kirche und den Synagogen etc. I, P/135/1207. See also the archives of Dr. A. Freund, G.A.J. XVIII, M/2, M.S.S. Rechtsgeschichte etc., das Austrittgesetz, 1876. See also the series of May Laws of the *Kulturkampf,* according to G. Franz, pp. 224–225, to the state regulations which were represented in the Jewish press as constituting a danger to the continued existence of the Jewish communities: "Die neuesten Schritte auf Kirchenpolitischen Gebiete, etc.," A.Z.d.J., Vol. 39, 1875, p. 279.

scruples or denominational considerations, did not wish to be affiliated with the synagogue and who could therefore not leave Judaism, according to the law, without forfeiting their legal status as members of the Jewish faith.[91]

Orthodox Jewry continued to exert pressure on Eduard Lasker and other Liberal Progressive deputies to effect a change in this law. It was obvious to S. R. Hirsch and Israel Hildesheimer, as well as others, that the law as it was formulated in the version of May 14, 1873, prevented an Orthodox Jew from leaving the synagogue that had become too modern for his taste and forced him to become a member of a Liberal or Reform congregation. In March 1876, Kaiser Wilhelm authorized Adelbert Falk, the minister of education and public worship, Graf Eulenberg, the minister of the interior, and Leonhardt, the minister of justice, to submit a draft of an amended law to both houses of the Prussian Diet. As a result of the intervention of Eduard Lasker and the Liberal Progressives, and the pressure exerted by Orthodox Jewry, a new version of the Law of Separation was passed in May 1876 whereby the same law that applied to Christians was also valid for Jews, that is, a Jew could now withdraw from the congregation and not be considered as having withdrawn from Judaism as a whole.[92]

91. *Stenographische Berichte etc., achtundsechzigste Sitzung, 19. März 1873; Haus der Abgeordneten etc., Sweite Beratung.* Photographic copies of the minutes of these meetings are now in the General Archives for Jewish History in the S. R. Hirsch collection, HM, P 1, II, No. 42; see there also the argument of the Jewish deputy Warburg who regarded the Law of Separation, in its first version, as a special law that discriminated against the Jews (*Spezialjudengesetz*), and all such special laws, he observed, "of which there are many in Germany . . . are for me nothing but a small ghetto." See above, minutes of the meeting, p. 1750 ff, see also A. Z.d.J., Vol. 37, 1873, pp. 219, 385, 401, 417, 433, 497, 531, 581, 643, and especially the open letter of Ludwig Philippson to Eduard Lasker of Nov. 13, 1873, p. 871.

92. *Haus der Abgeordneten etc., 3 Session 1876, Anträge zu dem Entwurf eines Gesetzes betreffend den Austritt aus der jüdischen Synagogengemeinde,* the above collection of S. R. Hirsch, No. 39; see also the different versions of the Law of Separation and the appended political, legal, and ideological argumentation in the above collection, No. 38–41. See also the essay criticizing Eduard Lasker's views and the speech of Professor Heinrich von Sybel condemning the Law of Separation, A.Z.d.J., Vol. 40, 1876, p. 279 ff; for the political activities of the leaders of the Orthodox communities in behalf of the new version of the Law of Separation of the year 1876, see copy of the Memorandum sent by the heads of the Gemeindebund to the president of the parliamentary Committee of Appeals, Professor Rudolf von Gneist, March 16, 1874, according to the photostat copy in the General Archives of Jewish History, G.A.J., P 135/1207. The work appeared in several editions, as a separate pamphlet, and as part of S. R. Hirsch, *Gesammelte Schriften,* Frankfurt a/M, Vol.

This Law of Separation conferred upon the Jewish community a new legal and public status that was characterized by Ludwig Philippson as an expression of "the intervention on the part of the cultural state [*Kulturstaat*] in the lives of its citizens and their freedom of conscience . . . and this was not our purpose in supporting the *Kulturkampf*." [93] The novel feature in the last version of the Law of Separation in 1876 is apparent when we compare it to the Law on the Status of the Jews of July 23, 1847, which obliged every Jew to be and to remain a member of the congregation in his local community (*Ortsgemeinde*). To withdraw from the congregation and still remain in the community, that is, to fail to pay taxes or fulfill other obligations imposed by the administration of the community, was tantamount to leaving Judaism. In short, according to this law one could not be a Jew without being a member of a congregation. [94] The civil status of a Jew in Greater Prussia was determined on the basis of membership in a congregation. The law of 1847 had also permitted a Jew to withdraw from the congregation, but consent for such separation was granted only for geographical reasons and on condition that he join another congregation in another locality; to withdraw from a congregation because of religious principles or beliefs without at the same time becoming a member of another congregation was against the law. After the Law of Separation in 1876, however, a Jew was able to leave the congregation and still remain a Jew without becoming a member of any other congregation. This new situation, Ludwig Philippson declared, was nothing but "a perversion of the liberal principles on which the May Laws of the *Kulturkampf* were based . . . for we did not join the struggle for the sake of disrupting the congregations [*Synagogengemeinden*] and church parishes [*Parochien*]; it is their freedom and continued existence that we had expected." [95] This was not an isolated or accidental reaction; it testified to the changes that had taken place in the attitude of the non-Orthodox Jewish community toward National Liberalism, in its evaluation of the changing status of the historical Jewish community, and in the relations between the leaders of this community and Orthodox Jewry.

---

IV, 1908, p. 239 ff, Nos. 4, 14, 47, 48; 1874, Nos. 2, 21 (1st Supplement); 1876, Nos. 18, 24–28. For the attitude of the leaders of the non-Orthodox communities, see H. Makower, *Die Gemeindeverhältnisse der Juden in Preussen*, Berlin, 1873.

93. *Zentrum*, p. 1.

94. L. Auerbach, *Das Judenthum und seine Bekenner in Preussen und in anderen deutschen Bundesstaaten*, Berlin, 1890, pp. 301 ff, 322 ff.

95. *Zentrum*, p. 1.

Soon after the Law of Separation had been passed in May 1873 the representatives of the leading non-Orthodox communities—including also rabbis, teachers, functionaries, and social workers—met in Leipzig to discuss, among other things, the Law of Separation which in theory was designed to abolish state intervention in the religious and cultural life of the citizen but which in practice represented a grave interference in the lives of the Jews. Now that compulsory membership in the religious community was no longer required, many Jews could freely leave their congregations but only few of these, it may be assumed, with the intention of joining an Orthodox congregation; the greater part would disavow all responsibility to the Jewish community out of apathy and indifference to religious tradition. It was feared that such a mass withdrawal from the religious community would result in a severe reduction of communal revenues in the form of taxation and contributions and that many communities would be unable to maintain basic services, such as synagogues and social welfare organizations, and even Jewish cemeteries would have to be abandoned because of inadequate financial support.

Ezekiel Caro, the rabbi of Dirschau, 1870–1879, asserted that the abolition of compulsory membership in a congregation (*Zwangsangehörigkeit*) would entail the dismissal of many veteran teachers; he also complained of the indifference of the Jewish communities and of the Gemeindebund and urged that pressure be brought to bear on the deputies of the various electoral districts to demand the repeal of the Law of Separation.[96] During the latter part of 1873 and throughout the following year there was a marked increase in the efforts of the heads of the Jewish community, under the leadership of the jurist H. Makower, Ludwig Philippson, and his son Martin Philippson, to persuade the Prussian authorities to retain compulsory religious affiliation. In a series of memoranda drawn up in 1874 by the leaders of the large Jewish communities to be submitted to the president of the Committee on Grievances in the Prussian Diet by the deputy Eduard Lasker and the leaders of the National Liberal and the Progressive Liberal factions, the spokesmen of the non-Orthodox Jewish community demanded that the state refrain from enacting any further legislation of this nature which, in their opinion, could only result in the complete disintegration of the Jewish communities.

96. Letter of Rabbi Ezekiel Caro to the heads of the Jewish Gemeindebund, March 6 and 27, 1874; see there also copy of the Memorandum sent to the Prussian Lower House, photostat copy in the General Archives, G.A.J., P 135/1207 (hereafter, "Memorandum").

The memorandum submitted by the leaders of the Gemeindebund to the Prussian Diet in 1874 pointed out, among other things, the similarity between Orthodox Judaism and "ultramontanism"—its intolerance and dogmatism and its adherence to outworn medieval traditions; the spiritual and perhaps also political allegiance of its leaders, such as Hirsch, Hildesheimer, Lehmann, and others, was primarily to the localities in which they grew up, that is, in such conservative centers as Hungary, Moravia, and Mainz, and their national loyalty was outside of Germany, in the land of Israel.[97] The Orthodox Jews were accused of endangering the very existence of the Jewish community in Germany. Their paramount concern was to maintain their inner unity at all costs, and this isolated them from the rest of the Jewish community; they therefore welcomed the Law of Separation, although by doing so, the spokesmen of the Gemeindebund argued, they undermined the basis on which the Jewish community was founded—and without this basis it was doubtful whether Jewish unity could be maintained or even whether intermarriage and conversion could be checked.

In a pronouncement issued by the Faculty of Jewish Teachers of the Hochschule in Berlin (Das Lehrercollegium der Hochschule für die Wissenschaft des Judenthums) on May 5, 1875,[98] Orthodox Jewry was censured for making the acceptance of formulated articles of faith (*formuliertes Glaubensbekenntnis*) a necessary condition for belonging to the Jewish people. Since this condition existed in Christianity, the pronouncement continued, new legislation was needed to define procedures for withdrawing from the various religious faiths. Judaism, however, had always taught that he who was born into Judaism was and remained a Jew as long as he did not abjure his faith and adopt another religion. In contradistinction to Christianity, verbal acknowledgment of adherence to the Jewish religion did not suffice to make one a member of the Jewish community; there was no way for the Jew to retain his Judaism other than belonging to the Jewish community as such, and not to an Orthodox or

97. "Memorandum," p. 5 ff. The heads of the non-Orthodox Jewish community declared, among other things, that German Jewry refused to be oppressed any longer by this medieval burden borne by the "ultramontanist" Jews; see copy of the above "Memorandum," p. 5 ff.

98. *Das Lehrercollegium der Hochschule für die Wissenschaft des Judenthums,* Berlin, Vol. V, 1875. In the above photostat copies, G.A.J., P 135/1207.

Liberal congregation. To isolate oneself from the Jewish community in general, asserted H. Makower in his talk at a meeting in Berlin in May 1875, and to accept the Christian tradition of sectarianism and "indulge in pompous talk about articles of faith that separate the Orthodox from the Liberals . . . are characteristics of the time caused by the excesses of the *Kulturkampf*." [99] From a historical point of view, the leaders of the Gemeindebund pointed out, "the Jews constitute not only a community that is held together by faith alone [*Glaubensgenossenschaft*] but one that shares a common destiny [*Schicksalsgenossenschaft*]; a history of suffering over a period of thousands of years has forged the bonds of solidarity that unite the Jewish community and inspires every Jew with a deep feeling of belonging to the people." [100]

The original version of the Law of Separation of May 8–14, 1873, the authors of the memorandum added, was perfectly proper within the framework of *Kulturkampf* legislation in regarding the status of the Jew as different from that of the Christian, since the latter could withdraw from the church and still remain a Christian whereas Jewish law made membership in a congregation a necessary condition for belonging to Judaism. The Law of Separation, with its supplementary amendments, clearly set forth the historical and theological reasons for this state of affairs in Judaism and justly stated that "a Jew who is not prepared to make his contribution to the community [*Gemeindebeiträge*] should declare his withdrawal from Judaism." [101] In contrast to the position taken by Eduard Lasker, Moritz Warburg, and other deputies who looked upon this special law (*Spezialjudengesetz*) as an "expression of the ghetto" and as discrimination against the Jews,[102] and also in contrast to the position of the Orthodox Jews, the leaders of the Gemeindebund declared that the Jews had an absolute right to demand from the state special legal guarantees to ensure the continued existence of the Jewish communities: "The history of Jewish suffering has affected Jews for, having been at the mercy of the majorities among whom they lived, they developed a peculiar sensitivity with respect to the legal rights of minorities." [103]

99. *Kultur*, pp. 4–5.   100. "Memorandum," p. 6.   101. Ibid., p. 7.
102. See, above n. 62.   103. "Memorandum," pp. 7–8.

## Conclusion

Our examination in this chapter of the relations between the *Kulturkampf* and the status of the Jews in the Second Reich has brought to light a number of basic historical problems which have helped us in clarifying the status of religion and of ecclesiastical institutions in the modern state and in particular the status of the Jews as a minority group.

With respect to the status of religion it became clear that, despite the pronouncements of Bismarck and the Liberals, the *Kulturkampf* was not exclusively concerned with liberating the constitutional state from church domination, or the national state from the rule of Rome; nor, as the Progressive Liberals thought, with conducting a campaign to achieve greater independence of society and culture from the influence of religion. It was also concerned with the efforts of the church to secure for itself safeguards against intervention by a constitutional state and with the struggle of the religious elements in the community, both Catholic and Jewish, to obtain favorable conditions, politically, economically, and spiritually, that would permit them to observe their respective religions as they deemed proper and preserve their uniqueness in a modern industrial society.

At the beginning of the struggle the state championed the liberal principles of social and political equality and religious freedom. With the intensification of the struggle, however, the Liberals supported the policy of the regime in imposing political and spiritual freedom on the population by the power of the state, by means of propaganda, and by economic and political coercion. In practice the principle of equality became egalitarianism, civil liberty was determined by national identity, and spiritual freedom ended in cultural uniformity. It was, paradoxically, the antiliberal, antinational, conservative "ultramontanist" Catholics who now found themselves in the vanguard of the struggle in defense of the rights of particularistic groups within the Reich for self-determination. This liberal attitude, however, was limited to the Protestant regions where the Catholics were in the minority; nor did it continue beyond the late eighties when the Catholics were completely integrated into the national imperial regime of the German Reich.

In these movements we can see clearly the shift of authority that took place in those days—in the political sphere, from the rationalistic to the romantic and mythical; in the religious sphere, from the traditional to the rationalistic and liberal. Liberalism became a conservative force, and Catholicism pursued liberal goals; rationalistic authority was invested with traditional significance, and traditional authority was enlisted in support of rationalistic reforms. This inner dynamic movement within the *Kulturkampf* helps us to explain the special status of the Jews.

At first German Jewry supported liberalism, for in this movement they hoped to find favorable social, political, economic, and spiritual conditions that promised complete emancipation. This for the majority of German Jewry had a twofold significance: absolute integration into the dominant Christian society, that is, integration into the daily social life of the country but at the same time preserving their separate status as members of the Jewish faith while remaining Germans. In actual practice, however, as the struggle grew more intense, it became increasingly difficult for the Jews to achieve this double aim of the emancipation, namely, complete integration and the preservation of their identity. The Liberals opposed it on the grounds that it defeated their basic principle of egalitarianism; the Catholics objected because of their general anti-Jewish attitude which was evident at the beginning of the *Kulturkampf* and grew more hostile as the struggle proceeded until it ended with their complete integration into the German nation.

As a result of these changes, some leaders of the Jewish community and a number of scholars of the Wissenschaft des Judenthums began to feel that the historic mission of the Jews was after all to preserve their status as a minority as a value in itself, as an ideal expression of the moral obligation of the citizen in the modern national state, the obligation to preserve his distinctive individuality while adapting himself to his environment.

The special status of the Jews in Germany, as defined by the leaders of liberalism, served both Liberals and Christians as a kind of barometer to gauge the merits of their cause and the degree of aberration from the liberal principles of freedom and equality and the Christian principles of love and tolerance. Even in the modern national state, then, the Jew had been regarded as a disruptive and disturbing force. His very existence made the Christians apprehensive of their exclusive claims, compelling them to a painful spiritual stock-taking and to a re-examination of the basic concepts hitherto taken for granted in all spheres of life. This role of the Jew contributed little to the growth of brotherly love between Christians and Jews. It was a potent ingredient in inflaming a spirit of dissension and even hatred between them; but it also had a chastening influence on both religions that would lead them to discover the road back to their unified selves.[104]

104. An important work has recently been published concerning the relations between Catholicism and Judaism in Germany and Austria in the period from the end of World War I until the middle of the 1930's, Hermann Greive, *Theologie und Ideologie: Katholizismus und Judenthum in Deutschland und Österreich (1918–1935)*, Heidelberg, 1969, 320 pp. The Preface and Introduction of this book ( pp. 9–18, 19–30) deal primarily with the period which is central to our study. The conclusion that the author comes to is that the anti-Jewish attitude in Christian tradition and the racial attitude of modern anti-Semitism are not to be regarded as contradictory but rather as complementary attitudes. He does not close his eyes to the anti-Christian elements in racial anti-Semitism; and, indeed, he distinguishes clearly between tendencies directed to an institutional organic structure, i.e., the church, and tendencies directed against Christianity as a system of opinions and beliefs, i.e., religion. But his conclusion is that "the Aryan-Semite opposition does not preclude the Christian-Jewish opposition, but rather presupposes it and absorbs it," p. 16. In this matter the author relies on one of E. Sterling's central theses, p. 141. Further on, Greive collects historical data connected with the anti-Jewish and anti-Semitic activities of A. Rohling and J. Rebbert, p. 20 ff, see below, Chap. 5. Important historical source material may be found in Greive's book (p. 22 ff) not utilized in our present study, such as the writings of Albert Maria Weiss and Hans Rost, and are therefore invaluable for the student who desires a comprehensive view of the entire subject. I take this opportunity to express my indebtedness to Dr. Greive for helpful comments in connection with the *Kulturkampf*, which were also invaluable in helping me to verify the accuracy of the relevant quotations. See his instructive critical essay "Zu den Ursachen des Antisemitismus im deutschen Kaiserreich von 1870/71" in *Judaica*, Vol. 27, No. 4, December 1971, 184–192. Prof. Greive correctly emphasizes the importance of the socioeconomic analysis of the Bismarck era by Hans Rosenberg, *Grosse Depression und Bismarckzeit, Wirtschaftsablauf, Gesellshaft und Politick in Mitteleuropa*, Berlin, 1967.

# 3 | The Christian State and the Jewish Citizen

The Christian State—Watchword of Conservatism

"In our day 'the Christian state' has become a conservative slogan" [1] was the terse phrase with which, in 1876, Johann Caspar Bluntschli, one of the most influential of the liberal political scientists of that period, characterized the changing attitude within the Conservative Protestant community and, to a certain extent, within the German national movement as a whole. This new attitude was most apparent in the attempt to adapt the Christian political principle of the first half of the nineteenth century to the new reality that had been created with the establishment of the German Empire.

In this attempt the conservative leaders went back to a number of different and often contradictory authorities, such as Friedrich Julius Stahl, August Villmar, Victor A. Huber, Ludwig von Gerlach, and Heinrich Wilhelm Thiersch. At the beginning of the seventies they set forth the two central principles of their political philosophy. First, in the spirit of Luther's grievances against the Roman church and papal rule, and in the face of the new social realities of modern Europe, the German Empire with its particularistic historical states, some of which were Catholic, must be transformed into one national state under the aegis and hegemony of the kingdom of Greater Prussia; at the same time the parliamentary political regime and the modern industrial society must not be permitted to restrict the authority of the church or jeopardize the political and economic interests of the historical social classes. Second, the new Reich would derive its sovereignty not from abstract rational principles—such as the theory of "natural law" from the days of the Enlightenment or the

1. J. C. Bluntschli, *Lehre vom Modernen Staat,* Stuttgart, 1876, Vol. III, pp. 221–229.

"social contract" theory from the days of the Jacobins, nor even the metaphysical Hegelian conception whereby the state and Christianity attained freedom by virtue of the absolute, metareligious, rational spirit— but from the principle of "the Christian state" which derived its authority and justification from the Lutheran doctrine of the state whose source was Luther's *Of Earthly Government* (*Von Weltlicher Obrigkeit*) of the year 1523 and his *Larger Catechism* (*Der grosse Katechismus*) of the year 1529.

In his criticism of these conservative views Bluntschli went on to say that "the modern state is not a Christian state, for it is not a theocracy ruled by priests as in the Middle Ages, nor are the adherents of the Christian religion in our day supreme and able to use force or to discriminate against those who are not Christians." [2] Moritz Lazarus, a leading spokesman of German Jewry and one of the founders of the school of *Völkerpsychologie,* declared that Conservative Protestantism was renewing the traditional antagonism between Christianity and Judaism and that "this return to the Middle Ages presents a danger to all of us, Jews and humanists alike, for it reasserts the supremacy of the Christian consciousness over the rationalistic consciousness . . . and with this Christianity has declared war against humanism, liberalism, and also Judaism . . . for Judaism is the social or religious vesture of that rationalistic consciousness." [3] But these and similar criticisms did not deter the conservatives from becoming a potent force in the Reich, especially from the time of the coalition crisis in 1878 until the parliamentary victory of the Social Democrats in 1912, a force whose social and political implications had been recognized even before the turn of the century by Max Weber when he pointed out that the dynasty in the Prussian state rested on the Prussian Junker class, and its political acumen was a powerful source of strength that could be used in the service of the power politics of the state. [4]

In the light of this historical testimony derived from a variety of different sources we shall examine in this chapter the attitude of the Conservatives toward Judaism, the Jews, and the efforts of the Jews to be in-

2. Ibid., p. 229.

3. These words were spoken in 1881, but appeared in print only in 1906 in the polemical collection *Protestantismus und Liberalismus,* pub. by Verein der deutschen Juden, Berlin, Leipzig, 1906, pp. 4–5.

4. M. Weber, *Gesammelte Politische Schriften,* 2d ed., Tübingen, 1958, p. 25; see also: Friedrich Meinecke, *Weltbürgertum und Nationalstaat* (*1907*), München, Berlin, 1919, p. 517.

tegrated into German society, and then attempt to discover what conclusions may be drawn from this attitude with respect to the relations between the Conservatives and the national state and modern society.

## Internal Politics and Conservative Protestants

The principal social and political forces of the Conservative Protestant community which served as a barrier between this community and the Jews were embodied mainly in the following social groups: (1) the Deutsch-Konservative Partei which after 1876 included the relatively moderate Conservatives who supported Bismarck's policy, the Neue Konservative Fraktion, and also the rightest groups that wished to curb the growing power of the Reich, the Alt-Konservative and the circles of the *Kreuzzeitung;* (2) many adherents of the Christian-Social movement led by Adolf Stöcker, especially after 1878, together with the followers of Heinrich Wichern, V. A. Huber, and Rudolf Todt; (3) the Farmers' League (Bund der Landwirthe) after 1893; (4) members of the Inner Mission; (5) many groups that moved between the Conservatives and the Free Conservatives, the principal group being the Freikonservative Reichspartei; (6) the circles that gathered around the chief periodicals of the Conservative Protestants—the *Neue Preussische Kreuzzeitung;* the influential *Allgemeine Evangelische Lutherische Kirchenzeitung,* edited by Professor Luthardt, a prominent theologian and one of the heads of the Mission unter Israel; the *Neue Evangelische Kirchenzeitung,* edited by Professor Hermann Messner; and a series of small popular journals published in rural districts; (7) many prominent figures of the intellectual classes, scientists, writers, artists, leading educators, like L. Wiese, and a number of people who were active in the Evangelisch-Sozialer Kongress (E.S.K.) together with the Liberal Protestants.[5] The political backbone of the Conservatives was the Deutsch-Konservative Partei or, as it was generally called, the Konservative Partei, whose members were recruited also from the aristocratic circles, Junkers who had remained on their landed estates, and those who had left for urban centers to enter the civil service and the professional army. This party counted among its members farmers,

---

5. An important systematic study in this connection is Hans Booms, *Die Deutsch-Konservative Partei: Preussischer Charakter, Reichsauffassung, Nationalbegriff,* Düsseldorf, 1954; To complete the picture, see H. Kohn, *German History: Some New German Views,* London, 1954, pp. 16, 21, 28, 160.

craftsmen, merchants from the middle and lower middle classes, as well as intellectuals and members of the liberal professions.

In May 1873 the extreme right wing of this conservative community, which was to be found chiefly in the kingdom of Prussia when the *Kulturkampf* was at its height, announced its opposition to "all legislation that made for the disintegration instead of the unification of organic relations," [6] and demanded that the imperial government, which still had a Liberal majority, refrain from interfering in the affairs of the church and in the educational policies of the public and confessional schools and to do so, moreover, not in the interest of some liberal principle but because of the danger that threatened to weaken the particularistic power of the Prussian Kingdom within the empire and of the conservative circles within Prussia. To counteract this danger, the Alt-konservative declared, required a unified regime capable of cultivating the "Christian personality." This attitude was summed up by the *Kreuzzeitung,* the principal organ of the extreme conservatives, in the following words: "It is our first and foremost duty to reconstruct with greater energy the religious and ethical foundations of German life. We do not want a Christian state in the old sense; but at the basis of all its ordinances and laws the state must put Christianity . . . we must again regard state sovereignty as a principle that emanates from a divine source." The periodical then gave examples from civil life, such as marriage laws and school regulations, which should be reformed in accordance with Christian-German tradition; above all, the people must be imbued with a respect for authority and with a feeling of piety for the national historical tradition in order to counteract the newfangled ideas of liberalism and rationalism: "Furthermore, it is our task to curb unbridled freedom . . . rigid discipline must be restored to all areas of life." [7]

With the intensification of the struggle against liberalism and the industrial revolution in the middle of the seventies the various factions of the

6. The document was reprinted in *Politisches Handbuch der N.L.P.,* Berlin, 1907, p. 627.

7. *Kreuzzeitung,* No. 195, Aug. 22, 1878; for attempts to apply these principles to current economic and social questions, such as protecting the interests of artisans or those requiring credit against the industrial economy or against Jews, see No. 194, Aug. 21, 1878; Nos. 168–170, July 21–23, 1878; Supplement to No. 177, July 31, 1881. For sources for the legal background, see K. Kupisch, *Quellen zur Geschichte des deutschen Protestantismus, 1871–1945,* ed. W. Treue (Quellen-Sammlung zur Kulturgeschichte), Göttingen, Berlin, Frankfurt, 1960, pp. 45–47.

Conservative party drew closer to one another. The Deutsch-Konservative Partei, which was founded in the fall of 1876, emphasized in its platform the principle of Christian historical exclusiveness and declared the aims of the party to be the following: (1) to strengthen German nationalism, whose political and social nucleus was to be the Prussian monarchy, its dominant religion Lutheran Protestantism, and the source of its ideological authority historic organic growth; (2) to combat the liberal democratic principle of civil equality as expressed in universal suffrage and to preserve "not universal franchise but the natural groupings and organic structures of the people"; and (3) to preserve "the religious life of the German people, maintain and strengthen the Christian ecclesiastical institutions . . . and, above all, the Christian confessional school." [8] To the founders of the party these aims seemed to provide an effective bulwark against liberalism and socialism which they claimed were nourished by "Jewish separatism . . . arrogant Jewish anthropocentrism . . . the typical Jewish illusion that man can and should live without an organic-historic framework . . . as if man alone is endowed with reason and capable of freedom . . . true freedom, however, permits man to become integrated into a structured organism of family life, religion, culture, and spirit in which man has been placed by a supreme Providence and by divine grace." [9]

An important factor that contributed greatly to strengthen the Conservatives politically was the *Kulturkampf,* for this struggle not only witnessed the failure of liberal idealism to achieve its basic aim, the separation of church and state, but it succeeded in making the Conservative party a powerful political force in Prussia and in the Reich. After 1878 the public influence of the Conservatives had risen considerably, especially in Greater Prussia, Hessen, Würtenberg, and in the northern states of Germany. In the eighties and nineties the Conservatives established cordial relations with the Free Conservatives as well as with the National Liberals. After the Reichstag was dissolved in January 1887 this rapprochement between the Protestants and the National Liberals was reflected in the local electoral agreements and in the coalition of the three

8. "Nicht auf das allgemeine Wahlrecht sondern auf die natürlichen und organischen Gliederungen des Volkes." "Gründungsaufruf der Deutsch-Konservativen Partei, 1876," in Wilhelm Mommsen, *Deutsche Parteiprogramme,* München, 1952, pp. 24–25.

9. *Konservative Blätter für das Christliche Deutschland,* Berlin, 1897, p. 4. I have seen only one issue, but a complete series may have been published, apparently by circles of the *Altprotestanten.*

partners of the Right, which was known as the "Kartell." This was the period in which Prussian nationalism, and to a certain extent the entire Reich, was being more deeply influenced by the Protestant character, a tendency that was aptly described by E. Fuchs, who subsequently became one of the leaders of the Central Verein: "Since the establishment of the Kartell I do not know whether the National Liberals support Protestant rule over our German people or whether Protestantism has come to terms with the National Liberals and is absorbing them." [10]

In the period of the Kartell the dispute between the extreme wing of the Conservative Protestants, led by A. Stöcker, von Hammerstein, Hans Kleist-Retzow, and the circles of the *Kreuzzeitung* on the one hand, and the greater part of the Deutsch-Konservative Partei and the Free Conservatives on the other grew more acute. The extreme wing demanded that the church and the clergy be made less dependent on state institutions, but most of the Conservatives preferred to have the regime retain broad powers in ecclesiastical and educational affairs. Although the proposals of the Conservatives were designed to restrict state intervention, they still regarded the authority of the state as higher than that of the Protestant church. The opposition did not advocate the separation of church and state in principle. The extreme group among the Conservatives wished to have the state relinquish its authority over the church through Parliament, the Reichstag, and the chancellor, and to have it transferred to the kingdom (in Prussia) or the empire (in the Reich).

In this dispute Bismarck refused to yield to the demands of the extreme group and insisted that a distinction be made between the status of the Protestants and the Catholics in Prussia and in the Reich as a whole for, whereas the highest Catholic authority was in Rome, the head of the German Protestants was the king of Prussia, who was also the Kaiser of the Reich. Furthermore, there had always been an identity of interests, especially in Greater Prussia, between the state and the Protestant church. The Lutheran church had always been an organic part of the state, so that it was inconceivable that differences should arise between them, whereas in the case of Catholicism the state and not the church was sovereign. In a circular to the Jewish communities in 1889 the leaders of the Gemeindebund expressed their reaction to these arguments:

10. *Der D.I.G.B. und die christliche Bevölkerung Deutschlands*, Leipzig, 1887, p. 14.

Let not the members of our communities be misled by the outmoded interpretations that prevail at present among the Conservatives, namely, that the state,
being Christian, is sovereign over the church, as was the status of the Landeskirche in the early days of Protestantism. . . . We are citizens with equal
rights in a constitutional state, and our status is determined by rational, natural
law by virtue of which we are obligated to continue to integrate into our German
fatherland. . . . We cannot consent to the perversion of the constitutional principles expressly laid down in 1869, nor will we aid and abet in restoring medieval
conditions when the sovereign was the ruler of the church because both the sovereign and the religion were Christian.[11]

The Protestant representation in Parliament, as well as the party organization, was of an exclusive character and did not admit the social classes
to which most of the Jews belonged. There were no Jews among the Conservative parliamentary representatives and active political figures, not
only because of their religion but because they belonged to social classes
that were only slightly represented in the Conservative party. Among the
Reichstag representatives we find aristocrats and landowners [12] and also
former senior officials and army officers. The files in the archives of the
Ministry of Justice clearly indicate that in the period we are studying the
authorities carefully investigated the religious affiliation of senior government officials, showing a marked preference for Conservative Protestants
and an undisguised bias against Jews and, to a certain extent, against
Catholics.[13] In Greater Prussia the number of Protestants and Catholics in
the senior and middle categories of officials in the governmental bureaucracy was determined on a proportional basis in accordance with the
number of members of the two religions in the population. The Prussian
government adhered to this proportional composition in its appointments,
particularly in the judicial and executive departments. Religious affiliation was a determining factor in appointments to government positions,
especially to those which represented the Christian Protestant character of
the state. And if this was the case with respect to the Catholics, how
much more in the case of the Jews who were known to be hostile to the
principles of the Christian state and of Christian exclusiveness in both

11. *An unsere Gemeinden,* pub. by Committee of D.I.G.B., Berlin, Leipzig, 1889, p. 2.
12. Rittergutsbesitzer-Majoratherren. This fact also emerges from the biographical details
of active Conservatives, according to *Handbuch der Deutsch-Konservativen Partei,* 4 rev.
ed., Berlin, 1911.
13. See, below, n. 45.

public and private life. This attitude was attested to by the Reichstag deputy Heinrich Rickert, one of the heads of the League to Combat Anti-Semitism (*Verein zur Abwehr des Antisemitismus*): "Have we Liberal Protestants, even the most secular among us, examined ourselves to see whether we have completely effaced every vestige of Christian exclusiveness in our daily life, in our homes, and in our families? Is it possible to remove the last barrier between the members of the two religions when the fact of belonging to another religion keeps us apart, even when we have recognized the fact that the age of religions is past?" [14]

After 1884 the number of deputies that came from the small landowners and farmers increased, and with the founding of the Farmers' League (Bund der Landwirthe) in 1893 the Conservatives became the party that represented agrarian interests. There were very few representatives in this group before the nineties who were close to the Jews socially or politically, such as merchants, industrialists, or members of the liberal professions. This was also true of the liberal faction in the Conservative party, the Free Conservatives (also called the Deutsche Reichspartei), although it had deputies who came from the commercial and industrial classes, especially after the seventies, as well as some jurists, but relatively few members of the liberal professions. The exclusive character of these political parties can be inferred from their deference to the opinions and judgment of the aristocrats and landowners. [15] Liberal economists and sociologists, among them Max Weber, pointed out the danger of this anachronistic, pseudofeudal, romantic veneration of the nobility (which was especially widespread in Prussia at the end of the century) to the technological and social development of German industry.

The nobility was characterized by Kaiser Wilhelm on a number of occasions as "the pearl of the nation" and as a potent factor in curbing the power of the Social Democrats and other disruptive, anarchistic elements in society. In one of the Conservative publications (*Handbuch der Deutsch-Konservativen Partei*) the nobility was defined as a vital social and cultural force even at the end of the nineteenth century, the symbol of the ideal Germanic, Prussian, and Protestant virtues, and hence a force

---

14. H. Rickert, *Irrationales Gefühlswesen als Hinderniss etc.*, pub. by V.A.A., Berlin, 1894, p. 4.

15. In the language of Max Weber, "verächtliches Streben nach Adelsprädikaten." See Wolfgang J. Mommsen, *M. Weber und die deutsche Politik*, Köln, 1959, pp. 103, 106, 111 (hereafter, W. J. Mommsen); M. Weber, *Gesammelte Aufsätze zur Soziologie und Sozialpolitik*, Tübingen, 1924, p. 380.

capable of uniting all citizens, army officers, civil servants, and farmers. The qualities distinguishing the nobility were self-respect, unreserved loyalty to Kaiser and fatherland, intrepidity, self-control, harmonious physical perfection, and intellectual alertness—qualities which in the propaganda of the election campaign of 1893 were described as "not acquired but handed down as a heritage from generation to generation; their source is in the German landscape, in its mountains and valleys, its rivers and lakes; their inspiration comes from the magnificent church steeples that are found in every town and on every estate; and their purpose is to safeguard the historic and organic German purity." [16]

With the waning power of the nobility at the beginning of the twentieth century, economically, socially, and as a Prussian-Germanic national ideology, the Farmers' League (Bund der Landwirthe) became more and more influential within the Conservative party. This body, which was founded in 1893 as a political bloc for the landowners and farmers, advocated protective tariffs, lower taxation for farmers, and similar goals,[17] and opposed trade agreements that resulted in reducing the price of local products. From the social point of view this league served as a mouthpiece for the impoverished nobility that had failed to be integrated into the modern industrial society, as well as for the landowners who, economically and socially, had drifted away from their original aristocratic class. Conscious of its decline and rapid deterioration, this group now desired to find a refuge for its despair in a Bund that would preserve its proud past and dwindling hereditary status. About a year after the founding of the Bund, in November 1894, E. Fuchs, one of the leaders of the Jewish Central Verein, declared: "As Germans of the Mosaic persuasion our existence depends on an open, free, and liberal society; every element that urges state intervention in order to preserve the Protestant character, every element that strengthens the traditional classes, must of necessity retard the full and final achievement of social emancipation." [18]

In its attitude toward the Jews the Farmers' League fulfilled a special function: it indulged in an outspoken, rabble-rousing anti-Semitism, with-

---

16. *Wählt Konservative,* Berlin, 1893, p. 1.

17. Bund der Landwirthe, *Satzungen und Programm,* Berlin, 1894, pp. 2–4 (§§1–11); O. H. Böckler, *Der Bund der Landwirthe, Antisemitisches Jahrbuch,* Berlin, 1898, p. 105; S. R. Tirrel, *German Agrarian Politics after Bismarck's Fall: The Formation of the Farmers League,* New York, 1951, p. 144 ff.

18. E. Fuchs, *"Liberalismus und die Interessen des Bundes der Landwirthe,"* *Rede, November 1894,* pub. by C.V., Leipzig, Berlin, 1894, p. 4.

out the anti-Christian racial doctrines, while fomenting Christian-Jewish antagonism; it thus served as a bridge between "Christian Germanism" and the romantic elements in the renascent nationalism. This ideology was clearly formulated by the head of the League, the deputy Dr. Dietrich Hahn, whose slogan was: "War against the Jews" (Kampf gegen das Judenthum):

What we have in common with the anti-Semitic factions is that we have both exposed the polar antithesis of Germanism, that is, Judaism . . . rationalism instead of tradition, a vague universalism instead of historic nationalism; the freedom to crush the farmer instead of law and order . . . [and over against this] the love of the German soil instead of the breaking up of the estates [Güter-Schlächterei]; respect for the German historic myth instead of contempt for the deep-rooted German Volk; blind loyalty instead of perverse cunning; obedience to national-Christian authority instead of egocentric lawlessness; the love of one's fellow man instead of the love of abstract, dry legalism—these and similar virtues are the essence of Germanism, which is the very antithesis of the spirit of Judaism . . . this is the element we have in common with Liebermann von Sonnenberg and his colleagues.[19]

From the very outset non-Christians were excluded from membership in the League.[20] Its anti-Semitic character was also apparent in a speech that was given by Graf Leo von Caprivi, Bismarck's successor, in defense of his policy of international trade agreements on November 17, 1893, in the Reichstag.[21] Similarly, the president of the League, Alfred von Plötz, in advocating the amalgamation of the Deutscher Bauernbund with the League and with the Conservative party in general, urged the Conservatives to direct their policies against the three principal forces undermining the national economy and the Christian German state—Liberalism, Jews, and Social Democrats.[22]

With these ends in view the League supported the anti-Semitic factions in the Reichstag early in the nineties in their efforts to limit the entry of Jews into Germany, using the slogan: "Kampf gegen das Gross-Judenthum" (War against organized Jewish power).[23] In the League's publication (issue of July 19, 1894) that had proclaimed that its policy

19. Ein Wort an die Juden, Berlin, 1897, p. 6.    20. A.S., Danzig, 1900, p. 57.
21. Ibid., p. 63.
22. Ibid.; "Gegen die zerstörenden Mächte des Freisinns, des Judenthums und der Sozial-Demokratie."
23. Ibid., p. 65.

was based on Christian-German ideals, we now find an ideology to the effect that nonracial Christian anti-Semitism and anti-Christian racial anti-Semitism were complementary, reflecting the respective opinions of the Protestants and the atheists or racists. The League was to serve as the monarchy's chief support in the rural areas, and the Liebermann von Sonnenberg group was to defend the Christian-German national spirit against the Jews in the cities.[24] A comprehensive ideological explanation of outspoken anti-Semitism and Christian exclusiveness was given by Plötz in one of the sessions of the Wirtschaftliche Vereinigung (Economic Association) on March 11, 1904, when he stated that the members of this Association, especially the Social Christians, constituted a minority group like the Welfen of Braunschweig, the middle-class associations (*Mittelstandsvereinigungen*), and the members of the League—all of which had in common, outside of their economic interests, a deep desire to preserve the native vigor of the German spirit. The surest way of measuring the success of this undertaking, he added, was to compare their situation with that of the Jews:

As long as their position keeps rising above ours, we have a visible sign of our failure; we have failed in our economy . . . the tariffs do not provide sufficient protection for our products. Why? Because the errors of Jewish liberalism are still rife among us . . . trade agreements with Russia are about to deplete our internal market. Why? Because Jewish wealth has turned Caprivi's head . . . the farmer's taxes have risen and not decreased, and what is the reason? Because the industrialists, who are the prisoners of the Jews, have succeeded in throwing off their burden of taxes, which has now fallen upon us . . . we have failed to preserve the conservative foundations of our society; we have failed to preserve the historic purity of our culture.[25]

In the practical affairs of political life there were many points of opposition between the Farmers' League and the anti-Semites, especially after the end of the nineties. As a social force, however, the League fulfilled an auxiliary and complementary function in consolidating Christian exclusiveness among the nobility and the landowners and among the Con-

24. Ibid. Here a somewhat different version: "The Farmers League must be the support of the monarchy in the rural areas, while the anti-Semites will be the backbone of the people loyal to the king in the cities."

25. *Correspondenz des Bundes der Landwirthe* (*"Haus des Bundes"*), *Dessauerstr. 7,* Berlin, 1904. This circular differs in form and in size from the usual issues of the *Correspondenz,* and it may have been a special number issued only for a single occasion.

servatives in their various political activities. A series of practical political measures were envisaged by the Conservatives in their efforts to preserve the exclusive Christian character in those spheres in which the principle of the Christian state had been established: in education, civil service, the administration of justice, and the army. Almost all social and political spheres were regarded as proper places to introduce "practical Christian principles"—national insurance, improvement of the social status and material conditions of workers and tenant farmers, strengthening the middle class, state intervention to restrain unfair competition and unethical business practices, protective tariffs, the struggle against the domination of industrial manufacturing and the wholesale market, protection of the craftsman and his corporative, particularistic organization.[26]

"Practical Christianity" (*practisches Christentum*) was coined by Bismarck at the beginning of the eighties to justify the regime's social policy and to seize the initiative from the Social Democrats by showing the social concern of an antisocialist imperial regime for improving the condition of the workers by passing laws such as national insurance. Even as early as 1882–1883 the Liberal Progressives, the heads of the organized Jewish communities, and the intellectual circles around the *Nation,* published by Theodor Barth, were discussing the ideology of "practical Christianity," which was characterized by the *Nation* as a "veritable plague" (*völlige Landplage*), a slogan that was used to further the interests of conservatism, Christian clericalism, political, and social anti-Semitism. Moreover, behind this slogan they saw the increasing withdrawal of the state from the principle of nonintervention advocated by classical liberalism.[27]

A similar slogan was used by Bismarck on May 9, 1884, in defending his progressive social policy, and on this occasion he openly stated that the most effective means for curbing the power of the Social Democrats was for the state to show "a little more Christian concern (*christliche Fürsorge*) for the welfare of the workers." The term "Christian" was used by Bismarck in two senses: in its general current usage as humane or

26. Above, n. 17.
27. D.N., Vol. 6, 1888–1889, No. 38. In his article "Practisches Christentum," Theodor Barth states: "The slogan 'practical Christianity' was created by Prince Bismarck . . . Reichstag, April 2, 1881 . . . since 1881 'practical Christianity' has become one of the most popular political phrases . . . the entire group of social-political laws and drafts of proposed laws has gradually assumed this garb . . . and hence this phrase has become a veritable plague." See D.N., Vol. 8, 1891, No. 44.

charitable, and in a political sense as the antonym for socialist, atheist, revolutionary, radical. The citation in connection with the honorary degree conferred on Bismarck by the University of Giessen in 1888 clarified this slogan further by describing Bismarck, among other things, as a statesman who recognized that "only the Christian religion can redeem the social reality." In his reply of November 22, 1888, Bismarck acknowledged that his policy of "practical Christianity" was designed to deal effectively with the social reality, to assert the political power of Christianity, and to contain the non-Christian forces of socialism and "Manchester" liberalism.[28] This attitude was also reflected in the social legislation, in the parliamentary discussions, and in the propaganda campaigns of the Conservatives and the Farmers' League prior to the Reichstag elections of 1887, 1893, 1898, and 1907. The main plank of the Conservative platform was to uphold the Christian world view and to deepen its influence among the people and in the state administration, to realize its aims in the spheres of legislation, education, public affairs, and business ethics, this being the necessary condition for the future development of the Reich and its states.

The character of this propaganda did not escape the notice of some of the leaders of the organized Jewish community, whose principal objections were: (1) the anti-Jewish note in this propaganda was formulated more subtly and presented in a more restrained manner than in the publications of the "rabble-rousing anti-Semites," and hence was more likely to appeal to the Christian community; (2) the racial factor was slurred over and often omitted, and the emphasis placed on ethnic anti-Semitism, according to which the Jewish people were beyond all redemption or improvement as long as they retained their status as a separate nation which, being rooted in the Jewish religion, would continue to exist together with their ineradicable racial characteristics; (3) this propaganda contained two contradictory views of conversion: some Conservatives insisted on conversion as a condition for full integration into German society and culture; others had reservations regarding its efficacy, especially since many converts admittedly accepted the Christian principles of faith to facilitate their professional, economic, or social advancement; and then there were those who were convinced that conversion was not the way out for the Jew, for it could not penetrate to his tainted seed and redeem him; the

28. On Bismarck and the Liberals see W. M. Simon, *Germany in the Age of Bismarck,* London, New York, 1968, pp. 216–223.

baptismal font could not remove the deep stain. This latter idea induced many Conservatives to accept certain aspects of racial anti-Semitism.

The Reichstag elections of 1893 and 1907, the two most decisive elections in the political development of racial anti-Semitism, enable us to examine more closely the anti-Semitic views of the Conservative leaders and the anti-Semitic political parties with respect to the influence of their anti-Jewish propaganda. The outcome of the elections depended as well on factors of an economic, social, political, and psychological nature; but in considering these factors the views of the Conservative leaders must be analyzed and taken into account. In both elections the Conservatives made gains, and in this the propaganda we have been discussing was an important and at times a decisive element, especially in the districts where the religious or Conservative Protestants were concentrated and where the difference in the number of votes between the Conservatives and the official anti-Semites was small. In the election of 1893 the Tivoli Platform of the Conservative party was an important factor in reducing the number of supporters of official anti-Semitism. This platform, which was adopted the previous year at a convention of the Conservative party in Berlin (parts of it were retained in the subsequent platforms of 1889 and 1895), stated, among other things: "we are combating this ubiquitous Jewish influence which is disintegrating the life of our people." [29]

The members of the Conservative party, outside of its extreme wing, rejected the inflammatory propaganda of the anti-Semitic parties, regarding it as a violation of the principles of authority and monarchist conservatism.[30] This was the position taken in 1894 by the president of the regional branch in Saxony, Freiherr von Friesen: "Rabble-rousing anti-Semitism, especially of the anti-Conservatives, the followers of Oswald Zimmermann in the Reform Party . . . is opposed to monarchist rule and to the highest Conservative principle—authority . . . the purpose of the

29. In the original: "Wir bekämpfen den vielfach sich vordringenden und zersetzenden jüdischen Einfluss auf unser Volksleben" (P. Massing, p. 69); see also A.S., Danzing, 1900, p. 399; A.Z.d.J., Vol. 56, 1892, No. 10, p. 109.

30. *Die Anträge der Konservativen und der Reichspartei, etc. Par. 2, Die Bestimmungen des Vereins und Versammlungsrechts,* Berlin, 1899, pp. 14–16; *Konservative Agitation und der vierte Paragraph der Verordnung vom 11.3.1850,* ibid., pp. 28–29; *Der Bund der Landwirthe und die antisemitischen Parteien während der letzten Reichstagswahlen,* Berlin, 1908, pp. 8, 9, 11, 12, 13, 19, 20. The last work, which is programmatic and propagandistic, was published by one of the two anti-Semitic parties, the Reform Partei or the Deutsch Soziale Partei, probably by the former; its statistical data was taken for the most part from the official yearbooks of the Reich and the Prussian government.

anti-Semitic resolution adopted in the Tivoli Convention in Berlin two years ago was not to effect a union with the blustering anti-Semites but to prevent them from capturing many votes that belong to the Conservatives.'' [31] But in a number of electoral districts voters switched from the Conservatives (1890) and went over to the ranks of the political anti-Semites (1893) because "the Tivoli Convention had denied the Jews the right to dominate our country, our economy, and our education, but it failed to draw from this denial the basic conclusion—the basic racial conclusion that the very existence of the members of that race is harmful.'' [32] In the two elections the Conservatives captured almost all those districts in which the differences between the National Liberals and the Progressive Liberals had become irreconcilable. In this dispute a prominent place was given to a severe criticism of "Manchesterism" as "a Jewish expression of progressivist illusions," but only the Conservatives profited by this and not the anti-Semites (except in the kingdom of Saxony and in the Grand Duchy of Hessen).

The principle of "the Christian state" was applied in connection with the policy of admitting Jews to public posts and to high government positions and was put into force in the civil service, the administration of justice, jury service, army training and instruction, and, to a considerable degree, in the universities and in other institutions of higher learning. The arguments used by the Jews during this period of the Second Reich against this discriminatory policy differed from those used throughout the preceding century, not only because of the large increase in the number of educated Jews who were attempting to integrate into their various professions or because of the political organizations that had been formed to combat anti-Semitism and discrimination but, above all, because the legal basis on which the Jews could rely in this struggle had changed. At the beginning of the Second Reich the demand of the Jews that discriminatory practices be abolished in all these areas was based on a special law that was passed on July 3, 1869, within the framework of the Bundesgesetz which declared: "(special Paragraph) by virtue [of this regulation] all existing disabilities respecting civil and civil-political rights resulting from differences of denominational affiliation are hereby rescinded. It is specifically stipulated that the right to take part in communal and state representation or to hold government posts shall not be

31. *Der Konservative Landesverein in Sachsen,* Dresden, Leipzig, 1894, pp. 1–2.
32. *Staat und Kirche,* Berlin, 1900, p. 2.

dependent on religious profession." [33] The German Jews insisted that this constitutional right reflected the basic rational character of the state in which the "Christian principle" was not permitted to dominate the civil spheres. [34]

After the period of the *Kulturkampf*, in which these questions were dealt with intensively, [35] the question again arose regarding the relation between religious affiliation and the right of all citizens to be appointed to government posts. In 1880, after A. Stöcker and other political anti-Semites had demanded that Jews be excluded from all such posts, Professor Hänel raised this question in the Prussian Diet. The discussion took place on November 20 and 22, during which the Progressive Liberal deputies and also the deputy of the Center, Windhorst, warned that anti-Semitism would intensify discrimination in the appointments of Jews (or, in Windthorst's language, "non-Protestants") to public and government positions. [36]

During the eighties the Gemeindebund extended its activities and, with the help of the Progressive Liberals, greater pressure was brought to bear on the authorities, especially in Greater Prussia, to appoint more Jews to civil and administrative posts, especially in the primary and secondary schools, in the department of justice, and in the offices of the public prosecutor and of the judge in the various states of the Reich. Similarly, the leaders of the larger communities were protesting against the discrimination of Jews for jury service. In 1890–1891 these demands were again brought up in the Prussian Diet for discussion, chiefly as part of the polit-

33. An excellent although partisan summary of these legislative changes is J. Auerbach, *Das Judenthum und seine Bekenner in Preussen und in den anderen deutschen Bundesstaaten,* Berlin, 1890, p. 264 ff.

34. Above, n. 10, p. 10 ff. The concept "the Christian principle," which appears in this propagandistic work, is discussed in a short historical review of the history of the political struggle of German Jewry against the principle of the "Christian state"; the thesis was taken from a speech given by the deputy Briggemann in 1847 in a plenary session (*Kurie*) of the three classes of the Prussian Diet: Regierungskommissar Geheimrath Briggemann: "That the Christian principle contains within itself the right to pervade all areas of life." Two deputies, F. Naumann of the Posen district and Rudolf Campenhausen of the Rhineland, expressed themselves in similar terms, as did Bismarck early in his career; the words were reported in *Stenographischer Bericht,* Berlin, 1847, Vol. IV, pp. 1745 ff, 1755 ff, and reprinted in part in M.V.A.A., 1895, p. 391.

35. See below, "Conservatism and Modernism."

36. *Die Judenfrage: Verhandlungen des Preussischen Abgeordnetenhauses über die Interpellation des Abgeordneten Dr. Hänel, Abdruck der Stenographischen Berichte vom 20, 22, November 1880,* Berlin, 1880; see reports and evaluations in A.Z.d.J., Vol. 44, 1880, Nos. 47–53.

ical campaign of the Progressive Liberals against the Prussian Minister of Justice Dr. F. von Schelling, and at the end of the following year the Deutsch-Konservative party in Breslau passed the well-known resolution which stated that "a Christian state is dependent first and foremost on Christian authority, and the teachers of our people can only be Christians." [37] This resolution reflected a widespread mood, as was made plain at the so-called Tivoli Convention of the Conservative party held that same year. Also at the general meeting of the Conservative party in Dresden in the state of Saxony on June 13, 1892, the authorities were asked to take "constitutional measures which would enable them to erect effective barriers against the further spread of the materialistic world view of Social Democracy and of Jewish power." [38]

The political motto "the Christian state" served not only as an anti-Jewish but also as an anti-Liberal slogan, and this can be seen from the words spoken in the early eighties by Freiherr Friedrich Karl von Fechenbach, a right-wing leader of the middle-class Conservatives: "We wish to preserve the Christian and German foundation of our people, and to do this we must first get rid of the foreign elements that have infected our legislation and the life of our people." [39] The Conservative deputy Wilhelm von Minnigerode, in his parliamentary dispute in 1893 with the Progressive Liberal deputy Heinrich Rickert, declared that his party's slogan was: "Christian sovereignty in every sense" (*eine christliche Obrigkeit in jeder Hinsicht*). Professor Karl Walcker, a lecturer in political science in Leipzig, left the League to Combat Anti-Semitism (*Verein zur Abwehr des Antisemitismus*) in 1893, for he believed that anti-Semitism should be combated not in order to solve the Jewish problem but because it served the political interests of the Progressive Liberals; the Jewish problem itself would be solved only when the Jews decided to assimilate into the dominant society as Germans and Christians through "*Assimilierung, Germanisierung und Christianisierung.*" [40]

At the beginning of the nineties all these political activities were con-

---

37. "Der christliche Staat," A.S., Danzig, 1892, p. 346.        38. Ibid., p. 18.

39. From the above review in n. 10, p. 14; see there words of the Conservative deputies Wilhelm von Minnigerode and von Wackerbarth in the stenographic minutes of the sessions of the Prussian Lower House, Jan. 18–21, 1893, and Feb. 13, 1893. For these words of F. K. Fechenbach, see also A.Z.d.J., Vol. 44, 1880, No. 34, p. 529 ff.

40. Karl Walcker (Dozent der Staatswissenschaften an der Universität Leipzig), *Die Judenfrage vom staatswissenschaftlichen Standpunkte aus betrachtet*, Sondershausen, 1894, p. 11.

solidated mainly within the framework of the League to Combat Anti-Semitism (founded in 1891–1892) and, after 1893, in the Central Verein, the Jewish organization that actively opposed discrimination. The political struggle to eliminate discrimination, which had arisen from the principle of "the Christian state" or what the Jewish leaders called "unofficial anti-Semitism," began in the early part of the century with the founding of the parent organization, Verein der deutschen Juden, with the support of the Society of Jewish Statistics (V.S.J.). Many prominent persons in the life of organized Jewry also took an active part in this campaign, for example, Eugen Fuchs, Maximilian Horowitz, Martin Philippson, Samuel Kristeller, Hugo Preuss, Bernhardt Breslauer, and Martin Peltasohn. Besides the periodicals that were involved in this struggle, such as *Im Deutschen Reich,* the organ of the Central Verein, and the hundreds of circulars, manifestoes, and bulletins, a significant role was played by Jewish newspapers, such as the *Allgemeine Zeitung des Judenthums.*[41] At the beginning of the twentieth century the campaign against discrimination that had been conducted under the slogan of "the Christian state" or "the Christian society" was well organized and fairly effective. In 1901 a petition signed by almost three hundred Jewish communities was submitted to Bernhardt von Bülow, the chancellor of the Reich and the head of the Prussian government, protesting against the discriminatory policy of Prussian Minister of Justice, Schönstedt. A similar campaign was conducted against the minister of justice in the Grand

---

41. G.A.J. HM 1112, *Protokolle der Sitzungen des C. V. Vorstandes, 1894–1905,* Vols. I–II, E. Fuchs, Bericht der Rechtschutz-Commission, Berlin, 1894: "der Staat ist sowenig christlich wie das Christenthum staatlich ist." Also see the regular sections in the two special periodicals devoted to the struggle against Jewish discrimination, M.V.A.A. and I.D.R., and the minutes of the Association of German Jewish Teachers, at first confined to central Germany and after 1896 within the framework of the Verband der jüdischen Lehrervereine im Deutschen Reiche, G.A.J., G.A. M7/1, Minutes of the Third Conference of the Association of Jewish Teachers of the year 1904; see G.A.J. TD 34. For the activities of the general organization, Verein der deutschen Juden, including noninterference of Jewish communities in the matter of employment of Jews in public positions, see ample material in archives: G.A.J. G.A. M 21/4. An instructive example of the fears of the Jewish communities that a highly organized political campaign of the Jews would increase discrimination in this area of appointments to public posts is the answer of some of the communities to the circulars of the V.D.J. of Dec. 3, 1906, in the file, G.A.J. G.A. M 21/2, Korrespondenz des V.D.J. For inaccurate polemical statistical reports relating to Jewish discrimination in government posts, see Justizrath Bernhard Breslauer, "Die Zurücksetzung der Juden im Justizdienst," *Denkschrift im Auftrage des Verbandes der Deutschen Juden,* Berlin, 1907.

Duchy of Hessen, Dittmar; and in that same year the Jewish organizations initiated a political campaign against the Center in the Bavarian House of Deputies in protest against the proposal of one of its deputies, Dr. Heym, to limit appointments of Jews to the judiciary in accordance with their numerical representation in the population.

The arguments put forward by the Jews and the liberal statesmen, including the Catholic liberals, against discrimination and against the conception of "the Christian state" that justified or rationalized it were answered by the Conservatives with different and often contradictory arguments, depending on local political and economic conditions. In a number of essential respects, however, they were in agreement.

A distinction must be made between the professional and the essentially political aspects of this campaign to have more Jews appointed to public posts in government service. From the purely professional point of view, as was pointed out even by some moderate conservatives and foes of racial anti-Semitism, such as the clergyman G. Habermann, this highly organized campaign of the Progressive Liberal Jews was altogether disproportionate to the actual desire of the Jews to enter public or government service. The posts that were most coveted by the Jews were in the universities and other institutions of higher learning and research and in the judiciary; here the doors were often closed against them "because they are Jews, and education, teaching, or the judiciary are regarded in our culture as the product of the Christian spirit . . . or as an instrument of the Christian spirit, to which outsiders cannot contribute." [42] Few Jews showed any desire to enter the other branches of the government civil service, and mostly preferred private practice in the liberal professions where they earned a higher income and where they were not exposed to the unfriendly atmosphere in many of the public government serv-

---

42. From the words of Professor Hans Delbrück, the assistant editor of the *Preussische Jahrbücher* in his public answer to the D.I.G.B.: *Ein Wort über die Zurücksetzung der Juden auf unseren Universitäten und höheren Lehranstalten,* Berlin, 1885, p. 1. For a more aggressive statement, see his review of Martin Philippson's study, *Geschichte des preussischen Staatswesen vom Tode Friedrichs des Grossen bis zu den Freiheitskriegen,* Vol. II, Leipzig, 1880–1882. Among other things, Delbrück asserted that "one who has only a superficial idea of Protestantism" has no place in the intellectual life of Germany or among its historians, hence: "If, as happens in life, someone insinuates himself into a select society to which he does not belong, then a member of this society must take it upon himself to remove the intruder . . . which must be done if the society wishes to remain in good repute," P.J., Vol. 54, 1884, p. 578 ff; Vol. 55, 1885, p. 357.

ices. This, the Conservatives were quick to point out, was partly the fault of the Jews themselves because of their foreign ways and unpleasant manner and partly the result of the "historic and organic antagonism between the German-Christian mentality and that of the Jewish tribe." [43]

In the heat of the controversy, especially during the political campaign against Prussian Minister of Justice Schönstedt in 1901–1902, and following the statistical data issued by the Verein der deutschen Juden in 1906–1908, both sides used the available statistical information to buttress their respective positions. The officials in the Prussian judiciary acknowledged that the statistics as presented by the Jewish leaders were correct with respect to the small number of Jews employed in high government posts, especially in the administration of justice and in the field of education, but were misleading with respect to the number of those employed in lower positions or in those positions with only a professional character and not of a representative nature or on a decision-making level. But even in such instances the representatives of the Central Verein or the Verein der deutschen Juden were not justified in interpreting this situation as anti-Semitism in a political or racial sense. Aside from the fact that there was no great liking for Jews, conservative circles in Prussia observed, a more relevant consideration was the custom in Prussia and in other states of the Reich to regard high posts in the ministries of Justice or Education, for example, judges in the municipal, state, or national courts, or important posts in the legislative and executive branches of the government, not only in their technical or professional capacities but as symbols of the national spirit which, being universally acknowledged as Christian, could not be permitted, public opinion or political considerations notwithstanding, to be put into the hands of Jews.

These considerations arose in part from local political interests, but also from a general political conception, for which the heads of the Conservative faction in the Prussian Diet found support in one of Bismarck's early reflections, namely, that if the state were deprived of its Christian basis, there would be nothing left but a random collection of rights, and its legislation would no longer be derived from an ancient creative source of truth, but from a blurred and capricious concept of humanism. Thus, Bismarck continued, if a German were obliged to stand before a Jew who represented the sacred kingdom of Prussia, he would feel humiliated and

43. Above, n. 42, Delbrück's proclamation of the year 1885.

degraded and unable to serve his fatherland with self-respect, and "this feeling I share with the lower classes of our people." [44]

An examination of the archival sources at our disposal today indicates that the answers given by the Conservatives corresponded to the objective facts and for the most part reflected the public mood of that period. It is difficult to ascertain now whether most of the Jews in the liberal professions preferred private practice, as the Conservatives maintained, or to what degree they were compelled to do so by the "social boycott" (*gesellschaftlicher Boykott*), as the Conservatives themselves described the anti-Jewish atmosphere that prevailed in the public government services. The statistics in the archives of the Prussian Ministry of Justice regarding the religious affiliation of those appointed to posts after 1880 and the exclusion of Jews from government service after 1866 would indicate that the data published by the Jewish organizations to combat discrimination was not accurate (except, as already stated, with respect to the employment of Jews in the universities and secondary schools).

The number of Jews employed in government service does not, of course, reflect the real character of "the Christian state." It is clear, however, that the basic conception behind the discriminatory policy of appointments was to safeguard the professional interests of the Christian teachers, lawyers, and notaries public and to place Jews at a disadvantage, professionally and economically, with respect to their Christian colleagues. This is the view expressed in letters, manifestoes, newspaper articles, and minutes of meetings found in the archives of the Prussian Ministry of Justice from 1878 until the end of the era we are discussing which culminated in a series of petitions submitted in 1901 to Minister of Justice Schönstedt by the Progressive Liberals and the Jews demanding the admission of Jews to a number of high posts in the state judiciary.

A typical letter, dated February 15, 1901, was written by Professor A. Suchsland, a teacher by profession, the executive chairman of the Conservative organization in Halle, one of the leaders of the Protestant Farmers' League (Bund der Landwirthe), and a prominent theoretician of a middle-class anti-Semitic movement close to the group led by Lieber-

---

44. Spoken by Bismarck in the Prussian Lower House before the "Stände und Herren Kurien" on June 15, 1847, according to the official minutes, p. 1784. This is taken from a circular of the Conservative wing in the Prussian Lower House in 1908. On the parliamentary reports in Hessen regarding this question, "Über die Zurücksetzung jüdischer Justizaspiranten," and on its earlier historical development, see A.Z.d.J., Vol. 65, 1901, p. 566 ff.

mann von Sonnenberg. The argument of the letter is contained in the following two points: (1) the opposition of Christians to Jewish jurists, as members of the bar or as government officials, "is deeply rooted in the soul of the people [*Volksseele*]"; (2) there was fear of Jewish domination of the legal profession and the consequent de-Christianizing (*Entchristlichung*) of the nation's Christian character and the Christian meaning of law and justice. By combining the romantic, racially anti-Semitic key concept *Volksseele* with the dominant Protestant Conservative conception of the Christian character of law and justice, the letter succinctly expressed the double meaning that was bestowed on the concept "Christian state" in the period we are discussing. In another characteristic letter, apparently written by a member of one of the subsidiary branches of the Conservative party to Minister of Justice Schönstedt, dated February 1, 1901, we find: "One need not be an anti-Semite in order to confirm the fact that a Jew in the role of a magistrate, barrister, notary public, etc. awakens in a German a feeling of loathing . . . the very sight of a Jew is at times unbearable." [45]

45. B.A.K., P. 135/3529: "Generalien-Akten des Justiz-Ministeriums enthaltend Äusserungen der Presse und Eingaben betreffend die Konfessions-Verhältnisse der höheren Beamten, sowie die Judenfrage, 1893–1930," Vol. I, p. 152 (144). Rich documentation on conservative public opinion, especially in Greater Prussia, against the employment of Jews in the judiciary (and in different degrees also in education) for the reason given, because the administration of justice reflected and safeguarded the Christian character of the state, may be found, in addition to the file in this archive, in the following files: B.A.K., P. 135/11948: "Generalien-Akten des Justiz-Ministeriums betreffend: die Ausschliessung der Juden vom Staatsdienste, 1866–1921"; B.A.K., P. 135/11949: "Generalien-Akten des Justiz-Ministeriums enthaltend: Äusserungen der Presse über die Ausschliessung der Juden vom Staatsdienste, 1878–1900." Of special importance are the newspaper articles in the years 1891–1893 of the political campaign of the Jewish organizations against the discrimination of Jews in government service. The statistics of those years indicate that the spokesmen of organized Jewry, of the Progressive Liberals, and those active in the struggle against anti-Semitism reported the number of Jews appointed to government posts and especially to the judiciary after the early nineties to be less than the number actually employed: B.A.K., P. 135/11944, "Acta Generalia des Justiz-Ministeriums betreffend: die Konfessionsverhältnisse der Beamten, 1880–1926," p. 171 ff. See there also the minutes of parliamentary deliberations on questions of the Christian state and Jewish (or Catholic) appointments: "Haus der Abgeordneten . . . betreffend die konfessionellen Verhältnisse der Justizbeamten, 16. Sitzung, 10.II.1896; 23. Sitzung, 11.II.1901." Important testimony concerning the paucity or even total absence of Jews in high government posts in the first years of the Empire, 1871–1872, has been preserved in the file: B.A.K., P. 135/3258, "Acta Generalia des Justiz-Ministeriums betreffend: die Konfessionsverhältnisse der höheren Beamten, Hauptzusammenstellung," p. 990 ff. Concerning this entire chapter, see U. Tal, "Conservative Protestantism and the Status of Jews in the Second Reich" (Hebrew), *Zion*, Vol. 27, Nos. 1–2, 1962, pp. 87–111.

Conservatism and Modernism

The history of the political relations of Conservative Protestants to Jews, which we have discussed above, may serve as a framework for the study of the daily life of the community and its existential problems as revealed in popular folk literature, school studies, sermons, current phrases, habits, and manners. From all these we learn that conservatism was a complex movement that was subjected to two contradictory tendencies. On the one hand, the Conservative felt that the stable framework of his unified world view and the traditional forms of life had been swept away; on the other hand, he felt that it was imperative that he participate in the new order which he could neither reject nor ignore. To regain his lost unity he fled to the world of art and literature where he could indulge his private broodings and romantic nostalgia for the past; [46] and to participate in the new order he was tempted to join rightist groups and become

46. For intellectual and especially romantic roots insofar as they are reflected in the attitude of the conservatives toward the Jews, see E. Sterling, *Er ist wie Du,* München, 1956, chap. vi, p. 118 ff. On the conservative mentality, the important essay is Karl Mannheim, "Das konservative Denken," A.S.W.S.P., 1927, No. 57. Important also for the discussion in this chapter are the documents in Harry Pross, *Die Zerstörung der deutschen Politik, Dokumente 1871–1933,* Frankfurt a/M, 1959, chaps. ii, vii. Among the original sources of the period discussed in this chapter a prominent place is given to what in the second half of the nineteenth and the beginning of the twentieth century was known as scientific or popular-scientific literature, but which can no longer be regarded as such. Taken for what they are, they help us to understand the conservative mentality and the everyday thoughts of the German individual in all walks of life—the family man, the villager, the city dweller. See W. H. Riehl, *Über die bürgerliche Gesellschaft, Vortrag in der öffentlichen Sitzung der königlichen Akademie der Wissenschaften,* München, 1864, p. 9 ff; idem., *Die Naturgeschichte des Volkes als Grundlage einer deutschen Social-Politik,* Vol. III, Stuttgart, 1873, p. 267: "Our fathers emancipated themselves from the small town and we must emancipate ourselves from the big city." To this type of popular science that has become a historical source belongs the instructive series Evangelische Kirchenkunde, das kirchliche Leben der deutschen evangelischen Landeskirchen, ed. von D. Paul Drews, Professor of practical theology. See, for example, Part 1, *Die Evangelisch-Lutherische Landeskirche des Königreichs Sachsen,* Tübingen, Leipzig, 1902, chap. viii, "Das religiöse und das sittliche Leben," p. 348: "In its general character, history, and economic condition this people on the whole had a shrewd Lutheran piety with a strong admixture of rationalism that revealed itself in some as an aptitude for turning ecclesiastical rules into rational truths and in others as a dogmatic understanding of Christianity. . . . In short, they set a high value on an active, alert piety in conjunction with a zest for life . . . trust in God and professional rectitude; these were the poles around which the Christianity of most people revolved. . . . Superstition was regarded as the real religion of the people. To a certain extent it was the unofficial religion and took its place over against the Christian ecclesiastical (religion) as if it were the official one."

involved in political action. Suspended in a middle state between a world that was dead and one still unborn, he pressed forward to a jubilant age of conquest and progress, and at the same time looked back to the past for inspiration, to a world of mystery and wonder that was not accessible to reason and pure thought, irresolute whether to exchange progress for salvation, material bread for spiritual freedom, the spirit of revolution for the revolution of the spirit.

The Conservatives, then, adjusted themselves to the organizational forms of modern political realities, but their goals were confined to the particularistic interests of the historical social classes. Furthermore, as the central support of most of the coalition governments in the Wilhelmian period the Conservatives interpreted their governmental responsibilities and even their class interests not in terms of a constitutional state (*Rechtsstaat*) but in terms of authority (*Obrigkeit*) in the Lutheran Protestant sense, which was defined by Professor Adolf Wagner in a lecture on "Judaism and the Rise of Germany," delivered in 1878 under the auspices of the Municipal Mission in Berlin, as "the responsible guardian of the citizen's discipline, having two aspects like the two Tables of the Law, namely, the divine law (*jus divinum*) and the natural law (*jus naturae*); in the political rule of today, therefore, authority [*Regiment*] must be regarded as being responsible for order not only in the physical world." [47]

Two approaches to modern reality thus converged in conserva-

47. Wagner's words refer to Melanchton's principle of political authority, according to *Corpus Reformatorum* ed. by C. G. Bretschneider and H. E. Bindseil, Halle and Braunschweig, 1834–1860, Vol. 21. In a relatively late version of *Loci Communes*, i.e. his treatise on the main principles of religious faith, Melanchton attempted to introduce the theme of Aristotelian political authority as "law," using the symbol of the two Tables of the Law: "Aristotle has given a very apt definition of authority in a few words which, if explicated, will prove highly instructive: 'Authority is the guardian of the law.' If I say, however, that authority is the guardian of obedience, you will understand that it should guard the two Tables of the Law. That is, it is not only the guardian of peace, as a keeper of herds, and should not only serve the belly, but first and foremost the honor of God. . . . It is not permitted to kings, princes and those in authority to act contrary to the divine law [*jus divinum*] and the natural law [*jus naturae*]." The passage from Wagner's speech appeared in the manifesto issued by the League to Combat Anti-Semitism (Verein zur Abwehr des Antisemitismus), *Freunde und Feinde Ahlwardts,* pub. by V.A.A., Danzig, 1893, pp. 4–5. See the early numbers of A. Stöcker's weekly, *Deutsche Evangelische Kirchenzeitung, Wochenschrift zur Pflege evangelischen Gemeindelebens und zur Förderung kirchlicher Selbständigkeit,* 1887, 1888, 1889.

tism—the consciousness of being alienated from the past and an attempt to be integrated into the modern world with patterns and concepts borrowed from the past. At the beginning of the period we are discussing this consciousness of a deep cleavage between past and present was formulated in a leading article in the conservative journal the *Kreuzzeitung:* "A deep and unfortunate split characterizes our time, so that what is united in an inseparable unity in the Kingdom of God (religious life and natural life) is torn asunder in violation of nature. . . . Hence, there is no higher solution for the great contradictions and struggles of our time than the renewed teaching of the Kingdom of God." [48]

In a similar vein conservative theologians and writers of moralistic literature (such as General Superintendent L. K. Moeller or Bishop H. Martensen) preached the Lutheran principles of authority and discipline as a way of rejecting, absorbing, or overcoming modernism.[49] From a theoretical point of view the intellectual presuppositions that were laid down at the end of the eighteenth century and throughout most of the nineteenth century continued to serve as the basis for the conservative conception of "the Christian state" during the period of the German Empire, and these were principally the political-religious ideology of Adam Müller, Karl Ludwig von Haller, Karl Streckfuss, von Thadden, Ludwig von Gerlach, Julius Stahl, and also the official ideology of the Christian state in the days of Friedrich Wilhelm IV. In the spirit of the *Preussischer Volksverein* of the sixties, the extreme conservative periodical *Kreuzzeitung*

48. In the original: "Ein unglücklicher tiefer Riss geht durch unsere Zeit, dass das, was im Reiche Gottes als unzertrennliche Einheit verbunden ist (das religiöse und natürliche Leben) unnatürlich auseinander gerissen wird . . . Darum gibt es für die grossen Gegensätze und Kämpfe unserer Zeit keine höhere Lösung als die erneuerte Lehre vom Reiche Gottes." *Kreuzzeitung,* No. 115, May 18, 1878, "Die Christliche Weltanschauung," according to Dr. Mühlhäusser's lectures: "Über die biblische Lehre vom Reich Gottes" (Winter 1875–1876, Karlsruhe).

49. H. Martensen, Bishop of Seeland, *Die Christliche Ethik,* 3d rev. ed., second part: *Die Sociale Ethik,* Karlsruhe, Leipzig, 1886, p. 124 ff; L. K. Moeller, *Das Haus in unserer Zeit und in unserem Volke, seine Gefährdung, seine Bewahrung, und seine Erbauung: Ethische Zeitbetrachtungen,* Hamburg, 1892, pp. 6, 16 ff, 257 ff. See also, Moeller's words on the task of the Christian state with respect to heretics (socialists, atheists, and others), p. 47: "Also as a military power the state is in accordance with the will of God authorized to restrain the forces of evil. . . . Wherever the anarchistic spirit breaks out against the existing order . . . there authority does not wield the sword in vain: 'For he is the minister of God, a revenger to execute wrath upon him that doeth evil' (Romans 13:4) 'and for the praise of them that do well' (1 Peter 2:14)."

declared that instead of a parliamentary regime deriving its constitutional authority from the voters the country needed "personal kingdom by the grace of God and not by grace of the constitution." [50]

The principal innovation of the Conservatives was to adapt the idea of the Christian state to the political, social, and cultural reality of their time. In contradistinction to the first half of the nineteenth century it now became clear to most of the leaders of Conservative Protestantism that it was no longer possible to return to a preindustrial society, to the corporate system and methods of production and marketing prior to the industrial development—a return advocated by the extremists in the Conservative party as an expression of nostalgia of the social classes that now found themselves between the crumbling traditional world of the past and the modern world that had not yet been given visible shape. The new element of conservative ideology was to adopt a sober political approach to the realities of the modern world, and instead of withdrawing from the bureaucratic apparatus seek to dominate it by combining its inherent universalistic character with the interests of a particularistic group. Such an adaptation could only succeed at the end of the nineteenth century, with the growing bureaucratic complexity, the rise of modern political parties, and the conscious participation of the Conservatives in the inner politics of the Second Reich. Nevertheless, no essential change occurred in the basic ideological thesis, namely, that the state was a Christian state whose ethical and political legitimacy was derived not from the sovereignty of the people nor from any historical social contract between the state and its citizens, but from the principle of *civitas dei* as embodied in the person of the monarch.

Here we have one of the principal roots of the inveterate antagonism between the Conservatives (and, in varying degrees, the Protestants as a whole) and the Jews. In the internal polemical disputes between the Protestants and the Liberals following the publication of the *Katechismus des Protestantenvereins* in 1888 this antagonism was formulated by Dr. Mühlhäusser in the following words:

---

50. *Kreuzzeitung,* Aug. 21, 1878, No. 195, "Persönliches Königtum von Gottes und von Verfassungs Gnaden." Even at the end of the period we are discussing, in 1911, the periodical again proclaimed that F. J. Stahl's principle of the Christian state should continue to serve as the guide for the Conservatives. See *Kreuzzeitung,* Aug. 10, 1911, No. 271; see the ideological-political platform of the Conservatives in the Prussian Volksverein of the year 1869, W. Mommsen, *Deutsche Partei-Programme etc.,* München, 1952, p. 23.

No faith is to be put in the pronouncements of the Liberal and Reform Jews—who constitute the majority of Jews in Germany—that they accept the German state as their natural fatherland just as the Protestants. . . . We know as well as the Orthodox Jews that a people that does not acknowledge the grace of the Redeemer to have already been revealed, and that the task of the state is to bring about the social and political conditions that will enable every individual to absorb this Revelation, as it is said: "The time is fulfilled, and the kingdom of God is at hand: repent ye, and believe the gospel" (Mark 1:15); a people such as this is unable, nor should it be permitted, to regard itself as an organic part of our people, as though it were flesh of our flesh and blood of our blood.[51] Similar thoughts were expressed by Count Friedrich Albert Eulenburg, the head of the Conservative organization in East Prussia, on the eve of the Conservative Conference in Berlin in 1891: The Jews of Germany believe that the State was born only in the year 1869 with the granting of Emancipation . . . they forget that their right to dwell among us, although apparently conferred upon them by the emancipation, is not derived from an abstract, destructive French rationalism,[52] as they believe . . . this is the rationalism that has led to the disintegration of all the organic structures in that state and hastened the advent of Darwinism. . . . No! the source of their rights is nowhere but in the historical calumny of the Jews and in their power to impose their will on their rulers. This was already taught by Augustine who relates in the name of Seneca that "this perverse people took unto itself such great power that they were accepted in all countries, and as the defeated they dictate the laws to the victors" . . . beware of them.[53]

From the very beginning until the early nineties the basic ideology of the German Conservatives underwent a process of consolidation, including a reformulation of its basic tenets of historical organic structures and Christian exclusiveness in face of the rising masses and the "tyranny of

51. For this dispute between the Conservative and Liberal Protestants, see *Kreuzzeitung,* 2d ed., Jan. 22, 1888, No. 19A. The entire passage is from the bulletin, *Mitteilungen des Konservativen Vereins für Ostpreussen,* 1888, No. 2, p. 8.

52. The concept *"zersetzend"* (undermine) to describe the influence of the Jews in the history of nations from the ancient days down to the Second Reich was accepted under T. Mommsen's influence, see above, Chap. 1, p. 52. Another source for the concept "undermining force" is the speech of Stahl in Erfurt, May 15, 1850: "The chronic malady of Liberalism . . . I do not fear revolution but the undermining power of the 'Freisinn' (liberalism of the Left) led by Jews." The quotation is from the *Kreuzzeitung,* Aug. 10, 1911, to commemorate the fiftieth anniversary of Stahl's death.

53. *Mitteilungen des Konservativen Vereins für Ostpreussen,* 1891, No. 4, p. 16. The quotation from St. Augustine is from Civitas Dei VI, 11, and was familiar to the clergy and to the conservative political figures. To quote Seneca in connection with the Jewish question was customary for the spokesmen of racial anti-Semitism as well as for their opponents. See *Antisemiten-Katechismus,* Leipzig, 1893, p. 31; G. St[ille], "Die Juden im Römischen Reich," A. S., Berlin, 1899, p. 1.

egalitarianism'' which threatened to undermine the organic unity of Prussian Germanism and Germanism as a whole. The central symbol for these destructive, antiorganic manifestations was the Jews, as we learn from the words of Eulenburg: ''The concept of organism our political and social life reveals its real meaning when we contrast it with the Jews; in them are concentrated the forces that destroy organism, and hence in our war with them we find the tested means to consolidate our own organic essence.'' [54] The Jews, in their very existence, were considered the embodiment of what was ''strange'' and ''inorganic,'' having a separate religion, culture, and mentality and separate interests centered around trade, industry, capital, and liberalism. Their continued existence proved that it was possible to live in conflict with the ideology of organism. To oppose this aberrant, rebellious spirit—which also found its way into liberalism and socialism—return to the principle of ''authority and not majority'' was imperative.[55] The dissolution of traditional organic forms would in the end turn the Germans into a ''rabble of slaves who have just cast off their shackles.'' Unless these forms were preserved, Germany would be ruled by the vulgar masses and finally succumb to bureaucratic absolutism.

Against this danger of bureaucratic absolutism Lutheran Protestantism had in the past been able to protect itself by two methods which had stood the test of time but were now, the Conservatives feared, in danger of being abandoned: the preservation of the authority of the aristocratic class in every state and in every principality; and the preservation of the autonomy and independence of the state churches. The state was invested with authority over the church and was even its custodian, but did not encroach upon the jurisdiction of the church. The church was granted complete independence in its own sphere which was concerned with the individual, with the welfare of his spirit and the redemption of his soul, while the state concerned itself with the policies of the church and with the security of its members. The separation of church and state, the Conservative spokesmen declared, was foreign to the spirit of Protestantism, and the essential historical unity between these two authorities required a return to the principle of the ''division of tasks.'' Since the Peace of Augsburg in 1555 the feudal lord or king extended his protection to the church in his state, principality, or country estate; the church, which was

54. Above, n. 8, in the circular of the year 1891, pp. 6, 9.

55. ''Autorität nicht Majorität.'' This slogan was widely used in Conservative literature throughout the period we are discussing; see *Kreuzzeitung,* Aug. 10, 1911, No. 371.

restricted to these areas, became free to concern itself with the personal life of the individual, with instructing the ignorant, chastening the wayward, and comforting the penitent. Church and state together constituted the one *Corpus Christianum,* for whose continuity and stability they were both responsible.[56]

This Christian unity was now interpreted by Protestant ideology in two ways. First, the church and the state church being one body, the church was exempt from concern with the affairs of this world, its internal and external entanglements, and so forth, and was to function as a kind of clinic or convalescent home for the individual, the family, and society. This also represented the views of the Liberal Protestants, and because of this belief—not because of the principle of nonreligious natural law—they advocated the separation of church and state. Second, since the state and the state church constituted one body composed of two complementary members, there could be no separation between church and state and, whether the state was supreme or whether the church influenced the policies of the state, the state was and would remain Christian. Hence, Protestant ideology emphasized the words of Paul the Apostle in the Epistle to the Romans (13:1, 2, 6): "Let every soul be subject unto the higher power; for there is no power but of God; and the powers that be are ordained of God. Whosoever resisteth the power, resisteth the ordinance of God: and they that resist shall receive to themselves damnation . . . for this cause pay ye tribute also: for they are God's ministers, attending continually upon this very thing." In one of the Conservative pamphlets the following explanation was added: "The officials of the government are nothing but the ministers of God; can Jews who do not acknowledge Jesus, the Son of God, be appointed officials of our government? Are they not worse than atheistic socialists, for the latter ignore our faith whereas the Jews impugn it. Let us also bear in mind that according to the church law of 1873 the Prussian monarch is the bearer of the ecclesiastical rule of the state."[57]

56. For the place of the tradition of the *Corpus Christianum* in conservative ideology as well as in the history of religion and culture in Germany, see K. Matthes, *Das Corpus Christianum,* 1929, chap. iii, "Der am Corpus Christianum orientierte Typus der Forschung," p. 90 ff. Extensive bibliography, especially for the historical and theological study of the period under discussion here, is on p. 131 ff; see further p. 127 ff.

57. Words quoted in the propaganda pamphlet in the Conservative election campaign of 1893, *Zu den Wahlen,* Berlin, 1893, p. 2. Church law refers to the decree of Wilhelm I, as king of Prussia, issued Sept. 10, 1873: "Erlass betr. Kirchengemeinde und Synodalordnung für die älteren preussischen Provinzen." In the introduction to the decree the king of Prussia was called the "Träger des landesherrlichen Kirchenregiments," and in the decree itself,

A complementary expression of this principle of the unity of the *Corpus Christianum* and of Christian exclusiveness is also found in the conservative Christian conception of law as rooted in a basic primordial unity between *lex dei* and *lex naturae* in contradistinction to the conception of natural law as it was taught in the days of the Enlightenment. These two powers seemed separated only because of man's state of inherited sin. It was the mission of the church, through the redemptive power of Jesus, to remove this barrier, which was nothing but the product of man's erring cognition, and to restore the law to its pristine unity. This conception was essentially the continuation of the Protestant principles of Philip Melanchthon, Nicholas Taurelius, and, of course, the teachings of Luther, all of whom thought of state-ecclesiastical law as the road that would lead man back to his unified ethical self, to his prelapsarian condition prior to sin before the *lex naturae* was separated from the *lex dei*. By his own unassisted efforts and relying on his opaque reason alone, man was too feeble to unite that which had been torn asunder. He was nailed down by his finitude. Here lay the glory of Christianity and its superiority over Judaism: that by virtue of the divine revelation in Jesus, the Son of God, a suprahuman source had been made available to man to help him overcome his inner division. But the incorrigible Jews, driven by their rebellious temper, refused to partake of this divine medicine, and by their astonishing infidelity prevented man from keeping his covenant with God. When the Jews accepted the inestimable benefits of Christianity, man would complete his probation and enter into fellowship with essence—reason would be reconciled with religion, science with faith, divine law with natural law—and the words of the Apostle be fulfilled: "That ye be renewed in the spirit of your mind." [58]

In this spirit conservative ideology interpreted Luther's conception of the two kingdoms (*zwei Reiche*), according to which all men are divided into two classes: (1) true Christians who believe in Jesus and in the Holy

---

par. 24, his religious-political dual authority was emphasized by having him, and not a member of the clergy, convene the Generalsynode of all the churches. See, newly published: Karl Kupisch, *Quellen zur Geschichte des deutschen Protestantismus, 1871–1945,* München, Hamburg, 1965, p. 49 ff.

58. Epistle to the Ephesians 4:23. This entire manner of thinking is reflected in the literature of conservative ideology from the seventies to the nineties; see my article "Conservative Protestants," (Hebrew) *Zion,* Vol. 27, Nos. 1–2, 1962, p. 99 ff. The relationship between this literature and the basic theological principles of Lutheran conservatism was treated in 1872 by L. Wiese, a Prussian educator, *Gegen den Katechismus des Protestantenvereins,* 1888, p. 16 ff (place of publication unknown).

Spirit, subject only to a spiritual religious authority (*geistliches Regiment*), endowed with grace not by virtue of works or their piety but by the power of God's free will, citizens of the kingdom of heaven and as such also members of the ruling class of the kingdom on earth; (2) those who are not citizens of this celestial kingdom, that is, heretics, un-Christian, or evil men, for whom God has ordained a worldly political authority (*weltliches Regiment*), and who are subject to the law and the sword.[59] This Lutheran principle was set forth by the Conservatives more plainly with the establishment of the German Empire: "It is written: 'For rulers are not a terror to good works, but to the evil' (Epistle to the Romans 13:3) . . . and this is the basis of our political rule . . . our duty as citizens in the kingdom of God is to observe the commandment of Peter addressed to the believers to take upon themselves the yoke of this kingdom, and these in our day are the Jews and other heretics, such as atheists or socialists." [60] In reality, the citizens of both kingdoms were subject to worldly rule, which meant the national state in whose hands the welfare of the citizens in both kingdoms had been entrusted, just as a father is entrusted with authority over the members of his household.

This arrangement into two kingdoms was not believed to be the product of human initiative or social contract but ordained by those called by the grace of God to perform the duties of their office and bear its responsibilities. A non-Christian society or state appoints its rulers not by the grace of God but by social contract, majority vote, or a rational decision. But these human sources of political authority are invalid, being an expression of human pretension that seeks to usurp God's wisdom, "an un-Christian deification of human arbitrariness, rationalistic legislation . . . an absolutizing of the relative, an eternalizing of the temporal . . . a Jewish exaltation of the human." [61] The conduct of the state was not to be entrusted to the arbitrary judgment of voters or political parties. Only

59. From Luther's letters in *Von Weltlicher Obrigkeit wie weit man ihr Gehorsam schuldig sei,* 1523. See new edition, Martin Luther, *Ausgewählte Werke,* ed. H. H. Borcherdt and Georg Merz, 3d ed., München, 1948, pp. 5, 13, 14. This source for the Lutheran theory of the state was an accepted part of conservative ideology, especially in the circles of the *Kreuzzeitung* and also among the pietists. The quotation here is from a series of lectures to secondary school teachers by L. Wiese in the early seventies in Berlin but was frequently quoted even a decade thereafter: L. Wiese, *Der Staat und das Persönliche: Pädagogische Fragen in unserem höheren Schulwesen,* F.A., No. 2.

60. F.A., No. 2, p. 17.

61. In the source: "unchristliche Vergötzung menschlicher Willkür, rationaler Gesetzlichkeit . . . eine Absolutierung des Relativen, eine Verewigung des Zeitlichen . . . eine jüdische Überhebung des Menschlichen" (ibid.).

those possessing grace, even if only by virtue of inherited social position as, for example, the members of the aristocracy and their offspring, were "God's ministers, and all who rise up against them resist the ordinance of God . . . and only they are fit to exercise power as office holders in the service of Christ, his congregation and his state . . . servants of the members of his holy body in grace, authority, and dignity." [62]

At the same time, however, with the establishment of the Second Reich, this development was beginning to be looked upon with misgivings by the Conservatives, especially by the Alt-Lutheraner, the *Kreutzzeitung,* the leaders of the right-wing Evangelisch-lutherische Conferenz, the clergy, the landowners, aristocratic circles, and the cadre of officers. Even before the establishment of the Reich and during the *Kulturkampf* these circles pointed out the dangers that the modern world presented to the traditional values of society, to the interests of the historical social classes, and to the organic German character; in the words of Count Krassow, Kleist-Retzow, and Freiherr von Hammerstein: "The Leviathan, the modern state, with its impersonal administrative apparatus, its secular political parties, must be restrained, for they all undermine the individualistic tradition of the historical cells of our nation; we must therefore begin by limiting the power of the Jews, since they are the ones who demolished our tradition." [63]

Another Lutheran theme which was reinterpreted by conservative ideol-

62. In the original: "Amtsträger im Dienste Christi, seiner Gemeinde und Staat . . . Diener an den Gliedern seines heiligen Körpers mit Gnade, Vollmacht und Würde" (ibid., p. 15). The beginning of the quotation is from Paul's Epistle to the Romans 13:2, 6. The Conservative leaders went on to praise the "95 Theses" written by the Universitätsprediger Claus Harms of Kiel at the celebration of the Protestant "Union" formed that year between the Reform and the Lutheran Church. Harms belonged to the extreme *altlutherisch* Orthodox circles that opposed the Union and were also against political and secular interference of the state in the affairs of the church. Quotations from Harms in the political writings of the Conservatives in the early years of consolidation after the establishment of the Empire indicate the strong influence of the extreme Orthodox circles in this movement at that time and its ambivalent attitude toward the state.

63. From the proclamation issued during the election campaign of 1878, signed by Baron Freiherr von Mirbach: "Zur Lage der conservativen Partei," p. 1. For clarification of the political background of this proclamation, see Mirbach's public denial of having said in his election campaign speech that "Juden, Kaufleute und Halsabschneider sind der Ruin der Landwirtschaft," *Kreuzzeitung,* Supplement to No. 171, Aug. 3, 1878. For the theoretical interpretation of the Christian character of the state by these circles, and the actual conflict between the state and Conservative interests, see the series of articles by Mirbach entitled, "Preussische Gedanken," *Kreuzzeitung,* Supplement to No. 179, No. 187, and others, 1878.

ogy was the principle "authority of the father." Basing themselves on Luther's *Larger Catechism* of 1529 concerning "Obedience to Superiors" (*Gehorsam gegen Oberpersonen*), the Conservatives preached the need to return to the principle of authority of the father in its composite sense as "a condition having the many-sided authority of the father" (*mehrfache Vaterstand*). This authority included the duty of the individual to internalize the teachings that came down to him from the church, the state, the father, or the home, in the words of Luther: "From the three divine hierarchies or primordial powers, namely, the Christian churches, worldly rule, or the police, and the chaste, bourgeois household." [64]

Despite these authoritarian tendencies, the distrust and fear of imperial sovereignty in the Second Reich kept increasing. In the face of non-Christian political power and the corroding forces of modernism—chiefly Jews and liberals, industrialization and socialism, secularism and materialism—we no longer find the authentic bearer of Lutheran *Obrigkeit* in the political sphere or a trustworthy source to justify the introduction of discipline and authority in the life of the individual. The last refuge of the Conservatives in this rear-guard action in defense of traditional values centered around the home and the family. The home was to become again a kind of family society (*Hausgenossenschaft*), to which the individual could repair when threatened by feelings of alienation, loneliness, and homelessness, when "subjected to political and economic forces with which he has no connection and which—being Jewish forces, openly or disguised—present a grave danger for every Christian." [65] An extensive literature of articles, sermons, and exhortatory essays appeared in Conservative periodicals and booklets extolling the Christian virtues of piety, temperance, industry, discipline, contentment, sobriety, self-sacrifice, the

---

64. In Luther's language: "den dreien göttlichen Hierarchiis oder Ertzgewalten, nämlich von den Christlichen Kirchen, vom weltlichen Regiment oder Polizey, und von bürgerlichen und züchtig Haushaltung." The quotation is taken from "Zirkulardisputation über das Recht des Widerstandes gegen den Kaiser," May 9, 1539. It is difficult to know which editions were in the hands of the authors; see the critical Weimar edition of 1883 ff, Vol. II. The authority of the father as the expression of an external authority that has been internalized is a reference to the *Great Catechism* of 1529 and also to Luther's words of 1539 in *Von den Konzilis und Kirchen*.

65. Above, n. 2, in the proclamation issued by the Verein zur Abwehr des Antisemitismus. On p. 6 the editor states that these words were spoken by Bishop H. Martensen in a talk to theologians in 1878.

love of the *Heimat,* and the love of God in whom we find our felicity and eternal bliss.

In a widely read book L. K. Moeller, the principal court preacher of Magdeburg, summed up the conservative view of the home as follows: "The home . . . is a self-contained unit of different levels of equality, of an order that proceeds from above and an acceptance of the yoke from below, of strict order and unrestricted love, of authority and the fear of God . . . a place of love in all its forms which aids, consoles, and chastises . . . the earliest stage of vital development, and the school that is the best preparation for the state, the church, society, and, finally, for the kingdom of heaven . . . the home contains, as in a bud, all other forms of sociability." [66] The state should ensure the existence and preservation of the home, for the state was not only a *Rechtsstaat* based on law but also a *Kulturstaat* designed to promote education and morals among all the people. But since the state was not perfect, the home became the last stronghold where the child could be imbued with the Protestant personality, trained to withstand the allurements of pleasure and sordid gain, and, as a responsible citizen, to obey appointed officials in positions of administrative authority.

Opposition to Judaism and to Jews had a well-defined place in this conservative ideology. Judaism, and especially modern Liberal Judaism, was taken to be an important factor in this destructive process of undermining the traditional values of society; it reflected and embodied this process and, to a certain extent, was also its victim. This was noted by Professor Heinrich Thiersch at the beginning of the seventies:

Modern ways of life, insofar as they have been adopted by Jews, make for a relatively rapid disintegration of Israel's ancient culture. . . . Modern heretical Judaism is a stumbling block for the people of Israel and, at the same time, it is also a thorn in the flesh of the Christian nations. . . . Together with the loss of faith, they also lost their homeland, and nothing is holy in their eyes. . . . Even when all we possess goes to rack and ruin, they will continue to dream of future Jewish domination, this being the last paltry remnant of their ancient faith. . . . It is difficult to determine who has caused more injury to whom, whether the Christians of little faith to the Jews or the faithless Jews to us, the Christians.[67]

66. L. K. Moeller, *Das Haus in unserer Zeit und in unserem Volke seine Gefährdung, seine Bedeutung und seine Erbauung: ethische Zeitbetrachtungen,* Hamburg, 1892, p. 6.

67. Heinrich W. J. Thiersch, *Über den christlichen Staat,* Basel, 1875, pp. 76–77.

This formulation by Thiersch points to a basic conservative conception that was adhered to throughout the period of the Second Reich. In the conservative criticism of Judaism and the Jews we find that Orthodox Judaism did not occupy a central place, the bulk of the criticism being directed against modern Judaism which was regarded as the embodiment of modernism itself, the focal point of the antireligious rationalistic views threatening the traditional order. In an important series of articles in criticism of liberalism the *Kreuzzeitung* in 1878 presented this conservative view in a clear and explicit form:

The real leadership of Liberalism, especially in its opposition to ecclesiastical religious life, has been taken over by modern Judaism, which dominates the press and plays its part in the parliaments of the Reich and the states. . . . All honor to the loyal religion of ancient Judaism that rests on Old Testament revelation; but modern Judaism that denies its ancient faith and its ordinances, vaunts its enlightened liberalism and marches everywhere in the vanguard of progress, is a real misfortune for our people. Judaization is making giant strides, and this is furthered by liberalism. Originally, the children of Israel were destined to be a blessing for all the nations, but they have forfeited their mission and, because of their modern heresy and lack of faith, have become a curse to the nations.[68]

Similar views, although differently expressed, were voiced by the leaders of various conservative groups, including educators, members of the liberal professions, aristocrats, government officials, army officers, members of the Christlich-Sozial movement, and even ordinary folk in provincial towns.[69] Bishop H. Martensen in his book on Christian social ethics defined modern Judaism as one of "the principal powers in the disintegrating process of the Christian state and in the life of Christians"; the source of the destructive power of Judaism was not in its early religious essence but in its rationalistic development, whereby Judaism became a "religion of humanism . . . in the realization of which it hopes to establish a messianic kingdom on earth."[70]

---

68. *Kreuzzeitung,* No. 189, Aug. 15, 1878.
69. A.E.L.K.Z., Leipzig, 1871, p. 252; 1880, pp. 83 ff, 1156 ff, 1216 ff, 1237; 1893, pp. 235, 862 ff; N.E.K.Z., Berlin, 1871, pp. 152 ff, 736, 765, 778; 1880, pp. 420, 436, 453, 753; *"Der alte Glaube: Evangelisch-Lutherisches Gemeindeblatt,"* feature editor, Freiherr Ernst Röder von Wiersburg, Leipzig, 1901, pp. 1073, 1096.
70. H. Martensen, *Die christliche Ethik,* 3d rev. ed., second part: *Die sociale Ethik,* Karlsruhe, Leipzig, 1886, p. 128.

Conclusion

Toward the end of the nineteenth century the conservative views discussed in this chapter were consolidated and found expression in the following attitudes toward Jews.

The state was Christian and also constitutional, and all citizens enjoyed equal legal rights; hence, Jews wishing to be citizens of this state and still clinging to their Judaism had to be prepared to relinquish the distinctive social status separating them from the German Christian citizen. They could not expect to be treated by society like citizens who could embody and promote the Christian character of the state. They therefore had to find employment in social and economic spheres not relevant to Christian character. At the same time many Conservatives did not believe that conversion could annul the special status of German Jews, especially since it was mostly undergone in bad faith, not with the intention of accepting Christianity as a religion or as a historical culture but as a means for social and professional advancement. For this reason, and perhaps also because of the prevailing racial theories from the beginning of the eighties, conservative ideology interpreted the peculiar character of the Jews as being of a hereditary, historical, or mythical nature, rooted in fossilized religious forms on the one hand and in a crafty, parasitical character seeking to dominate the environment on the other, hence ineradicable and impervious to conversion.

Accordingly, Conservatives after the end of the nineteenth century adopted a positive attitude toward political Zionism, a characteristic expression of which may be found in the *Kreuzzeitung* at the time when the First Zionist Congress met in 1897.[71] In its criticism of German Jewry's negative attitude toward political Zionism, as expressed in the declaration of the Rabbiner-Verband that "the aspirations of the Zionists are opposed to the messianic hopes of Judaism," [72] the *Kreuzzeitung* described the views of this declaration as "hypocritical" and added:

71. *Kreuzzeitung,* Aug. 13, 1897, Supplement to No. 375, "Der Widerspruch gegen den Zionisten-Kongress."

72. The proclamation of the Rabbiner-Verband in Deutschland was issued in Berlin on July 6, 1897, and was submitted by Rabbi Dr. Sigmund Maybaum for publication in the newspapers. The proclamation was signed by the Executive Committee of the Verband, Dr. Sigmund Maybaum, Dr. Marcus Horovitz of Frankfurt, Dr. Jakob Guttmann of Breslau, Dr. Leopold Auerbach of Halberstadt, and Dr. Mose C. Werner of Munich. The third paragraph of the proclamation stated that the opposition of the Rabbis to Zionism was only

One would think that to the modern Jew who complains of anti-Semitic oppression and fabrications nothing would be more welcome than the idea of obtaining political support for his separate religious existence and ethnological peculiarity that would assure him the blessings of international law which, in these days of persecution that is not merely imaginary, can be of far-reaching consequence. At present the Jew is dependent on the moral tolerance of the nations in whose midst he has settled; the Jewish press complains that the rights granted to Jews (Israelites) and guaranteed by the state are recognized only grudgingly, and that the Jews continue to be exposed to many further insults.[73]

The periodical then asked: "Why are they spurned?" and its answer was that in an era of nationalism in which the national state had become one of the highest values in human society and an important factor in the family of nations the citizens of a national state could not wholeheartedly trust those who deny their nationality.

The avowals of the German rabbis that "Judaism enjoins its adherents to serve the fatherland to which they belong with utmost devotion and to promote its national interests with all their heart and all their might" [74] would not likely inspire trust in a German who saw his state as national *and* Christian. Moreover, the declaration of the Chief Rabbi of England expressing the fear that Jewish support of political Zionism "might create

directed against its political-national aspect and not against "those lofty aspirations of Jewish workers of the soil to establish a settlement in Palestine." The appended document contained the reactions of Jewish and Christian circles, and may be found in the archival file G.A.J. G.A. M 4/1, "Akten des reorganisierten Rabbinerverbandes in Deutschland, 28.XII.1896–1899." See ibid., the correspondence of the heads of the Rabbiner-Verband before and after the First Zionist Congress in which they expressed the fear that political Zionism might jeopardize the existence of German Jewry. In a letter of May 11, 1897, to his colleagues in the Rabbiner-Verband, Rabbi Werner asked that a public proclamation be issued before the Congress convened to the effect that: "Our religion has nothing to do with nationality." In a letter of January 21, 1897, Rabbi Maybaum of Berlin stated that there was little prospect for success in the efforts of the Rabbiner-Verband to check the destructive influence of political Zionism; as for the possibility of having talks with Theodor Herzl the letter stated: "I see no reason . . . for negotiations with T. Herzl, the man who suffers from delusions of grandeur and imagines he is a second Bar Kochba," ibid., G.A.J. G.A. M 4/1.

73. Above, n. 71.

74. "das Judenthum verpflichtet seine Bekenner dem Vaterlande, dem sie angehören, mit aller Hingebung zu dienen und dessen nationalen Interessen mit (soll heissen von) ganzem Herzen und mit allen Kräften zu fördern" (from the above Rabbinical Proclamation, par. 2). The linguistic correction in parenthesis appears in the text of the *Kreuzzeitung* to ridicule the Jewish style of writing German. Parallel linguistic notes, from the national Zionist point of view, are in Herzl, "Protest-Rabbiner" in *Before the People and the World* (Hebrew), Vol. I, Jerusalem, Tel Aviv, 1961, p. 101 ff.

the impression that we Jews are not loyal to the state in which we live'' [75] had the opposite effect than the one intended. Those who were loyal to their national origin were trusted and esteemed; and in Judaism religious affiliation and national identity were inseparable, for the Jewish religion had a national (*volkstümlich*) character. Contrary to the views of the anti-Zionist Jews, national states believed that:

Whoever is imbued with the hope for the future of his fatherland or his religion and refuses to do what is required of him to realize this hope is a fool or a traitor who has forgotten his duty. If the Jew wishes to think as a German national, then he must also be open to this form of thinking. If we and other nations permit the Jewish people to live within our borders as guests, does this mean that we wish to erase from the hearts of these guests the memory of their nationality [*Volksthum*]? On the contrary, it is precisely here that anti-Semitism finds the nourishment on which it thrives . . . the Jews alone in the Christian states claim that they wish to preserve their religious but not their national separateness . . . and from this fraud against the people that grant them the rights of the fatherland they derive their means of subsistence . . . pretending to belong to a foreign nationality but without in fact relinquishing their peculiar stubborn character.[76]

A similar opinion was expressed by the extreme anti-Semitic periodical in Dresden, *Deutsche Wacht,* in the issue of July 9, 1897, in answer to the declaration of the rabbis:

What the rabbinic gentlemen have in mind is clear: to erase from people's minds the fact that the Jewish people exist at all, so that in the future as in the past the Jewish rabble will be able to continue to spread secretly and under cover of ''religion'' their dubious ethical and economic influence. . . . To dwell on the soil and on its own piece of land as an independent nation under sovereign rule is what the Jewish people fear . . . and this means sacrificing themselves on the altar of destruction through a self-imposed limitation. Nevertheless, for the good of the world this must be drawn out into the open. The question is whether this will be done by the Jews of their own free will or whether they will be forced to do so.

75. Above, n. 71. These words of the rabbis of England, the United States, and others, are in the files of the Rabbiner-Verband, G.A.J. G.A. M 4/1; see also ibid., answers of the Zionist organizations in Germany: *Flugblatt* No. 2, pub. by Berliner Ortsgruppen der Zionistischen Vereinigung für Deutschland. For Herzl's answer to these rabbis, see *Before the People and the World,* Vol. I (Hebrew), Jerusalem, Tel Aviv, 1961, pp. 75 ff, 98 ff. Herzl's answer to the Rabbi of Vienna, Dr. M. Güdemann, is in ibid., p. 43 ff. On this entire affair, see A. Bein, *Theodor Herzl: Biography* (Hebrew), Jerusalem, 1961, p. 175 ff.

76. Above, n. 71.

The Mission unter Israel, pietistic and evangelical circles, and also relatively moderate groups among the Conservatives, such as the Freikonservative led by Freiherr von Zedlitz, had ambivalent feelings with respect to this positive attitude toward political Zionism and also with respect to the power of conversion to eradicate the uniqueness of the Jews and to integrate them completely into the dominant society of German Christians.

The admission that the German Jews, despite their equal civic status as citizens, could not be completely assimilated into German society cast some doubts not only on the effectiveness of German legislation but also on the Christian character of the state. For not only had Christian charity and love (tempered with rigor) proved ineffective, but even conversion had failed to redeem the Jew, and this cast a heavy shadow on classical Christian faith in the efficacy of baptism and the theological structure of the *Heilsgeschichte*.

This dilemma was recognized as early as 1881 in Professor C. E. Luthardt's important periodical *Allgemeine Evangelische-Lutherische Kirchenzeitung* (in the course of a critical review of E. Dühring's book *Die Judenfrage als Racen- Sitten- und Culturfrage,* Karlsruhe, Leipzig, 1881), in which it was pointed out that German Christians were unable to accept Dühring's racial views negating Christianity and religion in general, but also "for many people baptism is a purely external ceremony that serves their material interests. . . . We on our part do not share Dühring's attitude toward religion, nor do we underestimate the efficacy ascribed to baptism; but to our regret we cannot deny that the number of those for whom baptism has had a redeeming effect is relatively small compared to those for whom it has the opposite effect." [77]

In these respects Conservative Protestantism was in agreement with racial anti-Semitism. This agreement itself, however, was ambivalent, for racial anti-Semitism included not only anti-Jewish tendencies and activities, but also anti-Christian elements—a dilemma to which the last chapter in this book will be devoted.

---

77. A.E.L.K.Z., Leipzig, 1881, p. 1217; to complete the picture, see in this periodical, 1871, p. 252 ff; 1880, pp. 83 ff, 1156 ff, 1167, 1216, 1236 ff; 1893, pp. 209, 235, 802.

# 4 | Protestantism and Judaism in Liberal Perspective

Liberals among the Protestants and Jews

Liberal Protestantism during the Second Reich was nourished by two currents of thought, one religious and one scientific, which had their roots in the late eighteenth and in the first half of the nineteenth century. The religious impulse went back to Johann G. Herder and Friedrich Schleiermacher with their repudiation of rational argument and institutional forms and insistence on the theology of devout feeling which sought to renew Christian Protestant faith as a bulwark against the pure rationalism of the Enlightenment. The scientific movement, led by Ferdinand Christian Baur and, after his death in 1860, by the Tübingen school he had founded, abandoned the doctrinal attitude to Holy Writ in exchange for the rigorous application of Hegelian ideas to the development of Christianity, especially primitive Christianity, and to the problems of biblical criticism.

The consolidation of these two currents of religion and science became immensely important in the intellectual and cultural life of Germany in the latter half of the nineteenth century and was accomplished by a number of theologians, historians, philologists, jurists, educators, literary men, and journalists as well as public figures in the political life of the country. Foremost among these were the followers of Schleiermacher and Baur, such as Richard Rothe, Daniel Schenkel, the first president of the Protestantenverein, and Albrecht Ritschl, who exerted a strong influence on his generation and gave rise to the Ritschlian school of theology toward the end of the century. The latter included Julius Kaftan, Johannes Gottschick, Ferdinand Kattenbusch, Wilhelm Herrmann (the teacher of Karl Barth), Adolf von Harnack, in whom Liberal Protestant theology found its strongest proponent, Martin Rade and Wilhelm Bornemann, the editors of the influential organ of this group *Christliche Welt,* Paul Drews, one of the founders of the movement called "Practical Theology," and A. Hausrath, who transmitted to his generation in a more popular form the spiritual legacy of Richard Rothe (and who also wrote historical romances under the pseudonym of George Taylor). Besides these, there was a group of scholars, led by Ernst Troeltsch and Max Rischle, who directed their criticism against the "meaningless general concepts" of the neo-Kantian school and who attempted to develop a scientific approach deriving normative values from the *Geisteswissenschaften* or social sciences that were more congruous to an age grown weary of Hegelianism.

Despite inner contradictions and quarrels all these circles were animated by a desire to find a common ground between faith and knowledge, between science and religion, that could withstand rational, empirical scrutiny from the *Geisteswissenschaften* on the one hand and the modern anthropological interpretation of Lutheranism on the other, and thus serve as a possible rational basis for the religious life of the Christian community. These efforts on the part of the Liberal Protestants constituted an important cultural factor in the growing industrial society of Germany and in its renewed nationalism which transformed ideological elements borrowed from history into authoritarian patterns in order to enhance the prestige of the power state.[1] The social and intellectual influ-

---

1. An authentic picture of the various currents in Liberal Protestantism can be gained from the central organ of these circles, *Die Christliche Welt: Evangelisch lutherisches Gemeindeblatt für die Gebildeten,* which first appeared in Leipzig in 1887. Supplementary to this source is the popular semiscientific series of publications at the beginning of the twentieth century called *Hefte zur Christlichen Welt.* The contributors to this series were the most eminent scholars of the Protestant community, such as Adolf von Harnack, W. Herrmann, Julius Kaftan, K. Köhler, Friedrich Loofs, and others. A typical example of this source is the work of Hans Weichelt in No. 49 of the series, *Der moderne Mensch und das Christenthum,* Tübingen, Leipzig, 1901, p. 36: "Christianity is endowed with a remarkable ability for assimilation. In the consciousness of every individual it assumes a different form." Christianity could adapt itself, Weichelt continued, to various cultures, regimes, and ways of thought, however different, and herein lay the secret of its historic strength. It had been able to ally itself with different nations and traditions without forfeiting its own special character or its peculiar mission. "And this is also true with respect to the relations between Christianity and the life of modern man and his problems," Weichelt concluded. An almost identical attitude was taken toward liberal Judaism, as this movement developed in the course of the last century and the beginning of this, by Kaufmann Kohler in his clarification of the concept "assimilation"; see *Grundriss einer systematischen Theologie des Judentums auf geschichtlicher Grundlage,* Leipzig, 1910, chap. ii, par. 5. Another primary source is Karl Kupisch, *Quellen zur Geschichte des deutschen Protestantismus, 1871–1945,*

ence of Liberal Protestantism was first felt in the institutions of higher learning. By the end of the nineteenth century, however, its ideas were widely discussed in learned circles and in most of the important periodicals that dealt with religion, science, culture, and politics, thus exerting a strong influence on the recrudescent nationalism of the Second Reich. Nevertheless, Liberal Protestantism was not specifically organized to seek political power, and for the most part it kept aloof from political activity. Its aim was rather to prepare the ground for a more rational conception of religion and to gain support for the vital principles of Christianity by reasserting its ethical and practical aspects. Many of its adherents, like J. C. Bluntschli and Rudolf von Bennigsen, were active in the Deutscher Protestantenverein (D.P.V.) since its founding in 1863, as well as in the Innere Mission, the Evangelisch-Sozialer Kongress (E.S.K.), and the Christlich-Sozial movements. For the most part they supported the liberal parties, the National Liberals (N.L.), the Progressive Liberals, and later, to a certain degree, the party of Friedrich Naumann. On the whole, however, the members of these liberal circles, just as the other intellectuals of that period, kept aloof from engaging in active politics.[2]

The relations between the Liberal Protestants and the Jews in the Second Reich are revealed in a number of characteristic historical documents. At the beginning of the period we are discussing, in 1862, Richard Rothe declared that the task of Protestantism was to cleanse Christianity of its dogmas, sacraments, belief in miracles, and other primitive notions, and to come to terms with modern science and culture. In the eyes of the enlightened men of his generation the dogmas of the Athanasian Creed (also called *Quicunque-vult* from its opening words) and other traditions relating to the Trinity, as well as the teachings of the ecumenical Council of Chalcedon (451 A.D.) concerning the divine nature of Christ and his sacramental body, could no longer stand the test of ra-

---

München, Hamburg, 1960, 1965, p. 9 ff (hereafter, Kupisch). Relevant sources there are especially Nos. 4, 8, 17, 24, 26, 29. General studies important for our discussion are W. Nigg, *Die Geschichte des religiösen Liberalismus*, Zürich, Leipzig, 1937, p. 207 ff (hereafter, W. Nigg); K. Leese, *Der Protestantismus im Wandel der neueren Zeit*, Stuttgart, 1941, p. 12 ff (hereafter, K. Leese). See also the general study, Horst Stephan, *Geschichte der deutschen Evangelischen Theologie seit dem deutschen Idealismus*, 2d newly rev. ed. by Martin Schmidt, D.D., Berlin, 1960, Parts III, IV (hereafter, Stephan-Schmidt); and for currents of thought in biblical criticism relevant to our discussion, see Hans-Joachim Kraus, *Geschichte der historisch-kritischen Erforschung des Alten Testaments*, Neukirchen Kreis Moers, 1956.

2. See Chap. 1, n. 1.

tional criticism. Rothe saw in this a hopeful sign that the ideals of Christianity would ultimately be realized, and that the rational truths it contained *in potentia* would emerge as a trustworthy guide for enlightened men.[3] Almost four decades later, at the turn of the century, Martin Rade defined Liberal Protestantism as a system of beliefs and opinions that had developed from a religion into a scientific attitude and then into a secular theology and was therefore eminently suited to serve as the main support of the new German nationalism. This notion, Rade added, was welcomed by enlightened Germans for it utilized the historical Christian sources of German nationalism in the struggle against the disintegrating forces of the revolutionary Left, the conservative Right, and the "ultramontanists." [4]

This new formulation that was presented by an eminent spokesman of Liberal Protestantism reaffirmed the exclusively Christian character of German society, nationality, and culture which as such could tolerate the Jew only if he became completely assimilated. This represented the general attitude of Liberal Protestantism at that time, and we find it expressed in a series of articles that appeared in the influential periodical of this movement, the *Christliche Welt* (which Rade edited from 1886 to 1931) as part of the general subject of "the spiritual struggle with enlightened Judaism." In this series of articles the writers called upon the Jews to relinquish their singularity and become an integral part of Christian culture, addressing this appeal not to the Orthodox Jews or to the Zionists, but to those modern Jews who shared the Liberal Protestant way of life and who accepted the same advanced views regarding the historical and philological criticism of the Old and New Testaments, the anthropological approach to religion, and the civic emancipation of man in modern society, including the Jew as a full-fledged member of that society.

The desire of German Jewry to retain its identity was therefore a severe blow to the Liberal Protestant principle of unity, for it was precisely the educated and emancipated Jews who, despite their strong intellectual affinity with liberal Christians, spurned the consolations of the dominant faith and insisted on remaining Jews. That this unity to which the Liberal

3. R. Rothe, *Gesammelte Vorträge und Abhandlungen aus seinen letzten Lebensjahren*, ed. Freidrich Nippold, 1886, p. 15; see W. Nigg, pp. 208–209.
4. *Symposium der Freunde der Christlichen Welt*, Berlin, 1904, pp. 14–18. For a more comprehensive definition of these characteristic terms, see Fritz Stern, *The Political Consequences of the Unpolitical German*, in *History*, No. 3, a Meridian periodical, New York, 1960, p. 104 ff; Hajo Holborn, "Der deutsche Idealismus in sozial-geschichtlicher Bedeutung," H.Z., Vol. 174, 1952, p. 366 ff.

Protestants aspired failed to include the Jews as a separate body was prejudicial to the truthful exposition of their deepest convictions and productive of their deepest disappointment. Jewish recalcitrance had deprived them of a quick harvest of success and revealed the impotency and inadequacy of Christian liberalism. The main hope and purpose of Liberal Protestantism, namely, the national and cultural unity of the Second Reich based on historical and Christian principles, had broken against the stiff neck of Judaism. This disappointment was voiced in an article in the *Christliche Welt* which recalled the early expectations of Liberal Protestantism that the emancipation of the Jews and their admission into the spiritual life of Germany

would bring about a peaceful and gradual fusion . . . but such a fusion with the Christian nations had not taken place nor had Jewish thought adapted itself to the national Christian way of thinking . . . Judaism, to be sure, had appropriated the treasures of Christian culture and its external material benefits, but it did not succeed in finding a way of penetrating the religious-ethical thinking out of which this culture grew. . . . No one can be completely at home in the life of a nation or genuinely feel that he is participating in its activities, aspirations, and hopes as long as he remains untouched by the spirit of Christianity . . . the Jews have not reached the point of acknowledging Christianity as a vital source of culture; they have appropriated Christian culture, but have refused to acknowledge that this culture is the product of the religious-ethical spirit of Christianity.[5]

"Liberal Judaism" is here defined not only as the Reform movement and those circles around the rabbis that called themselves liberal, but includes those groups, whether actively organized or only passive, that did not belong to the Orthodox community nor identify themselves with it but which nevertheless defined their Judaism as a religion and wished to maintain some kind of a tie with the Jewish community or with the Jewish religion. To these groups belonged most of the men of the Wissenschaft des Judenthums, writers, journalists, and members of the liberal

5. "Der Weg zur Verständigung zwischen Judenthum und Christenthum," Ch. W., 1893, No. 17, col. 397 ff. The words of M. Teichmann are taken from a critical article on the work of Dr. Johannes Müller, one of the leading figures in the Mission unter Israel and one of the founders of the anti-intellectualist school in personalist Protestantism. Müller's work, which bears the same title, appeared in Leipzig in 1892. Teichmann himself was a member of the right or "biblicist" wing of Protestantism, as is evident from his criticism of Reform Judasim and political Zionism. See Ch. W., 1900, No. 40, Col. 945 ff. The attitude of the writer of the article was also typical of the more moderate liberal Protestants; see Ch. W., 1900, No. 13; 1906, No. 40; 1907, No. 27; 1909, No. 33.

professions, whether they regarded Judaism as a religion or as an ethnic group to which they happened to belong not as a result of any deep conviction or emotional attachment but simply by accident of birth or by the arbitrary definition of the outside world. The Liberal Jewish community also comprised the members of the communal and intercommunal organizations, such as the Deutsch-Israelitischer Gemeindebund (D.I.G.B.), the Central Verein, consisting of German citizens of the Jewish faith, the Verein der Deutschen Juden (V.D.J.), the Hilfsverein (H.V.) or the German Aid Society, and the Rabbiner-Verband in Deutschland (R.V.D.). Liberal Judaism, then, included the majority of non-Orthodox and unaffiliated Jews (except for an increasingly large number that belonged to leftist movements), some of whom did not explicitly avow their Jewish identity, some who openly defined themselves as liberals, some who moved between the Liberals and the Conservatives, and some who adhered to a traditional way of life in the spirit of conservative Judaism but who did not identify themselves with Orthodox Judaism. This wide classification of the Liberal Jewish community was also based on the definition set forth in the declaration of the Council of the D.I.G.B. in 1884 which was distributed among its member congregations shortly after the public dispute had broken out between the Orthodox rabbis who remained faithful to the Law (*Rabbiner der gesetzestreuen Richtung*) and the non-Orthodox rabbis, the members of the Rabbiner-Verband. The declaration stated that since the Orthodox constituted a negligible minority that had separated itself from the larger community the Jewish community as a whole might be characterized as liberal: ''We use the designation liberal here as an adjective and not as a noun or as the name of some organization or movement . . . the designation liberal describes the nature of one's relationship to Judaism . . . a relationship that is open and free and yet seeks to be attached to the Jewish tradition.'' [6]

6. F.A., No. 2. Supplementary information concerning the various elements within the non-Orthodox Jewish-liberal community is in archival files: G.A.J., G.A. M1/2, Protokolle von Ausschussitzungen des D.I.G.B.; M1/3, Akten des D.I.G.B.; M1/9, Zur Geschichte des D.I.G.B.; T.D. 171/b, Mittheilungen des D.I.G.B.; G.A. M1/33, Schriftwechsel D.I.G.B.; Protokolle der Vorstandssitzungen des C.V., Filmreel 124 (1b), 1901–1905; G.A. M2/1, Hilfsverein 1901–1913; T.D. 34, Verband jüdischer Lehrer-Vereine in Deutschland; T.D. 353, Arbeitsamt für jüdische Akademiker 1909–1912; G.A. M4/1,4/2, Rabbiner-Verband in Deutschland 1896–1899, 1909–1911; G.A. 21/2, V.D.D.J. Korrespondenz 1904–1922; G.A. M/36, Vereinigung für das liberale Judenthum in Deutschland; T.D. 913, Die Gesamtorganisation der deutschen Juden; T.D. 23, V.D.D.J. Further information about the Jewish organizations is in *Die Jüdischen Gemeinden und Vereine in*

At the beginning of the period we are discussing the intellectuals as well as the religious and lay leaders of the great Jewish congregations still assumed that "the liberal tendency in Protestant theology is a fortunate result of changing historical conditions; it has much in common with Judaism and will soon find itself able to acknowledge the eternal value, the unique character as well as the continuing mission of Judaism." [7] In the preface to his work on the history of Israel, *Einleitung zur Geschichte Israels,* which appeared a few years later, B. Stade professed to detect in the movements that arose in Judaism since the past century under the influence of Christian civilization hopeful signs that Judaism would recognize Christianity as the true continuation of the religion of the Old Testament. In the first decade of the twentieth century the spokesmen of the Liberal Jewish community and of the Wissenschaft des Judenthums— among them Martin Philippson, Leo Baeck, Martin Schreiner, and Gustav Karpeles—appealed to the public and warned it of "the Leviathan danger" that would attend the rapprochement of the two religions under the cloak of liberalism. [8] The new tension in the relations between the two religions was not the result of age-old theological and mythological differences but rather of their common outlook and cultural convergence— an unexpected development in the relations between Christians and Jews that will concern us in the following pages.

---

*Deutschland,* pub. by Bureau für Statistik der Juden, Berlin, 1906. These sources, although compiled by the heads of Jewish organizations, include data concerning Jews who did not belong to these organizations, which constituted the greater part of the non-Orthodox liberal Jews. Additional information regarding the *Zeitgeist* of this community is in *Jahrbuch für jüdische Geschichte und Literatur,* pub. by Verbande der Vereine für jüdische Geschichte und Literatur in Deutschland, Berlin, 1898 ff; Further information is given by Gustav Karpeles in his annual survey *Literarische Jahreswende,* Vol. 5, 1902, pp. 21–22: "Our learned men waver irresolutely between Haeckel and Harnack, between the natural sciences that reject everything and Protestant theology which humiliates Judaism, between one world view that dismisses all religion and another that relegates Judaism to a national cult." To complete this picture, see an Orthodox interpretation, Dr. M. Cahn, Provinzial-Rabbiner in Fulda, *Die Religiösen Strömungen in der Zeitgenössischen Judenheit,* Frankfurt a/M, 1912, p. viii ff; Part I, B; Part II, Part IV.

7. Joseph Eschelbacher, *Der konservative Protestantismus und das Judenthum . . . Rede 1884,* Berlin, 1898, p. 4. For the political aspects in this discourse, see U. Tal, "Liberal Protestantism, etc.," J.S.S., New York, Vol. 25, 1964, No. 1, p. 25.

8. Martin Philippson, *Konservative und Liberale Protestanten: Ein Wort über die Ritschlsche Schule,* Berlin, 1903, p. 4 ff.

Negation of the "Christian State"

One of the manifestations which from the outset seemed capable of bridging the gap between Christians and Jews was the opposition of the Liberal Protestants to the idea of the Christian state and the policy of the Catholics and Conservatives for its practical implementation. The Liberal Protestant attack on the Christian state was based on the principle laid down by Richard Rothe that the church would cause its own dissolution as an institution; but as a system of beliefs and opinions it would continue to exert a profound influence on secular reality to a point where society would be able to dispense with the church altogether as a separate institution. The church, as a community of the devout within the state, was a transitory phenomenon that would ultimately be absorbed by the state, which in turn would embody all the functions of the human spirit. The church was a tributary and not a patron of the state. In the social and political order envisaged by Rothe the state would not cease to fulfill its function as the center of political and judicial power, but would be imbued with ethical and religious principles derived from the gospels. The state would thus become converted from an instrument of brute political power into a "moral being" (*ein sittliches Wesen*): "The ecclesiastical stage in the historical development of Christianity has passed and gone, and the Christian spirit has entered its ethical, that is, its political stage." [9] Rothe contrived to incorporate in his exposition Hegelian principles which he applied in interpreting the kingdom of God on earth as a process in which Christianity would culminate in a secular society on the one hand and in which the political state would be thoroughly imbued with the spirit of Christianity on the other. [10] Therefore, the task of Christianity in the modern world was to complete the process begun by the church when it infiltrated and conquered the heathen world.

9. R. Rothe, *Theologische Ethik,* Vol. III, Wittenberg, 1848, p. 1010, par. 477. See also W. Nigg, pp. 207–208, and especially K. Leese, p. 160; Leese analyzed Rothe's book and concluded that in Rothe's view the days of the church as a separate institution were numbered, "and that it will surely be gradually absorbed in the state, that is, in a worldy political-moral communal body. He no doubt had in mind a state imbued with the moral and religious forces of Christianity, more accurately a 'totality of states'—the Christian world."

10. This has been competently dealt with by Christian Walther (hereafter, Walther) in his basic study, *Typen des Reich-Gottes Verständnisses,* München, 1961, p. 117. The author likewise cited the above-mentioned source from Rothe's *Theologische Ethik,* p. 134; see also Stephan-Schmidt, p. 197 ff.

This interest in the world and in material things had long existed in the ecclesiastical hierarchy of the Catholic church; in Protestantism, however, the center of gravity shifted from the church proper to all of human existence until it became coextensive and even identical with Christianity. Religion as "feeling" would be a formative impulse destined to influence the intellectual life of the age and indeed the entire sphere of human activity. Christianity was seen as entering upon a career of greater freedom and finding an ever-expanding expression in the developing life of man. In this enlargement of the Christian sphere and in the enrichment of its character the things of this world would not be opposed to the life of the spirit but would be spirituality pressing toward utterance; and thus the state, within whose borders this process takes place, would be "the last precursor of God's kingdom."

Rothe's approach combined elements taken from the teachings of Schleiermacher and Hegel. From the former Rothe borrowed the principle of "the total impress of Christ" (*Totaleindruck von Christo*) whereby the effect of the Incarnation in the physical world was absolute, all-embracing, boundless, and eternal, hence governing all human and cosmic experience. From Hegel, especially as interpreted by Ferdinand Christian Baur, he took the principle of self-consciousness as a spiritual force realized in universal reality which, however, and here Rothe followed Baur in opposition to Hegel, would be inspired with a vital, that is, historical Christianity which, although not perfect, had attained full freedom. Scholars have thus far paid scant attention to this deviation from Hegel's teachings, and yet it is precisely here that we find one of the reasons for the widespread public interest shown in this aspect of Rothe's thought. Most Liberal Protestants did not accept Rothe's teaching in its entirety, and in particular did not subscribe to its far-reaching consequences regarding the disappearance of the Church as an institution. But they supported his central thesis that the task of the church was to infuse all areas of life with Christian consciousness, and that this was to be done not through political and ecclesiastical institutions, conformity to external standards, or participation in established rites, but by "accepting the yoke of the kingdom of heaven and the knowledge of God within and through Jesus the Messiah." [11]

This view of the role of Christianity in the modern world was also that of Albrecht Ritschl who defined the state, from the Protestant point of

11. In the above-mentioned *Symposium* (n. 4), p. 2.

view, as nothing but an earthly framework which in itself could not be Christian, for Christianity concerned the things of the spirit. But since the task of the state was to enable this spirituality "to gain dominion over human reality," Christianity should not only make ontological statements in theology but also make value judgments respecting this world, with a Christian fear of God but also with full awareness that they were not the prerogative of the clergy alone but of all sovereign citizens.[12]

The political campaign that was conducted in the seventies by the Reich against the "ultramontanists" and to some extent also against the Conservative Protestants was regarded by the Liberal Protestants as a concrete expression of their opposition to the Christian state. After the end of the seventies and especially in the middle of the nineties, with the entrenchment of clericalism on the one hand and the intensification of the struggle against Social Democracy on the other, the opposition of the liberal groups to the principle of the Christian state grew more intense. An expression of this antagonism may be found in a series of lectures given in 1887 by Albrecht Ritschl on the occasion of the four hundredth anniversary of Luther's birth in which the essence of Luther's teachings was defined as having given Christianity an overarching and supereminent goal of "the spiritual domination of the world." The consciousness of this lofty goal constituted the superiority of Lutheranism over Catholicism which aspired to world domination through the political and universal authority of the church. Lutheran Protestantism emphasized the ethical and spiritual ascent of the individual, his vocation in the world, and the development of his moral character, and not submission to external authority and the unquestioned acceptance of given truths. Thus it was superior to all other religions, especially Judaism with its national segregation and confining ceremonialism dating from the Pharisees in the time of Jesus. Lutheranism thus preserved the authentic traditions of early Christianity and endeavored to create the conditions "in which the life of the spirit will truly govern the world in a spiritual manner." [13]

12. In the original: "der weltfrömmigen Werturteile ihrer souverainen Bürger" (ibid.); see Walther, chap. vii; also, for the philosophical roots of this conception, Paul Wrzecionko, *Die Philosophischen Wurzeln der Theologie Albrecht Ritschls,* Berlin, 1964, p. 199 ff.

13. In the original: "unter denen das geistige Leben in geistiger Weise wirklich über die Welt mächtig wird," Albrecht Ritschl, *Festrede zum 400 Geburtstag Martin Luthers,* 1887, p. 10 ff. The copy I consulted was transcribed (with many errors) by the Verband der jüdischen Lehrervereine im Deutschen Reiche, Magdeburg, 1888, p. 2 ff. See Walther, p. 145 ff; also K. Kupisch, p. 101 ff.

The arguments put forward in this series of lectures were answered by Rabbi Joseph Eschelbacher in an address to the Association of Jewish Teachers (Verband der jüdischen Lehrervereine im Deutschen Reich) in which he pointed out that the shift of religious authority in Liberal Protestantism from the church to all spheres of secular life would isolate the members of the Jewish religion from their German environment. Ritschl's thesis that Protestantism should rule the state and all spheres of social life in accordance with a pattern revealed in Christ as the bearer of civilization involved the danger of totalitarian rule no less grave than that of traditional clericalism. The view of Ritschl and his followers, Eschelbacher declared, that Protestantism had reached an evolutionary stage in which Judaism and Catholicism attained their perfection, and hence represented the final stage in the development of western Christian civilization, was contrary to liberal principles and a divergence from traditional Kantian principles that had been accepted by Ritschl himself.[14] As a result of Eschelbacher's outspoken views a Council was formed to serve as an adjunct to the Verband der jüdischen Lehrervereine im Deutschen Reiche and its functions defined as follows: to clarify and reformulate the theoretical and theological elements uniting and separating Jews and Christians and to investigate the practical possibilities of integrating the conclusions reached by this council into the curriculum of the Jewish schools.

In the course of the last two decades of the century this theme became an integral part of Liberal Protestant ideology, a theme that might be described in Ernst Troeltsch's phrase as "total Christianity." Liberal Protestantism opposed the idea of the Christian state as represented in Roman Catholicism with its clerical hierarchy and political domination from Rome, its miracles, irrational dogmas, and sacraments; it also opposed the Christian state as represented in Lutheran conservative ideology with its bias in favor of the clergy, the landed gentry, and the traditional cadre of officers, its "outmoded pietistic provincialism and romantic intoxication." Instead of this domination of German national culture through the imposition of institutionalized external authority, Liberal Protestantism

14. Eschelbacher's words were printed in a report of a discussion by teachers and rabbis (including those of the Orthodox group): J. Eschelbacher, Simon Dingfelder, S. Adler, F. Cohn, J. Klingenstein, S. Maybaum, S. Katz, H. Steinthal, M. Loewinson, J. Wohlgemüth, S. Audorn, *Der Jüdische Religionsunterricht und die soziale Lage der jüdischen Lehrer,* Magdeburg, pub. by I.W., 1889, p. 12.

would make religion an affair of the inner life of man and imbue him with a "consciousness of vocation" (*Berufungsbewusstsein*) rooted in the ethical world view of the gospels, the constant touchstone of daily conduct.[15] This was the view defended by Rudolf von Bennigsen in a discussion that took place under the auspices of the Deutscher Protestantenverein in 1888. It was also the position taken by the *Christliche Welt,* the central organ of Liberal Protestantism, during the last decade of the century when it urged that "Christian meaning" should govern the life of the citizen and the education of his children in the school. The clergy in the field began to use traditional conservative terminology more and more, although starting from contrary premises. In this spirit they also urged those circles connected with the *Christliche Welt* not to look upon education as the study of general humanity, which was the goal of rational liberalism and atheism, but as a tool for Christian character training and the inculcation of religious-ethical attitudes. Truth was not the product of rational thought but the reward of holiness, and hence it was imperative to strengthen Christian education "so that the entire educational system will be imbued with a Christian religious spirit." [16]

In contradistinction to the Conservatives, however, the *Christliche Welt* was opposed to the separate position of the church as an autonomous institution. The state need not be Christian, although it would necessarily be influenced by a society and culture that was in every respect Christian. The Liberals were thus opposed to having Christianity limited to a special subject or confined to the confessional schools, as if Christian education were nothing more than religious training. On the contrary, they pointed out that the attempts of the Conservatives to strengthen the confessional schools merely resulted in the exclusion of believing Christians from the German community and from the nation as a whole. The evangelical spirit should pervade all studies—mathematics and the natural sciences as well as the humanities—so that the student would acquire a Christian world view and a Christian character whereby "man's spirit will come to appreciate the wonderful lawfulness of the world of creation. . . . Jesus went to the life of nature for his language . . . his parables." [17] The basic problem of education, as defined by the educators and scholars of the *Christliche Welt,* was the application of what they called the "Christian principle," the principle that bestows value and a specific ideological

15. These words in the name of Bennigsen are quoted by Rabbi Eschelbacher, p. 22.
16. Ch. W., 1890, col. 1062–1067.        17. Ibid.

character on all professions and on all the studies in the school curriculum—the humanistic and scientific subjects, aesthetics, ethics, character training, the acquisition of a world view, and the formation of personality—all of which must derive their inspiration and validity from the gospels.[18]

From the Liberal Protestant point of view the state and its citizens should be influenced by Christianity only indirectly through the human personality which, raised to the highest ethical level by virtue of the gospels, must necessarily exert a strong influence on the social and political life of the nation. The political ethics of Christianity thus operates indirectly on the state through the ethical personality as it is shaped by evangelical training. This is the source of its strength. Since the state is nothing more than the expression of the sovereignty of the individual, the more an individual is inspired by Christian faith and its ethical principles the more will the state be elevated to the highest ethical level. Christianity acknowledges the existence of a separate political sphere, especially that of the state, but its contribution to the state is made through the individual in the form of a "religion of personality," whereby political morality is influenced indirectly, but all the more deeply since it is based on a new personality invested with high ethical value. The state is a tributary and not the patron of the church. This is the spirit of the modern interpretation of the answer that Jesus gave to the Pharisees: "For lo, the kingdom of God is within you" (Luke 17:21).[19]

These views were also reflected in the attitude of the Liberals toward the relations of state and church. After the end of the *Kulturkampf* in the middle of the eighties, and with the strengthening of the Christian political parties, the Conservatives and the Center, a new campaign was launched by the Conservatives of the extreme Right to curtail state intervention in the affairs of the church and its institutions. Methods of increasing the power of the Lutheran church were discussed in the various parliaments, especially in the Prussian Lower House, in the political deliberations of the church as in the Assembly at Barmen on October 20, 1886, and in the leading journals. The right-wing Conservatives, led by Freiherr von Hammerstein and Kleist-Retzow, advocated greater organi-

18. Ibid.
19. Ch. W., 1889, col. 694; 1890, col. 195 ff, 621 ff. At the beginning of the twentieth century this concept was authoritatively treated by E. Troeltsch, *Politische Ethik und Christenthum*, Göttingen, 1904, pp. 8, 11–12, 22–26, 32 (hereafter, Troeltsch).

zational and juridical power for the church. Just as the Catholics had been granted greater freedom in ecclesiastical and state affairs at the close of the *Kulturkampf,* so also should the Lutheran church be restored to its historic subjection to the king and not to Parliament.[20]

To this end the right-wing groups were prepared to change the ecclesiastical law (*Synodalordnung*) that had been in effect in Greater Prussia since June 3, 1876, and make the clergy less dependent on the state. The Conservatives demanded freedom from state interference in the following areas: the inner regulations of the church, its public and educational activities, appointments of the clergy, legal authority for inner reforms through royal sanction, including the right of taxation, without having this sanction subject to state or parliamentary approval. This policy was evidently intended to strengthen the principle of the separation of church and state, but the Protestants saw it as an obvious pretext under the cloak of religious freedom for granting greater power to the orthodox clergy and weakening the parliamentary rule in favor of the conservative social classes by placing the particularistic interests of the clergy and of the aristocratic conservative circles above the interests of the national state. This was regarded by the Liberal Protestants as ''using the church in the struggle against social democracy in order to exchange one despotic form for another.'' [21]

The Liberal Protestants, on the other hand, supported a policy that would grant the state, and especially the parliamentary institutions, broad supervisory powers and the right of intervention in ecclesiastical and educational affairs, conceiving this to be the best method for safeguarding the priority of universal national interests against the particularistic interests of separate groups. The nature of these universal interests did not diminish the growing influence of Christianity as the Jews had assumed or hoped for at the outset. On the contrary, the struggle against the Conservative policy and the separate status of the church was calculated to make Christianity a dominant force in the national, cultural, and educational life of the country and, indeed, in the government and its institutions. In this struggle the Liberal Protestants developed a twofold aim: on the one hand they wished to weaken the Conservatives as a political and religious force and to strengthen parliamentary institutions over the impe-

20. Ch. W., 1887, col. 76 ff.
21. In the *Symposium der Freunde der Christlichen Welt,* (n. 4), p. 18. See also remarks of Hauptpastor D. Heinrich Röpe, Hamburg, Ch. W., 1889, col. 672, 694.

rial circles; on the other hand, however, they hoped that this policy would facilitate the introduction of a historical national culture into public and private life whose evangelical Christian content would create a new kind of citizen.

Those who subscribed to this policy included many of the active members of the Inner Mission, at the head of which were, among others, Oberkonsistorialrath Dr. Löber and Missionsinspektor Dr. Theodor Zahn of Dresden, as revealed in the reports of the meetings that took place in Dresden in 1895 and two years later in Barmen. The leaders of the opposition to a Christian state were the active members of the Deutscher Protestantenverein and also theologians and scholars, such as Rudolf Sohm, Theodor Kaftan, and Friedrich Paulsen. Despite many internal differences, there was general agreement on a number of basic issues: (1) Christianity is primarily concerned with the redemption of the soul and the welfare of the spirit; it is thus by its very nature apolitical, and the intrusion of politics in religion is prejudicial to its truthful exposition; Christianity is not confined to any one class or nationality, but has a divine commission to promote justice and to ensure the freedom of moral action under every regime and within every social reality; (2) to confer religious or suprarational validity on ethics, science, politics, or matrimonial affairs is unwarranted and can only lead to tyranny and the denial of religious liberty and freedom of conscience; the concern of Christianity is to foster man's love of God and of his fellow man, whereas the state and politics are concerned with the consolidation of power toward the attainment of material ends and *terrena felicitas;* (3) since man's autonomous rational authority theoretically resides in morality, society, and the state, it is common to all men and all citizens and therefore not restricted to the communicants of any particular church; (4) to make of Christianity a political instrument is to vitiate its religious purity; from an educational and even political point of view the extraneous intrusion of politics is injurious to religion and will of necessity provoke an atheistic reaction: "The result of the Christian state in the forties and fifties was Social Democracy." [22] In this spirit Professor Rudolf Sohm at the Congress of the

22. From the discourse of Rudolf Sohm at the Congress of the Inner Mission in Dresden, Sept. 24, 1895, M.V.A.A., 1895, No. 39, pp. 307–309. For the background of the views of Sohm and the members of his circle, see Dieter Stoodt, *Wort und Recht: Rudolf Sohm und das theologische Problem des Kirchenrechts,* München, 1962, p. 111 ff. Similar views in these circles of liberal scholars in the Inner Mission movement appear in M.V.A.A., 1895, No. 46, p. 367, No. 52, p. 415; 1897, No. 11, p. 83, No. 41, p. 324; "Vom

Inner Mission in Dresden in September 1895 stated that "the questions that dominate public life, prominent among which today is the social question, have to do with justice and the distribution of power, that is, questions of this world that cannot be solved by Christianity . . . which is concerned only with questions of the world to come. . . . Luther burned Christian law so that Christianity might be free. 'Away with Christian law' is the verdict of the Reformation. 'Away with the Christian state' is the verdict of world history. . . . The hatred of the masses against Christianity, against Christ, against the church . . . is the consequence of the idea of the Christian state." [23]

At the end of the last century and during the first decade of the present century we find less emphasis being placed on the principle of the separation of church and state and a greater emphasis on the need to cultivate Christian personality and a Christian society. To Harnack, Troeltsch, and a growing number of Liberal Protestants the separation of church and state on an institutional level seemed possible; but no such separation was possible in any of the other spheres of human activity—political, cultural, professional—since these spheres were presumably entirely permeated with Christianity. In this spirit Troeltsch concluded his well-known work on the separation of church and state, *Die Trennung von Staat und Kirche:* "Today we no longer understand our civil duty to be a form of service for the benefit of the church alone, but also a form of scientific work in the vital religious question which also embraces the nation." [24]

This attitude of Liberal Protestantism toward the Christian state created a deep contradiction within the movement between its theoretical principles and its practical policy, a contradiction that is more easily understood when compared to a similar dialectical tension among the Conservative Protestants. The Conservatives began with an explicit ideology in favor of the Christian state and then went over to a policy designed to restrict state intervention in the affairs of the church and its institutions and to extend the influence of the particularistic classes of society. The Liberals, on the other hand, began with a firm stand against state intervention in religious, educational, economic, and social affairs and then went over

---

Christlichen Staat und Christlicher Obrigkeit," No. 50, pp. 399–400; 1899, No. 16, p. 121 ff: "Just as the love for the Christian religion served as the basis of the Christian state, so is the national state based only on the will to power."

23. From the above report of Sept. 24, 1895, above n. 22.

24. See *Die Trennung von Staat und Kirche,* Göttingen 1907, p. 68; also, Troeltsch, p. 32.

to a policy in favor of state control in all these spheres. Although the Conservatives desired to consolidate their particularistic position, they governed the Reich for the greater part of its existence; the Liberals, who wished to strengthen their universalism by cultivating the citizen's sense of responsibility to the nation and to the state as a whole, entrenched themselves in particularistic and oppositional positions or, as was customary among many intellectuals, disassociated themselves entirely from political activities and the burdens of public office. The Conservative Protestants subscribed to the principle of compulsory religious education for the youth, but in actual practice pursued a policy in favor of separate parochial institutions of education to enable various segments of the population to receive religious instruction along confessional lines. The Liberal Protestants, on the other hand, defended the freedom of the individual and society to conduct their own educational affairs without external interference, but in practice they denounced confessional and private schools and thus impeded the free development of autonomous particularistic education in the state, especially that of the Jewish minority.

That the German Jews decided to remain Jews and that the Liberals among them adhered to their ancestral faith was a bitter disappointment to the Liberal Protestants and interpreted by them as a deep betrayal by their closest friends in Germany. At the same time they recognized this Jewish defection as demonstrating the weakness of Liberal Protestantism itself and as a challenge to its adherents to inquire into the foundations of their faith and the validity of its central ideal that looked forward to the day when "Germanism, the Reich, and the nation, the state and society, that is, our whole public life, will be imbued with a vital ethical Christianity." [25]

The Common Denominator

Toward the close of the nineteenth century the Liberal Protestants and Jews began to recognize that their relations had become more complicated, more involved in contradictions, and more fragile than had been

25. *Symposium,* above n. 4, p. 19. See similar formulation by K. Kupisch, p. 53: Zusatz vom 22 April 1892, Programm der Freunde der Positiven Union, 1873. The quotation is from Troeltsch's lecture of Oct. 3, 1901, see E. Troeltsch, *Die Absolutheit des Christenthums und die Religionsgeschichte, Vortrag auf der Versammlung der Freunde der Christlichen Welt zu Mühlacker,* Tübingen, Leipzig, 1902, p. 94.

suspected. The alliance of these two groups, in contradistinction to the unambiguous relations between the Jews and other Christian movements, was characterized by an ambivalent feeling that arose not from mutual hatred or anti-Semitism but rather from similarities in social conceptions, political views, and in the conduct of daily life. As these common interests grew stronger, the contradictions between the two groups became more apparent, contradictions that neither side sought nor desired, but could not avoid as long as they insisted on retaining their respective identities. They had both suffered a common disillusionment in the high hopes and ideals of the Enlightenment with its optimistic trust in the power of universal education and civic equality to bring about the rule of reason in all areas of life and to redeem the human spirit from authoritarian social patterns, from superstition, prejudices, and vain hatreds, including of Jews.

But at the height of this convergence of common interests at the turn of the century both groups became aware of the precarious nature of their affinity, the various points of dissension and divergence hitherto unnoticed because of the imperfect comprehension of the intellectual and moral forces by which the progress of the modern world was being molded. The circumstances that contributed to this change of mood and interest have already been examined. The Liberals had put their faith in the ideals of the Enlightenment, in education, rational morality, tolerance, humanitarianism, cosmopolitanism, the redemptive power of reason, and the perfectibility of man and society, but these, they felt, had failed to provide adequate answers to the questions of an age in search of some base of assurance. In the cultural despair of this period (*Kulturpessimismus*) we perceive the unmistakable influence of Nietzsche who as early as 1867 declared: "What is there in history except the endless war of conflicting interests, and the struggle for self-preservation?" [26] The ideas that men believed to be the substance and goal of the struggle for survival were but the faint echoes and worn-out answers to man's basic animal needs. This was also the theme of the anti-intellectualist and anti-Semitic proponents

26. F.A., Nos. 6, 7, 8; from personal testimony of talks in intellectual circles in Berlin, Frankfurt, Leipzig, including the testimony of secondary school teachers under Professor Schwalbe, who was one of the signers of the anti-Semitic petition of Nov. 21, 1880; see Leopold Auerbach, *Das Judentum und seine Bekenner in Preussen und in anderen deutschen Bundesstaaten*, Berlin, 1890, p. 39. The source is to be found in Nietzsche's *Aufzeichnungen über Geschichte und historische Wissenschaften* (1867) Musarion Gesamtausgabe, München, 1922, Vol. I, p. 286.

of racial theories who were deeply influenced by social Darwinism as interpreted by E. Haeckel, according to which the struggle for survival was not a means toward a spiritual or historical goal, but an end in itself and the quintessence of all history. Such was the struggle that was now being waged by the Aryan race and by the German people who embodied the highest value, brute physical power—the struggle against weakness, irresolution, morbidity, self-mortification, and all the other unwholesome qualities known as "morality" in the Jewish and Jewish-Christian heritage. Fritz Bley expressed this view in 1897 when he spoke of the place of Germanism in the world: "God, who breathed living breath into man . . . desires the war of all against all, so that the best, the ablest may emerge as victors. The strong man is destined to rule. He should transmit his qualities to posterity and spread out into a clan, into a nation, and finally into all mankind." [27] Similar despairing views were expressed by Eduard von Hartmann in his *Philosophy of the Unconscious* as early as 1868–1869, and following him by an increasing number of intellectuals and educators, who raised the unconscious to a dynamic power that providentially fashions all phenomena and guides all issues to a predetermined end to a point where it completely eliminates the more vitalizing truths of enlightened rationalism. In a symposium at the end of the eighties in Leipzig on the subject of "Matter and Spirit in Our Day" students, under the evident influence of Schopenhauer, reflected the mood of that day when they declared: "Instead of the ideal of harmony as formulated by Leibniz and Lessing, the truth is that existence is nothing but a torment, culture nothing but a rationalistic illusion, being will be redeemed by nonbeing, the conscious will is but a faint shadow of the arbitrary primordial *Urwille,* all existence is an affliction, a vain pillar of smoke; the world will be redeemed by a return to the primordial Nothing, to the will that desires nothing and to that which is not desired." [28]

The principal problem that now faced liberal religion was whether it could provide the youth with a more robust doctrine that might dispel this dismal estimate of life. Could it find an answer to Jakob Burckhardt's prophecy of the rising masses and the vulgarization that threatened to engulf modern man? Could it still serve as a guide for the common man

27. Fritz Bley, *Die Weltstellung des Deutschtums,* 1897, col. 23–24. This appears again in the collection of sources, Harry Pross, *Die Zerstörung der deutschen Politik, Dokumente 1871–1933,* Frankfurt a/M, 1959, p. 60.

28. F.A., No. 8/b.

who was being crushed between the wheels of bureaucracy and mechanization, subjected to the arbitrary demonic powers of big business, political parties, and a highly centralized state which he failed to comprehend and over which he had no influence? Could the Liberal Protestants and Jews provide a rival interpretation that would prove a more abiding redemption from the growing wave of pseudoromanticism, anti-intellectualism, and race theories, from a mythological world of unmediated experience in which modern man had found refuge from the treadmill round of experience and its attendant responsible decisions? In short, the challenge to the Liberals was to provide a theory to counter the arguments advanced by the racial anti-Semites who advocated "unbridled, genuine, natural feelings in which alone and in complete surrender to which is there an escape from the degenerate effects of sterile rationalistic concepts, that is, from a petrified Judaism or its offspring, Christianity." [29]

The liberals in both religions vaguely felt and sometimes acknowledged that they could find no answers to the fateful questions of their generation, for they themselves had fundamental doubts concerning the force and relevance of their own rationalistic liberal tradition, the tradition on which their future existence depended. In his well-known letter to Elkan Herz of July 23, 1771, Moses Mendelssohn was still able to write with pride: "We have no dogmas that are repugnant to reason or above reason. We add nothing to natural religion beyond rational laws, judgments, and ordinances. The elements of our religion and its articles of faith rest on a rational basis; they are compatible with scientific inquiry in every respect without conflict or contradiction." [30] At the same time, however, a growing distrust of pure reason and the principles of the Enlightenment was reflected in the terse comment of Dr. Joseph Eschelbacher, a vigorous apologist of that period, namely, that "the Enlightenment, which has reached its peak in our day, has not brought the expected blessings." [31]

29. Ibid.

30. Moses Mendelssohn, *Gesammelte Schriften,* ed. by G. B. Mendelssohn, Leipzig, 1843, Vol. II, p. 321. See also Nathan Rotenstreich, "Mendelssohn's Understanding of Judaism" (Hebrew), *The Writings of Moses Mendelssohn,* Vol. I, Tel-Aviv, 1947, p. 17 ff.

31. Rabbi Dr. Joseph Eschelbacher, *Das Judentum und das Wesen des Christentums,* pub. by der Gesellschaft zur Förderung der Wissenschaft des Judentums in Berlin (1905), 1908, 2d ed., p. 7 (hereafter, Eschelbacher). Another important book is J. Eschelbacher, *Das Judentum im Urteile der modernen protestantischen Theologie,* pub. by der Gesellschaft zur Förderung der Wissenschaft des Judentums, Leipzig, 1907. This work, which is an elaboration of the lecture that Eschelbacher gave under the auspices of the above *Gesell-*

Eschelbacher's disillusion in the Enlightenment was more than a specifically Jewish matter concerned with equal status and Jewish identity. It was part of a widespread feeling of discontent among the intellectuals—educators, rabbis, students, public leaders—the feeling that the failure to integrate Judaism with Germanism without surrendering Jewish particularism was a reflection of a general spiritual and social malaise, characterized by one of Rabbi Eschelbacher's followers as "the impotence of the Enlightenment to answer the question of freedom from the standpoint of self-determination within the sphere of human reality." [32] Similarly, the intellectuals within the Liberal Protestant community expressed their distrust in the power of human reason to liberate man from ignorance, social, and economic oppression, or indeed from the irrational beliefs of Christianity itself. A report of the discussions that took place among the students of Professor Friedrich Loofs plainly stated that "the part of the ancient dogma of *Confessio Augustana* which condemns to perdition all those who have not experienced the cleansing power of baptism . . . or the purifying influence of the Holy Ghost" was so deeply ingrained in the Christian that no rational considerations could uproot these beliefs from his heart. If indeed rationalism should be successful in cleansing and in purifying faith of its irrational dross "men would again be enslaved to reason with the same irrational fervor with which they believed in the myth of baptism." [33]

---

*schaft* on Jan. 5, 1907, discusses in an explicit and systematic manner the standpoint of modern Protestantism, which continued to regard the reason for Judaism's existence, in the words of Julius Wellhausen, as an early preparatory stage of Christianity, ibid. p. 11. The studies by K. A. Wünsche, *Neue Beiträge zur Erläuterung der Evangelien aus Talmud und Midrasch,* Göttingen, 1878, and by G. Dalman, *Die Worte Jesu,* Vol. I, Leipzig, Darmstadt, 1898, were approved by Eschelbacher since in his opinion they were derived from a direct understanding of the original biblical and talmudic sources. Eschelbacher criticized a considerable number of Protestant historiographers, theologians, and biblical scholars of his day, including C. H. Cornill, F. Weber, J. Wellhausen, H. Gunkel, E. Schürer, and W. Bousset. His chief criticism of these scholars was that they presented their Christian anti-Jewish views in modern scientific garb in order to justify the Christian principle that the continued existence of Judaism was an anachronism; there was no reason for Judaism to exist after the rise of Christianity, when Election was transferred from Israel in the body to Israel in the spirit, that is, to Christianity. From Eschelbacher's words here we can perceive the universal significance he attached to the dispute between modern Protestantism and Judaism as an expression of deep disappointment that followed the sanguine hopes that the generation had placed in education and science.

32. F.A., No. 14/a.

33. F.A., No. 8; the discussion among the students arose following a study of *Die Bekenntnisschriften der altprotestantischen Kirche Deutschlands,* Cassel, 1885, p. 335 ff.

It was plain to many Christians that the acquisition of legal equality and an enlightened education did not help Jews find their way to Christianity and thus hasten the eschatological process foreseen in the universalistic *Heilsgeschichte*. A special relationship had developed between the Liberal Protestants and the Jews that was characterized by a mutual dependence and criticism, often severe and even aggressive, which no doubt stemmed from their mutual disappointment. This was apparent even at the beginning of this relationship, as may be deduced from the remarks in a lecture given by Abraham Geiger on Christianity as a universal force:

It is not my intention to criticize Christianity, and even less to take issue with a faith that has given and still gives happiness to so many millions of people, nor indeed to affront pious souls. Nevertheless, it is our duty to state candidly how those who do not share this faith regard it from the standpoint of its origin and as a world-historical factor, and this justifies us to continue to support and maintain a spiritual abode side by side with it.[34]

In this new relationship both sides were united by a common attitude toward religion which they regarded not as a metaphysical system possessing dogmatic authority, but as a social product that embodies ethical principles of suprahistorical validity. At the center of both religions stands man who is seen from two points of view, first, as a reasonable being and as such capable, by virtue of what Ritschl called *Werturteile* (value judgments), of amending and clarifying those historical religious ideas which in the eyes of that generation could withstand rational criticism. In his *Ethics of Judaism* (par. 87), which was accepted by Liberal Judaism at the beginning of the century as a kind of theoretical platform, Moritz Lazarus expressed this thought in popular form: "Every age is justified in disregarding, more, is in duty bound to disregard, the written law whenever reason and conviction demand its nullification." [35] The second manner in which man is regarded as the center of religious experience is historical and psychological. Man, as a system of needs, desires, and impulses, formed and nourished by religion, is the product of

34. A. Geiger, *Das Judentum und seine Geschichte,* Berlin, 1865, Vol. 1, p. 139. See also Jacob Fleischmann, *The Problem of Christianity in Modern Jewish Thought (1770–1929)* (Hebrew), Jerusalem, 1964, p. 106 ff.

35. M. Lazarus, *The Ethics of Judaism,* Philadelphia, 1900, par. 87; see also, Nathan Rotenstreich, *Jewish Philosophy in Modern Times, From Mendelssohn to Rosenzweig,* New York, Chicago, San Francisco, 1968, p. 45 ff (hereafter, Rotenstreich).

what the school of *Völkerpsychologie* (Wundt, Lazarus, Steinthal) called the *Volksgeist,* which serves to bridge the gap between historical tradition and suprahistorical transcendence.[36] This living source of religious authority and moral judgment in Judaism is to be found, according to Lazarus (par. 66 ff), not only in the Bible nor in the traditional rabbinical laws. The ethical core of Judaism, the source that provides the elements to construct modern historical reality, is to be found in the anthropological characteristics of the Jews, in their customs, conduct, and aspirations as these have been formed in the course of history—in short, what at that time was called the *Volksgemüth,* the innermost essence of a people's spirit.

The two religions, in their liberal form, defined the human essence as a unity in which theoretical speculative knowledge is combined with sensible experience, religious faith with rationalistic thought, revelation arrived at through faith with moral principles arrived at through rational autonomy. This integration is rooted in the bipolar nature of man as both object and subject. As object man is the product of historical, physiological, and psychological conditions in which he is born and reared; as subject, however, he is able to create meaning, so that not the conditions in themselves but their meanings express man's unique position and determine his place in historical reality in theory and in practice. Both liberal

36. M. Lazarus, H. Steinthal, *Einleitende Gedanken zu einer Zeitschrift für Völkerpsychologie und Sprachwissenschaft,* Z.V.P.S.W., Berlin, Vol. 1, 1860, p. 6 ff. This *Völkerpsychologie* was developed by Lazarus and Steinthal in the last third of the nineteenth century under the influence of J. F. Herbart's school of *angewandte Metaphysik* in psychology and also of W. Wundt's psychology and ethnography. The periodical published by this school was highly respected for its high standard of scholarship in the field of the history of cultures. The exponents of this school were opposed to the mythological, romantic conception of the *Volksseele;* see an early but mature work by M. Lazarus, *Einige synthetische Gedanken zur Völkerpsychologie,* Z.V.P.S.W., Vol. 3, 1865, No. 5, and Lazarus' definition: "der Staat ist eine moralische Persönlichkeit" (the state is a moral personality), p. 30. The many-sided activities of Lazarus and Steinthal in the fields of philology, mythology, the philosophy of history, and the origins of religion have as yet been only inadequately investigated. For an evaluation of their system by contemporaries, and also as a method of refuting the relativity of values, see P.J., 1881, Vol. 48, No. 5, pp. 451, 461 ff. For the place of Lazarus in Jewish thought, see Julius Guttmann, *Philosophies of Judaism,* London, 1964, pp. 350–352; his treatment of the question of nation and nationality, see Rotenstreich, pp. 34, 51, 56 ff; also, the recent study, D. Baumgardt, *The Ethics of Lazarus and Steinthal.* L.B.Y., Vol. II, 1957, p. 205 ff. For general evaluations of this system and its place in the history of the social sciences, see Helmut Schoeck, *Soziologie: Geschichte ihrer Probleme,* München, 1952, pp. 131 ff, 188 ff; Armand Cuvillier, *Manuel de sociologie,* Paris, 1958, p. 33, par. 6.

religions emphasized man's reflective nature, a being conscious and also aware that he is conscious, subject to experience and fashioned by it but also the master of his experience in that he determines at the outset the speculative instruments with which the empirical world is apprehended and constructed and which make experience possible.

From the theoretical or cognitive point of view the two religions conceived man's ethical rationality to reside in his free will; from the historical or anthropological point of view it was conceived as residing principally in the recognition of truths and their realization in the cultural and empirical world in which man finds himself. The cognitive approach is chiefly concerned with deductive reasoning and the criticism of the internal logical and analytical structure of the concepts constituting religious beliefs and with eliminating or modifying those elements which do not conform to the criteria of mathematical thinking or to the analytical concepts of the natural sciences and which are therefore defined as irrational, illogical, and lacking objective validity and autonomous status with respect to ethical thinking. The historical or anthropological approach sought by induction to interpret historical reality conceived as the revelation of suprahistorical truths; it hopes to corroborate faith through the findings of the historical and philological sciences and, to an increasing degree, through psychological and anthropological analogies or, as in the systems of Wilhelm Windelband, Wilhelm Dilthey, Heinrich Rickert, and Ernst Troeltsch, through the *Geisteswissenschaften* or social sciences as opposed to the natural sciences. Thus, by means of these two methods, that of pure thought and that of empirical scientific findings, the Liberal Protestants and Jews attempted to create what Harnack called "a world view and a historical life view" and Troeltsch a "culture type" (*Kulturtypus*).[37] The purely theoretical approach was cultivated from the sixties

37. The attitude of the Liberal Protestants from the time of Ritschl's teachings is summarized by Stephan-Schmidt, p. 251 ff: "It bore within itself the promise that it was possible to be a Christian in good conscience even in the modern world so full of realism, natural science, and historical criticism . . . thus were the disciples of Ritschl imbued with a confident sense of its triumphant mission." Harnack's methodological approach insofar as it affected the problem under discussion is in A. Harnack, *Die Aufgabe der theologischen Facultäten und die allgemeine Religionsgeschichte,* Giessen, 1901, 3d ed., Rectoratsrede, Aug. 3, 1901. In a much later work Harnack gave a clearer summary of his basic attitude toward the positivistic historical approach as it existed in theory and practice during the period we are discussing, especially at the end of the nineteenth and the beginning of the twentieth century: *Über die Sicherheit und die Grenzen geschichtlicher Erkenntnis,* München, 1917, p. 4 ff. For Troeltsch's views concerning the normative validity of the

on by the schools of thought that returned to the transcendental systems—
such as those of Kuno Fischer, Eduard Zeller, Hermann Lotze, and especially the influential system of Albrecht Ritschl—and reached the height
of its development at the end of the nineteenth and the beginning of the
twentieth century in the Marburg school and in the system of Hermann
Cohen.

A discussion of the purely theoretical aspects of the neo-Kantian school
of philosophy and of Hermann Cohen's system falls outside the scope of
this study. We are here concerned with the historical expression of these
teachings and their influence which dominated the discussions of this
period, and we shall therefore confine ourselves to a clarification of those
ideas that found a response among the public, chiefly through the popu-
larizations of M. Schreiner, I. Goldschmidt, and Moritz Lazarus. We
shall also discuss the polemical discussions of Moritz Lazarus and in the
Orthodox camp those of the regional rabbi, M. Cahn.[38]

---

social sciences, which had a deep influence on the methodological attitude of both Jews and
Protestants, especially in view of their disillusionment in the purely rational-cognitive approach of the neo-Kantian school, see E. Troeltsch, *Die Absolutheit des Christentums und
die Religionsgeschichte,* lecture at the Assembly of the Freunde der Christlichen Welt at
Mühlacker Oct. 3, 1901, Tübingen, Leipzig, 1902: "The doctrine of the purely causal process of the sum-total of phenomena in consciousness seems to me an unwarranted analogy
. . . from external to inner experience" (p. 6). Among Jewish thinkers the question of the
normative validity of historical studies and the social sciences had been discussed since the
time of the Wissenschaft des Judenthums. For the beginning of the period discussed here,
see M. Lazarus, "Über die Ideen in der Geschichte," lecture of Nov. 14, 1863, in
Z.V.P.S.W., 1865, Vol. 3, No. 4, p. 386 ff.

38. Hermann Cohen, *Die Nächstenliebe im Talmud,* Marburg, 1888; "Liebe und
Gerechtigkeit in den Begriffen Gott und Mensch," J.J.G.L., Vol. 3, Berlin, 1900; *Religion
und Sittlichkeit,* J.J.G.L., Vol. 10, Berlin, 1907; *Religiöse Postulate,* Report of the second
plenary session of the V.D.J., Berlin, 1907; *Innere Beziehungen der kantischen Philosophie
zum Judenthum,* 28th annual report of the Lehranstalt für die Wissenschaft des Judenthums,
Berlin, 1910; *Die Bedeutung des Judenthums für den religiösen Fortschritt,* Proceedings of
the 5th Weltkongresses für freies Christenthum, Vol. II, Berlin, 1911; *Das Gottesreich,
Soziale Ethik des Judenthums,* Berlin, 1913; *Der Nächste,* Korrespondenzblatt des V.D.J.
No. 14, Berlin, 1914. For the response to this school, insofar as it affected the relations be-
tween Protestantism and Judaism, see I. Goldschmidt, *Das Wesen des Judenthums,* Frank-
furt a/M, 1907, pp. 107 ff, 119. For critical reactions from the Orthodox group, see M.
Cahn, Provinzial-Rabbiner in Fulda, *Die Religiösen Strömungen in der zeitgenössischen
Judenheit,* Frankfurt a/M, 1912, p. 371 ff. For comprehensive studies, see Julius Guttmann,
*Philosophies of Judaism,* London, 1964, p. 352 ff; Nathan Rotenstreich, p. 31 ff; also A.
Altmann, *Theology in the Twentieth Century, German Jewry,* L.B.Y., Vol. I, 1956, p.
164 ff; H. Liebeschütz, *Jewish Thought and Its German Background,* L.B.Y., Vol. I,
1956, p. 22 ff. The influence of leading Liberal Protestant personalities on Hermann Cohen
has been treated by Robert R. Geiss in a documentary collection, *Dokumente jüdisch-*

The theoretical approach in liberal critical thought attempted to reduce religion to a pattern of logical relationships in conformity to the structure of the transcendental deduction. Just as the a priori categorical presuppositions come to liberate cognition from its dependence on its objects so as to ensure its objective validity, so also does the liberal conception seek to liberate religion from its dependence on irrational elements so as to ensure the objective validity of faith. Even as the theoretical emphasis in transcendental logic is transferred from the cognized object to the a priori conditions that make it possible for the object to be cognized in a synthetic structure, so also liberal religion transfers its central emphasis from belief or the observance of the commandments to the a priori conditions that make a religious relationship possible between man and God, between man and his fellow man, and between man and his own self.

In Cohen's teachings religion is ancillary to philosophy as such and does not constitute a theoretical system in itself. Since philosophy has its roots in mathematical thinking, the theoretical structure of religion, its validity, and verifiability must be subjected to rational criticism. Since the root of philosophical judgment is ethics, the root and end of religion is exhausted in ethical judgment. Hence, the ethical judgment which is the root of both religion and philosophy is possible only within the limits of mathematical thinking and must therefore be prepared to submit to the stern test of logical criticism. Those presuppositions that fail to stand this logical test cannot be included in the system of philosophical judgments and are hence not susceptible to religious judgment. In Cohen's system, therefore, ethics is conceived as analogous to logic. Even as logic is at the center of the mathematical sciences, so is ethics at the center of the humanistic disciplines based on religious and even historical thinking. In this structure logic and ethics serve as functions of "correlation," logic being a correlative of mathematics, ethics of religion. The two terms of the correlation assure their freedom and autonomy. Logic safeguards the natural sciences and mathematical thinking from unmediated and uncritical experimentation; ethics prevents historical studies

---

*christlicher Begegnung,* Theologische Bücherei No. 33, München, 1966, p. 40: "Sein Bild von Luther, der Reformation und der protestantischen Theologie seiner Zeit bezieht er ausschliesslich von Ritschlianern, deren Schule während seiner Marburger Jahre (1873–1912) in Marburg durch T. Brieger (1876–1886), W. Herrmann (1879–1916), in Giessen durch J. Gottschick (1882–1893), F. Kattenbusch (1878–1904) und B. Stade (from 1875) sehr repräsentativ vertreten war."

and the social sciences, and especially religious judgments, from falling prey to irrationalism.[39]

In this manner Cohen was able to demonstrate the liberating nature of Lutheran Protestantism, especially in the historicocultural sphere, the affinity between Protestantism and Judaism, as well as the uniqueness and superiority of the latter. The liberating power of Protestantism is reflected in the separation of the two spheres of religion and science.[40] After Luther this separation was effected by Kant, who based ethics on logic which is the source of the cognitive system of ethical judgments in conformity to the mathematical pattern of the natural sciences. This superiority of logic, in Cohen's view, in no way constitutes a disparagement of ethics or a diminution of its value. On the contrary, the dependence of ethics on the logical cognitive system guarantees its sovereign position in the realm of practical reason.[41]

The affinity between Protestantism and Judaism, according to Cohen, is based on the fact that both experienced what may be called a religious Copernican revolution. God is no longer the focal point of religion, which is confined to the logical and ethical spheres. He is no more than a symbol for the unity of the ethical world and the moral order of existence, the guarantee for the progressive ethical development of mankind. ''The essence of God is and remains the essence of human ethics, but this essence is now fraught with a deeper significance whereby man, by virtue of his own unassisted efforts, is obliged to create his own ethics.'' Hence

39. A succinct analysis of this approach is given by H. Cohen in his work, *Der Begriff der Religion im System der Philosophie,* published in 1915, that is, after the period we are discussing, but was also dealt with in the early days. In speaking of the ''unity of the culture-consciousness'' (*Einheit des Kulturbewusstseins*) Cohen explained the inner logical need to have religion conform to the cultural consciousness in other spheres, such as science, ethics, and aesthetics. Religion did not constitute a separate discipline (*Lehrgebiet*) to be cultivated instead of systematic philosophy, but a complementary sphere, so that ''true religion is based on the truth of systematic philosophy and hence from a subjective point of view genuine religiosity [is based] on the maturity and lucidity of systematic cognition,'' p. 137. See also H. Cohen, *Religion und Sittlichkeit,* J.J.G.L., Vol. 10 (hereafter, R.u.S.), p. 104 ff. See Cohen's lecture mentioned above, ''Die Bedeutung des Judenthums, etc.,'' p. 2: ''The end of all the monotheistic religions is moral progress . . . until their completion (*Vollendung*) in scientific ethics.'' The use of the German word *Vollendung* from the verb ''vollenden,'' to ''terminate'' and to ''perfect,'' best expresses the classical Christian attitude toward Judaism as a religion that is ''finished,'' that is, has brought things to an end and come to an end with the birth of Christianity; on the relation between this thought structure and Hegel's conception, see Nathan Rotenstreich, *The Recurrent Pattern, Studies in anti-Judaism in Modern Thought,* London, 1963, p. 72 ff.

40. R.u.S., p. 113.       41. Ibid.

man, and not God, is responsible for his deeds and ethical decisions. For man to maintain his autonomous position he need not be endowed by a divine power with ethical uniqueness or, as in Christianity, by divine grace *gratia inspirationis* or by mediation *auxilium gratiae,* physical or spiritual. Man as a rational being is the source of his own morality with the power of independent decision and the possibilities of moral renovation.[42]

Having demonstrated the affinity between the two religions, Cohen demonstrated the superiority of Judaism. In Judaism, God is the basis of the unity of nature and ethics, but He stands outside of both and cannot be absorbed by either. Every confusion of the limits between God and man, such as exists in pantheism, every mediation between the two, as in Christianity (for example, the Johannine incarnation of the logos), deprives God of his absolute transcendent essence and man of his autonomous status as a moral being. The irrational penetration of God's saving grace or his Son's redeeming love into the human plane separates religion from morality. God loses his unique status as absolute, and man his moral autonomy. Judaism addresses itself exclusively to man's moral will. It does not regard man as depraved by original sin and in need of God's grace as does Pauline Christianity, but as a being capable of *selbstständige Sittlichkeit* (independent ethics), that is, of directing his impulses toward ethical goals. By resisting the preferred boon of God's unmerited grace, Judaism is more faithful to the principle of autos-nomos and hence to man's ethical essence.[43]

Apparently, some of the spokesmen of Liberal Judaism, such as I. Goldschmidt in his polemical work against A. Harnack, and Moritz Lazarus in his major work *Ethics of Judaism,* wished to retain Cohen's view of man as the focal point of logical philosophical speculation, religious consciousness, and moral conduct. But Cohen's system treated the concept of man and not man himself, the concept of God and not God, concepts that serve as the bearers of pure intellectual thought, whereas an increasing number of scholars of that period were less interested in abstract intellectual systems than in the possibility of the anthropological or existential application of religious and ethical thought to social problems.

Cohen insisted that scientific knowledge and logical speculation alone

42. Ibid., p. 124.
43. H. Cohen, *Der Begriff der Religion im System der Philosophie,* Giessen, 1915, p. 66. See Rotenstreich, p. 71 ff, and esp. 85 ff.

can guarantee objective certainty and consequently the freedom of ethical decision. True ethics, autonomous ethics, is possible only within the confines of speculative cognition,[44] for only pure reason and logical thought can save man from being enslaved by myth and irrationality. This strenuous philosophical endeavor of Cohen and the Marburg school to expound and justify moral conduct and religious consciousness on logical principles did not satisfy the demands of an age eager to penetrate historical, psychological, and anthropological reality and not only the cognitive conditions of that reality. This was perhaps one of the principal reasons for the growing influence of the rival systems of Windelband, Dilthey, Troeltsch, Weber, and also of Paul Natorp and Wilhelm Wundt, all of which recognized the inadequacy of neo-Kantian idealism to construct a theory of knowledge capable of appreciating the needs of modern civilization and of liberating the generation from the notion that natural science was the archetype of all knowledge.

Neo-Kantian philosophy seemed to have had a profound influence in the sense that it provoked sharp criticism and opposition, and thus unintentionally strengthened the positivist historical approach and the "philosophy of life," associated with the names of Dilthey and his disciples, including Leo Baeck. Even in the early days of the neo-Kantian movement in the sixties the exponents of the school of *Völkerpsychologie* criticized Kantian schematism on the ground that it failed to reach empirical reality by restricting consciousness to an immanent analysis of the concepts of consciousness instead of studying the products of the collective intellect as objectively manifested in myth, language, religion, customs, and laws.[45] The deductive analogical structure of the neo-Kantian approach was felt to be inadequate by an increasing number of Christian and Jewish liberals who looked to their religious culture for positive answers to the existential questions of their day, to the pessimistic teachings of Schopenhauer, Nietzsche, and Hartmann, and to the widespread belief in the relativism of values as taught by positivism and social Darwinism. An instructive and characteristic expression of this general mood has come down to us not only in the writings of prominent persons but also in the testimony of average educated men, students, teachers, and members of the various liberal professions, Christians and Jews alike, such as the

---

44. R.u.S., p. 105 ff.    45. Z.V.P.S.W., 1866, Vol. 4, No. 4, p. 483.

students of Friedrich Paulsen at the end of the last century and of Paul Natorp at the beginning of this century. These testimonies are important for our discussion in that they indicate that we are dealing not only with an abstract intellectual problem but with the intellectual struggles of a historical, living community, important aspects of which we shall have occasion to refer to in the following paragraphs.[46]

In the neo-Kantian analogical deductive structure speculative thought seemed to be tautological and entangled in its categorial presuppositions. The failure of schematism in the transcendental critique to effect a transition from consciousness to phenomena themselves seemed to imprison man in an ivory tower, completely cut off from all empirical reality. The systematic efforts of the neo-Kantians to liberate consciousness from the restraints of cognized phenomena in themselves were achieved by evading the encounter with reality, and it was precisely this encounter that the generation of that day expected religion to undertake. To achieve objectivity the thinker had to enclose himself in a deductive circle of concepts devoid of phenomena and hence alien to reality, and to put concepts of cognition and their forms in the place of phenomena themselves which deductive and mathematical thought now treated as reality itself. It is hence not surprising that the generation at the turn of the century was disillusioned with the achievements of pure reason and turned to the popular philosophies of pessimism, nihilism, and materialism wherein it found relief from the rigorous and austere principles of neo-Kantian philosophy. The youth of that day had demanded a courageous response to their problems and not what they considered to be only abstractions, and in its *Auswegslosigkeit* embraced an irrational philosophy that was expressed in an inordinate veneration of materialism, in a pathetic affirmation of evil, in a denial of free will and all spiritual certainty, in a cynicism that despaired of moral improvement, and in pseudo-Schopenhauerian slogans of blind will as the inexhaustible source of suffering, as if the world and its history were nothing but fraud and futility and the life of man "solitary, poor, nasty, brutish, and short." Dr. Sigmund Gottwohl, one of the participants in a conference of Jewish teachers that was held in the winter of 1902, characterized this mood as the result of "a one-sided system that turns everything into a theory in

46. F.A., No. 8, 6-4/a.

which deductive thought revolves around itself, leaving man bereft of true reality and imprisoned within himself.'' [47]

In the face of the insufficiency of this purely rational approach, there arose in Protestantism and in Judaism another tendency, referred to at the beginning of this chapter, namely, the historical, philological, and, to a certain extent, anthropological approach which, as formulated by Ernst Troeltsch and subsequently by Leo Baeck in a relatively late work, hoped that history would be able to erect a scientific system which would do justice to objective scientific truth and at the same time enable us to deduce from historical research normative values relevant for our present day. [48] Hermann Cohen had denied all possibility of deducing normative values from empirical or historical investigation since normative authority presupposed rationality, autonomy, and freedom from all external conditioning and the use of a priori instruments, uninfluenced by a posteriori findings. On the other hand, the school of Dilthey, Troeltsch, Harnack, and a considerable number of Liberal Jews, including the adherents of the school of *Völkerpsychologie* and the apologists of the Wissenschaft des Judenthums, wished to proceed by analogy from the given to the desired, from the past to the present, from knowledge gained by empathy through participation in historical experience to the existential life of the here and now. As early as 1860 the young Dilthey felt that it was his mission to gain a deeper apprehension of the inner life of religion as it developed in the course of history through identification and experiential participation (*Erlebnis* and *Verstehen*) and bring his findings to the knowledge of his contemporaries whose horizon was limited to ''state and science.'' [49] Similarly, Steinthal during that same period felt that intellectual concepts

47. F.A., No. 4/a, recollections of a discussion among teachers on ''Zur Kritik der Herbart-Zillerchen Schule.'' In the same spirit, influenced by the views of Moritz Lazarus on Jewish ethics, discussions took place in the Association of Jewish Teachers, May 21–22, 1899, in Halberstadt; see discourse of Dr. Spanier of Magdeburg on ''Die Ethik des Judenthums und Herbarts ethische Ideen''; parts of the discourse and the discussions were printed in the literary journal, *Lehrerheim*, Breslau, 1899, Vol. 5, No. 282, p. 274; for the Jewish public aspect behind these discussions, see archival file G.A.J., G.A. M7/1.

48. In the original: ''die Gewinnung normativer religionswissenschaftlicher Erkenntnisse.'' E. Troeltsch, *Die Absolutheit des Christenthums etc.*, Tübingen, Leipzig, 1902, p. 4; for the development of Troeltsch's theses concerning the relativity of values as influenced by historicism and the derivation of positive values from history, see Leo Baeck, ''Theologie und Geschichte (1938)'' in *Aus drei Jahrtausenden, Wissenschaftliche Untersuchungen und Abhandlungen zur Geschichte des jüdischen Glaubens*, Tübingen, 1958 (trans. Michael A. Meyer, ''Theology and History'' in *Judaism*, Vol. XIII, No. 3, 1964).

49. *Der junge Dilthey*, ed. Clara Misch, Leipzig, 1933, p. 40.

and rules had no reality unless they were subjected to life itself and thus became personally relevant to the individual. Toward the end of the century we find that the two liberal religions were beginning to doubt whether a detached and objective method of interpretation could interpret the inner meaning of religious ideas and were seeking for a way to break away from "the closed circle into which the transcendental critique had fallen." [50]

The two liberal religions now turned to historical and philological studies in the hope that they would yield values relevant to the modern situation without forfeiting objectivity. This common effort, however, also gave rise to the rift which estranged the liberals in both religions, a rift whose dialectical development will be discussed in the pages that follow.

## Conflict within Unity

By the end of the nineteenth century Liberal Protestantism had become an explicit ideology that derived many of its conclusions from the critical historical and philological study of the Old and New Testaments and from the historiography of Judaism and Christianity. Behind this ideology was the attempt to make Christianity more palatable to the educated classes as a religion and as a component of German national consciousness and culture. With this end in view it conceived its principal task to be the renewal in modern form of the traditional Christian conception of the church fathers, according to which Abraham's birthright and blessing passed from the Jews to the believers in Jesus: "And the scripture, foreseeing that God would justify the Gentiles by faith, preached the gospel beforehand unto Abraham, saying, In thee shall all the nations be blessed. So then they which be of faith are blessed with the faithful Abraham. For as many as are of the works of the law are under a curse . . . no man is justified by the law in the sight of God . . . for, The righteous shall live by faith" (Epistle of Paul to the Galatians 3:7 ff). Israel in the spirit, that is, Christianity, was the true heir to the chosen people; but Israel in the flesh, which stubbornly refused to acknowledge

50. Or, in the words of Rabbi S. Maybaum at the beginning of the eighties: "To comprehend the reality of historical religious life systematically and critically illumined, and thus restore to the formal principles of knowledge, which have authority for the determination of rational necessities only within the limits of inner sense, their material content in its historical individuality." From F.A., No. 4/e, the fragment opens with "gegenstandsgleichgultiger Aprioprismus der neukantianischen Schule."

Jesus Christ as the Redeemer, Messiah, and Son of God, was the heir of a petrified pharisaism; and the historical existence of Israel as an abject, oppressed, and degraded people was a witness to the truth of the Christian faith.[51] Thus, by relying on biblical criticism and scientific findings derived from the study of history and philology, and by incorporating them in a historical structure (*Geschichtskonstruktion*) in the spirit of the age, Protestantism was able to renew the traditional conception of the ethical and religious superiority of Christianity in its role as the legitimate heir to the Law of Israel. Israel itself was destined to live on, sterile and incorrigible, as a petrified remnant of the days of the Second Temple, from the Return to Zion until the rise of ''talmudic rabbinism'' down to the present.

Christianity, then, is the authentic historical heir of biblical monotheism or of the original early religion of Israel as revealed in the ethical teachings of the prophets and in the Psalms, reaching its fulfillment in the glad tidings of Jesus Christ, the Messiah. Judaism, as distinguished from Israel, is a relatively late product of a long process of petrification and decay. In this connection Moritz Güdemann (in his *Jüdische Apologetik,* p. 63) pointed out: ''From the standpoint of the church, Judaism is only the withered branch of the religion of the Old Testament whose sap and vitality, by virtue of the New Dispensation, have passed to the side of Christianity.'' Güdemann went on to say that even in his day of scientific studies attempts were still being made, as by Julius Wellhausen and Eduard Meyer, to fix the date of this process of deterioration in Judaism (*Abwelkungsprozess*) as early as possible, in the days of Ezra and Nehemiah, so as to confirm the modern theological conception that Christianity represents the fulfillment and completion of the religion of Israel.

This historical explanation of the classical theological conception of the transference of election from an unfaithful Israel to Christianity was based on the scientific conclusions of the most prominent theologians—such as Friedrich Loofs, F. Weber, R. Smend, K. Marti, H. Holzmann, J. Wellhausen, W. Bousset, E. Meyer, H. Gunkel, and E. Schürer—who proved that Christianity was the rightful heir of Israel's original prophetic

---

51. Against this thesis the Jewish leaders stressed the opposite conception of R. Travers Herford: ''This is by no means to say that Judaism stands condemned by its rejection of Jesus'' in *Christianity in Talmud and Midrash,* London, 1903, p. 360; see also, Moritz Güdemann, *Jüdische Apologetik,* pub. by Gesellschaft zur Förderung der Wissenschaft des Judenthums, Glogau, 1906, p. 238 (hereafter, M. Güdemann). The words are quoted in opposition to the views of W. Bousset and E. Meyer, see ibid.

religion, of an Israel whose vitality had been exhausted by the time of the Babylonian exile and the Return to Zion as a result of successive wars, political crises, and economic hardships which increased the power of the privileged classes and the priesthood, but which impoverished the population and depleted the social and spiritual resources of the country. This malignant process had begun, according to these scholars, between the ninth and seventh centuries, that is, in the days when the prophets were still vigorously denouncing a corrupt society. The political and spiritual decline of the country had therefore begun with the Assyrian campaigns of conquest in the eighth century, especially those of Tiglath-Pileser in the third decade of that century. This process was accelerated by the expeditions of Sennacherib against Philistia and Judah at the end of the seventh century and by the wars between Egypt and Babylonia in the days of Jehoakim, who reigned at the end of the seventh century, and especially during the period when the Babylonian kingdom was at the height of its power in the first half of the sixth century and by the campaign of Nebuchadnezzar against Judah in 587–586. The political and moral life of the country also declined as a result of internal dissension, of which we have ample evidence in the account of the prophet Jeremiah and also in the murder of Gedaliah ben Ahikam in the 680's. The nation's rapid decline became evident in the social and economic entrenchment of the privileged classes and the priesthood, beginning with the Return to Zion in the third decade of the sixth century, in the days of Ezra and Nehemiah, until the middle of the fifth century. The lowest point was reached in what was called "the rule of Pharisaism," with its sterile legalism that extinguished all hope of deliverance and made the dissolution of faith certain. The Jewish settlement continued to be visited by unending calamities during the Greek rule in Palestine between the Seleucid and Ptolemaic dynasties, beginning with the conquests of Alexander the Great in the third decade of the fourth century. These disasters were followed by the conquest of Palestine by Antiochus III (the Great), the wars of Judah Maccabee, the wars of liberation of Jonathan and Simon from 167–135 B.C., and throughout the period of the Hasmoneans, from Alexander Jannai to the Roman subjugation of the country in 63 B.C. and, finally, the internal wars during Herod's reign on the eve of Jesus' appearance as the Messiah. All this reduced the nation to such a state of despair that it seemed it could be saved only by supernatural power; and this prepared the ground for the coming of the Redeemer and the rise of Christianity.

In his famous work *Das Wesen des Christenthums,* Harnack, relying on the researches of Wellhausen, summed up this perpetual suffering of the Jewish people from the historical and theological point of view: "For two hundred years one blow followed another, beginning with the dreadful days of Antiochus Epiphanus, and the people have still found no rest." Harnack then enumerated the causes for the economic, cultural, political, and religious crisis, such as the civil war in the days of the Hasmoneans, the persecution by the Romans, the cruel reign of Herod, the Edomite, and so on. These crises produced a moral and material decline so devastating that the only salvation to be hoped for was God's redemptive grace. This historical interpretation of the deterioration of pre-Christian Judaism was directed against modern Judaism and supported by the indefatigable researches of biblical scholars who were highly esteemed by both Christians and Jews, among whom was E. Schürer who characterized the exegetical methods and the pilpul of the halacha as repugnant "especially to the modern consciousness." [52]

Another scholar who looked upon Christianity as the continuation of ancient Israel before it degenerated into Judaism was Julius Wellhausen who, in his *Pharisäer und Sadduzäer* (1874), maintained that the authentic traditions that have come down to us in the early gospels clearly indicate the degenerate character of Judaism on the eve of Jesus' revelation. In his exposition he drew a sharp contrast between the formalized sterile worship of postexilic Judaism and the natural religion of the early Israelites for whom religion was the very breath of life. Jesus was therefore not opposed to genuine biblical Judaism but to a Judaism which, under the corrupt influence of the scribes and pharisees (as related in Matthew 23), had ceased to be true to itself. A similar approach was taken by R. Smend who regretted that the place of the living message was taken by the holy book; the conscience of Israel so clearly perceived in the prophetic utterances was not fully and distinctly expressed in Holy Writ and often departed, sometimes deliberately, from conscience thanks to the holy book (*Lehrbuch der alttestamentlichen Religionsgeschichte,* 2d ed.

52. E. Schürer, *Geschichte des Jüdischen Volkes in Zeitalter Jesu Christi,* Leipzig, 1898–1902, Vol. II, par. 28, "Das Leben unter dem Gesetz." In this chapter Schürer speaks of the talmudic halacha which "because of its excessive casuistry, which is in part ludicrous and in part morally questionable, is particularly offensive to the modern consciousness."

Freiburg i.B., 1899, p. 290). Although the holy writings deplore the nation's moral decline and castigate sin it was still possible, Smend said, to interpret the laws, prescriptions, and ordinances to suit one's convenience and allay one's conscience—which could not be done with the personal, unmediated message of the prophets and Jesus.

Scholars like F. Loofs and C. H. Cornill contributed to this historical construction on the highest scientific and intellectual level and with due circumspection in making value judgments. In their opinion prophecy ended after the Return to Zion and was not renewed until the time of John the Baptist. A similar approach that emphasized the persecution of the prophets by the Pharisees is also found in Cornill's *Introduction to the Old Testament* (1905); in his exposition of this historical period Eduard Meyer also gave a prominent place to the decline of Judaism.[53] Since Judaism had begun to deteriorate at an early period, whatever Jewish religious or philosophical creations existed in the Hellenistic period must have originated in Hellenistic culture; even Philo was absorbed by this culture and could not have influenced the development of Judaism, which was then completely dominated by the Pharisees and the talmudic legalistic spirit, but only the development of Christianity and western civilization.

Christian biblical scholars were thus able to prove that the national and ethnic isolation within Judaism began with the Return to Zion, as testified by the ordinances of Ezra and Nehemiah in such matters as the relation to the Samarians, the expulsion of foreign wives, or the cessation of prophecy. As a result of these changes faith, as understood by the Christians in the sense of ''the duties of the heart'' or as ''devotion to the revelation of

---

53. Friedrich Loofs, *Leitfaden zum Studium der Dogmengeschichte,* Halle, 1906, p. 36 ff; C. H. Cornill, *Der Israelitische Prophetismus,* 3d ed., 1900, p. 177. Among the replies of the Jewish apologists, see Eschelbacher, p. 22 ff; the essay of Felix Perles, ''Die Welt,'' 1899, No. 15, pp. 13–14, which later appeared in his book *Jüdische Skizzen,* Leipzig, 1912 (hereafter, Perles), p. 239 ff; see there additional critical remarks by both Jewish and Christian scholars. In this collection by Perles we find critical essays on E. Schürer, pp. 242–250; also interesting bibliographical material on many of the critics but also of scholars who supported Schürer's interpretation, including Harnack, ibid. p. 246. See also the critical reaction of Schreiner, ibid., p. 33 ff. On Eduard Meyer and the other Christian historians, see the instructive study, Hans Liebeschütz, *Das Judenthum im deutschen Geschichtsbild von Hegel bis Max Weber,* Tübingen, 1967, chap. ix, p. 269 ff, also Liebeschütz's analysis of the difference between the systems of Wellhausen and Meyer, ibid. p. 277 (hereafter, Liebeschütz).

grace in the gospels,'' began to decline and instead of a religion of love we find ceremonial worship dictated by primitive fear which, after the Destruction of the Temple, departed further and further from its ancient source in Israel and finally atrophied under the burden of talmudism and an elaborate system of harsh laws.[54] This process of degeneracy within Judaism was interpreted by the new historiography as retribution for the impenitent Jews who refused to acknowledge Christian salvation. Moreover, from the very beginning Providence had assigned to Judaism the task of preparing the ground for the advent of the Redeemer and so should be regarded as nothing more than the preliminary stage of Christianity. Its continued wretched existence, however, as was taught by the church fathers could only serve as a living witness to the true faith of Christianity.

This view of Jewish existence was reinforced by Hegel, who was convinced that the Absolute Spirit had been made manifest in history and that the truths of Christianity had already penetrated the real world through the agency of the state. Judaism had exhausted its initial vigor and had no reason to survive, so that historiography could rehabilitate the old belief that Christianity was the legitimate heir to ancient Israel. At the beginning of the twentieth century this same idea was elaborated in a collection of popular essays, edited by Hermann Gunkel, devoted to the relevancy of Christianity to the spirit of the age. Several prominent persons representing various schools of Protestant thought contributed to this collection, among them Adolf Deissmann, Rudolf Eucken, Wilhelm Herrmann, and Georg Wobbermin. From his analysis of the various types of literary composition in the Old Testament and his study of the popular origins of religious belief, Gunkel concluded that ''ancient Israel was at the outset not a people of the Torah, as has been commonly assumed until now, but happened to fall under the rule of the Law only in the period after the Babylonian exile, when the country was devastated and when its people

54. A typical expression for this conception current among the Conservatives is Gerhard Uhlhorn (Abt zu Loccum), *Der Kampf des Christentums mit dem Heidentum: Bilder aus der Vergangenheit als Spiegelbilder für die Gegenwart,* Kloster Loccum, 1885, 7th ed., Stuttgart, 1924, p. 68: ''Israel had a twofold task. It had to provide a place for the birth of Christianity, and it also had to pave the way to the pagan world.'' Although this work by a conservative priest had no scientific pretensions and was rooted in Lutheran theology and even intended for religious edification, there is a striking parallel between its conception of Judaism's task, namely, to make way for Christianity, and the conception of Protestant historiography discussed above, despite the different terminology and criteria of the latter; see ibid. p. 69 ff.

(*Volkstum*) were in the gravest danger.'' [55] Such a degeneration, Gunkel continued, need not be regarded as a disparagement of Judaism, for it is a common fate of nations and cultures and a typical historical pattern whenever people lose their political independence or suffer a national tribal dissolution. The life of such a nation, especially when driven into exile, becomes fixed in rigid, institutionalized forms as happened, for example, to the Patriarchate of Constantinople. This process also explains the decadence that set in with the establishment of the Second Temple, the principal cause of which was the conversion of ''the life of the people into a church.''

A new trend arose that exerted a profound influence on Liberal Protestant ideology and on the theological thought—the literary, philological, and critical studies undertaken by higher criticism, including the New Testament.[56] The investigation of the sources and the various layers of the Bible began in the middle of the eighteenth century when the French physician Jean Astruc discovered the presence of two interwoven narratives running through the book of Genesis that used the two different names of God, Jahwe and Elohim—and hence called the J (Jahwistic) and E (Elohistic) narratives—a discovery that proved that the Law of Moses was not the product of a unique revelation possessing metaphysical authority. This conclusion was confirmed by later studies in the course of the following century which deciphered these narratives with greater precision, especially by the school of Graf Wellhausen and even more radically with the publication of Eduard Meyer's historical study *Die Israeliten und ihre Nachbarstämme* (1906). The Law was not given by Moses; it was the product of a complex historical process, and hence the source of its authority was not absolute but relative. Only some parts, such as Exodus 18–24, can be considered to be of a relatively early date, the end of the tenth or ninth century B.C., and even these chapters have come

55. H. Gunkel, ''Das Alte Testament im Licht der modernen Forschung,'' in *Beiträge zur Weiterentwicklung der Christlichen Religion,* ed. A. Deissman, et al., München, 1905, p. 43 ff.

56. In the analysis of this subject we are not concerned with biblical criticism as such but with the relations between Protestants and Liberal Jews insofar as they were influenced by biblical criticism, which has been our procedure with respect to the other currents of thought in the critical historiography of those days. Our interest here is in sources that reflect the mood of the community and the prevailing climate of opinion, not in the methods of professional investigators primarily; hence, for background we refer to only one such study, Hans Joachim Kraus, *Geschichte der Historisch Kritischen Erforschung des Alten Testaments, von der Reformation bis zur Gegenwart,* Neukirchen, 1956, chaps. vii–viii.

down to us in a later revision in which the Judaistic tendency was already conspicuous. The greater part of the Pentateuch was composed about the middle of the eighth century B.C. and contains the first expression of priestly consolidation whose center was in Ephraim. These sources also have come down to us in a much later Judaistic revision, as is testified by the Elohistic names from Genesis 15:5 to Joshua 24:33. These Jahwistic and Elohistic layers are skillfully interwoven to reflect "the Jahwistic historical view," as in Genesis 37:12 ff, especially after the middle of the seventh century B.C., and in this layer some of the early sources in the books of Deuteronomy, Judges, Samuel, and Kings were edited in the spirit of the Deuteronomist.

The last stage in the redaction of those layers in which there is still a breath of the authentic prophetic spirit of Israel was concluded in the days of Josiah in the last quarter of the seventh century with the codification of Deuteronomy and with the centralization of sacrificial worship in the temple at Jerusalem (2 Kings 23), a theory that was generally accepted by Old Testament scholars and by the Liberal Protestant intellectuals. Thereafter, in the Babylonian exile and with the Return to Zion, the priestly code was dominant, that is, after the sixth century Judaism began to displace Israel: the priesthood silenced prophecy, the ritual law and its barren forms drove out genuine religious and ethical feeling. The early sources were again subjected to revision, this time in the spirit of the priestly code whose principal aim was to extend the influence of the priests and scribes. The ground was thus prepared for the rule of the Pharisees on the one hand and for the growth of Christianity as the heir of Israel in the spirit on the other.[57]

The Psalms also were now interpreted as the product of a much later period. The Davidic Psalms 3–46, with the possible exception of Psalms 10:6 and 23, were assigned to the days of Ezra and Nehemiah, and Psalms 41–71 to the middle of the fourth century. The novel aspect of this exegesis was not only its chronology, but the need to make these psalms an authentic spiritual source of Christianity. Such an interpretation required a later chronology. Since both historiography and biblical criti-

---

57. Liebeschütz, chap. viii, p. 245 ff. Of the many typical Jewish reactions, which apparently attempted to remain within the confines of scientific study but which reflected apologetical tendencies, see H. Steinthal, Z.V.P.S.W., Vol. 11, p. 1 ff; Vol. 12, p. 253 ff; Vol. 20, p. 47 ff. For the scant interest shown by Jews in biblical criticism, see Perles, p. 102 ff: "Judentum und Bibelwissenschaft."

cism wished to prove that the Jews were incapable of creating or absorbing ethical values, profound literature, or inspired songs during the period of the Babylonian exile or the Return to Zion (called the exilic and post-exilic periods in the language of biblical criticism), it was imperative that they be regarded as early, perhaps indirect sources of Christian inspiration.

In connection with this subject we consulted not only well-known relevant studies, but also the testimony of students and well-informed individuals, mostly members of the liberal professions with literary, cultural, and what some of them called "educational-national" interests. The testimony derived from these sources confirmed the general theological tendency of scholarly research in that period that Christianity was the legitimate successor of ancient Israel, with all its claims and prerogatives, charged with the task of developing and preserving the ethical elements in the religion of the prophets and in the psalms, the finest flower of the Israelite religion before it degenerated into sacrificial worship, the halacha of the Schulchan Aruch and the other traditions of the oral law.[58]

Thus the prophet Isaiah was called "the evangelist among the prophets" on the basis of the messianic prophecy in 7:14, 9:1 ff, 11:1 ff, and especially Deutero-Isaiah 40–66. The book of Isaiah was now considered to be an amalgam of different layers originating in the eighth to the fourth or even third century before the common era. Here as well Liberal Protestant ideology was dependent on the investigations of scholars, some of whom employed entirely different methods in arriving at their conclusions, like Julius Wellhausen and Eduard Meyer. The upshot of these conclusions was that the literature of prophecy and the psalms is not Jewish but Israelite; hence, its theological essence is Christian and its historical teaching pre-Christian. Hermann Gunkel in his *Ausgewählte Psalmen* (1904) described Psalm 103 as "a piece of the New Testament within the Old Testament." The New Testament also speaks of Judaism's rejection of prophecy, as: "Woe to you, scribes and Pharisees, hypocrites! for you build the tombs of the prophets. . . . Thus you witness against yourselves, that ye are the sons of those who murdered the prophets. . . . You serpents, you brood of vipers, how are you to escape being sentenced to hell? Therefore I send you prophets and wise men and scribes, some of whom you will kill and crucify, and some you will scourge in

58. F.A., Nos. 1, 4.

your synagogues . . . that upon you may come all the righteous blood shed on earth . . . O Jerusalem, Jerusalem, killing the prophets and stoning those who are sent to you'' (Matthew 23:29–37). These sources served as a kind of scientific verification of Liberal Protestant theological doctrines and were taught as such in the nation's schools. In addition, A. Harnack elaborated the basic conception of Daniel Schenkel, one of the fathers of Liberal Protestantism and the author of the *Charakterbild Jesu,* according to which the decisive step in alienating the Jews from the prophets was ''the internalizing of the God idea.'' [59]

On the basis of the researches of biblical scholars, including Friedrich Bleek, Friedrich Loofs, and C. H. Cornill, Liberal Protestantism assumed that since legal talmudism rejected prophecy as early as the Persian period or the beginning of the Second Temple, we must regard the period after the Babylonian exile as an early source of Christianity. In this it was also influenced by the researches of Ernest Renan which placed the theological beginning of Christianity in the eighth and seventh centuries B.C., the centuries in which the great Hebrew prophets arose and in which were enunciated the basic religious ideas: Israel as a people of God, monotheism, and the worship of God with devotion and pure faith. Whereas Renan's words were cited by Jewish apologists to prove the dependence of Christianity on its Jewish origin, Liberal Protestant ideology interpreted them in an opposite sense, namely, that the original Israel from which the great early prophets sprang ended in ritual legalism, rigid formalism, and narrow-minded particularism, with the rise of Judaism. Only with the renewal of prophecy which began with John the Baptist, contended C. H. Cornill and his followers, was Israel an authentic continuity, so that ''those among the Israelites, the sons of Abraham, who preceded the Jews and who as yet knew nothing of the Law . . . were already Christians . . . as was proclaimed by Paul the Apostle: 'The promise to Abraham and his descendants, that they should inherit the world, did not come through the law but through the righteousness of faith.' '' [60]

59. The source of Daniel Schenkel's definition in his book *Charakterbild Jesu,* Göttingen, 1864, appears in a more elaborate form in his *Bibellexicon, Realwörterbuch zum Handgebrauch für Geistliche und Gemeindeglieder,* Leipzig, 1869 ff, Vol. II, p. 515; see Julius Wellhausen, *Israelitische und jüdische Geschichte,* Berlin, 1895, p. 213.

60. This conclusion is summarized by the Freunde der Christlichen Welt in a conference held in 1905, F.A., No. 6/b. The New Testament source is Epistle to the Romans 4:13; for a discussion of Renan's conception see, Eschelbacher, p. 21. For Renan's school, see

Historical and philological studies and biblical criticism had undermined many of the accepted beliefs of the New Testament and historical Christianity as they had many of the traditions of the Jewish heritage as well as many social conventions. By the end of the nineteenth century Liberal Protestants had accepted the scientific conclusions of Ferdinand Christian Baur and the Tübingen school and, with reservations, those of D. F. Strauss as to the relatively late date of the Epistles attributed to Paul which were assigned to a period not earlier than the second century. Similarly, after the studies of K. J. Weizsäcker, W. Wrede, A. Jülicher, and others, the generally accepted view was that the Fourth Gospel of John had been composed at a much later date, so that Liberal Protestantism based its contentions almost solely on the first three gospels. These early sources generally agreed that the testimony of Mark, as revised by Matthew and Luke and with additions of relatively early traditions derived from Peter, is one of the earliest of all the documents and one of the most authentic. The middle of the second century was thus taken to be an important stage that separated a Christianity that was still attached to its Jewish origin from a Christianity that had embarked on the successful mission of the Apostles to the heathen or that had made a sharp distinction between the observance of the Torah and its commandments on the one hand and their nullification for the sake of the redemptive faith in the Messiah on the other by adopting the redemptive faith of the Messiah in the spirit of Paul's Epistle to the Galatians 2:20–21: "It is no longer I who live, but Christ who lives in me; and the life I now live in the flesh I live by faith in the Son of God, who loved me and gave himself for me. I do not nullify the grace of God; for if justification were through the law, then Christ died to no purpose." [61]

The conspicuous element that emerged from these chronological investigations was the intellectual and ideological impulse that brought with it new turns in the reciprocal relations between the two liberal religions. As the historical point of view became more widespread and the literary and philological study of the New Testament more acceptable, it became clear

---

Shmuel Almog, ''The Racial Motif in Ernest Renan's Attitude to Judaism and Jews'' (Hebrew), *Zion,* Vol. 32, Nos. 3–4, 1967, p. 184 ff. The excerpt from Cornill from the above F.A., No. 6b; see C. H. Cornill, *Der Israelitische Prophetismus,* 3d ed., Strassbourg 1900, p. 177.

61. From discussions in the conference, above n. 59; see also W. Nigg, p. 253 ff; Stephan-Schmidt, p. 233 ff.

to the Protestants themselves, including the circles of the *Christliche Welt,* that the early sources were not only early chronologically and still attached to their Jewish source, but that in them and not in the later post-Pauline traditions were to be found the values to which modern liberal man could still respond. Prominent among these sources is the Sermon on the Mount with its prophecies of consolation and its beatitudes in praise of the meek, the poor, the merciful, the pure in heart, and the peace-makers; also the sentiments and beliefs in the Paternoster, including the verse (Deuteronomy 14:1) that is regarded as the universal principle of Israel's religion: "You are the sons of the Lord your God," and also the commandment: "Thou shalt love thy neighbor" in its early version before it was changed in Matthew 5:43, 44: "You have heard that it was said 'You shall love your neighbor and hate your enemy,' But I say to you, Love your enemies." The traditions that modern man found difficult to accept, even in their new interpretations, were those that arose when Jewish Christianity separated from post-Pauline Christianity, especially with the ascendancy of the heathen Christians, for example, the magical and irrational traditions, such as the sacramental nature of the body of Jesus as the basis on which the church was founded (Epistle to the Romans 12:5) or the principle of apostolic succession, against which the liberals fought with great determination, these being principles from which—as Harnack, Loofs, and others pointed out—even the conserva-tive Lutheran Protestants could not free themselves. In the vehemence of this struggle Friedrich Loofs publicly accused the Conservatives of "saint worship" (*Heiligendienst*) and of succumbing to spiritual decay: "The leavened Catholic dough deserves to be swept away . . . the gospels in essence ask of man nothing beyond faith . . . and to be possessed by Jesus the Messiah." [62] These traditions reflected "not only the chrono-logical transition from Judaism to Christianity, but the spiritual transition from a consistent monotheistic to a syncretic or even pagan faith." [63]

After the nineties some of the Liberal Protestant leaders—principally, the historians and theologians Adolf Hausrath, Wilhelm Herrmann, Fer-dinand Kattenbusch, and Adolf Harnack—summed up the contributions of modern research by stating that if Protestantism was to free itself from the remnants of paganism and idolatry of historical Catholicism which had not been entirely removed even by Luther's Reformation, and if it

---

62. Friedrich Loofs, *Leitfaden zum Studium der Dogmengeschichte,* Halle, 1906, p. 948.
63. Above, n. 57.

was to be a living force in the life of modern man, it must return to the original authentic sources of Christianity, to Jesus the man, to his life and message. In contrast to the approaches of the early critics in the schools of the life of Jesus, led by D. F. Strauss, it was now declared that this inner renewal also required a renewed acknowledgment of the historical and intellectual sources of the life of Jesus and his message, that is, of Judaism.[64] In the collection of essays mentioned above (n. 55), which was designed to strengthen Christian faith, A. Deissmann in 1905 stated this view as follows (p. 52): "Between the Old Testament and the New Testament there is no gap that cannot be bridged. Those who wish to sever the gospels from the Old Testament and from Judaism cut down the vine at its root." The evident purpose of Deissmann's discussion was to demonstrate that this continuity between Judaism and Christianity was not based on discord or contradictions, but on a refining process within Judaism itself until it attained the messianic consciousness of Jesus as one of Jewish origin who realized, completed, and thus ended the Old Testament and as the one in whom the New Dispensation was fulfilled.

For Liberal Protestantism, then, that which at the time was called "the essence of Christianity" found its chief expression in Jesus as revealed in the early gospels and in the historical Jewish sources. Historical and even chronological questions now assumed an importance with respect to the relations between the two liberal religions that went far beyond the scientific and historical sphere, questions as to whether Jesus departed from Judaism or whether such a departure was a later Pauline or post-Pauline phenomenon; when and why such a transition took place from the time of the message that announced the coming of the kingdom of God, which was still addressed to "the lost sheep of the house of Israel" (Matthew 10:6) to the Judaized dispersion and thereafter to the heathens; how the change occurred from the time that John the Baptist accepted immersion until the High Priest arose in the Sanhedrin and asked: "Art thou the Messiah?" and the fateful answer that Jesus gave concerning his mes-

---

64. This approach was clearly expressed in the struggle of the Liberal Protestants for reforms in the dogmatic traditions of the church, especially *das apostolische Glaubensbekenntnis*. The struggle became acute in 1891–1892, following the affair of the pastor Schrempf, see W. Nigg, pp. 279–283. Harnack's call for reforms in the dogmatic symbols in the church from a historical-critical approach (in 1892) was characterized by A. Stöcker as nothing but "liberalisierendes Gezücht," that leads to a "poisoning of the *Volksseele*"; ibid., p. 281 ff, for the views of the liberal theologians Ferdinand Kattenbusch and Wilhelm Herrmann.

sianic mission: "And Jesus said, I am" (Mark 14:60–62). In the eyes of the Liberal Protestants, then, the "Christian essence" was to be found in the early stages of Christian development and in the life of Jesus, that is, in Judaism and in its transition to Jewish-Christianity.[65]

The question of the separation of Christianity from the mother religion was a crucial question also for Liberal Judaism. It was clear from the polemical and apologetical writings that if it were established that Jesus and his message were rooted in Judaism and if Liberal Protestantism would realize the extent to which the synoptic gospels were bound up with biblical, prophetic, and pharisaic sources, the Christian strictures against the narrow-minded particularism and spiritual sterility of Judaism would lose their justification, at least in the eyes of the more enlightened and educated Christians. Since the opinions of the Liberal Protestants about Jews and Judaism as well as the scientific conclusions of Liberal Protestant scholarship greatly influenced the conceptions that the Jews had of themselves, their history, and religion, a confrontation of the two religions was inevitable as a condition of survival and as a necessary means of assuring their continued existence as friendly rivals.

A focal point for an extensive discussion of this subject was provided by a series of lectures given by A. Harnack at the University of Berlin during the winter semester of 1899–1900 on "Das Wesen des Christenthums." By the term *Wesen* Harnack and his contemporaries desired to indicate not the metaphysical substance of Christianity but its "essence," the ethical and spiritual elements in the gospel of Jesus which, despite the changes throughout history, remained constant, and were hence still relevant for contemporary man. The lectures represented an attempt to do justice to the moral and religious content of the gospels in the light of the secular culture of the nineteenth century. Harnack's intention in these lectures was to give a critical exposition of the unfolding Christian spirit, to define its essential faith, and to give it intelligible form for modern Protestantism and, to a large extent it consequently affected Lib-

65. At the center of these discussions we have the two different but complementary approaches of Wellhausen and Harnack. The question as to whether Jesus looked upon himself as the Messiah and thus erected an impassible barrier between himself and the other Jews while he was still alive or whether his disciples attributed messiahship to him is discussed in Harnack, p. 85; see these explanations in Eschelbacher's Jewish interpretation, pp. 11, 14, and especially beginning pp. 35 ff, 127 ff. Both Harnack and Eschelbacher stressed the authenticity of the gospels that attributed to Jesus himself his messianic consciousness, as Matthew 10:37; 11:2 ff; 16:13–20.

eral Judaism and the Wissenschaft des Judenthums. Harnack's work, which went through fifteen editions and was translated into fourteen languages, created a sensation from the moment of its appearance, soon became the subject of extensive discussions and controversies both among Christians and Jews, and was vigorously refuted in 1903 by Alfred Firmin Loisy in his famous work *L'Evangile et l'église*. Many leading members of the Jewish community took part in this debate—Leo Baeck, Joseph Eschelbacher, Moritz Lazarus, Israel Goldschmidt, A. Ackermann, Moritz Güdemann, Martin Schreiner, and others—for it was felt that Harnack's work and the polemics to which it gave rise were of vital importance for the future destiny of German Jewry.[66]

66. A. Harnack, *Sechzehn Vorlesungen über das Wesen des Christentums vor Studieren-den aller Fakultäten im Winter-Semester 1899/1900, an der Universität Berlin,* Leipzig, 1900 (*What is Christianity?* trans. T. B. Saunders, London, 1901). This work was considered after its publication an important expression of modern Liberal Protestantism. Professor Delbrück, the editor of the *Preussische Jahrbücher,* theological critics, and other scholars hailed the book as a signal achievement of its era, as the definitive answer of religion to the claims of science, a valiant defense of religion against the onslaughts of materialism, skepticism, and religious indifference, and as a renewed inspiration to Christianity in a form that appealed to modern man. The work engaged the best minds among the Christian and Jewish scientists, theologians, writers, and political figures, and in the first decade of the twentieth century became the source book for the development of modern theology and Liberal Protestant ideology. It also constituted a principal subject for public and private discussions among the leaders of the community, among Jewish scholars, apologists, teachers, and educators. For Christian reactions from the period we are discussing, see *Christliche Welt,* 1901, col. 931, 959, 963. Also important for our discussion is the criticism of W. Bousset, *Theologische Rundschau,* 1901, Vol. 4, p. 102 ff. An additional source, including the reactions of Harnack, is Introduction of Rudolf Bultmann to the new edition of the book, 1964, p. 7 ff. The principal Jewish reaction was Joseph Eschelbacher, *Das Judentum und das Wesen des Christentums,* pub. by the Gesellschaft zur Förderung der Wissenschaft des Judentums, Berlin (1905), 1908. The book was originally the author's lectures to Jewish students in 1904 in answer to Harnack's lectures on "Das Wesen des Christentums," 1899–1900. Of the Jewish answers, explanations, and studies the most important, in addition to the above work by Eschelbacher, is Leo Baeck, "Harnack's Vorlesungen über das Wesen des Christentums," M.G.W.J., 1901, No. 45, and thereafter his book *Das Wesen des Judentums,* 1905, which appeared in several editions, undergoing basic changes in keeping with Baeck's spiritual development; see 3d ed., Frankfurt a/M, 1923. For Leo Baeck's personality and teachings, see the interesting study by Akiba Ernst Simon, "Leo Baeck, Last Representative of German Jewry," which appeared as the introduction to the Hebrew edition of Baeck's *The Essence of Judaism: Elements and Beliefs* (Hebrew), Jerusalem 1968, pp. 7–54. In our discussion here of Harnack's attitude toward Judaism we have not touched on an important subject, namely, his views of Marcion and his negative attitude toward the Old Testament. We did not include this subject since most of the reactions of Christians and Jews appeared at a much later date, for the most part after the period we are discussing. But since Harnack's views of Marcion's negation of the Old Testament were al-

The question of Jesus and his relation to Jewish roots, as most of the questions that engaged the minds of theologians during the period we are discussing, arose in the middle of the eighteenth century. This question was systematically treated in the first half of the nineteenth century by Samuel Hirsch and Ludwig Steinheim; its basic historical clarification began in the fifties and sixties and attained its greatest public interest at the end of the nineteenth and the beginning of the twentieth century when the "essence" of Christianity and of Judaism became the subject of widespread discussion. In his well-known work, *Das Judentum und seine Geschichte* (2d ed., 1865), A. Geiger returned to the arguments that had been advanced by Joseph Salvador, Samuel Hirsch, Ludwig Philippson, and H. Graetz, and asserted that the message of Jesus, from the standpoint of its ethical essence and historical roots, was in no sense original.

---

ready formed at the beginning of his scientific career, the omission of this subject may impair the historical picture we wish to describe and analyze here. Hence, E. Simon's words are particularly important in this connection, see ibid., p. 21 ff. For Baeck's views on the question of the essence of Judaism and Christianity, see also Reinhold Mayer, *Christentum und Judentum in der Schau Leo Baecks,* Stuttgart, 1961, chaps. i, iii. An important book in the disputation that followed the publication of Harnack's famous work is Martin Schreiner, *Die jüngsten Urteile über das Judentum,* Berlin, 1902, pp. vii, 14–48. This apologetic work carries on the dispute also with the systems of Paul de Lagarde, Eduard von Hartmann, Eduard Meyer, Houston Chamberlain, and Professor Hermann Strack, one of the most distinguished scholars of his day in the historicotheological field and one of the leaders of the Mission to the Jews. The latter also wrote a highly instructive work on "Das Wesen des Judentums," based on a lecture he gave to the International Society of the Mission to the Jews in Amsterdam in 1906. The work first appeared in the *Jahrbuch der evangelischen Judenmission,* Vol. I, Leipzig, 1906, and was well received both by Christians and Jews. In the introduction to his booklet Strack observed that the dispute with Harnack helped both sides, Jews and Christians, to clarify the problem of their "essence," and with this in mind he mentioned a number of polemical works written by Jews against Harnack. Strack's lecture was reprinted in *Schriften des Institutum Judaicum in Berlin,* No. 36, Leipzig, 1906. Among the works cited by Strack, in addition to the above-mentioned works by Eschelbacher, Baeck, and Schreiner, a marked influence was exerted by books (with the same title, *Essence of Judaism*): Jelski, Berlin, 1902; Simon Mandel, Frankfurt a/M, 1904; Jakob Fromer, Berlin, 1905. Other books that caused a stir in intellectual circles were A. Ackermann, *Judentum und Christentum,* Leipzig, 1906, and much later a work that appeared after Strack's lecture, J. Eschelbacher, *Das Judentum im Urteile der modernen protestantischen Theologie Schriften,* pub. by the Gesellschaft zur Förderung der Wissenschaft des Judentums, Leipzig, 1907, p. 5 ff. Another polemical essay against Harnack, written in a popular style, appeared in German and in English, Felix Perles, *Was lehrt uns Harnack,* Frankfurt a/M, 1902, reprinted in his collection of essays, *Jüdische Skizzen,* Leipzig, 1912, pp. 208–231. Another polemical book following Harnack that was bitterly attacked by Orthodox Jewry was Israel Goldschmidt, *Das Wesen des Judenthums, nach Bibel, Talmud, Tradition und religiöser Praxis,* Frankfurt a/M, 1907.

The teachings of Jesus were only a continuation of biblical, prophetic, and pharisaic ethics, expressed in the language and spirit of our sages, of blessed memory, and especially of Hillel. What was new in the teachings of Jesus, whether introduced by himself or by Paul, was essentially the product of compromises with heathen worship or its acceptance. In this connection Geiger stated that Jesus "was a Jew, a pharisee Jew of Galilean stock, who shared the hopes of his time and who believed that these hopes were embodied in him. He walked in the ways of Hillel; in no way did he express a new thought." [67] Similar opinions were stated by Emmanuel Löw, Manuel Joel, Ludwig Philippson, and by many popularizers in the Jewish press. In the *Jüdische Zeitschrift* of 1872 (Vol. 10), which was still being edited by A. Geiger, we find this extreme view simply

---

67. Also quoted in Franz Delitzsch's polemical essay *Christentum und jüdische Presse,* Erlangen, 1882, p. 32 (hereafter, Delitzsch). The third edition of Graetz's *History of the Jews,* 1888, omitted significant portions of the original chapter on Jesus; see *Geschichte der Juden,* 2d ed., Vol. III, chap. xi. See also Vol. IV, chaps. v, viii, ix, and n. 9–14, 19. The original chapter is also in fragmentary form and is appended by Moses Hess to the end of his *Rome and Jerusalem,* Köln, 1862. On the dispute between Graetz and some members of the Wissenschaft des Judenthums and heads of the Jewish community, see archival file, G.A.J. G.A. M1/24, Historische Commission: Correspondenz mit D.I.G.B. In this correspondence between the heads of the D.I.G.B. and the Historische Commission, and between them and the leaders of local Jewish communities, the question concerning Graetz's not being a member of the Commission's Board of Directors was also discussed. Among the determined opponents of Graetz's nomination for such membership was Professor H. Breslau who, in his letters to Dr. Kristeller, the president of the Executive Committee of the D.I.G.B., dated Nov. 20, 1885, and Nov. 30, 1885, urged the directors of the D.I.G.B. not to yield to the pressure of the communities to appoint Graetz to the Historische Commission, his argument being that "our Jews have no idea what even the philosemites think of this man." In the course of his argument he characterized Graetz as one of those who had not yet liberated himself from the subjective approach to historical studies, an approach marked by a strong emphasis on Jewish nationalism and an aggressive attitude toward Christianity. Hence, Breslau added, non-Jewish historians had disassociated themselves from Graetz's historiography whereas the larger Jewish public had evinced great interest in his writings and even accepted his method. In reality the opposition to Graetz, aside from personal considerations, stemmed from the fear of "what will the Gentiles say"; indeed, Dr. Kristteller, in his various letters in the above-mentioned file, such as his letter of May 28, 1886, to the Jewish community of Hanover, commented: "The history of the Jews is at the same time the defense of Jews." A circular of the D.I.G.B. of Nov. 28, 1887, asking the local Jewish communities to support the Historische Commission publicly and financially stated: "There is no need to point out that these works, besides having scientific value, also have social significance. The latest agitation, designed to conceal hate and vulgarity under a mask of scientific terminology, found us unprepared. However, human affairs being what they are, we must expect to our sorrow that future generations will not be spared these conflicts and, hence, it is our duty to mobilize means of defense while there is still time."

stated: "Since he [Jesus] after all did nothing, they had to make of him a kind of God." [68]

In the course of this debate a public letter of protest by Franz Delitzsch was published (July 17, 1872), together with Geiger's answer. In this letter Delitzsch stated, among other things, that since Christianity had not ceased to defame Judaism and Jews in a vile manner, and since it had made every effort to persist in its offensive missionary work, especially among Jews who were ill-prepared to defend themselves either intellectually or psychologically, and since Christians "spend millions to subvert Judaism," German Jewry had no choice but to combat it. [69] Exchanges of this kind were common in the seventies and eighties. The edition of *Hizzuk emunah* of Isaac ben Abraham Troki, translated and annotated by Rabbi David Deutsch was published in 1865, with a second edition in 1873, and was well received by a large circle of readers in the last third of the nineteenth century. In the Introduction to this edition Rabbi Deutsch stated his belief that his contemporaries should familiarize themselves with Troki's refutations of Christian arguments, as well as of his criticism of the nonmonotheistic elements in Christianity, not only for purely scientific-historical reasons but also as a protection against missionary activities. [70] Martin Philippson, Gustav Karpeles, Felix Perles, and other popularizers of Jewish studies added that this was also necessary because an increasing number of Jews owed their knowledge of Judaism solely to Christian sources and knew nothing of the Jewish elements in Christianity or of the non-Jewish elements that were added to Christianity which, for the most part, were of an irrational, pagan, and hence nonmonotheistic nature. At the same time Martin Philippson warned against excessive polemical zeal in pursuing this line of argument which might well lead readers to heresy and atheism.

The Association of Jewish Teachers (Verband der jüdischen Lehrervereine im deutschen Reiche) and the Rabbinical Association (Rabbinerverband in Deutschland) recommended this edition by Rabbi Deutsch on several occasions and suggested that particular attention be paid to the following aspects: (1) the Christian doctrine of Incarnation, whereby the

---

68. Delitzsch, p. 36: "Da [Jesus] doch am Ende garnichts gethan, musste doch eine Art Gott aus ihm gemacht werden."

69. Ibid., p. 38.

70. David Deutsch, *Befestigung im Glauben von Rabbi Yitzhak,* 2d ed., Sohrau, Breslau, 1873: "It is in no way my intention to attack Christianity, but the Christian missionary zeal directed to Jews," p. iii.

Deity descended from the throne to the cross to make himself known to man through the ignominy of the Crucifixion, blurs the distinction between time and eternity, between man and God, endangering both the conception of an indivisible God and that of man's moral autonomy; (2) the Jewish sources of the gospels should be compared to the texts in the New Testament to show the distortions introduced by post-Pauline Christianity into the authentic biblical and pharisaic sources; (3) the large place occupied in the New Testament by tales of sorcery, signs, and evil spirits; and by the miracles and wonders performed by Jesus should be stressed until they were recognized as repugnant to common sense, rational thought, and pure monotheism.[71]

In the seventies and eighties the Jewish press devoted itself to this question with great zeal and often in an aggressive and provocative spirit. The efforts of Jewish scholars and apologists to disparage the impure and inconsistent monotheism of Christianity were essentially made to justify the continued existence of Judaism in modern times. This was pointed out by Shmuel Ettinger in his discussion of Graetz's historiography: "If we agree that Christianity is a monotheistic religion and that it contains the basic elements of ethics, then Judaism's task is finished and completed. The approach common to Graetz and to the great majority of those who advocate the Jewish mission with respect to Christianity is their devastating criticism of the Christian religion." [72]

At this stage of the controversy the question of Jesus as the Son of God and as the Messiah became acute, and hence also the concept of his incarnation and divinity. Jewish scholars—H. Steinthal, M. Güdemann, Leo Baeck, Joseph Eschelbacher, A. Ackermann, and Martin Schreiner—

71. F.A., Nos. 6, 7; see similar material in the archival file G.A.J., G.A. M7/1; for the historiography of this subject, see G. Lindeskrog, *Die Jesusfrage im neuzeitlichen Judenthum, ein Beitrag zur Geschichte der Leben-Jesu Forschung,* Uppsala, 1938, 369 pp.; idem, "Jesus als religionsgeschichtliches und religiöses Problem in der modernen jüdischen Theologie" in *Judaica,* Vol. 6, No. 3–4, 1950; Schalom Ben Horin, *Das Jesubild im modernen Judentum,* Z.R.G.G., Vol. 5, 1953, No. 3.

72. Shmuel Ettinger, *Graetz's Historiographical Achievement* (Hebrew), in the collection of lectures *Historians and Historical Schools,* pub. by Israeli Historical Society, Jerusalem, 1963, p. 89. A similar need was felt by the leaders of Liberal Protestantism, for whom even the attack against Judaism served as a means for strengthening their faith or even justifying their unique mission. At the height of the dispute with Harnack, following his lectures on *Das Wesen des Christentums* the Jewish apologists argued that Harnack in his efforts to renew Christianity by means of Liberal Protestantism was the one "who had dethroned the people of Israel and its religion in history, uprooted the gospels from its Jewish soil, and transplanted it to the soil of mankind," J.J.G.L., Vol. 6, 1903, p. 22.

maintained that these beliefs constituted the basic difference between Judaism and Christianity, between pure monotheism and a monotheism vitiated by pagan influences, between a religion that could withstand the scrutiny of modern man's rational and existential criticism and a religion that repelled modern man and drove him to materialism and atheism or at least to religious indifference. The traditions of the supernatural events in the life of Jesus, the miracles he performed in the sight of the Galileans and his disciples, his appearance in Jerusalem as the king of the Jews and as the redeeming Messiah of mankind, his sacrificial death that erased the sins of the community of believers (Matthew 26:26 ff), and, finally, his resurrection and ascension to the right hand of God—in all this the leaders of the Jewish community saw the essential differences between the two religions.

Protestant scholars, such as A. Hausrath, H. L. Strack, and A. Harnack, hastened to point out that Liberal Protestantism itself was engaged in a struggle within the church to purify Christianity, to cleanse it of its spurious accretions and alien traditions. At the height of the dispute with Harnack this view was summarized in the pages of the *Christliche Welt* (1901) in the following points: the essence of Christianity as revealed in the gospels consisted of the belief in the coming kingdom of Heaven through complete identification with Jesus the Messiah; in God who was symbolized by the image of the Father; in the absolute and unconditioned value of the human soul; in justice, righteousness, and the commandments of love. In this conception of Christianity, declared the *Christliche Welt,* there was no room for such outworn dogmas as the Trinity as expounded by Tertullian and formulated by the Council of Nicaea in 325 and in Constantinople in 381 A.D., the magical belief in Jesus as the Son of God, the Pauline doctrine of justification through the operation of irresistible grace without the moral test expressed in actual works, or the anthropological interpretation of the Johannine Logos that became flesh.[73]

One of the principal arguments put forward by Jewish apologists was that Liberal Protestantism in its criticism of Christian dogmas was actually returning to Judaism, which from the very beginning had rejected Christianity for the same reasons. In reality, however, Christianity could not disencumber itself of its pagan or irrational traditions to meet the temper of the new age as the Liberals hoped. These traditions were embedded in

73. Ch. W., 1901, col. 963.

the Christian calendar according to which the Christian lived, moved, and had his being, independent of his genuine beliefs—the holidays commemorating the Immaculate Conception, the Epiphany in memory of the three wise men before the cradle in Bethlehem, Good Friday in celebration of the sacrificial death of Jesus, Easter and the day of Sunday to mark the miracle of the Resurrection, and other holidays determining the life-rhythm of the Christian. The same is true regarding the belief in the divinity of Jesus, particularly the dogma of the Logos that became flesh, according to which God descended from heaven to enter into corporate union with man: "And the Word became flesh and dwelt among us, full of grace and truth; we have beheld his glory, glory as of the only Son from the Father" (John 1:14). These contradictions between Judaism and Christianity could be neither reconciled nor ignored by modern liberalism; but they could help the liberals in both religions to clarify their respective commitments and rival merits in their struggle for self-identification.[74]

After the seventies the dispute was exacerbated by a more aggressive attitude on the part of the Jewish spokesmen that did not shrink from using abusive and opprobrious language. Many traditions from the New Testament were singled out for ridicule, such as those depicting Jesus as a wonder-worker to demonstrate the truth of his teachings and his messiahship; also the answer that Jesus gave to two of John's disciples who asked him, "Are you he who is to come, or shall we look for another," that he had come to redeem and save, and a sign of that was that "the blind receive their sight and the lame walk, lepers are cleansed and the deaf hear, and the dead are raised up, and the poor have good news" (Matthew 11:2 ff). Criticism was also directed against Christianity's accommodation to paganism, whereby the faith in Jesus was corrupted to a kind of idolatry, for example, the word of the Lord spoken by the prophet Isaiah: "I am the Lord, and besides me there is no savior" (Isaiah 43:11) and the words in the psalm: "And he will redeem Israel from all his iniquities" (130:8) are attributed in the New Testament to Jesus as the Son of God, as Divinity incarnate from his birth until the full redemption

74. The words of Rabbi S. Maybaum at the conference of rabbis, teachers, and active members of the local Jewish communities, Berlin, 1884, according to the memoirs in the F.A., No. 1/b. A similar but stronger public statement was made twenty years later by Martin Philippson in his annual survey, in the Yearbook, J.J.G.L., 1902, pp. 2–3; see also M. Güdemann, in the Introduction, p. xi.

that came into the world through him: "She will bear a son, and you shall call his name Jesus, for he will save his people from their sins" (Matthew 1:21).

At the beginning of this period of polemical intensification Treitschke wrote in the pages of the *Preussische Jahrbücher* (1879) that the calumny, malice, and ridicule of the Jewish "journalists" in attacking Christianity "have been presented to our people as the latest achievements of the illuminati." We find similar views expressed by Eduard von Hartmann and by the clergy in both the rural areas and in the large urban centers.[75] Also the spokesmen of the Jewish community, its scholars, and spiritual leaders, foremost among whom was Moritz Lazarus, deplored the form that the dispute had taken as inappropriate and unprofitable and contrary to the basic thesis of those who defended the "essence of Judaism," according to which Jesus and his teachings were rooted in Jewish tradition and in the school of Hillel and his contemporaries.

An additional element in this controversy was introduced by Franz Delitzsch, one of the leading figures in the Mission unter Israel and one of the great biblical scholars of his generation. At the end of his days (1882) he expressed his disapproval of the abusive polemics of the Jewish press in defaming Jesus with such vulgar and paltry criticism, such as comparing the celebration of his birth with Astarte worship, or drawing a parallel between Jesus and Balaam (following the midrashic homilies to Numbers 22:5 ff) in the manner of the Jewish apologist Joseph Stier, in his villifying essay in the *Jüdisches Literaturblatt* of August 3, 1881, according to which our sages, of blessed memory, applied Balaam's words to Jesus and compared him to a sorcerer, an interpreter of dreams, and a false prophet.[76] In his comments Delitzsch confessed that despite his vigorous and consistent opposition to scientific and racial anti-Semitism, including the anti-Protestant anti-Semitism of August Rohling, he could not help agreeing with the latter's denunciation of the arrogant anti-Christian polemics indulged in by the Jews of Germany, Austria, France, and even the United States, which was a manifestation of Jewish national particularism and a presumptuous expression of Liberal Jews proclaiming their modern Judaism as the universal religion. Delitzsch's reference to Rohling was in connection with the polemical exchanges that followed the latter's popular anti-Semitic work *Talmudjude*. In his reply, *Franz*

75. P.J., Vol. 44, 1879, p. 573; Vol. 56, 1885, p. 429 ff.    76. Delitzsch, p. 18.

*Delitzsch and the Jewish Question* (1881), Rohling declared that his exposé of Judaism was provoked by the Jewish attack against Christianity, and it was necessary since many Christians were still unaware of the outrageous revilements against Christianity by the spokesmen of German Jewry.[77] Delitzsch reminded these Jewish spokesmen that a vindictive attitude on their part could only provide fuel for anti-Semitic propaganda, which was not only anti-Jewish but also anti-Christian and antireligious as was evident, for example, in *Babyloniertum, Judentum, Christentum* (Leipzig, 1882) by the well-known Orientalist, Professor Adolf Wahrmund, one of the leading exponents of racial anti-Semitism. Jewish criticism of the nonrational or pagan character of Christianity, continued Delitzsch, could only serve to strengthen the antimonotheistic tendencies in racial anti-Semitism, and it would be in the greater interest of Jews to make common cause against this danger together with the Christians. He agreed that the abusive language used by Jewish polemicists was understandable in the light of the Christian hatred of Jews throughout the centuries. Nevertheless, the time had come for the two religions to desist from this form of disputation and to discuss their common problems with dignity and scientific impartiality, animated by an enlightened and generous spirit, as indeed had been done by some Jewish scholars such as Moritz Steinschneider, Abraham A. Berliner, and Adolph Jellinek, and writers such as Berthold Auerbach and Ludwig Gompert.

Under the influence of scholars and apologists, such as A. Geiger, M. Joel, T. Reinach, M. Schreiner, and M. Güdemann, the dispute was confined to two aspects: the miracles of Jesus on the one hand and his divine nature on the other, this being incompatible with authentic monotheism and with man's moral autonomy and responsibility. Protestantism interpreted the teachings of the New Testament as a vindication of the purity and force of man's moral character that gathers strength from the life of Jesus and his redemptive death. Moreover, it appealed to the modern temper by its emphasis on the social factor in religion and on man's ethical vocation, and was thus authorized to speak to contemporary man about justice, philanthropy, progress, equality, moral rectitude, and freedom. The renewal of faith in Jesus and in his message could also serve, as Hausrath observed, to safeguard man's individuality against the corrosive influences of modern society.

---

77. F. *Delitzsch und die Judenfrage,* Erlangen, 1881, p. 49.

These same ideals were regarded by Liberal Jews as the essence of Judaism in its modern form. But to base such ideals on the religious or historical image of Jesus was in their opinion "a kind of personification of monotheistic values whose nature does not suffer any human likeness . . . and a transference of the source of man's ethical responsibility for his deeds from himself to a supernatural authority that deprives him of autonomous responsibility." [78] Joseph Eschelbacher, under the influence of Manuel Joel, examined in greater detail the irrational traditions about Jesus as well as the magical and demonic images as recorded in Mark 1:23 ff, 3:11 ff, 5:2 ff, 9:25 ff, and in Matthew 8:28 ff, 11:28 ff, 12:22 ff, and other sources that testify to the fact that the Christian interpretation of Jesus stressed the belief that "wherever he turned he drives out evil spirits, and these were the first signs to announce that he was the Son of God; he describes their ways, enumerates them, uses them in his parables, and also confers upon his disciples the power to drive them out." [79]

Together with this monotheistic impurity in the teachings of Jesus as the result of concessions to pagan influences, the Jewish apologists showed that the ideal qualities found in the character and sermons of Jesus were rooted in Jewish tradition, in biblical, prophetic, and psalmist literature, and in the teachings of the sages. Scholars like Harnack, Wellhausen, and Eduard Meyer agreed that the original contribution of Jesus consisted of his ability to extract from the sterile Judaism of his day, encumbered by national particularism and arid legalism at least since the time of the Babylonian exile, ethical treasures hidden in the Law of Israel and in the teachings of the prophets. Most of the Jewish leaders, however, whether scholars, popularizers, or public figures, agreed that the message of Jesus contained nothing that was not to be found in the ethical teachings of the Pharisees or of Hillel. That which may be considered new, they maintained, was introduced as an accommodation to the pagan world. [80]

---

78. A. Geiger, *Zur Kritik der Bibelkritik, Vortrag . . . Berlin, 1891,* pub. by Central-Anzeiger für jüdische Literatur, Frankfurt a/M, 1891, p. 2 ff.

79. J. Eschelbacher, p. 40; additional New Testament sources cited to show the irrational character of Jesus' images are: Matthew 12:43 ff, 13:39, 15:22, 17:18; Mark 5:8–14, 6:7 ff; Luke 8:2, 10:17 ff; Acts 8:17, 38, 19:13 ff; 1 Thessalonians 2:18; 2 Corinthians 6:15, 12:7; Ephesians 2:2, 6:16 ff; John 12:31, 14:30, 16:11.

80. Of the many works that deal with this subject, see M. Schreiner, *Die Jüngsten Urteile über das Judentum,* Berlin, 1902, pp. 6, 14 ff, 19 ff; also Eschelbacher's book for the

At this stage of the controversy there was general agreement that the source of Jesus' teachings was Jewish law and prophetic ethics, but disagreement arose as to whether Jesus liberated these sources from narrow national particularism and barren pharisaic legalism. Thus, for example, B. Stade and A. Harnack were of the opinion that the commandment to love one's neighbor gained in universalism and ethical force when it was transferred from Leviticus 19:18 to Mark 12:28-32. It was pointed out by Heinrich Graetz, Ludwig Philippson and his son Martin Philippson, Abraham Geiger, Leo Baeck, and others that the source of the ethical elements in Jesus' message was the Law of Moses, in Jewish teachings in at least one or two generations before the time of Jesus, and in Hillel's answer to the heathen who wished to become a Jew; "What is hateful to thee, do not unto thy fellow man: this is the whole Law; the rest is mere commentary" (*Talmud Babli,* Tractate *Shab.* 31a). In Hillel's dictum is to be found the universal human value of the commandment of brotherly love, and it was to this Jewish tradition that Jesus returned, only without Hillel's virtue of humility: "A man should always be as humble as Hillel" (*Talmud Babli,* Tractate *Shab.* 30b). These arguments were consciously polemical and ideological, for the purpose of the dispute was not only to discover historical or literary details or to investigate new sources, but to strengthen the faith and inner unity of the two rival yet closely related religions. In this connection Harnack argued that the tradition of the kingdom of Heaven as an ethical ideal that man should seek with all his heart and soul, the conception of God as Father, the universal principles of justice and love were the new ideas in the gospels as opposed to a petrified legalistic Judaism. To this Jewish apologists replied that the belief in miracles, in Jesus as the Messiah and as the Son of God, and other pagan influences found in the New Testament could not be attributed to Jewish sources, but the principle of the kingdom of Heaven in its monotheistic purity and historical roots was surely derived from the tradition of Israel, without making a distinction between Israel and Judaism. This idea was familiar to the Pharisees, and they even discussed it with Jesus (Luke 17:20 ff); it is also found in the Pentateuch (Deuteronomy 4:29): "But from there you will seek the Lord your God, and

---

most part; and Felix Perles' answer to Harnack, "Was lehrt uns Harnack," 1902, in *Jüdische Skizzen,* Leipzig, 1912, p. 208 ff; in ibid., p. 232 ff, "Die Jüdische Schriftgelehrsamheit zur Zeit Jesu, Besprechung des Gleichnamigen Vortrags von Prof. Oskar Holtzmann, Orient, Lit. Zeitung, 1902, No. 3, Spalte 114 ff."

you will find him, if you search after him with all your heart and with all your soul''; and also in Jeremiah 29:13: "You will seek me and find me, when you seek me with all your heart." Jewish prayers are replete with references to the kingdom of the Almighty, as is also the Pharisaic Aggadah even before the time of Jesus. The only new elements in Christianity, according to this argument, were some nonmonotheistic ideas introduced by Jesus, or some non-Jewish ideas, such as when he called himself the Son of Man, that is, the Son of God. Jesus thus became the only path to the kingdom of Heaven, or even to a metaphysical being identical with this kingdom; so that only he who believes in him and clings to him is eligible to be a member of this kingdom.

In answer to Harnack's argument I. Goldschmidt, Joseph Eschelbacher, and Martin Schreiner declared that the belief in "God as Father, and the absolute value of the human soul"—a belief that Harnack related to the concept of *Gotteskindschaft,* and which received its finest expression in the Lord's Prayer—was not original with Jesus, but deeply rooted in Jewish tradition. All the ideas of this Christian prayer (as it has come down to us in Matthew 6:9 ff and Luke 11:2 ff) are nothing but a continuation of what the Protestants call biblical Judaism and are derived from Jewish sources: Deuteronomy 14:1: "Ye are the sons of the Lord your God"; Psalms 103:13: "As a father pities his children, so the Lord pities those who fear him." In this connection Rabbi Joseph Eschelbacher quoted the words of Hugo Grotius to the effect that Jesus derived his thoughts and manner of expressing them, whether in the Lord's Prayer or in his ethical parables, from Hebrew sources, that is, from the biblical and pharisaic traditions in which he grew up.[81] The source of the idea of divine holiness in the Lord's Prayer was given by the apologists as Leviticus 22:32: "And you shall not profane my holy name, but I will be hallowed among the people of Israel"; and for the other verses of this prayer (Matthew 6:10 ff) they cited Jewish sources such as Mechilta to Exodus 15:4, tractate Berachot 16b, 17b, 29b, 70b. The apologists also discovered some sources in the Prayer Book, like the Blessing of the New Moon, some of the prayers of Rabbi Jochanan, R. Zira, R. Chaya, and Rab, which included the same motifs as in the Lord's Prayer: "May it be thy will, O Lord our God, to grant us long life, a life of peace, goodness, blessing, and prosperity, a life of freedom without fear of sin, shame or

81. J. Eschelbacher, p. 52 ff.

disgrace.'' And for the verse: ''For thine is the kingdom, the power, and the glory forever, Amen'' (Matthew 6:13) the apologists cited biblical and midrashic sources and also traditions found in the Prayer Book, among them the words of King David, which are recited by the cantor on taking the Scroll from the Ark, and repeated after him by the congregation: ''Thine O Lord is the greatness and the power, and the glory and the victory and the majesty'' (1 Chronicles 29:11). In this manner the apologists cited Hebrew and Jewish sources for the Sermon on the Mount and for other Christian motifs taken from the Psalms.

Jewish scholars of the Wissenschaft des Judenthums and spokesmen of the Jewish community maintained that the principal new idea introduced by Christianity was the antimonotheistic symbol of the ''Son of God''— which was only a translation of a pagan Greek motif. Influenced by Christian theologians, such as Oskar Holtzmann, Gustav Dalmann, and Adolf Hausrath, Jewish scholars stressed the fact that in the Christian-pagan tradition the image of Jesus as the Son of God was developed to a point where it became the complete Godhead. This line of argument was continued by Ludwig Geiger, Joseph Eschelbacher, Moritz Güdemann, and others who insisted on the essential historical connection between the concept ''Son of God'' and the antimonotheistic concept of the Logos. Philo of Alexandria still defined the Logos as the intermediary between God, as Creator and as absolute spiritual essence, and the world as creation and the essence of corporeality. The Logos thus served as the expression for creation, the power of the Creator, and the process of creation; it also served as an expression for the structure of emanation that made possible the transition from complete metaphysical being to incomplete ontic existence. But in the gospel of John the Logos is the Word that has become flesh; God himself, the invisible power of the Logos and its spiritual essence, is now incorporated in the body of Jesus as the *Deus visibilis,* and as a result we have the personification of God on the one hand and the deification of man on the other.[82]

A special place in the disputation was reserved for Harnack's argument that the New Testament, in contradistinction to the Old, introduced something new with respect to the commandment of love, the ''royal law'' (*nómos basilikos,* James 2:8) which is the basis of Christian humanism. The central point in this dispute was the Jewish criticism of the abolition

82. Ibid., pp. 59 ff, 112 ff, 144 ff.

of the observance of the commandments in Pauline Christianity and to a certain extent also in early Christianity. Most scholars and apologists relied on relatively later traditions, such as Paul's Epistle to the Galatians 3:10 ff, and argued that to assert the substitution of the belief in Jesus for the observance of the Torah and the Commandments constitutes not only a criticism of "pharisaic legalism" but a basic negation of the Law as the embodiment of ethics, and this is testified by Pauline Christianity, which places the Torah and the observance of the Commandments under a curse. It was pointed out by Leo Baeck, Joseph Eschelbacher, and others that there was a profound difference between the negation of the halacha in Pauline Christianity and Jesus' criticism of Pharisaic Judaism to which he himself belonged. Pauline Christianity, as expressed in the Epistle to the Romans 5:20 (see, ibid., v. 12 ff), effects a total breach not only with the Torah and the Commandments, but also with the principle of man's moral autonomy, for it regards man as incapable of self-responsibility or as qualified by nature to be the vehicle of rational and ethical powers. Before the superhuman figure of Jesus, man appears morally impotent to observe the Commandments, so that the negation of the Law and the Commandments in Pauline Christianity is in essence a total negation of man's ethical status.[83]

Joseph Eschelbacher, in adopting this extreme approach, relied on A. Hausrath's interpretation of Romans 7:14 ff, especially v. 23: "But I see in my members another law at war with the law of my mind and making me captive to the law of sin which dwells in my members"; and also Paul's words in the Epistle to the Galatians (5:17): "For the desires of the flesh are against the Spirit, and the desires of the Spirit are against the flesh, for these are opposed to each other, to prevent you from doing what you would." From this Eschelbacher concluded that "Paul totally denies that it is in the power of human nature to observe the law by its own strength, that is, to fulfill the ethical precepts. Sin dwells within man, in his flesh, and this is the law of his members." [84]

Pauline Christianity was criticized by both Liberal Protestants and Jews, although prompted by different motives. The criticism of Hausrath and other Liberal Protestants was made in order to strengthen Christian faith in Jesus' message as set forth in the first three gospels. The spokesmen of non-Orthodox Judaism, however, impugned Paul's attitude to-

83. Ibid., p. 146 ff.    84. Ibid., p. 147.

ward the law not because of a religious commitment to halachic ethics but because it regarded the law as a basic humanistic structure derived from purely rational categories and at the same time compatible with the historical truths of revelation peculiar to Judaism. Liberal Judaism thus found itself in a perplexing dilemma. In the negative criticism of the law in Pauline Christianity it recognized a basic motive for Jewish self-identity; on the other hand, however, it interpreted halachic law as a rational principle that had binding force in the daily life of the Jew only to the extent that it conformed to reason and only as it answered the needs of modern man.

Liberal Judaism took the view that Christianity, by holding that man can be redeemed from the bondage of sin only through Jesus, deprives man of his ethical autonomy and renders him powerless to fulfill the Commandments, as stated by Paul: "We know that the law is spiritual, but I am carnal, sold under sin. I do not understand my own actions. For I do not do what I want, but I do the very thing I hate . . . so then it is no longer I that do it, but sin which dwells within me. . . . For I do not do the good I want, but the evil I do not want is what I do." [85] In one of the discussions following the dispute with Harnack the Association of Jewish Teachers in Germany (non-Orthodox) summed up the Jewish view of Pauline Christianity as follows. The Christian doctrine of original sin and the miraculous status of Jesus as the Redeemer is irrational and antireligious, for it makes man a passive object caught in the coils of sin and unable to perform the Commandments; man is nailed down by his finitude and can only rise through the agency of indefectible grace, that is, by virtue of faith in Jesus the Messiah—and this can only lead to a stultification of his moral sense. The Liberal Jews were thus left in a position similar to that of their Protestant colleagues since for them neither the halachic tradition nor the principles of neo-Kantianism, according to which the theoretical source of religion resided in the concept of reason, had any binding force.[86]

85. Epistle to the Romans 7:14–20; the source and the above explanation were quoted in the program for teaching Judaism in the Sunday schools, published by the Association of Jewish Teachers (Verband der jüdischen Lehrervereine im Deutschen Reiche), Berlin, Leipzig, 1906, p. 4. The program itself was drawn up by Rabbi Leimdörfer of the Reform congregation in Hamburg for the purpose of "pointing out the theological weaknesses and inner contradictions within Christianity over against the consistent monotheistic attitude of Judaism," ibid.

86. Rotenstreich, p. 46 ff.

Conclusion

The relations between the Liberal Jews, who constituted the vast majority of German Jewry, and the Liberal Protestants, who were the most influential intellectual element in the German national movement, created new tensions between the two religions, tensions that arose not from contradictions or disagreements but from an affinity in their intellectual and theological outlook. Both groups had their roots in the rationalism of the European Enlightenment and in the neo-Kantian movement wherein they hoped to find an answer to the "value relativism" and the "culture pessimism" to which the intellectuals of that period had succumbed. But in the course of time both groups experienced a deep disappointment in the formal and purely theoretical approach of neo-Kantianism which they felt had failed to provide the solutions to the problems of that generation, and in their perplexity they turned to the historical schools of thought, especially in the fields of biblical criticism and philology, to find normative values relevant to modern existence.

In this common turning to historical religion we find one of the principal causes of tension between Liberal Judaism and Protestantism, both of which sought ideological justification for their separate existence and ethical mission, hoping in this mutual effort and confrontation to achieve a sense of self-identification. There were also significant political and social changes during this period, as has emerged from our study of the attitudes of the Conservative Protestants compared with those of the Liberal Protestants.

Conservative Protestantism took its point of departure in the principle of the Christian state and in its corollary that non-Christians or even non-Protestants, such as "ultramontane" Catholics and of course Jews, were excluded from holding public posts that symbolized the Protestant Lutheran character of the state. With the increasing intervention of the imperial regime of the Second Reich in the private sphere of the individual and in the religious affairs of the Conservatives, and with the increasing danger to the traditional framework of society as a result of the corrosive influences of the new industrial society and the rising Leftist movements, the Conservatives began to cooperate more and more with the "ultramontane" Catholics, and to some extent with Jewish Orthodoxy and political Zionism, recognizing their common interests based on a common religious and even national-religious heritage. The Liberal Protestants, on the other hand, took their point of departure in the negation of the Christian state and its right to exclude non-Christians from government posts. Since the Liberal Protestants did not surrender the ethical and historical principle that the Reich's renewed existence was based on the gospels, they insisted that the inculcation and preservation of Christian character be transferred from the citizen to the individual, from the regime to the educational institutions, and from the external authority of the state to impose the official religion to its acceptance by the conscience and ethical judgment of the individual.

From the classical liberal view which would limit state authority to the function of preserving normal social existence, Liberal Protestantism arrived at the opposite view which regarded the state not as an external protective apparatus (*äusserlicher Schutzapparat*) imposed on the citizen from without, but as an authority that the individual desired of his own free will as a result of an internalized process of identification with it. This was a very significant change of attitude and was discussed by Troeltsch in his influential lecture on "Politische Ethik und Christenthum" given in 1904 at the fifteenth Evangelisch-Sozialer Kongress in Breslau. In order to give this internalized authority more than the formal rational structure it possessed in the neo-Kantian system Liberal Protestantism filled it with positive content and with symbols borrowed from the "Christian idea of personality" and from German historical tradition; and in order that it might not become relative, to the historical and social conditions out of which Christianity arose, Troeltsch and growing circles within the Liberal Protestant community endowed Christianity with absolute value. In a lecture given on September 3, 1901, before a group of the Freunde der Christlichen Welt, Troeltsch expressed this view by describing Christianity as "the culmination of all previous religions." This exalted position of the Christian religion was not to be understood in the sense that it was the sum total of the fossilized remains of the religions that preceded it, including Judaism, as was maintained by the historical schools, higher biblical criticism, and to a certain extent by the Hegelians. The inevitable victory of Christianity was the result of a long historical process of interpreting and proclaiming the ultimate experiences of mankind, often with consummate power and beauty, in doctrines that answered to the highest aspirations of human reason and the deepest needs of the moral life. Its inestimable benefits and its immense effect on the minds of men were too apparent to require external corroboration, for their record was engraved in the whole course of human conduct and attested in the deep consciousness of man's nature.[87]

87. This discussion of Liberal Judaism needs to be supplemented by a special study of the efforts of Orthodox Jewry in Germany and in central Europe to integrate into the non-Jewish environment. The personal archives of Rabbi Samson Raphael Hirsch, preserved in the General Archives for Jewish History in Jerusalem, indicate that there were well-prepared institutionalized paths to facilitate the integration of Orthodox Jews into German Christian society. I hope to be able to devote myself to the study of this special problem.

# 5 | Christian and Anti-Christian Anti-Semitism

## Clarification of Terms

From our discussion thus far it is clear that the social, political, and spiritual factors that determined the status of the Jews in the German society of the Second Reich, into which they desired to integrate fully without, however, forfeiting their Judaism, had their roots in the Christian heritage. This heritage had undergone a process of secularization that began at the end of the eighteenth century [1] and in the period of the Second Reich had assumed an institutionalized social and political form.

The principal political parties that had been the main support of the regime during the greater part of the empire's existence described themselves as Christian. Other political parties, such as the National Liberals and even the Progressive Liberals, regarded the Christian historical heritage as the roots of the empire's national ideology and at the same time as a shield against Leftist and other subversive elements, including the Jews,

1. Eleonore Sterling, *Er ist wie Du: Aus der Frühgeschichte des Antisemitismus in Deutschland (1815–1850)*, München, 1956, p. 85 ff: "Das von der Religion für 'antichristlich' ausgegebene Judentum wird jetzt 'anti-sozial' und 'anti-national' genannt." See also p. 92 ff: "Das säkularisierte christlich-jüdische Verhältnis in der Geschichte etc." For the historical continuity of anti-Semitism from the early Middle Ages through a period of secularization in the eighteenth century and down to our own day, see Shmuel Ettinger, *The Permanent and Changing Elements of Anti-Semitism in our Time* (Hebrew), Institute for Contemporary Judaism, Hebrew University, Jerusalem, 1968, p. 11: "There is no doubt that in the European world of the Middle Ages the Jewish stereotype was a factor of paramount importance." For the historical and intellectual background of the transition from the traditional Christian heritage to the beginning of "that vast ferment, out of which emerged such powerful currents as Romanticism and Nationalism, the classicism of Goethe and Schiller . . . historicism and the evolutionary sciences," see Jacob Talmon, *The Unique and the Universal, Some Historical Reflections*, London, 1965, p. 91. For a general survey, see George L. Mosse, *The Culture of Western Europe: The Nineteenth and Twentieth Centuries*, Chicago, 1961, chaps. i–xi.

that were likely to injure the Christian character of German society or what the liberals called the ''spiritual unity'' of the renewed German nation.

An additional factor that influenced the status of German Jewry in the Second Reich was that of Christian and anti-Christian modern anti-Semitism, the subject of this chapter, to which historiography has until now given but relatively scant attention.[2] Since the political and cultural life of the Second Reich was deeply influenced by the historical sources of German Christianity, and even regarded itself as a modern secular manifestation of this historical heritage, the question is whether modern racial anti-Semitism was also part of the renewed German Christian heritage of the Second Reich. This anti-Semitism has been regarded as a direct result of Christianity's anti-Jewish tradition and an inseparable aspect of its attempt to adjust to a modern industrial society and to the imperialistic aspirations of the German Empire. Moreover, modern anti-Semitism may be regarded as a continuation *mutatis mutandis* of Christianity's hatred of the Jews who were held collectively guilty of deicide, a hatred that was cultivated for centuries by the church and implanted in the Christian heart in early childhood. This imputation of guilt for an unpardonable offense appears in the catechism for children, in ethical treatises, and in basic theological works, and has its source in the New Testament, as in Matthew 27:22, 25: ''Pilate saith unto them, what shall I do then with Jesus which is called Christ? They all say unto him, Let him be crucified. . . . Then answered all the people, and said, His blood be upon us, and on our children.'' Or, in the First Epistle of Paul to the Thessalonians 2:15 ff: ''Who both killed the Lord Jesus, and their own prophets, and have persecuted us; and they please not God, and are contrary to all men: Forbidding us to speak to the Gentiles that they might be saved . . . for the wrath is come upon them to the uttermost.'' Perhaps modern anti-Semitism in Germany, especially in Protestant Germany, can be understood as a continuation or a product of Luther's incitement to hate and vi-

2. The problem of Jewish integration among the Social Democrats or among the Leftist groups falls outside the scope of our study, as does also the phenomenon of anti-Semitism in these movements. This subject is of historical importance, for in the period of the Second Reich and thereafter during the period of the Weimar Republic there was a marked increase in the number of Jews who did not believe in identifying themselves as Germans of the Mosaic persuasion and who were attracted to those intellectual and social movements which supported the cause of cosmopolitanism. For the question of anti-Semitism in these movements, see Paul Massing, chaps. x, xi, xii.

olence against the Jews, particularly after 1543 when he realized that his efforts to convert them had been in vain. In his well-known works, *Vom Schem Hamphoras und vom Geschlecht Christi 1544* and *Von den Juden und Ihren Luegen 1544* the Jews come in for some scurrilous comments, and the Christian reader is even urged on to acts of violence, such as, "to set fire to their synagogue or school . . . and to do this for the honor of our Lord and Christendom, so that God will see that we are Christians . . . and so they know that they are not the masters in our land." [3]

Modern anti-Semitism, on the other hand, may also be understood as having been neither shaped nor reinforced by Christian anti-Jewish tradition, and being to a certain extent opposed to this tradition, especially when we consider that many of the leaders of modern anti-Semitism in the Second and in the Third Reich in their rejection of Judaism had also rejected Christianity. Furthermore, racial anti-Semitism was a denial of one of the basic tenets of the Christian *Heilsgeschichte,* the eschatological hope (in theory) and missionary zeal (in practice) as set forth by Paul (Epistle to the Romans 9–11) according to which the Jews are still eligible for salvation and election and will deserve to regain their lost prerogatives when they accept Jesus as the Messiah. On that day (the last before the Day of Judgment) the Jews shall step over to the side of the Savior and be delivered from the abject state to which their stubborn incredulity had reduced them. This courageous response will assure them of the enduring applause of mankind, for they will have thus consummated the final redemption of Christianity and humanity that had begun with the Incarnation. This view, which regards modern and especially racial anti-Semitism as different from and even opposed to the anti-Jewish Christian

3. "Erstlich, das man jre Synagoge oder Schule mit feuer anstecke und, was nicht Verbrennen will mit erden überheufe und beschütte, das kein Mensch ein stein oder schlacke davon sehe ewiglich. Und solches soll man thun unserm Herrn und der Christenheit zu ehren damit Gott sehe, das wir Christen seien. Zum anderen, das man auch jre Heuser das gleichen zerbreche und zerstöre . . . auff das sie wissen sie seien nicht Herren in unserem Land," *W.A.,* Weimar, 1883, Vol. 53, p. 523 ff. Martin Stöhr in his essay "Martin Luther und die Juden" points out that Luther's attitude toward the Jews had considerable influence up to and including the period of the Nazis and the holocaust. He quotes, among others, H. Graetz, *Geschichte der Juden,* 3d ed., Leipzig, 1891, Vol. IX, pp. 197, 316, which states that the poison of anti-Jewish hatred that Luther introduced into the Protestant world lasted a long time. Stöhr's essay is in *Christen und Juden,* ed. Wolf-Dieter Marsch and Karl Thieme, Mainz, Göttingen, 1961, p. 127 ff. Luther's words are also quoted in Stöhr's essay, p. 132. For the historical background of Luther's legacy with respect to the Jews, see Haim Hillel Ben-Sasson, "Jewish-Christian Disputation in the German Empire," H.T.R., Vol. 59, 1966, p. 369 ff.

tradition, finds corroboration in the historic fact that many of the leaders of racial anti-Semitic ideology were nourished by the critique of religion made popular by the teachings of Ludwig Feuerbach, Friedrich Daumer, and Nietzsche. The principle of "Dionysus versus the Crucified One" (passion and not martyrdom) that was preached by Nietzsche, the rejection of religion as a corrosive historic force that perverted, poisoned, and debased man's natural instincts, the attack upon Christianity as the religion of the poor, the weak, and the disinherited and their hypocritical ideals of selflessness, humility, renunciation, and sacrifice that seriously undermined all the vital forces tending to promote or elevate the life-enhancing qualities of pride, courage, fortitude, and vital spontaneity all nourished racial anti-Semitism and endowed it with a non-Christian or anti-Christian significance.

Toward the end of the period we are discussing this mood was expressed, without Nietzsche's apocalyptic tragic note, by Theodor Fritsch (also known by his pseudonym, Thomas Frey), one of the leaders of racial anti-Semitism in the Second Reich and at the beginning of the Third Reich, as follows:

The pure teaching of the Nazarene has degenerated and become a curse to the western people. It has swept over the countries like an ill-omened madness, unleashed the darkest emotions, and delivered the best to destruction. And it was precisely the blond races, from whose midst Christ emerged and whose daring free spirit inspired his teaching, that fell prey to the power-hungry church. For lower racial elements had found it possible to forge the Aryan doctrine of salvation into an instrument of spiritual subjugation and dark fanaticism.[4]

The third approach that seeks to clarify the relationship between Christianity and the rise of modern racial anti-Semitism does not regard this relationship as a single, unambiguous phenomenon, but rather as a complex system of diverse and even antagonistic forces that operated side by side during the period of the Second Reich. In this approach modern anti-Semitism is taken to be a bifurcated movement and the confluence of two streams—the continuation and the product of anti-Jewish Christian tradition and at the same time antagonistic to Christianity itself, including its biblical Jewish sources, its eschatological conception, and its ethical theological elements.

The concepts "Christian anti-Semitism" and "anti-Christian anti-

4. A.S., Danzig, 1911, p. 152.

Semitism'' thus represent two extreme types or patterns that help us to distinguish the historical reality in which they are found, although not always in a pure unambiguous form, but with varying intensity and dominance.[5] The designation ''anti-Christian anti-Semitism'' here refers to those movements, organizations, and schools of thought whose antagonism to Jews and Judaism went hand in hand with their antagonism to monotheistic religion in general and to Christianity in particular. The antagonism to Christianity expressed itself in different ways. It was directed against the institutions of the church and the clergy, chiefly against Catholicism; also against the political and economic views of the Christian political parties which, during the greater part of the period of the Second Reich, were the mainstays of the regime and a factor of considerable im-

5. For a description and bibliographical references of these various views in contemporary historiography and also within the framework of the theoretical and polemical discussions, including the schools of Jules Isaac, James Parkes, Hannah Arendt, and others, see Karl Thieme, ''Der religiöse Aspekt der Judenfeindschaft (Judentum und Christentum),'' in *Judentum-Schicksal, Wesen und Gegenwart,* eds. Franz Böhm and Walter Dirks, assisted by Walter Gottschalk, Wiesbaden, 1965, Vol. II, p. 603 ff. Among the sources of that period in which anti-Christian or non-Christian anti-Semitic concepts or expressions appear, see M.V.A.A., 1891, No. 17, p. 150 ff; 1896, No. 19, p. 149; 1898, No. 7, p. 54; 1899, No. 12, p. 9; 1901, No. 17, p. 329 ff; 1902, No. 23, p. 168; 1904, No. 4, p. 25 ff, No. 16, p. 126–127; 1906, No. 29, p. 220; 1909, No. 19, p. 166. P. Massing has also called attention to the differences between these anti-Semitic manifestations and has called the Christian anti-Semitism among the Christlich-Sozial ''anti-jüdisch,'' see there, p. 29, and also p. 99 regarding the difficulty of the conservative circles to distinguish between ''berechtigtem Antisemitismus und unchristlichem Judenhass'' (justified anti-Semitism and un-Christian hatred of Jews). K. Kupisch in the introduction to the collection of sources, p. 15, makes a distinction between Stöcker's ''Christian'' anti-Semitism, which was a kind of continuation of the ''early conservative anti-Semitism'' (*konservativen Frühantisemitismus*), and ''radical'' anti-Semitism. Hannah Arendt calls modern racial anti-Semitism ''antichristlichen Rassen-Antisemitismus'' as opposed to the traditional hatred of Jews (*Judenhass*); see Hannah Arendt, *Elemente und Ursprünge totaler Herrschaft,* Frankfurt a/M, 1955, p. 10. The part played by Christianity in the growth of modern anti-Semitism has been treated within the framework of the Christian-Jewish dialogue by A. Roy Eckardt, *Christianity and the Children of Israel,* New York, 1948; idem, *Elder and Younger Brothers: The Encounter of Jews and Christians,* New York, 1967, Part I, ''Anti-Semitism in Disclosure,'' p. 3 ff. Taking issue with Karl Thieme's approach Eckardt states: ''To refer to modern anti-Semitism as a 'post-Christian creation of pseudo-culture and mass-manipulation' is to utter a half-truth. Obviously, anti-Semitism directly violates Christian moral standards. But to identify modern anti-Semitism with something 'post-Christian' is to shut one's eyes to the intimate and centuries-long association of Christianity and anti-Semitism,'' p. 15. A different approach is Edward H. Flannery, *The Anguish of the Jews: Twenty-three Centuries of Anti-Semitism,* New York, London, 1965; ''anti-Christian anti-Semitism, that final fruit of anti-Semitic rationalism and in many ways forerunner of Nazi anti-Semitism,'' pp. 180–181.

portance in the political structure of such economic pressure groups as the Deutsch-Konservative Partei, the Bund der Landwirthe, some groups of the Freikonservative Deutsche Reichspartei, and the Catholic Center party. The anti-Semitic barbs were thus directed against Christianity as a historical and secular force in western culture and in particular in the rising German nationalism and even against Christianity as an ethical system and as a monotheistic religion.

The non-Christian or anti-Christian nature of this anti-Semitism is attested to by various types of testimony. One such type is evident in the utterances of the leaders of both racial and Christian anti-Semitism. The former included such persons as Eugen Dühring who, from the very inception of racial anti-Semitism at the end of the seventies, insisted that the hatred of Jews be recognized for what it was namely, a hatred of religion in general; and as long as this was not recognized, as long as "the opposition to the Jewish race is obscured by Christian slogans, and especially by the misleading contrast of Christian *versus* Jewish instead of Aryan *versus* Jewish," [6] man would be unable to free himself from the shackles of religion.

Other leaders of anti-Christian racial anti-Semitism were Wilhelm Marr, Theodor Fritsch, Friedrich Lange, and a number of propagandists

6. Eugen Dühring, *Der Ersatz der Religion durch Vollkommeneres und die Abstreifung alles Asiatismus,* Leipzig, 1881, p. 28. For sources for this conception among the early leaders of racial anti-Semitism in the criticism of religion among the Young Hegelians, like Friedrich Daumer, Bruno Bauer, and Arnold Ruge, see E. Sterling, *Er ist wie Du: aus der Frühgeschichte des Antisemitismus (1815–1850),* München, 1956, p. 111 ff. When the atheist Friedrich Daumer embraced Catholicism at the end of his days, he defined his criticism of religion in the 1840's as: "Entschieden Anti-Christliche Denkart" (a decidedly anti-Christian way of thinking); see G. F. Daumer, *Meine Conversion: Ein Stück Seelen und Zeitgeschichte,* Mainz, 1859, p. 3. This rare source is highly important for the study of the anti-Christian and anti-Jewish character of modern anti-Semitism as it developed during the last third of the nineteenth century. For this source, as for a number of others used in this book, I am indebted to Shmuel Ettinger; see his "The Roots of Anti-Semitism in Modern Times" (Hebrew), *Molad,* Vol. 2 (25), No. 9 (219), 1969, p. 323 ff; also the lecture of Shmuel Ettinger, "The Young Hegelians' Criticism of Judaism as a Source of Modern Anti-Semitic Ideology" (Hebrew), Israeli National Academy of Sciences, Jerusalem, 1969. For the criticism of theology and its conversion into anthropology in relation to the rationalistic principles at the basis of the European and Jewish emancipation, in the teachings of Bruno Bauer, Friedrich Daumer, and others, see Nathan Rotenstreich, *Judaism and the Rights of Jews: A Chapter in the Polemics on the Emancipation* (Hebrew), Tel-Aviv, 1959, chaps. i, iii, iv. See ibid., chap. vi for analytical discussion of the transition from the antirationalistic attitude toward the objectivization of empirical characteristics in racial theory; see also Zvi Rosen, "Anti-Jewish Views of Bruno Bauer (1838–1843), Sources of Influence and their Significance" (Hebrew), *Zion,* 1968, Year 33, Vol. 1–2, p. 59 ff.

whom we shall have occasion to discuss in the course of this chapter. These leaders repeatedly proclaimed the superiority of "pre-Christian Germanism" over the culture, religion, and ethics of ecclesiastical Christianity, especially of Catholicism. Christianity subjected man to a debilitating morality and imbued him with the hypocritical qualities of renunciation, humiliation, and the subordination of self to others instead of cultivating the aboriginal Germanic virtues of self-mastery, candor, and fortitude, qualities befitting those who aspired to be masters of the world. This was the view that prevailed in the circles of the *Alldeutsche,* a view that was summed up by Friedrich Lange, one of the prominent leaders of the movement, in his anti-Semitic periodical *Deutsche Zeitung* of April 15, 1896, as follows: "We are convinced that wherever a practical Christianity could weaken the physical or spiritual energy of our people, we have to curb Christianity through Germanism and not vice versa." The students of E. Dühring, speaking of the unwarranted dependence of the New Testament on the Old Testament and of the injurious morality contained in both, expressed themselves in a similar vein in their periodical, the *Moderner Völkergeist* of May 1897. Since the New Testament was a continuation of the ethics of the prophets and since it did not come to nullify the law and the commandments but to fulfill them, it could not serve as a guide "for the nations that stand on a higher plane."

Anti-Semitic antagonism toward the Christian clergy emerged at a much later date, in the issue of March 24, 1900, of the anti-Semitic periodical, the *Westphalische Reform,* which inveighed against "international gold" controlled by Jews who fleeced the small man, against the "Red International" which enslaved the small man through the all-powerful apparatus of socialism, and against the "Black International" (the clergy of all religions, Catholics, Protestants, and Jews) which made of every religion a corrupt business and turned it into a pressure group of interests.[7] At the end of the period that we are discussing, however, the anti-Christian aspect of racial anti-Semitism became more influential so that we find a vigorous campaign being conducted against the church as an institution in publications by Theodor Fritsch and members of his circle, as in the pages of the *Hammer.* In one issue of this periodical (January,

7. "Gegen den Antisemitismus der Geistlichen," A.S., Danzig, 1900, p. 302 ff. See additional sources, some of which are to be found in the periodical *Moderner Völkergeist,* which declared that Christianity was invalid since it was nothing but "Neujudentum," in Joseph S. Bloch, *Israel und die Völker nach jüdischer Lehre,* Berlin, Wien, 1922, p. 505.

1911) Dr. Ernst Wachler-Weimar, an intimate friend of the anti-Semitic literary critic Adolf Bartels, proclaimed: "Away with fables and legends, the laws and ethical teachings of the Jews as of the Christians"—for these traditions, among other things, inhibited the free and unrestrained development of "the basic Aryan instincts." [8]

The second type of source material that helps us to distinguish the Christian from the anti-Christian or non-Christian motifs in modern anti-Semitism consists of documents, statements, official announcements, casual conversations, educational discourses, and public debates that have come down to us from Christian clergymen, theologians, historians, statesmen, and other members of the intellectual class who among themselves sought to make a distinction between the two types of anti-Semitism. The reasons, both tacit and avowed, for this distinction between the anti-Jewish attitude that was compatible with Christian tradition and the racial or political anti-Semitic attitude that was injurious to Christianity are highly complex. Among these Christians some subscribed to economic or political anti-Semitism but refrained from adopting it as a policy for they were convinced that it would prove harmful to Christianity and to religion in general. They also feared that the Christian population would suffer politically and economically if such anti-Semitism were permitted outside the framework of the political parties, such as the Deutscher Reichspartei or the Bund der Landwirthe or the Center party. Many Christians were opposed to all forms of rabble-rousing anti-Semitism (*Radauantisemitismus*) for this plainly reduced the prospects of successful missionary activities among the Jews and obstructed the path to conversion. Others felt obliged to disassociate themselves from racial anti-Semitism on the ground that the hatred of one's fellow man was contrary to Christian ethics, at least in theory, and if permitted to take root would have a pernicious effect on general moral education and on Christianity itself. Still others rejected racial and political anti-Semitism since, by its advocacy of violence, it constituted a grave danger to the stability of the

8. A.S., Danzig, 1911, p. 203; see, p. 194, for reaction to the speech of the priest Alfred Fisher at the general meeting of the Verein zur Abwehr des Antisemitismus, Berlin, 1910, on the subject "Is Christianity Compatible with Anti-Semitism?" See also lecture by Salo W. Baron at the World Jewish Congress in Brussels, August 4, 1966, *Deutsche und Juden, Beiträge etc.,* Frankfurt a/M, 1967, p. 85: "There was an unmistakable increased resistance since the seventies of the nineteenth century against everything that Judaism and Christianity stood for, and it is no exaggeration to say that this development paved the way for the Nazi seizure of power."

traditional social order and to the existent political regime. Then, finally, there were those who repudiated the racial elements in anti-Semitism because they did not conform to modern scientific-rationalistic or human-istic-ethical criteria, or because they deprived baptism of its meaning and prevented the conversion of Jews, thus violating one of the central theo-logical principles of the Christian conception of salvation.

Public critical reaction against the non-Christian or anti-Christian char-acter of this anti-Semitism first became evident in connection with the rise of anti-Semitic incitements at the end of the seventies and especially in the eighties. The criticism was directed against A. Stöcker's brand of anti-Semitism and to a certain extent against H. Treitschke's public influ-ence, and came from men such as Theodor Mommsen, Paulus Cassel, and Franz Delitzsch among the Protestants and Friedrich Müller among the Catholics. The argument against Stöcker was summed up by De-litzsch in 1881 as follows: "From the side of the Christians an un-Chris-tian race hatred that cries to heaven has been subtly introduced into this movement; and since the roots of Christianity are the same as those of the Old Testament, we are presented with the unedifying spectacle of a bird that besmirches its own nest." [9]

In the sphere of domestic politics the conservative Christians kept aloof from political and racial anti-Semitism and were only in favor of Chris-tian anti-Semitism that was dictated by political considerations and party interests. Even at the beginning of 1883, before racial anti-Semitism had become a distinct political force, Landrath von Rauchhaupt, a Conserva-tive deputy in the Prussian Lower House, declared that anti-Semitism should not be permitted in those segments of the population that were not subject to the authority of the Conservative party so as not to endanger the concept of Protestant monarchist rule. Instead the Christian parties should encourage anti-Semitism for purposes of political expediency: "We have taken into our own hands all the enmity of the anti-Semitic movement in order to revive the Christian consciousness of the people and thus make it possible to establish the ethical basis for the solution of the social question." [10] In the course of the following years this attitude became more prominent in the Conservative parties in those states where anti-Semitic sentiment had increased, as in the kingdom of Saxony and in

9. The source is given in Leopold Auerbach, *Das Judenthum und seine Bekenner in Preussen und in anderen deutschen Bundesstaaten,* Berlin, 1890, p. 19.

10. A.Z.d.J., Vol. 47, 1883, No. 10, p. 152.

the interstate party organization within the Reich. Conservative opposition to political anti-Semitism was prompted by the fear that it was likely to undermine law and public order, Protestant monarchism, and the national Lutheran tradition. This was explicitly stated on various occasions and laid down in the platform of the Conservative state organization of the kingdom of Saxony as early as 1883, that "we Conservatives have no interest in international anti-Semitism." [11] Accordingly, the Conservatives again pointed out the danger of political anti-Semitism to the Christian state, and that the Jewish question was to be solved, in the words of Friesen, a Conservative leader in Saxony, "by excluding Jews from all governmental posts, from representative public positions, and from the teaching profession," [12] and not by the "rabble-rousing anti-Semites" (*Radauantisemiten*) whose proposed solution was unworthy of a Christian and even immoral.

Another characteristic note in the criticism directed against modern anti-Semitism was sounded by Pastor Gruber of Reichenback in Silesia in his book *Christ und Israelit,* in which he warned that the anti-Semitic propaganda which in 1880 had not yet become widespread could easily become popular among the masses, and then, "where there are fists, thinking quickly becomes superfluous" and is soon followed by "coarse acts of violence," a danger "by no means impossible even in this century of education and enlightenment." Similarly, the theologian Hermann Baumgarten in his work *Against Court-Preacher Stöcker,* which he had presented to the heir apparent Friedrich Wilhelm early in 1881, characterized anti-Semitism, including the kind advocated by Stöcker, as contrary to Christianity. Baumgarten warned his contemporaries that propaganda of this nature could lead to a blood bath, for the anti-Semitic movement "is called Germanic but is also Christian; former murderers of Jews also wore the cross, if not in their hearts, at least on their outer garment. We have been brought so low by these wild outbreaks of anti-Semitism that our humane century reminds us of the terror of medieval Jewish massacres." [13]

At the beginning of the era of political anti-Semitism in the early nine-

11. A.Z.d.J., Vol. 47, 1883, No. 39, pp. 627–628.
12. A.S., Danzig, 1892, pp. 18, 269. See p. 158 for the source of Pastor Gruber's words quoted below in the text.
13. A.S., Danzig, 1892, pp. 158–159.

ties these diverse approaches, in which religious and ethical conceptions as well as political and economic interests were involved, had exponents in the church and among the clergy. A conspicuous example of this was the circular that was issued on October 3, 1890, by the Supreme Consistory of the principality of Hessen, expressing its opposition to the clergy's support of the political anti-Semitic movement headed by Otto Böckel. It was thus clear that the members of the clergy in that area had indeed supported political and racial anti-Semitism at the time of their annual conference in Upper Hessen in August 1890. The Supreme Consistory resolved that while there was some justification for criticizing the economic practices of Jews, especially in the agrarian sector, the entire Jewish community could not be held responsible for this nor Judaism as such. It must be borne in mind, the Supreme Consistory argued, that Christian tradesmen and financiers took part in these questionable activities, including exorbitant rates of interest and profiteering, so that to blame the Jews alone would be tantamount to exonerating the Christians and thus deprive them of the opportunity for self-criticism and moral reform. Furthermore, anti-Semitic racial policy was built on "the fateful dark instincts of the German Christian people that lead it astray." This movement therefore tended to corrupt Christian morality from within and to undermine social discipline, law, and order among the population: "A spirit of insurrection and lawlessness, lust and hate thus unloosed . . . could profit only those whose revolutionary plans against the political and ecclesiastical establishment are based on the growing dissatisfaction among large segments of the population." [14]

14. Ibid., pp. 149–150. This view was an integral part of the concept of the "Christian state" discussed above in Chap. 3; see the attitude of the Conservatives in the Prussian Lower House on the question of the place of Jewish students in educational institutions. In one of the discussions of this problem in the Herrenhaus, May 8, 1890, the spokesmen of the Conservative faction argued that an increase of Jewish students in the higher institutions of learning "was a social danger . . . for the Christian-national education of our youth." Hence, "It is not right to relegate Christianity to a course in the curriculum of studies; it is rather the basis on which the entire educational system from grammar school to the universities must be erected. The idea of Christianity must be grasped by the pupil and become an active principle in the grown man. According to Par. 4 all Prussians are equal before the law; every group within the population is guaranteed free and unrestricted development. What happens to this free development when such irreconcilable conflicting elements as Christians and Jews are huddled together in schools? . . . It is Christianity which is the world's moving force, and in the Christian spirit we are all united. . . . If, however, we

In the political realities of everyday life, however, we find abundant indications of cooperation between the Conservative Protestants and the anti-Semitic organizations and political parties. Conspicuous instances of such cooperation are to be found as early as in 1893 between the conservative Bund der Landwirthe and the anti-Semitic parties, when local branches of the Conservatives in the various German states, especially in the rural areas, frequently entered into electoral agreements with the anti-Semites headed by Max Liebermann von Sonnenberg.[15] The followers of Eugen Dühring, however, repudiated the attempts of racial anti-Semitism to absorb Christianity as part of the German national racial doctrine and during that same period were unalterably opposed to all Christian motifs, asserting that:

For us Christianity is nothing but neo-Judaism which, because of its characteristic Jewish features—we mention only the hypocrisy of loving your neighbor and your enemy—cannot be reconciled with the thought and feeling of more recent and better nations . . . spiritual Jews are all those who regard the Bible as holy writings in which a Lord is revealed to mankind and who are hindered by the unnatural Christian commandment to love one's fellow man and even one's enemy from doing what needs to be done to free the people of the world from the pestilence of Judaism. . . . It is Christianity that has really made possible the Judaization of our people and prevented its de-Judaization . . . the ancient Germans were artificially stupefied and their senses blunted . . . Christianity impaired the understanding and the spirit; it unleashed wild fanaticism and engendered heinous crimes. Christianity has been, and is still today, the greatest obstacle to progress.[16]

---

must everywhere have a special regard for the Jewish element, the Christian future is endangered and we shall cease to be a Christian state." These and similar statements in the Prussian Lower House by Conservative delegates—Graf von Pfeil, Graf von Schulenburg-Beetzendorf, and also Hans Hugo von Kleist-Retsow—have come down to us in an article in the *Vossische Zeitung,* 1st Supplement, No. 215, May 10, 1890. This point of view that Jews should be removed from political, social, and even religious interests, interests likely to conflict with those of the anti-Semites, considering that both camps had more or less common circles of potential voters, becomes clearer in the light of the proclamation of the Conservatives in the Prussian Lower House on January 28, 1893, "Verhandlungen des Preuss. Abgeordnetenhauses, Amt. Stenograph. Bericht, 28.1.1893," M.V.A.A., 1899, p. 296; 1906, p. 220: "We cannot use terms strong enough to repudiate this anti-Semitism; it is not German and it is not Christian . . . and has nothing to do with any religious need. The desire to strengthen and deepen our ecclesiastical-religious life directly contradicts this activity and this disparagement of religion."

15. P. Massing, chaps. ii, iii, ix.    16. A.S., Danzig, 1900, p. 284 ff.

## Christian Anti-Semitism

In the first stage of the modern anti-Semitic movement in the German Empire, from the seventies until the middle eighties, we find two forms of anti-Semitism—the Christian anti-Jewish (*Judenfeindlich, Judengegnerisch*) and the racial political anti-Semitism which combined the rejection of Judaism with an antagonism toward Christianity—these two tendencies being sometimes in conflict and sometimes in harmony with one another. To the extent that it was imbued with a hatred of Jews and did not espouse Social Democracy most of the community retained the traditional Christian anti-Jewish attitude, although in its secular, economic, political, and social interpretation. These circles, especially those from among the lower middle class and from among the agrarians, feared that the anticonfessional aspect of anti-Semitism, as formulated in this early stage by H. Naudh-Nordmann, Wilhelm Marr, Eugen Dühring, and Christian Radenhausen, would remove the last remains of the preindustrial traditional structure of society. Hatred of the Jews combined with the rejection of religion and morality had already been repudiated by some conservative circles as early as 1878 as a reaction to Marr's anti-Semitic propaganda which they denounced as promoting the growth of atheism, materialism, and socialism and which ultimately "leads to ethical anarchy among our children who grow up in urban areas without restraints or discipline." [17]

The anti-Jewish attacks which began in the early seventies were not unwelcome to the spokesmen of the Conservative Protestants, for example, the *Kreuzzeitung* or the *Allgemeine Evangelisch-Lutherische Kirchenzeitung,* edited by the distinguished theologian Christian Ernst Luthardt. These conservatives continued to cultivate the traditional anti-Jewish view according to which the foreign Jews who controlled the country (*jüdische Fremdenherrschaft*) were the embodiment of antichrist. They were also supported by some of the provincial papers which defended the traditional Christian anti-Jewish arguments, like the *Deutsche Reichs-*

---

17. "Die subsidäre Regelung der Schulunterhaltungspflicht und die Schulsozietäten in Preussen," p. 2. These minutes of the Parents Meeting of the Conservatives have been preserved in F.A., No. 8/d. For a reserved anticonfessional reaction of Wilhelm Marr, see ibid., p. 5 ff.

*glocke.* Among the Catholics as well we find men such as the well-known political philosopher and publicist Constantin Frantz, a sworn enemy of Bismarck's Reich (which he characterized as the embodiment of Jewish materialism), who exerted great influence on Richard Wagner, Jakob Burckhardt, and Moeller van den Bruck. These views were also represented in some of the issues of the Catholic periodical *Germania* in 1875 and again in 1878.[18]

In all these cases the accusations against the Jews were chiefly of an economic, political, and social nature, so that there was as yet no distinction between the general policy of the conservatives and that of a considerable part of the Catholics. The Jews, together with the Liberals and the "Manchesterites," were made responsible for the economic disaster that followed in the wake of the financial crash of 1873, for the economic distress of the agrarians in the seventies after the repeal of the protective tariffs, and, in conjunction with the *Kulturkämpfer,* for the breakdown of traditional moral values and cultural ideals. Whatever the Jews touched withered; they turned bread into stones. Not content with controlling the economy of the country, they infiltrated and dominated its cultural life and the press. The Jews introduced the venom of the serpent into German society—the love of money, material gain, the cult of success—and thus planted in the heart of the ordinary man the seeds of dissatisfaction with himself and his station in society "assigned to him by Providence, which was a universally respected tradition until the Jews infected us with their baleful influence." [19]

In this series of arguments, which more or less reflected the general anti-Jewish sentiment among the Christians, different aspects were emphasized by different groups. The views of the agrarians were expressed

18. *Allgemeine Evangelisch-Lutherische Kirchenzeitung,* Leipzig, 1871, pp. 252–253; 1880, pp. 83 ff, 1156 ff, 1167, 1217 ff. An interesting reaction of the D.I.G.B. leadership of the year 1878 to the anti-Jewish tone of this periodical has been preserved in the archival file, G.A.J., G.A. M1/13, Antisemitica, Anträge in Bekämpfung des Antisemitismus, D.I.G.B., No. 44. In a draft of a letter dated June 1, 1878, addressed to the Ministry of Justice in Saxony, the D.I.G.B. complained of the insulting tone of the article, "The Economic and Moral State of Affairs at the Beginning of the Year 1878," which appeared in issue No. 5 of that year. Since the editor of the periodical was in government service, the heads of the D.I.G.B. stated that the article was likely to create the impression that the Kingdom of Saxony was behind this incitement against the Jews. From a note added later to the draft of the letter it is clear that the letter was not sent on to the authorities addressed. For other sources mentioned in this paragraph, see following notes.

19. No. 17 above, p. 5.

in an editorial in the *Deutsche Reichsglocke* of December 24, 1876, which stressed the part played by Jews in formulating the economic policy of the Liberals, a policy that had impoverished the agrarians and enriched the parasites—which was not surprising for "to reap without sowing, that is the Jew's profession." [20] Other groups among the Conservative Protestants, early disciples of Adolf Stöcker, engaged in heated discussions in 1878–1879 on the nature of the Jewish question and on the importance of Jewish persecutions in awakening renewed interest in Christianity and Germanism as basic elements in the new empire and German nationalism. Some of the discussions have been summarized in a programmatic article, "Das junge Deutschland," published in 1878 in the well-known anti-Semitic periodical *Reichsbote,* and the principal questions that were raised were also discussed at the meetings of the Parents Association and the high school teachers during that same period.[21] These discussions revolved around the following main points: the gravity of the Jewish question as a means of helping the Christian and the German recognize his own weaknesses and gain an insight into the emptiness and superficiality of modern life, the immaturity of German nationalism, and the loss of traditional values especially among the younger generation. In face of the hostile (Jewish) forces that menaced the life of the spirit—irreligion, materialism, egalitarianism, rationalism—it was the duty of the Christian German to assert his self-identity by going back to the Christian world view, to the heroic deeds of his early history, and to the unsullied virtues of the German spirit. To achieve this identification he would have to abandon the abstract rationalism of Judaism and liberalism that only served to separate man from nature and overcome his alien-

20. "Ernten ohne zu säen, das ist der Beruf des Juden" (*Deutsche Reichsglocke,* Dec. 24, 1876). The source is cited in L. Graf von Westphalen, *Geschichte des Antisemitismus in Deutschland im 19 und 20 Jahrhundert, Quellenhefte zur Geschichte und Gemeinschaftskunde,* No. 4259, Stuttgart, p. 23 (hereafter, Westphalen).

21. The essay, "Das junge Deutschland," appeared in the issue No. 287 of this periodical and was preserved in the file of the D.I.G.B., G.A.J., G.A. M1/38, Antisemitica Varia. Excerpts from this essay, translated into Hebrew, were printed in the collection of sources in the archives of Otto Dov Kulka, *Antisemitism in Europe during the Years 1848–1914* (Hebrew), Akadamon, Jerusalem, 1968, pp. 66–67. The views of the *Reichsbote* circle were accepted by other conservative groups among the Protestants and Catholics; this emerges from the correspondence carried on in the second half of the 1870's and in the 1880's between the leaders of the D.I.G.B. and the Ministry of Justice and the Office of the Public Prosecutor of the Reich and several of the states; see G.A.J., G.A. M1/13, Antisemitica, Anträge in Bekämpfung des Antisemitismus, D.I.G.B., No. 44; G.A. M1/16, Strafanträge in Bekämpfung des Antisemitismus, D.I.G.B., No. 45.

ation by returning to the bosom of his *Volkstum,* to the "natural historical cosmic organism."

The Catholic arguments stressed the Jewish anti-Christian influence (*Entchristlichung*) on the nation's economy and culture. These arguments became more widespread after the publication in 1871 of Professor August Rohling's popular work *Der Talmudjude,* which contained a series of quotations culled from the original sources to prove that the oral law permitted and even obligated the Jew to lord it over the Christian, to take advantage of him, to exploit, deceive, and even destroy him. These criticisms of Judaism and liberalism were repeated after 1874 in the works of the political philosopher and prolific publicist Constantin Frantz, and thereafter, in addition to the series of anti-Jewish articles in the periodical *Germania* in 1875, in the defamatory pamphlet published in 1876 in the Rhineland and Westphalia called *Not the Hatred of Jews but the Defense of Christians,* written by a Catholic priest by the name of Schröder.[22]

22. See above, Chap. 3. An important work relevant to our subject is Constantin Frantz, *Der Nationalliberalismus und die Judenherrschaft,* München, 1874, pp. 6, 10, 15 ff, 21, 46. See also, in the collection of essays, the clarification of the question of religion and the state, important for the new background of the Jewish question, *Literarisch-Politische Aufsätze,* München, 1876. For the part played by the periodical *Germania* and the political circles connected with it in the rise of political anti-Semitism, see P. Massing, p. 14 ff. Massing's opinion (p. 18) that this periodical concluded its anti-Semitic propaganda in 1875 is not correct. After a short interval the anti-Semitic articles continued; see the correspondence between the leaders of the D.I.G.B. and the chairman of its Executive Committee J. Nachod and the public prosecutor of the state court in Berlin in the period January to February 1878 in G.A.J., G.A. M1/13, Antisemitica, Anträge in Bekämpfung des Antisemitismus, D.I.G.B., No. 44. Another instructive example of a later period is provided by *Germania* in its issue of September 20, 1899, which announced that in the face of the intensification of the struggle against anti-Semitism on the part of Jewish organizations, there was no other choice but to establish "a central organization of German citizens of the two Christian faiths for the purpose of defending Christianity against Jewish defamation." The declaration was formulated in imitation of the recognized style of the central organization of German Jewry for combating anti-Semitism (C.V.). Testimony in support of this is found in the archival file B.A.K., P. 135/8225, Acta Generalia des Justiz-Ministeriums betreffend die Vergehen welche sich auf die Religion beziehen, B.St.G.B. par. 166, 168. The above booklet, published by the vicar of the cathedral, Schröder, and called *Nicht Judenhatz— aber Christenschutz—ein Volksbüchlein,* Paderborn, 1876, served as a pretext for the D.I.G.B. to institute legal proceedings. In their petition to the Prussian Ministry of Justice the heads of the D.I.G.B. stated that this abusive booklet was calculated to stir up hatred against the Jews among the Christian population, especially among the ultramontanists, and even to incite acts of violence, and this justified the public prosecutor to bring charges against the author and publishers of the booklet. This was still the period of the *Kulturkampf,* and the Prussian government seized the opportunity to strike a blow against the

The arguments advanced by the Catholics clearly reflected their desire to assimilate into the Second Reich as equal citizens and loyal supporters of the new nationalism no less than the Lutheran Protestants. Their anti-Jewish propaganda was the same as that of the *Kulturkampf,* that the domination of liberal doctrines and policies over the "Christian-German principle" brought about by the Jews or by the "spirit of Judaism" had greatly reduced the social influence of the church and made of religion a private affair of the individual. This insidious ascendancy of the Jewish spirit had not only destroyed the Christian basis of the state but had also deprived the individual of his moral autonomy, his reverence for tradition and authority, and his inner resistance to the blandishments of the modern world. As the educational and social influence of Christianity weakened and the destructive energies of modern big business and capital grew stronger, the individual lost his bearings and was no longer able to understand or cope with the material factors that shaped his daily life. This confusion was aggravated by the new constitution of the German Empire, which had turned the Christian state into a *Rechtsstaat* governed by secular laws and thus severely weakened the historical Christian character of the particularistic German states. The inevitable consequence of this process was to reduce the political, social, and spiritual power of the Catholics over against the Protestant majority not only in Greater Prussia but also in those states where they constituted a majority of the population, as in the kingdom of Bavaria and in the Rhineland. In this development anti-Jewish feeling was found to be a useful weapon in the struggle against liberalism, as was observed by the circles around the *Westphälischer Merkur:* "And hence it is our duty to combat liberals of the Center party led by Ludwig Windhorst . . . who has for some reason determined that anti-Jewish activities are not compatible with the political interests of

Catholics. The court found Schröder guilty and banned further publication of the booklet. See G.A.J., G.A. M1/16, Strafanträge in Bekämpfung des Antisemitismus, D.I.G.B., No. 45. To complete the picture, see Reports of the secretary of the D.I.G.B. in B. Jacobsohn, *Der Deutsch-Israelitische Gemeindebund,* Leipzig, 1879, p. 29 ff. Strong public reaction to this anti-Jewish literature from the conservative elements among the Catholics—especially to the above-mentioned works of Rohling, Schröder, and others put out by the Catholic publishing house of Bonifacius, and the important anti-Jewish periodical in Münster, the *Westphälischer Merkur*—was summed up in the wake of the public proceedings against the *Judenspiegel* by Justus, that is Aron Briman, in the copious material in the archives, G.A.J., G.A. M1/17, Antisemitica, Process Contra Justus, Münster, 1883, D.I.G.B., No. 45; G.A. M1/20, Gutachten über Schulchan Aruch, 1883, D.I.G.B., No. 48.

Catholics. . . . We are defending the Christian national spirit and not the interests of the politicians in the Reichstag.'' [23]

Until the second half of the eighties this anti-Jewish attitude developed in two directions at once. It aided conservative Protestants and Catholics in their efforts to integrate into the new German Empire and to increase their political and economic strength in its modern industrial society. At the same time, however, this anti-Jewish attitude prepared the ground for modern anti-Semitism as a social and political movement in which the concept of race was to emerge as a prominent element. Many of the early organizations of this movement, also those that subsequently cultivated non-Christian or anti-Christian attitudes, had their roots in this Christian anti-Jewish revival of the seventies and early eighties. These were small organizations which for the most part thought of themselves as societies for social reform or for the protection of artisans and manual workers. Many of them arose at the beginning of the eighties and flourished for only a short period, for example, the Soziale Reichspartei under Dr. Ernst Henrici, the Deutscher Reform Verein in Berlin and Breslau, the Deutsche Reformpartei in Dresden under Alexander Pinkert-Waldegg, the Sozialer Reichsverein in Leipzig and Berlin, and also the original parent association of these anti-Semitic organizations, the Allgemeine Deutsche Antisemitische Vereinigung. After 1886 these were joined by the anti-Semitic circles under Otto Böckel, who entered the Reichstag in 1887 as the first deputy of the anti-Semites as a result of the regional elections in Upper Hessen (district of Marburg-Frankenberg-Kirchhain).[24] These first cells of political and racial anti-Semitism regarded themselves as organizations that were primarily concerned with the preservation of Christian society, economy, morality, and nationalism.

One of the first political organizations in this anti-Semitic movement was the Deutscher Volksverein (D.V.V.) which arose soon after the lack

23. Anon., *Bismarck's kleindeutsche Politik,* Münster (?), 1881, p. 1. The allusion to the leadership of the Center refers to the statements concerning Jewish disabilities made by Ludwig Windhorst in the discussion on anti-Semitism that took place in the Prussian Lower House on November 20, 1880. The discussion was initiated by the Liberal-Progressive delegate, Dr. Hänel, and both the Jewish and the general press published the extensive minutes of this parliamentary discussion. Excerpts of Windthorst's remarks were published again at the beginning of the 1890's by the V.A.A. See "Katholische Stimmen über die Judenfrage," Flugblatt No. 14, p. 1.

24. On the weak organizational framework of anti-Semitism at the end of the 1870's and at the beginning of the 1880's, see K. Wawrzinek, *Die Entstehung der deutschen Antisemitenparteien, 1873–1890,* Berlin, 1927; also P. Massing, p. 80 ff.

of success of the Antisemitenliga (1879) under the leadership of Max Lie-bermann von Sonnenberg and Bernard Förster who had left the Soziale Reichspartei (S.R.P.). In its platform of March 14, 1881, this organiza-tion adopted a resolution to the effect that it was not concerned with religious questions since its aim was to improve the living conditions of the middle class and the farmers, but it nevertheless honored "the Chris-tian world view . . . and appreciated the reciprocal influence between the national and religious life among our people." [25] Further publications of the D. V. V. spoke of the religious and especially the Christian-Conserv-ative attitude toward culture and the national experience (*Religiosität der Gesinnung*) as the only guarantee for the preservation and renewal of his-torical German uniqueness and the purity of the national heritage. Only by preserving the nation's social, economic, and moral character could the artisan and the manual worker be saved. Unless the traditional per-sonal values in the life of the German Christian were safeguarded, mod-ern industrial society with its large financial corporations and stock-market speculations would swallow up the small artisan and tradesman. This was the constant refrain in scores of speeches, in pamphlets, and in inflammatory articles published in the periodicals of these social reform organizations, such as the *Deutsche Wacht* edited by A. Hentze, 1879–1881, the *Deutsche Reform* edited by A. Pinkert-Waldegg for a short period after 1880, the *Deutsche Volkszeitung* edited by Ernst Henrici, especially in 1881, and *Die Wahrheit* edited by Lieberman von Sonnenberg until 1885. Only Christian or historical Germanism could provide an escape from the destructive influences of modern society and save Germany from capitalism, "Manchesterism," and liberalism and their hypocritical infatuation with humanitarianism and the fraudulent morality of *Nivellierung* and *Verpöbelung* (egalitarianism and massifica-tion)—all of which were different expressions for the rule of Judaism over Germanism. The state was an integral part of the life of the people and permitted no distinction between people and state, between society and state, or between religion and state; and since the ground and origin of this total unity was Christian, there was no place in the national state for a civil group that adhered to a non-Christian religion. In this spirit the

---

25. *Die Fälschung der öffentlichen Meinung, nachgewiesen durch stenographischen Bericht über die erste öffentliche Sitzung des neugegründeten Deutschen Volksvereins, am 14.III.1881, im Grossen Concert-Saale der Tivoli-Aktien-Brauerei*, pub. by Vorstande des D.V.V., Berlin, 1881, par. 1.

second part of the platform and its appended explanations were formulated in 1882, proclaiming the need to combat Jews and Judaism, the principal menace to the national historical foundations of the country and to the peculiar character of the German soul, which was individual freedom in conjunction with a loyal and disciplined sense of responsibility.[26]

This mixture of romantic motifs and promises of social felicity to "the small man" together with protection against contaminating Jewish influences characterized the propaganda of the anti-Semitic organizations of the lower middle class at the end of the seventies and during the eighties. The leaders of these organizations during this period were astute political and ideological propagandists, but only rarely did they succeed in creating permanent political or economic pressure groups of public significance. Typical of such leadership was C. Wilmanns, a municipal judge in Berlin and the author of *Die goldene Internationale und die Notwendigkeit einer sozialen Reformpartei* (Berlin, 1876), one of the first anti-Semitic works that found a responsive chord in middle-class urban circles and, after the seventies, also in rural areas. An interesting reason for the wide currency and public influence of this work was given by Rabbi S. Munk of Magdeburg in a letter of March 1887 to Arnold Budwig, one of the leading figures of the Gemeindebund, in which he wrote of the need of the Jews themselves to combat the practices of their own coreligionists who charged exorbitant rates of interest in rural areas; he pointed out, among other things, that this anti-Semitic work by Wilmanns owed its influence not to the author's organizational talents but to "his unique ability as a propagandist to combine the classical Christian accusations against the Jew who cheats the Gentile in obedience to the oral law [the author in this matter relying on the information provided by August Rohling] . . . with the new racial anti-Semitism according to which even conversion cannot effect a change in the Jew since his racial nature is infected with radical evil." [27]

26. Ibid., par. 2, 3, 4, 6; and, especially, *Judentum und Liberal-Kapitalismus,* pub. by Vorstande des D.V.V., Berlin, 1881, pp. 18, 42.

27. The words of Rabbi Munk's letter quoted in the text are found in F.A., No. 2/a. See the original work of Wilmanns, pp. 63 ff, 83 ff. For efforts of the leadership of the D.I.G.B. in Berlin to induce the public prosecutor to take legal action against Wilmanns on the grounds that his book incited acts of violence (Penal Code, par. 130) and/or on the grounds that he defamed or vilified the Jewish community as a *Religionsgemeinschaft* (Penal Code, par. 166), see Auerbach, p. 101 ff. The part played by the Jews in the 1870's and 1880's in the economic difficulties of the farmers and landowners in general and in the

A similar method characterized the propagandistic activity of the other anti-Semitic organizers of the Social Reform movement, such as Alexander Pinkert-Waldegg, editor, journalist, and the head of the Central Council of the Deutscher Reform Verein in Dresden. His work, *Die Judenfrage gegenüber deutschen Handel und Gewerbe,* which reached its third edition in 1880, contained a collection of anti-Jewish opinions by various personalities representing different and even opposing currents of thought, such as Kant, Fichte, Herder, Schopenhauer, on the one hand, and A. Rohling, W. Marr, Otto Glagau, on the other. The book served as a pragmatic guide not only for the Social Reform organization in Dresden, but also for the anti-Christian racial anti-Semites in Leipzig under the leadership of Theodor Fritsch after the middle of the eighties. Among these leading propagandists we also find Dr. F. Perrot, who seems to have been the author of the series of anti-Jewish articles which appeared in the *Kreuzzeitung* in 1875, and also Freiherr von Fechenbach, a member of the impoverished aristocratic circle who was at the head of a number of small temporary organizations called Vereine zum Schutze des Handwerkes.

The spokesmen of the early anti-Semitic Social Reform movement pointed out that the liberal political forces which at the beginning of the nineteenth century had emancipated the farmer and the artisan from feudalism were the same forces behind capitalism in the industrial society of the seventies. Since liberalism's political strength was also derived from its economic power, the liberals and their prototype, the Jews, turned from liberators into exploiters, from the proponents of equality into the originators of social discrimination.[28] It was evident to the Social Reform

---

shortage of agrarian credit in particular has not yet been objectively studied. In the archival sources at our disposal today we find important testimony to the effect that Jews during this period were charging the rural population exorbitant rates of interest. In the correspondence between the leaders of the D.I.G.B. and Rabbi Munk of Magdeburg and other active members of the communities in central and southern Germany it was even acknowledged that the findings concerning the part played by Jews in the economic impoverishment of the farmers and in the huge debts incurred by them as a result of exorbitant rates of interest, as summarized by the Verein zur Sozialpolitik and published in the report, *Der Wucher auf dem Lande, Berichte und Gutachten,* Leipzig, 1887, corresponded at least in part to the reality. See G.A.J., G.A. M1/14, D.I.G.B., Antisemitismus, Verein gegen Wucher; especially the letters and circulars of Arnold Budwig and Samuel Kristeller in March and July 1887. This file also contains apologetic newspaper excerpts on this problem, J.P., Vol. 18, 1887, Nos. 30, 31, 32, 33; I.W., Vol. 18, Nos. 31, 32.

28. The development of liberalism from a revolutionary movement in a preindustrial society and economy into a conservative force that sought to preserve its achievements is

circles that the process of industrialization under liberalism had been the cause of a large migration of workers from the village to the large city which was unable to absorb them, thus creating an impoverished and disillusioned urban group. As a result of these migrations the small towns and villages suffered from a shortage of workers, and those who remained lost their natural organic relationship to the soil. The agrarian middle class, after the breaking up of the landed estates, became deeply in debt due to the lack of credit. A similar dissolution took place in the city where the middle class was caught in a wedge between the capitalists and the proletarians, where it was subject to systems of mass production, marketing methods, monopolies, and financial corporations that put finance capital above capital needed for creating the means of production and for increasing production, a system of credit that nearly ruined the farmer and the middle class. All this created a large urban class that had no social or economic security and no political representation. The traditional family and community ties had grown weaker together with a general laxity of public morality. The unfair conditions of competition created by the political pressure groups behind big capital were, according to the Social Reformers, a potent factor in undermining true Christian morality and the Christian principle of brotherly love.

The anti-Semitic antiliberal groups took the material for their propaganda indiscriminately from Fichte, Herder, Stein, Humboldt, Hegel, Marx, Rudolf von Jhering, Treitschke, J. K. Rodbertus, and others. The principal argument of these groups, apparently borrowed from Marxist ideology, was that man had become a slave to the economic system and had thus lost his basic status as a free man with natural rights to his own productions. He was hopelessly entangled in meaningless economic functions and no longer master of himself. An analogous argument, borrowed

---

perhaps one of the basic questions in the history of the modern period. The dispute between the Progressive Liberals and the National Liberals in those years provides the background to this problem; see Friedrich Lütge, *Deutsche Sozial und Wirtschaftsgeschichte,* 2d ed., Berlin, Göttingen, Heidelberg, 1960, p. 448 ff. This development is testified by the Liberals themselves, especially in the 1870's and 1880's; see Friedrich Facius, *Wirtschaft und Staat,* Boppard a/Rhein, 1959, p. 74 ff. See the debate carried on by the National Liberals against the Progressive Liberals, P.J., Vol. 52, 1883, p. 92; Vol. 53, 1884, p. 426. A detailed analysis of this development as seen by contemporaries, especially by the National Liberals who sought to justify the policy of state intervention and also the transition from the proclaimers of industrial progress to the conservers of its achievements, is in E. Philippi, "Die Schwankungen des Volkswohlstandes im Deutschen Reich," P.J., Vol. 52, 1883, pp. 221–314; Vol. 54, 1884, pp. 216, 418–443.

from conservative Christianity, was that a political constitution based on the principle of equality of all men and adopted under liberal and Jewish pressure must perforce undermine the traditional structure of society and consequently the principles of morality and obedience, the German tradition of serving "throne and altar," and the German ideal, "Mit Gott, für Kaiser, Reich und Recht." [29]

The proponents of the Social Reform movement were also convinced that the pernicious effects of modern industrial society were reflected in the laws and in the legal system of the Second Reich. The legal principles derived from Roman law were foreign to the German national spirit. According to this interpretation, which became popular in the eighties, Roman law—that is, the law that had been foisted on the Second Reich by the Jews and liberals—was based on an abstract legal equality, a notion foreign to the traditional class inequality of German society. Roman law was ignorant of corporative bodies, so that in its eyes the juridical person who served as the bearer of Roman laws was not a social organic body but an isolated individual who was morally responsible to himself alone and to an abstract system of rationalistic concepts that had no meaning for the uncorrupted German. Having lost his strong traditional ties with his family, his township, his tribe, or corporation, the German became an egoist involved in constant competition with the other members of society, without security, stability, or faith and without the support of the moral community that formerly gave him a sense of belonging. In this unfriendly atmosphere he despaired of his ability to restore the lost unity of his mind. He experienced a vertiginous imbalance which plunged him into a deep melancholy, the romantic mood par excellence of modern man.

These attempts to arouse and organize the lower middle classes of ar-

29. C. Wilmanns, p. 54 ff, also the beginning of the book. See also, nn. 9, 10 above. The summary of the entire argument in the collection of pamphlets and speeches in which many of the spokesmen of the various schools of thought we have already discussed took part is in *Judenfeindliche Anschauungen und unsere Wirtschaftspolitik,* Chemnitz, Sachsen, 1882, p. 4 ff. The same ideology appears in the collection of pamphlets, *Kapitalistische Wirtschaft und jüdische Geldmacht,* Dresden, 1885, pp. 1–3, 4–8, 12–19; also in the anti-Semitic catechisms published by Theodor Fritsch. The need to defend the Christian artisan and the fruits of "Christian diligence" against the Jewish capitalist was stressed in a series of pamphlets by Freiherr von Fechenbach in 1880–1881; some were appended to the booklet, F. Perrot, *An die deutschen Handwerker: Aufruf zur Bildung von Vereinen zum Schutze des Handwerkes,* Frankfurt a/M, 1881, par. vii, par. viii, 2d supplement. A manifesto is preserved in the archival file, G.A.J., G.A. M1/38, Antisemitica-Varia, 1880–1884.

tisans, small merchants, clerks, and, to a certain extent, teachers and the impoverished class of aristocrats with the help of the bogey of the Jewish menace constituted the basis of the race doctrine and of anti-Christian anti-Semitism. The concepts used during this period by the anti-Semitic propagandists differed from those used by the leaders of racial anti-Semitism. Whereas in some of his writings, as in his popular work published in Berlin in 1876, *Religiöse Streifzüge eines philosophischen Touristen,''* Wilhelm Marr included under the concept "Judaization of mankind" (*Verjudung der Menschheit*) also the malignant products of Christianity, such as pantheism, a weakening of the moral fiber, man's distrust of his own powers, and other such products of the Christian spirit that had brought Germany to the brink of destruction, we find that in the Social Reform movement the blame was put upon the Jew alone, and on liberalism as a manifestation of the Jewish spirit, for the economic, social, and even psychological plight of modern society.

Similarly, at the beginning of the eighties Eugen Dühring accused Judaism, Christianity, the Semitic spirit, and religion in general of perverting human nature, of making men slaves to conscience and other Jewish inventions inimical to human nature and especially to that of the racially pure Nordic and Aryan types. He regarded the New Testament as a "Jewish-racial tradition" inspired by a deep resentment against superior races such as the Germans whose thought and feeling were basically incompatible with those of Jewish or Christian origin.[30] In contradiction to this the first cells of the anti-Semitic movement in these early organizations of Social Reform still confined their anti-Semitism to Judaism. An example of this attitude was provided by a series of talks given in 1881–1882 in the Breslau branch of the Deutscher Reform Verein by one of its leaders, Edmund Winterfeldt, and by Wilhelm Pickenbach, the head of the Berlin branch and after 1890 a deputy in the Reichstag representing the anti-Semites in the electoral district of Giessen. In these talks it was emphasized that true social reform was possible only if German children were brought up in the spirit of the classical tradition of "German essence" which was now incorporated in the traditional class of agrarians and government officials, the class that had inherited the

30. "Deutsche Art und Weise des Denkens und Fühlens kann auf die Dauer mit der palästinensisch-christlichen nicht zusammen bestehen," Eugen Dühring, *Der Ersatz der Religion durch Vollkommeneres und die Ausscheidung alles Judentums durch den modernen Völkergeist,* Leipzig, 1886, pp. 61, 63.

functions of the charismatic religious leaders of old, the apostles, the bringers of good tidings, and the priests, appointed to assume the nation's executive authority and to supervise the daily life of the German people.[31] At the same time, however, we note certain non-Christian and even anti-Christian features characteristic of racial anti-Semitism. The second formulation of the official platform of the D.R.V. in 1881, apparently drawn up by Alexander Pinkert-Waldegg in Dresden, stated that "anti-Semitism is the only answer of the members of the middle class to the calamity that has befallen our culture due to the petrification of Jewish law and to the irresolution, pusillanimity, and unmanly hypocrisy inculcated by the New Testament." [32]

As a result of these developments there was renewed interest in the first international congress of the anti-Semitic movement that convened in Dresden on September 11–12, 1882. From the organizational or political point of view no great importance can be attached to this congress. The designation "international" is misleading, for mainly active members from Germany and Austria-Hungary participated. For our present discussion, however, and for the study of the reciprocal relations between Christian anti-Semitism and anti-Christian anti-Semitism this congress and the work of its Standing Committee are not unimportant. The documents that have come down to us of its brief ideological activity reflect the tension that existed between these two types of anti-Semitism. Among the participants in the congress were the active heads of the temporary organizations of the Social Reform movement at the beginning of the eighties and also some of the leading Christian anti-Semites who were in-

31. Above, n. 29, in the collection *Judenfeindliche*, p. 6.

32. Above, nn. 10, 26, *Judentum*, p. 41; the leadership of the D.I.G.B. urged the public prosecutor of the state court in Dresden to prefer charges against Pinkert-Waldegg on the basis of par. 130, 160, of the R.St.G.B. which prohibited defamation of religions or religious organizations or incitement to violence; see G.A.J., G.A. M1/16; D.I.G.B., No. 45, especially the correspondence between the Council of the D.I.G.B., signed by Jacob Nachod, and the public prosecutor of the Kingdom of Saxony and other courts of jurisdiction in the period 1880–1881. The public prosecutor refused to comply with the request of the D.I.G.B. on the ground that the testimony concerning degenerate Jewish morality and corrupt manners set forth in the Talmud and Schulchan Aruch, as quoted from Rohling's *Talmudjude* (pp. 73, 80), was also cited by such men as K. Martin and J. Rebbert or Treitschke so that "for reasons of preservation of the state and in the interests of morality it is imperative to combat them" (Decision of the Public Prosecutor of Dresden, July 3, 1880). On the documentation of Martin-Rebbert against the Schulchan Aruch referred to here, see above, Chap. 3. For further attempts to take legal action against anti-Semitism in Dresden, see Mittheilungen des D.I.G.B., 1881, No. 9, p. 7.

terested in promoting racial anti-Semitism. Conspicuous among the latter was Adolf Stöcker who at this time was at the height of his career and who, in addition to being the court preacher, was a member of the Reichstag, a member of the Prussian Chamber of Deputies, and the head of the Social-Christian party. Other participants included some of the leaders of Conservative Protestantism who were related to the aristocracy and some of the leaders of anti-Semitic Christian circles. Among the latter was Friedrich Karl von Fechenbach of Bavaria who during this period was the head of the societies organized for the protection of the rights of workers and also the honorary chairman of the Artisans Association in Westphalia. The congress itself and its activity was not characterized as "anti-Semitic," and even its official manifesto did not include this designation. It was called the "anti-Jewish Congress" (*antijüdischer Kongress*); its manifesto, which was drawn up by Victor von Istoczy, a member of the Hungarian Reichstag, and published by Ernst Schmeitzner, was called *Manifesto to the Governments and Peoples of the Christian Countries Endangered by Judaism.*[33] These designations were not accidental; the word "anti-Semitism" was avoided by these circles since it was associated in the public mind with the anti-Christian views of H. Naudh-Nordmann, Wilhelm Marr, Eugen Dühring, and Christian Radenhausen. The active members of the congress, led by Adolf Stöcker, disassociated themselves from all anti-Jewish tendencies that in any way suggested the negation of the Christian world view.[34]

The Jewish question was therefore defined in the spirit of Stöcker's conception as arising from the uniqueness of the Jews as an element with a different ethnic origin and religious identification, but the question nevertheless did not arise as purely racial or religious, "but as one having a universal, political, sociopolitical, and moral-religious character."[35] Judaism was also defined as a national group that existed by reason of its

33. *Manifest an die Regierungen und Völker der durch das Judentum gefährdeten christlichen Staaten, laut Beschluss des Ersten Internationalen Antijüdischen Kongresses, zu Dresden am 11 und 12 September 1882,* Chemnitz, Sachsen, 1882 (hereafter, *Manifest*). Of the activities of the Standing Committee, especially the discussions concerning the outcome of the case against Pinkert-Waldegg and the future of the anti-Semitic paper *Deutsche Reform* in Dresden, we have the testimony of the organizers of the congress and of the Standing Committee of July, August, and September 1882, in F.A., No. 5/d.

34. F.A., No. 5/d, according to Karl Freiherr von Thüngen-Rossbach, a landowner and an active member of the Christlich-Sozial; he also used the term *Vereine anti-jüdischer Tendenz.*

35. *Manifest,* par. II.

international solidarity based on a common origin, language, culture, dietary laws, and so forth—particularistic factors that conferred upon the Jews dwelling in Christian nations the separate or even isolated status of a caste. The designation of the racial character of the Jews as a caste, nationality, religion, or *Volkstamm* were all intended to indicate that no change in the conditions of their existence could change their basic nature, and hence "the Jews are incapable of being an organic part of a Christian people." [36] Those whom the anti-Jewish movement sought to defend from the ravages of Judaism and particularly from the domination of modern Jewry that strove "to dominate the Christian cultural world and corrupt it" [37] were not yet called the Aryan or Germanic race but the "Christian world," the "Christian life of the state and society," the "essence of the idea of the Christian state." [38] One of the few concepts borrowed from racial anti-Semitic terminology and accepted by the Standing Committee on the recommendation of A. Pinkert-Waldegg, W. Pickenbach, and E. Schmeitzner was "Christian-Aryan progeny" to characterize those who were to be defended against Jews and against Semitic exploitation.[39] The ideological and political tension between Christian anti-Semitism and race doctrine, together with its anti-Christian motifs, was seen most clearly at the beginning of the eighties with the political ascendancy of Adolf Stöcker and the Christlich-Sozial circles, which were later joined by Professor Adolf Wagner, an economist and *Kathedersozialist,* and by Freiherr von Hammerstein, the chief editor of the *Kreuzzeitung.*

Until a short time ago historiography was principally concerned with Stöcker's activities in behalf of political anti-Semitism. However, some recent works [40] have stressed other aspects of Stöcker's anti-Semitism,

36. Ibid., par. IV.
37. Ibid., "die christliche Kulturwelt zu beherrschen und zu zersetzen,"
38. "Christliche Welt," "Christliches Staats-und Gesellschaftsleben," "Wesen der christlichen Staatsidee," ibid., par. I, II, V, VI, VIII.
39. "Die christlich-arischen Eingeborenen," "die christlich-arische Bevölkerung gegen die semitische Ausbeutung zu schützen," ibid. in the conclusion of the minutes; also above, n. 34, F.A., No. 5/d.
40. Walter Holsten, "Adolph Stöcker als Symptom seiner Zeit, Antisemitismus in der evangelischen Kirche des 19 Jahrhunderts?" in *Christen und Juden,* ed. Wolf Dieter Marsch and Karl Thieme, Mainz, Göttingen, 1961, p. 182 ff (hereafter, Holsten). See also Wanda Kampmann, "Adolph Stöcker und die Berliner Bewegung" in *Geschichte in Wissenschaft und Unterricht,* Vol. 13, No. 9, 1962, p. 558 ff. See also the quotation in K. Kupisch, p. 15.

some of which have their roots in Lutheran anti-Jewish tradition, contrary to the anti-Christian tendencies of racial anti-Semitism. Paul Massing, whose study of the roots of modern anti-Semitism is also concerned with Stöcker's contribution to the political development of this movement, gives prominence to Stöcker's admission in his letter to the Kaiser of September 23, 1880: "In all my talks against Judaism I have openly proclaimed that I do not attack the Jews but only that light-minded Judaism that is without fear of Heaven, that pursues material gain and practices deceit, that Judaism which is the real misfortune of our people." [41] In this connection Massing pointed out that Stöcker's anti-Jewish attitude differed from the political and racial anti-Semitism of his day in that Stöcker never regarded himself as an anti-Semite; his avowed aim was to kindle the flame of Christianity in the hearts of his followers and to establish his movement on the rock of Christian faith and not on the hatred against Jews. [42] Nevertheless, and contrary to their original intentions, Stöcker, Wagner, and part of the Christlich-Sozial group served as an important factor in strengthening political and racial anti-Semitism, even including the anti-Semitism that rejected Christianity. The inner tension between theory and practice, between ideology and the actual political development of racial and non-Christian anti-Semitism, a tension which Stöcker and Wagner were well aware of, was one of the main points of discussion within this group.

At the time when Stöcker founded the Christlich-Soziale Arbeiterpartei in 1877–1878 together with the former Social-Democratic propagandist Emil Grünberg and other active members of the Inner  Mission in Berlin, he still did not indulge in anti-Jewish hate propaganda, nor are any traces of it to be found in the party's opening meeting on January 3, 1878, or in Stöcker's programmatic speech of January 25, 1878, held in the Berlin headquarters of the Artisans Association. The principal enemy of Christianity, the Christian state, the Christian fatherland, and the social order derived from the gospels was Social Democracy and its corollaries atheism, empiricism, and materialism. Stöcker even expressed himself favorably concerning the social ethics of the Old Testament, especially the prohibition against usury, the laws of the sabbatical year, and the jubilee year which was designed, in his opinion, to prevent wealth from accumulating in a few hands. The Old Testament was no longer regarded as Jewish but as Christian, for its promises had passed into the New Tes-

41. P. Massing, p. 31.        42. Ibid., pp. 30–31.

tament; Judaism had become "the lowest stage of divine revelation," [43] a stage that had attained its completion and perfection in Christianity in general and in German Christianity in particular. The umbilical relationship between the Old and the New Testament, and the complete fulfillment of the one in the other, kept Stöcker and Wagner, during this era of the national awakening of the German Christian state, from identifying their anti-Semitism with the racial doctrines formulated by H. Naudh-Nordmann, E. Dühring, W. Marr, T. Fritsch, C. Radenhausen, and A. Wahrmund. In the first platform of the Christlich-Soziale Arbeiterpartei of 1878, Stöcker had still not included anti-Jewish motifs. The basic principle of the platform was to integrate the social reforms demanded by the workers with the patriotic claims of German nationalism which were based on Conservative Protestantism and Prussian monarchism. [44]

In the fall of 1878, with the ill-success of the new party and the rise of

43. From one of Stöcker's early anti-Jewish pamphlets which was disseminated during the electoral campaign of 1878. To Stöcker's ideas, discussed above in Chap. 3, a new note was added, namely, the defense of the Christian worker: "We respect the Jews as our fellow citizens and honor Judaism as the lower stage of divine revelation. But we firmly believe that a Jew cannot be a leader of German workers, neither from the religious nor the economic point of view. The Christian Socialist Workers party has inscribed Christianity on its banner." (Wir achten die Juden als unsere Mitbürger und ehren das Judentum als die untere Stufe der göttlichen Offenbarung. Aber wir glauben fest, dass ein Jude weder in religiöser noch in wirtschaftlicher Hinsicht ein Führer deutscher Arbeiter sein kann. Die Christlich-soziale Arbeiterpartei schreibt das Christentum auf ihre Fahne), A. Stöcker, *Christlich-Sozial, Reden und Aufsätze,* 2d ed., Berlin, 1890, p. 127 (hereafter, A. Stöcker). This source is also quoted by P. Massing, p. 29; testimony of the impression that Stöcker's words made on some of the leaders of the large Jewish communities is also found in F.A., No. 1/b. Dr. A. Mossner, a Jewish lawyer active in the D.I.G.B., entered into negotiations with the Office of the Public Prosecutor in Berlin to determine whether Stöcker's words could be interpreted as damaging to the legal position of the Jews as citizens enjoying equal rights by virtue of the legal emancipation granted them in 1869. In his reply to Mossner and the members of the D.I.G.B., including Jacob Nachod, the chairman of the Executive Committee, at the end of the 1870's, the public prosecutor stated that the opinions expressed in the Christlich-Sozial circles sincerely reflected the sentiments of many citizens in the Kingdom of Prussia and indeed throughout the German Empire.

44. Stöcker's speech at the founding of the party, January 3, 1878, is in A. Stöcker, p. 3 ff; the first party platform was printed in A. Stöcker, *Reden und Aufsätze,* ed. R. Seeberg, 1913, p. 21 (hereafter, R. Seeberg). The two documents were reprinted in the collection of K. Kupisch, pp. 68–74; scc ibid., pp. 74–75, for Stöcker's conccption of thc church's social and political responsibility in face of the danger threatening Christianity and Christian-German culture as a result of the growing power of socialism. Here as well anti-Jewish allusions were as yet not introduced. The document appeared in the official ecclesiastical organ, *Kirchliches Gesetz-und Verordnungsblatt,* No. 2, 1877. See also dissertation in the Library of the University of Erlangen by Hans Engelmann, "Die Entwicklung des Antisemitismus im 19ten Jahrhundert und Adolf Stöckers Antijüdische Bewegung," 1953, p. 24.

the conservative Christlich-Sozial movement, Stöcker began to insert anti-Jewish slogans in his propaganda. After his important anti-Jewish speech of September 9, 1879, "Our Demands of Modern Judaism," he became one of the mainstays of political anti-Semitism, including the kind which after the mid-eighties developed anti-Christian tendencies. In the following year he was one of the main figures involved in drawing up the anti-Semitic petition that was submitted to the chancellor of the Reich (March 1881) demanding that Jews be denied access to any public position that symbolized the Christian character of the state, especially in the spheres of law and education. The petition also included the demand to discontinue or at least restrict Jewish immigration.[45]

Writers of this period have assumed that the marked increase in the number of those who now attended Stöcker's meetings was due to the attraction of his anti-Jewish ideology which was taken to characterize his ecclesiastical activity, his political attitudes, and his renewed Christlich-Sozial movement.[46] It is no doubt true that anti-Semitic propaganda, especially in Berlin in those days, added to Stöcker's popularity; but this does not explain the complex nature of his anti-Semitic ideology and that of his followers in the Christlich-Sozial movement nor the relation between his Christian anti-Jewish attitude and his contribution to racial political anti-Semitism. His demands and his proposals for the solution of the Jewish question constitute a complex system of theological, biblical, pietistic, and racial motifs. But the basic aim that he inflexibly pursued from the time when he first turned his attention to social problems was the defense of the Christian nation against the inroads of Leftist ideology. This singleness of purpose stemmed from his Conservative Protestant world view according to which it was the task of the German Empire to realize in the empirical political sphere those ideals which, after Israel's defection and deep betrayal, passed from Israel in the body to Israel in the spirit, that is, from the Jews to the Christians.

Even in his early speeches immediately after his political defeat in the summer of 1878 (examples are his first important speech in which he introduced anti-Jewish motifs on September 19, 1879; his speech in the Prussian House of Deputies on November 20–22, 1880; and again a

---

45. See above, Chap. 3; Stöcker's speech of Sept. 19, 1879, is in A. Stöcker, p. 367 ff. Part of this speech was reprinted in Westphalen, Document No. 26, and in P. Massing, pp. 238–239.

46. P. Massing, p. 31.

speech at a public gathering on February 3, 1882), Stöcker emphasized the distinction between the anti-Jewish attitude that was consistent with Christianity or derived from it and the anti-Semitic attitude that was likely to injure the Christian ethics of the gospels as well as the political interests of the Conservatives. In the above-mentioned speech of September 19, 1879, Stöcker warned his hearers that "a hatred against the Jews that is contrary to the gospels is beginning to flare up here and there." [47] Even in his most outspoken discourses, when he employed the term "race" with reference to the Jews, he continued to believe that their conversion was the only authentic Christian solution to the Jewish question. Only by confronting the Jews with their stubborn infidelity and persuading them of the inestimable benefits of baptism could the derelict Jews be redeemed from the graceless state to which their impenitence had brought them. Without such redemption, moreover, it was not possible for Christianity, and now the German state in which it was embodied, to complete its mission of universal salvation that had been promised to Israel of old, even Israel in the flesh, "when the full number of the Gentiles come in" (Romans 11:25). Israel, incorrigible and obtuse, was the only obstacle in the path of the destined meeting between man and God at the foot of the cross. On this Pauline promise Stöcker based his conviction concerning the nature of salvation awaiting the Jews:

A final salvation . . . not a future glory that will raise Israel above the other nations as envisaged by the Old Testament . . . and every believing Christian understands how great this moment will be in God's kingdom when the ancient people of the Covenant will finally acknowledge its sin against Jesus and repent. This event will resound throughout Christendom and the angelic empyrean like a triumphal song of victory. Also the church will be imbued with a new vital impulse when Israel will put at her service its uncommon religious gifts and intellectual talents.[48]

This inner tension between the theological conception that saw the solution to the Jewish question only when the Jews renounced their faith and the racial conception which held that no solution was possible as long as the Jews continued to exist in the flesh—in short, the choice between destroying Judaism to save the universal man or destroying the particularistic Jew to save the principle of universalism—this tension was inher-

47. A. Stöcker, p. 367; also in Westphalen, No. 26, and in P. Massing, p. 238.
48. R. Seeberg, pp. 141–142; in Holsten, p. 199.

ent in the structure of Stöcker's argument since the late seventies. He did not characterize the Jewish question as racial, and yet he found it to be rooted in the racial and ethnic peculiarity of the Jew. He did not define it as an exclusively religious question, and yet it was the result of a preposterous theological error on the part of the Jews whereby they lost their status as the chosen people, and indeed their whole wretched existence bore witness to the truth of the parable of the vineyard (Matthew 21:43): "The kingdom of God will be taken from you and given to a nation producing the fruits of it." [49] Similarly, the Jewish question was a political one, for the emancipation could not be abolished or ignored; but it was also a favorable ground for missionary work among the Jews. Finally, he stated that the Jewish question was essentially a social and ethical question, for the modern Jew was the living embodiment of everything that endangered the existence and welfare of the indigent classes of society; at the same time this socioethical problem could not be divorced from religion since the morality, economy, and culture of German society were but the external forms in which the German-Christian spirit expressed itself.

From one point of view Stöcker endorsed traditional conservative demands, such as the prohibition or restriction of Jewish immigration, the exclusion of Jews from official posts that symbolized the Christian essence of the nation, curbing the power of the Jewish press and Jewish financial activity—in a word, to deprive Jews of their influence and to render Judaism innocuous, so that it could no longer contaminate the German working class and *christliche Arbeit* and obstruct the long-awaited flowering of the Christian-German spirit. From another point of view, however, Stöcker's method differed from that of the agrarian elements among the Conservatives. Like Bismarck at the beginning of the eighties, Stöcker emphasized the need for a new social policy that would take away the initiative from the Social Democrats in their efforts to achieve social reforms. He was convinced that the Christian-German people could not fulfill their spiritual mission unless the economic, social, and political conditions of the masses, the workers and the lower middle class, were improved. The distressful conditions in which these lower classes lived

49. From a meeting of teachers, supporters of the Christlich-Sozial, in Berlin at the end of 1880, F.A., No. 1/b. The New Testament source is Matthew 21:43; a parallel source cited by the teachers is Mark 2:9 ff.

were the result of their false ideals, the worship of mammon, the pursuit of material gain, and other corrupt capitalistic ideals largely derived from Judaism, especially modern Judaism which had departed from its biblical and prophetic source and no longer observed the Law and the Commandments. The social struggle of the Germans against economic exploitation thus became the national struggle of the Christian against Jewish domination. From this Stöcker drew the obvious conclusion that one who impugned religion or Christianity or repudiated the New Testament was *ipso facto* an enemy of the German nation and its universal messianic mission. The enemy that Stöcker referred to was socialism, atheism, communism, anarchism, and, of course, the Jews, the archenemy on two counts, as masters of the financial world and the capitalist press and as the insidious underminers of ecclesiastical authority and of the traditional social order.

The ambivalent nature of Stöcker's thinking constitutes an instructive chapter in the development of modern anti-Semitism. On the one hand he was deeply influenced by previous attempts to create a Social Christian movement that would attract the working class, foremost among which were those of Johann Heinrich Wichern, Rudolf Todt, Carl Witte, among the Protestants, and Franz Josef Boss and Bishop W. E. von Ketteler, among the Catholics—men in whose spirit he continued to work, but whose pitfalls he was determined to avoid. On the other hand, however, he was influenced by the extreme wing of Lutheran conservatism and its traditional doctrine of election according to which salvation passed from Israel in the flesh to Israel in the spirit which, in its modern manifestation, was the "throne and altar" of Germany. Stöcker endeavored to organize groups similar to those of the Social Democratic party from the standpoint of the professional, economic, and social status of its members, but the indifference to religion and Christian tradition of those he sought to recruit presented a serious obstacle to his undertaking. These were workers in the various branches of industry and public utilities, mostly nonprofessionals, sons of farmers who had migrated to the urban centers but could not integrate into their economy or social structure, as well as artisans and tradesmen who were crushed by the large corporations.

Like his predecessors Stöcker proceeded on the assumption that the industrial revolution and the rise of the national state, with the consequent growth of socialism, atheism, and materialism, presented a new challenge to religion and the church. Religion was not confined to the inner life of man; it must become a factor in promoting the welfare of the masses and in redressing social evils. Religion and economics were not two worlds, but different aspects of the same world. The church must come to grips with man's alienation and lost sense of unity in a capitalistic regime that had absorbed his vitality, damaged the divine image within him, and destroyed his belief in redemption through faith in Jesus the Messiah who sacrificed himself for all mankind. Christianity, as the heir to the promises of the Old Testament, was called upon to realize the claims of its election in the modern world not only by comforting the disinherited and exploited in their sorrow and reconciling them to their humble station, but by engaging in the social struggle and helping the worker, the peasant, and the uprooted aristocrat find an answer to their existential perplexities.

Stöcker accepted Rudolf Todt's thesis that social, economic, and moral criticism of the Social Democrats against capitalism was justified. But contrary to the views of Social Democracy and the movements of the Left, he believed that the solution to the distressing social problems of his day was not to be found in the spirit of revolution that would change the basic social and economic order but in a revolution of the spirit through the gospels and the spiritual authority of the monarchy in the Christian state. Stöcker's attempts together with those of his friend, Adolf Wagner, to realize an economic social policy for the lower classes in the Christlich-Sozial movement were not politically successful, except in his own electoral district of Siegen in Westphalia. This was partly the result of a more realistic attitude on the part of his Leftist rivals and partly the result of his realization (and in this he differed from his predecessors) that it was difficult to reconcile the contradictions between a workers' movement that desired to change the basic social order and the methods of production and Lutheran conservatism which by its very nature sought to preserve the established traditional order with its cultural patterns and its insistence on the absolute authority of the church and state.

Another deep and perhaps decisive influence on Stöcker's thought and policies was the traditional Lutheran Orthodoxy. The investigator of this aspect of German anti-Semitism has access today to Stöcker's collected speeches and sermons, the testimony of his students and political supporters, especially in the districts of Marburg and Siegen, including the testimony of the man on the street, teachers, clerks, merchants, and the rural clergy. The overall picture that emerges from a close examination of these different sources will be summed up in the following pages.[50]

Stöcker's political ideology was governed by the fundamental theological conviction that the Christian-Germans, and not only the Christians in general, were God's people and had inherited the place of the postbiblical Jews who rejected the gospels brought to them by the Messiah and his apostles, as we read in Stephen's sermon (Acts 7:51–52): "You stiff-necked people, uncircumcised in heart and ears, you always resist the Holy Spirit. As your fathers did, so do you. Which of the prophets did not your fathers persecute? And they killed those who announced beforehand the coming of the Righteous One, whom you have now betrayed and murdered." The Jews were despised for they had rejected salvation and the Savior, and hence the rage of the prophet against them: "Hear and hear, but do not understand; see and see, but do not perceive" (Isaiah 6:9); this is repeated in Mark 4:12 and in Acts 28:25. When Israel rejected the message of salvation, it forfeited its election and *raison d'être,* and all its claims and prerogatives passed from Israel in the flesh to Israel in the spirit, that is, to the early Christian-Jews and the heathen Gentiles: "This salvation of God has been sent to the Gentiles; they will listen" (Acts 28:28). The modern Gentiles were the Germans, for they had been found worthy to establish a Reich that had renewed the tradition of the Carolingian Empire. Since the Jews, in their obstinacy and impenitence, rejected not only the message of salvation but also its author, and in malice crucified him, they had called down on themselves a curse of everlasting abhorrence. When Pilate washed his hands in front of the people to show that he had no responsibility for spilling the blood of the Messiah, the Jews proclaimed their own historical verdict: "His blood be on us and on our children!" (Matthew 27:25). This was followed by endless persecution, moral and physical decline, and even hyprocrisy—"So you also outwardly appear righteous to men, but within you are full of hypocrisy and iniquity" (Matthew 23:28)—all this as punishment for their unpardonable sin and for the justification of those who believed in Jesus the

50. F.A., Nos. 1/b, 1/c, 1/d; also Holsten, chap. ii, "Völkisches Christentum," p. 188 ff; chap. iii, "Missverstandenes Gottesvolk," p. 196 ff. For a balanced picture, see series of articles in the Jewish press and also in Stöcker's own publications, A.Z.d.J., Vol. 44, 1880, Nos. 47–53; Vol. 52, 1888, Nos. 3, 49, 69, 83, 99, 116, 149; D.E.K.Z., Vol. 1, 1887, pp. 91, 107, 120, 313, 323; Vol. 2, 1888, pp. 403, 490, 503.

Redeemer. The Jews testified against themselves: "Thus you witness against yourselves, that you are the sons of those who murdered the prophets" (Matthew 23:31).[51]

Stöcker was animated by the desire to renew and perpetuate the Lutheran tradition in which he was raised, and like Luther (as in his *Von den Juden und ihren Lügen*) he believed that the persecution and humiliation of the Jews redounded "to the honor and the strengthening of our faith, and to the shame of the stubborn unbelief of the benighted stiff-necked Jews." In this same spirit Stöcker asserted, as in his first important anti-Jewish speech of 1879, that the removal of Jews from positions of power and influence was necessary for "the strengthening of the Christian spirit." [52] At the same time, however, this religious-national terminology served as a fruitful ideological source and as a political incentive in fomenting racial and even anti-Christian anti-Semitism. The place occupied by Stöcker in the development of anti-Semitism of his time is perhaps best characterized by this tension between theoretical intentions and actual political influences. The Christian tradition to which he owed the force of his inspiration urged him to hope and work for the conversion of the Jews, for only with the final disappearance of Judaism could Christianity complete its own redemption. He thus felt from the very beginning of his anti-Jewish public career that "Jews and Christians must endeavor to find the proper relationship to one another." [53] With the spread of inflammatory anti-Semitic propaganda in Berlin, and with the outbreak of pogroms in Russia in the early eighties he repeated this admonition: "We do not wish to solve the Jewish question in a radical manner with violence, but gradually in a quiet, peaceful manner. To avoid the lamentable excesses such as in Russia is precisely the reason for the existence of our movement; it is an outlet for the bitterness among our people. We must keep the wound open until it is healed." [54] Nevertheless, Stöcker

51. From words of appreciation for the ideology of Stöcker and the group of active supporters of the Christlich-Sozial following a discussion concerning the place of the Jews in the educational system which took place in the Prussian Lower House on March 20–21, 1890, F.A., No. 1/d. For the public opinion concerning this parliamentary discussion, see *Vossische Zeitung,* 1890, No. 135 (supplement), "Stöckers neue Judenhetzreden im Abgeordnetenhause nach Abgang Bismarcks" (the issue is preserved in the above file).

52. For his words, see A. Stöcker, p. 367; the parallel between the quotation from Luther's *Von den Juden und ihre Lügen* in 1543 and Stöcker's words in 1879 was pointed out by Pfarrergehilfe A. Freilich at the meeting of active members mentioned above.

53. A. Stöcker, p. 367, and also Westphalen, Document No. 26.

54. Westphalen, Document No. 27.

and his circle were not averse to using popular anti-Jewish sentiment to promote the cause of the Christian state and the Christian-German national ideal which in the last two decades of the century was connected with questions of race consciousness, national destiny, Aryan supremacy, the purity of the German language, and the struggle to keep moral values and cultural ideals unsullied by Jewish influences.

The principles espoused by Stöcker and the followers of the Christlich-Sozial abounded with inner contradictions that stemmed from the desire to promote the cause of Christian anti-Semitism without at the same time being misled into anti-Christian tendencies. Testimony reflecting this dilemma has been preserved in reports published in newspapers of the meeting of the Christlich-Sozial in Berlin on October 21, 1892, at which Stöcker warned his hearers of the danger that faced Christianity, as well as German culture and nationality, not from anti-Semitism as such but from ''rabble-rousing anti-Semitism'' (*Radauanti semitismus*) conducted on racial grounds divorced from the political struggle of the Conservative Protestants against the Jews: "Anti-Semitic ideas should remain on conservative soil, otherwise they will become more dangerous than useful . . . I also see a great danger in having the struggle against Judaism detached from Christian soil. . . . Such an error is to treat the Jewish question as a racial question. This is not a Christian treatment. . . . There are anti-Semites who say that Jesus was not a Jew but an Aryan. This, however, is the height of folly.'' [55]

## Anti-Christian Anti-Semitism

The anti-Semitism in the Second Reich that sought to absorb Christianity into its racial ideology, which also included non-Christian or anti-Christian tendencies, sprang up side by side with Christian anti-Semitism, sometimes in conjunction with it and sometimes in political opposition to it. The complex relationship of racial anti-Semitism to Christianity goes back to the beginning of this movement and is evident in many of its early exponents, especially H. Naudh-Nordmann, Wilhelm Marr, Eugen Dühring, Christian Radenhausen, Adolf Wahrmund, Otto Glagau, Theodor Fritsch, and others of whom we shall speak in the course of this chapter.

55. A.S., Danzig, 1892, p. 273. A similar view held by Professor A. Wagner is in ibid., p. 179, according to the report in *Vossische Zeitung,* April 30, 1892.

Under the influence of Feuerbach's criticism of religion and more popular works in the first half of the nineteenth century, such as Friedrich
Daumer and Hundt von Radowsky, these early racial anti-Semites censured Christianity for having failed to overcome Judaism, for fostering
the same hypocritical "virtues" of humility, egalitarianism, and brotherly
love that sapped the vitality of the superior German Aryan race. Both
religions alienated man from his native soil and original nature, filled him
with fanaticism, morbid anxieties, and superstitions, and weakened his
confidence in his ability to be master of his own fate. All this was the
result of abstract rationalism shared by both religions, expressed in the
petrified law of Judaism and in the evangelical brotherly love of Christianity. Christianity was but the bitter fruit of the Jewish tree on Christian
soil.

One of the important early factors that served as a kind of connecting
link and regulator between these two types of modern anti-Semitism was
the amorphous and for the most part unorganized lower middle classes
that rallied around Otto Glagau in the early days of the Second Reich. At
the time of the financial crash of 1873–1874, the so-called *Gründerkrach,*
and throughout the period of the *Kulturkampf* until the mid-eighties,
Glagau carried on his publicistic campaign against the big industrialists,
investors, and financial speculators. His aim was to protect the small artisan, the petty tradesman, the low-income groups, teachers, disillusioned
intellectuals, and all those who felt the brunt of social and economic discrimination. In the eyes of all these groups the Jew was the tangible personification of all the forces in modern society that determined the fate of
the small man, forces he could neither control nor dominate and against
which he was unable to defend himself.

Glagau and the circles associated with the organ of the middle class,
the *Gartenlaube,* [56] were well aware that the members of the lower middle
class, insofar as they did not join the Social Democrats, were for the most
part loathe to relinquish their traditional Christian affiliations even if they
were nothing more than a secular and functional expression of their per-

56. See Introduction by Friedrich Sieburg to the photostatic edition of selected issues of
the *Gartenlaube: Facsimile Querschnitt durch die Gartenlaube,* ed. Heinz Klüter, Bern,
Stuttgart, Wien, 1963, pp. 1 ff, 17–18. Despite the undue importance that *Gartenlaube's*
anti-Semitic aspect has acquired in the historiography of anti-Semitism, we find that the Introduction and the balanced selection of this collection justly fail to confirm the erroneous
impression that the principal aim of this periodical was to incite anti-Semitic feeling.

sonal, family, and social identity. At the same time Glagau realized that the church had little influence on these frustrated groups in the urban centers in enlisting their enthusiasm for social causes, in enhancing the intellectual and moral quality of their lives, or in alleviating their fears. On these disappointments and frustrations Glagau built his anti-Semitic propaganda to serve as a kind of bridge between the traditional anti-Jewish anti-Semitism and the new racial anti-Semitism.[57] He desired to rally the moral forces of the community and to instill in the "small man" a feeling of belonging to the modern community which he called "We Christians," so that he might resist the forces of evil that had alienated him and made him insecure. The time had now come, Glagau proclaimed, for the Christians to express their passive repugnance of the Jews and expose the deceit, cunning, and chicanery of these parasites who "always push us aside, press us to the wall, rob us of the air we breathe." [58] Some of the basic concepts of racial anti-Semitism were already apparent in these words of Glagau. The Jews were a homeless tribe without a native country and hence the symbol and embodiment of alienation and instability; the Germans were a Christian *Volk,* a noble race that sought to be rooted in a stable Reich that had permitted itself to be dominated and hoodwinked by the malevolent and degenerate Jews.[59] The subtle and tenacious power of the Jews was a portent not to be disregarded. Glagau therefore urged his countrymen to exclude the Jews from all positions of influence, for they not only adhered to a foreign religion but constituted a foreign race, so that even if they should change their religion and become Christians they would still retain their offensive racial traits, their desire for dominion, their parasitic nature and inveterate

---

57. Otto Glagau, *Der Börsen und Gründungsschwindel,* Berlin 1876, pp. xxx–xxxi, first printed in *Gartenlaube* in 1874–1875 and again in the collection of sources, Harry Pross, ed., *Die Zerstörung der deutschen Politik—Dokumente 1871–1933,* 4th ed., Frankfurt a/M, 1963, p. 253; Westphalen, pp. 22–23. See also Kurt Wawrzinek, *Die Entstehung der deutschen Antisemitenparteien (1873–1890),* Berlin, 1927, p. 33 ff, and P. Massing, pp. 9 ff, 232, no. 28.

58. Westphalen, pp. 22–23. This view that the aim of the anti-Jewish struggle was to defend German Christianity, including both Catholicism and Protestantism, appeared in some of the issues of the periodical published by Otto Glagau, *Der Kulturkämpfer, Zeitschrift für öffentliche Angelegenheiten,* Berlin, 1879, p. iii, "Vorwort"; 1880, p. 5 ff, "Zur Emancipation der Eingeborenen"; 1885, p. 441 ff, "Hofprediger Stöcker und sein Prozess."

59. Westphalen, pp. 22–23.

insolence: "What will Christianity profit them; racial nature [*Rassennatur*] does not seek the counsel of priests, and blood does not attend to the sound of church bells." [60]

While Glagau's propaganda served as a kind of bridge between Christian anti-Semitism and the anti-Semitism that also included anti-Christian tendencies, a considerable number of the leading political and racial anti-Semites in the Second Reich stressed the anti-Christian aspects of their propaganda. A conspicuous representative of this latter group was Wilhelm Marr who, even at the beginning of his anti-Jewish campaign in 1862, negated Christianity in conjunction with his attack on Judaism. In his polemical work against Marr's *Judenspiegel,* called *Der Christenspiegel von Anti-Marr,* Moritz Freystadt of Leipzig pointed out that Marr was indebted to Voltaire and Feuerbach for his derogatory views of religion, monotheism, and Judaism as nothing but visionary anthropological projections, and then asked:

If the basis of Judaism is so decadent, as the modern Haman of Hamburg boldly proclaims, how can Christianity be built on it? How could the Redeemer of the world again and again return to this basis? Is not ancient Judaism the preordained basis of all Christianity? . . . Did not all the apostles continually testify to the truths of the Old Testament? . . . Does he not thereby clearly express his antipathy for Christianity, which is founded on it [the Old Testament]? Will not also his Christian brethren suffer as a result of this unnatural hatred of their fellow men? . . . No one does greater harm to Christianity than Marr himself, this young Jew-baiter of Hamburg. [61]

The growth of racial anti-Semitism was accompanied by an increasing criticism of Christianity as a religion and as an established church. In one of his more popular works, *Religiöse Streifzüge eines philosophischen*

---

60. From a public address of a secondary school teacher in Dresden about his Jewish students, according to excerpts of the minutes preserved in the collection of anti-Semitic addresses at the end of the 1870's or beginning of the 1880's until the end of the 1890's under the auspices of the student organization Deutsche antisemitische Studentenschaft; the collection is entitled "Reden studentischer Agitatoren," F.A., No. 6/a.

61. Moritz Freystadt, *Der Christenspiegel von Anti-Marr, ein offenes Sendeschreiben an die modernen Judenfeinde,* 2d ed., Königsberg, 1863, pp. 20–21, 39. The first edition was evidently published in November 1862. For a similar earlier reaction against the definition of Jews as a race and against the anti-Christian conclusion derived from W. Marr's anti-Jewish attitude, see the pamphlet *Der arme Jude wie ihn der grosse Demokrat Herr W. Marr besp.* [richt], beleuchtet von keinem Juden, Hamburg, Leipzig, 1862, pp. 5, 8, 9, 11. See also an aggressive anti-Catholic pamphlet by W. Marr, *Streifzüge durch das Koncilium von Trient: Voltairefrei nacherzählt,* Hamburg, 1868.

*Touristen* (1876), Marr stated, obviously influenced by Voltaire, Feuerbach, and the younger Bruno Bauer, that we must regard "Christianity, as every religion, with its dogmas and articles of faith, as a disease of human consciousness. . . . The philosopher defines every religion as a product of human self-consciousness, and relegates to the realm of phantasy the so-called 'revelations' of which every people is so proud, each according to its cultural development." [62] In a similar vein Marr asserted that Christianity is nothing more than a manifestation of Judaism and as such a source of corruption and fanaticism. Both Judaism and Christianity are "abstractions," that is, they regard man as a separate being, apart from reality, and hence "since Judaism and Christianity are the only religions that seek to rule society in an abstract manner . . . I find them detestable. . . . The zeal to kill and persecute one's fellow man seems to be inherent in Christianity from its birth." [63] Nevertheless, Marr maintained, the criticism of Christianity should not be confused with anti-Semitism. Such criticism was part of the more comprehensive indictment of religion in general as a web of superstition that had hastened the process of the degeneration of German life. Anti-Semitism, however, was not only a negation of a religious phenomenon and not only a reaction to deicide and the nonacknowledgment of Christian redemption on the part of the Jews, as was still believed by Stöcker and his followers; such a conception was an anachronism as well as a methodological error, and its advocate "has wrongly turned the empirical-scientific question of race into a religious question . . . and not treating the Jewish question in a sufficiently scientific manner. He forgets that the racial question respecting the Jews had already existed before the birth of Christianity and before the Christian church was founded, and that this physiological and

62. "Das Christenthum, sowie jede Religion in ihrem Theile der Dogmen und äusserlichen Satzungen als eine Krankheit des menschlichen Bewusstseins . . . der Philosoph erklärt . . . jede Religion für ein Product des menschlichen Selbstbewusstseins und erweist die sogenannten . . . 'Offenbarungen' deren sich alle Völker je nach ihrem Culturzustand verschieden, rühmen, in das Gebiet der Phantasie," W. Marr, *Religiöse Streifzüge eines philosophischen Touristen,* Berlin, 1876, pp. 95–96; also pp. 12 ff, 16, 19, 104 ff, 128, 192: "wir . . . verwerfen das Christenthum wie das Judenthum, verwerfen . . . alle Religionen." For the source called "anti-Semitism" in the works of W. Marr, see Alexander Bein, "Der moderne Antisemitismus und seine Bedeutung für die Judenfrage," *Vierteljahrshefte für Zeitgeschichte,* Stuttgart, 1958, pp. 345–346.
63. This excerpt became well known through the publications of the Verein zur Abwehr des Antisemitismus; see "Die Antisemiten und das Christenthum," A.S., Danzig, 1892, p. 137 ff. The excerpt is taken from the above work by Marr, pp. 8–12, under the title "Aufzählung der Schlachtopfer des Christenthums."

psychological phenomenon cannot be explained away by Christian-ecclesiastical abstractions. Stöcker thinks that it is possible to improve the Jews. . . . Did not God, did not Providence itself create this racial distinction?'' [64]

Marr's anti-Semitic argument lacked inner consistency and on more than one occasion he abandoned the anti-Christian note to defend the Christian and the policy of ''practical Christianity'' (as proclaimed by the Kaiser and the Bismarck regime on November 17, 1881) against Jewish domination.[65] Marr was inclined to formulate his views pessimistically and attributed the Jewish domination of Europe and Germany to ''a world-historical fate,'' so that now there was nothing left for the Germans but to confess ''that we are conquered, enslaved.'' [66] Eugen Dühring, on the other hand, formulated his views on a different intellectual level and proposed a well-defined alternative to religion and religious culture, both Jewish and Christian, namely, the alternative of race. In his anti-Jewish works after 1880, Judaism served as the prototype of religion, and this also included Christianity. The basic principle of Dühring's anti-Christian anti-Semitism was that the struggle against Judaism and the Jews was intimately bound up with the struggle against monotheistic religion and hence also against the forces suppressing the free and natural impulse of life itself. In his antireligious work *Wert des Lebens* (1877), especially in the third edition (1881), Dühring asserted that ''the religious systems . . . are a chapter in the study of the diseases of the universal history of the spirit . . . for religion, including Christianity, is the quintessence of the 'hatred of life'. . . and the eradication of the natural instincts.'' [67]

64. W. Marr, ''Der Judenkrieg, seine Fehler und wie er zu organisieren ist,'' 2d Part of *Der Sieg des Judenthums über das Germanenthum,* Chemnitz, 1888, pp. 2–3. These words also appeared in the series *Antisemitische Hefte,* No. 1. See also W. Marr, *Der Sieg des Judenthums über das Germanenthum von nicht confessionellem Standpunkt aus betrachtet,* 5th ed. Bern, 1879, pp. 7, 46, 48.

65. W. Marr, *Lessing: Contra Sem, allen Rabbinern der Juden und Christenheit . . . gewidmet,* 2d ed., Berlin, 1885, pp. 26, 39, 41.

66. W. Marr, *Der Sieg des Judenthums über das Germanthum, von nichtconfessionellem Standpunkt aus betrachtet,* 5th ed., Bern, 1879, p. 46 ff. In a later work called *Der Weg zum Siege des Germanenthums über das Judenthum,* Berlin, 1880, which was the fourth edition of a pamphlet *Wählet keine Juden,* Marr completely abandoned this pessimistic view and returned to an anti-Semitic style more likely to appeal to the Christian public, and he declared that the war against the Jews was directed to ''Christian emancipation,'' for the German Reich was a Christian state and to preserve this character it was imperative to combat the danger of a general Judaization.

67. Eugen Dühring, *Wert des Lebens,* 3d ed., 1881, p. 5 ff. In this connection Dühring also criticized his teacher Ludwig Feuerbach for his too lenient attitude toward the exagger-

Hence, to use the traditional concept of Christianity with its debilitating ethics and its "paradoxical doctrine of the reversal or crucifixion of all desires of the flesh" [68] was absurd, for it was combating a degenerate condition with weapons that were themselves degenerate. The Christians who believed this were only deceiving themselves, for "their anti-Semitism ignores the basic truth that Christianity itself is semitic, a truth which should be . . . the point of departure for all true anti-Hebraism." [69] As long as the Christians failed to liberate themselves from their Jewish source, from the "Jewish notion of unity," or from the "Hebraic confinement to unity" which was nothing more than "the despotism of egotism," they would not liberate themselves from the forces that opposed nature; but since Christianity was indissolubly bound to its Jewish origin, there was no choice but to insist on complete emancipation from the crushing yoke of both Judaism and Christianity.[70] For the various people and cultures of the modern age to acquire a sense of self-identity they must cast off the degenerate influences of religion and return to their original racial nature. They would then see how far the New Testament had perverted the aristocratic spirit of the Germans, for the New Testament was nothing but "a racially Jewish tradition." As the renewed German culture freed itself from the corrupt heritage of the Old and the New Testament, the "peculiar, superior national character of the Germans" would assert itself and rejoice in the final release from its bondage to religion.[71] This process of liberation from the Jewish-Christian heritage on the one hand and the restoration of the Nordic-Germanic racial nature on the other was not a process that could be achieved through education or civilization; it could only be achieved through the scrupulous preservation of the purity of the "natural foundations in flesh and blood"

---

ated spirituality of Christianity, E. Dühring, *Kritische Geschichte der Philosophie von ihren Anfängen bis zur Gegenwart,* 3d ed., Leipzig, 1878, p. 461.

68. E. Dühring, *Wert des Lebens,* 3d ed., 1881, p. 5.

69. Eugen Dühring, "Die Parteien in der Judenfrage," *Separat-Ausgabe von Hefte 7, 8, des ersten Bandes der Schmeitznerischen internationalen Monatsschrift,* Leipzig, 1882, p. 403 ff.

70. E. Dühring, *Die Judenfrage als Frage des Rassencharakters und seiner Schädlichkeiten für Exlstenz und Kultur der Völker* (1st ed., 1880), 6th enlarged ed., ed. H. Reinhardt, Leipzig, 1930, p. 32 ff. See there, p. 53 ff, a sharp criticism of the "paradox of loving one's enemy" in Christian ethics, an ethics that was nothing but hypocrisy. On Dühring's place in the racial anti-Semitic development of the hatred of Jewish religion and ethics, see K. Saller, "Die biologisch motivierte Judenfeindschaft" in *Judenfeindschaft,* ed. Karl Thieme, Frankfurt a/M, 1963, p. 181.

71. Eugen Dühring, *Der Ersatz der Religion durch Volkommeneres und die Ausscheidung alles Judenthums durch den modernen Völkergeist,* Karlsruhe, 1883, p. 63.

by prohibiting miscegenation and by adopting a policy of planned breeding.

The root of this misfortune that had befallen the German nation was not to be found in Christianity but in Judaism, so that the process of racial purification recommended by Dühring entailed first and foremost a process of "de-Judaizing" (*Entjudung*). Since Christianity remained imprisoned in its Jewish source and all of western culture had fallen prey to a "Judaization of the nations" (*Verjudung der Völker*), there was no way out of the impasse except to negate Christianity together with Judaism. The anti-Christian bias of Dühring's anti-Semitism is conspicuous in many publications of the Verein zur Abwehr des Antisemitismus many of whose leading members were Liberal-Progressive Christians. A typical excerpt from Dühring's works in their eyes was the following:

Christianity has no practical ethical precept that is unambiguously useful and salutary. Hence, the nations will rid themselves of the Semitic spirit only after they succeed in uprooting this second manifestation of Hebraism as well. . . . To go forth today to combat racial Judaism from the standpoint of Christianity is to attempt to turn evil into nonevil by means of one of its own offshoots, that is, by means of itself. Those who desire to strengthen the Christian tradition are in no position to combat Judaism with vigor. A Christian who understands himself cannot be a serious anti-Semite. The Nordic idols and the Nordic God contain a natural kernel and no thousand-year-old distraction can remove it from the world. . . . Here has reigned an imaginative spirit incomparably superior to the Jewish slave imagination.[72]

After the mid-eighties these attitudes of racial anti-Semitism that had an anti-Christian bias developed into an ideology with a marked public influence. This development began in 1884 with the establishment of a new Anti-Semitic Center in Leipzig under Theodor Fritsch and the appearance a year later of the influential periodical *Antisemitische Correspondenz,* which subsequently (1888) became the official organ of the D.A.P. under the new name of the *Deutsch-Soziale Blätter*. This center was an important factor in the struggle against Christianity or in making it an integral part of the Aryan race propaganda. This was officially announced as early as February 1887 when it declared that racial anti-Semi-

72. A.S., Danzig, 1892, p. 137 ff; see the same sources in the pamphlet issued by the Verein zur Abwehr des Antisemitismus, *Antisemitisches Christenthum und christlicher Antisemitismus,* Flugblatt, No. 7, pp. 1–2.

tism was to be "a pioneer in the creation of a new religion." [73] In connection with this new ideal the circles around Theodor Fritsch declared their opposition to baptism as a means of solving the Jewish problem, for baptism could not remove the deep-rooted stain in the Jewish or Semitic race, a stain identical with this race and its embodiment. This same point was emphasized in the anti-Semitic ideology of Eduard von Hartmann who asserted that the popular antipathy toward the Jew could not be removed by conversion and that the classical Christian conception of the efficacy of baptism was erroneous. His general argument was not consistent, however, for he still believed that if the Jews could succeed "in feeling Aryan inwardly" and in freeing themselves from their "Jewish tribal feeling," then a Jewish-German fusion might prove successful. Fritsch answered this argument in the early nineties by saying that although Hartmann had furthered the cause of anti-Semitism, he failed to understand that belonging to a race is not a matter of subjective feeling but an objective fact. [74] It is therefore not surprising to find that Fritsch's followers in the *Antisemitische Correspondenz*—in contradistinction to Liebermann von Sonnenberg's adherents who wished to disassociate themselves from anti-Christian anti-Semitism—were opposed to all attempts to absorb the Jews into German society on the ground that every admixture, especially intermarriage, could only lead to a "mixed Jewish-German race" to the detriment of the German Aryans and to all human culture.

The common thesis of the exponents of this type of anti-Semitism was that the Jews had been a problem for the Christians from the very beginning, and for the Germans ever since the days of Charlemagne, and they would continue to be a problem until Christianity freed itself from its dependence on Judaism. The very existence of Israel among the nations was an amazing anachronism, an antihistorical phenomenon that defied all logic and excited loathing in the heart of the German. Judaism was the

73. A.C., 1887, No. 10, p. 5; also in the same spirit, A.C., 1886, No. 5, pp. 2–3; 1886, No. 6, pp. 4–5; 1889, No. 55, p. 1. These sources are also quoted in a study written from the Nazi point of view, Joseph Müller, *Die Entwicklung des Rassenantisemitismus in den letzten Jahrzehnten des 19 Jahrhundert, dargestellt hauptsächlich auf Grundlage der "Antisemitischen Correspondenz,"* Berlin, 1940, Historische Studien, No. 372 (hereafter, Müller).

74. For Hartmann's attitude toward the Jewish question and the Jewish reaction to this attitude, see Hugo Bergman, "Eduard von Hartmann und die Judenfrage in Deutschland," *L.B.Y.*, Vol. V, London, 1960, p. 177 ff.

omnipresent ancient rival that Christianity must constantly confront, the cardinal point from which it diverged and to which it must bear constant reference. There was something diabolical in this absurd dependence of Christianity on Judaism, declared the distinguished Orientalist, Professor Adolf Wahrmund, and the only solution would seem to be the conversion of Jews which would mark the advent of the promised salvation as proclaimed by Paul (Romans 9:4 ff and 11:25). But this was a vain hope, Wahrmund continued, "because the Jews will never relinquish their stubborn attachment to the petrified law nor . . . the liberals among them . . . the delusion of grandeur in being the chosen people . . . and even if they become converts to Christianity, they will never be able to shed their peculiar Hamitic-Semitic racial traits which are for us, the Aryan-Christian people, so foreign and mysterious." [75] In the eyes of the Christian, Judaism remained a mystery. Even when he did not believe in the dogmas of the church or apprehended them imperfectly, the Christian was affected by the suggestive power of the graphic traditional locutions that surrounded this mystery. Only by overcoming and vanquishing Judaism, Wahrmund concluded, could Christianity save itself and the Aryan German people regain their identity. Israel's unyielding adherence to its historical and eschatological singularity, despite its wretched condition, was the primary cause of traditional anti-Semitism. The Christian who believed that he had earned God's grace through the self-sacrifice of Jesus would never be able to free himself from his dependence on the Jew. For it was the incredulity of the Jew and his faltering response in partaking of God's grace through Christ that had retarded the life of the spirit and kept the Christian from appropriating his rightful heritage.

These arguments were advanced and elaborated in both the popular Christian conservative and the racial anti-Semitic circles. The Jew's irrevocable commitment to preserve his historical uniqueness under pressure

75. These words of Professor Wahrmund have been preserved in fragmentary form in the collection *Reden und Aufsätze,* pub. by D.S.P., Leipzig, 1889, p. 4. This view was developed systematically on a seemingly historical basis and as an attempt to rescue Christianity by severing it from Judaism and by integrating it into a German-Aryan nationalism or into a German-Aryan national race theory in two popular books by Wahrmund; the first book, A. Wahrmund, *Babylonierthum, Judenthum, Christenthum,* Leipzig, 1882, chap. xvii, "Das Christenthum," p. 205 ff; see also chap. xviii, p. 213 ff, which is devoted to Christian anti-Semitism in the style of A. Rohling, "Der Talmud und die Entmenschlichung des Jahwismus." The second book that is pertinent to our discussion here is *Das Gesetz des Nomadenthums und die heutige Judenherrschaft,* Karlsruhe, Leipzig, 1887. See there, especially, "Vorwort," pp. v, 189, 232.

of every calamity not only obstructed the Christian's path to the kingdom of God on earth but thwarted all his plans in everyday life. The Jew was to blame for the high cost of living, unemployment, plagues, poor crops, excessive rain, drought, protracted frost, class exploitation, exorbitant rates of interest, the unfair distribution of wealth, the corruption of good manners, the increase in crime, the poor conditions in the factory, school, army, church, in the nation's internal and external relations—all because of the Jew's recalcitrance in refusing to acknowledge Jesus the Redeemer.[76] The Jew then not only interrupted the transcendental design, but he also did irreparable harm to the phenomenal order of things, for the protection of heaven had been withdrawn from the world because of him. The racial anti-Semites were not averse to adopting the anti-Jewish tradition of Christianity in order to gratify at once their resentment and piety. This, indeed, was the avowed aim of Professor Wahrmund: "The Aryan Christian or the Aryan as such sets himself ideal demands; the Semitic Jew or the Semite as such considers demands of this nature, insofar as he is capable of understanding them, as pure folly." [77] In this spirit the early exponents of racial anti-Semitism saw little hope that Christianity would liberate itself from its Jewish roots. In Christianity itself, not only in its Jewish sources which were shared by all Christians, but also in the structure of the established Catholic and Lutheran churches, there were rudimentary powers that enslaved the Christian by setting up impracticable ideals that could not be realized by finite man and thus imbued him with a lurking dread of sin, guilt, insecurity, and weakness. This structure of Jewish Christianity reinforced the dependency of the Christian on the church and its antiquated theological traditions and hastened the process of degeneracy in the Christian-Jewish man. This loss of natural vitality and original spontaneity obliged Christianity to rehabilitate itself

76. A. Werkstätter, *Der Antisemitismus auf dem Lande,* 1888, pp. 24, 29; Anon., *Otto Böckel und Adolf Stöcker: wir brauchen Beide! Aufruf zur judenfeindlichen Solidarität,* Dresden, 1889, p. 14 ff. A complementary summary of these arguments and points of view is in "Der Wucher und das Judenthum," A.S., Danzig, 1900, pp. 173–196; "Der Juden Antheil am Verbrechen," A.S., Danzig, 1900, pp. 197–224. See also Müller, p. 67 ff, "Judenthum und Christenthum im Blickfeld des Rassenantisemitismus": "der arische Christ, oder der Arier überhaupt stellt an sich ideale Forderungen, der semitische Jude, oder der Semite überhaupt, hält solche Forderungen soweit er sie verstehen kann, für ganz thöricht."

77. A. Wahrmund, *Babylonierthum, Judenthum, Christenthum,* Leipzig, 1882, p. 208 ff.

along Aryan lines that would liberate it from the coils of sin and the pangs of conscience. The freedom it would thus attain was called "idealism of Aryan Christianity." [78]

Some of the leading exponents of racial anti-Semitism—A. Wahrmund, C. Radenhausen, Theodor Fritsch, Oswald Zimmermann, Paul Förster, Hans von Mosch—proclaimed that their movement not only departed from Christianity but sought to overcome it by integrating it completely into the racial conception. Christianity itself, from its very inception, was anti-Jewish or anti-Semitic; its original and enduring impulse was to overcome Judaism, and this could not be accomplished by the conversion of Jews but by their extermination. Christianity, however, never completed its original task. It must now cleanse itself of its Jewish sources, of monotheistic abstraction that sundered man from nature and reality, of universalism and cosmopolitanism, the belief in immortality, reward, and punishment, and all the corrupt ethical principles that weakened the natural spontaneity of the German, his joyous affirmation of life, his instinctive attachment to concrete experience and to the soil of his native land. We find a typical expression of this sentiment in Paul Förster's anti-Semitic periodical *Freideutschland* (June 2, 1896):

From the historical point of view it is indisputable that the ancient Germanic power of the world-historical nation of heroes reached its purest state before its contact with Christianity; then in the course of centuries it receded more and more until it finally became the unfortunate people of today—and this under the influence of Christianity! No matter how well disposed we may be to Christianity, it will not help us to come to terms with this hard historical fact, a fact that must be squarely faced if one wishes to discuss the question "German or Christian." [79]

78. Ibid., pp. 212, 254 ff, for Wahrmund's request not to debate with Jews who abused their civic rights in order to vilify Christianity, such as Heinrich Graetz; Wahrmund's reference was to the Graetz-Treitschke debate, see above, Chap. 4. In this desire to liberate Christianity from Judaism, Wahrmund relied on Renan's conception according to which the Indo-European people must free themselves from the Semitic spirit if they were to preserve their Christianity, that is, the less Jewish the more Christian, E. Renan, *De la part des peuples sémitiques dans l'histoire de la civilisation,* Paris, 1889, p. 40.

79. "Geschichtlich ist unbestreitbar, dass die altgermanische Kraft des Heldenvolkes der Weltgeschichte völlig echt nur vor der Berührung mit dem Christenthum da war, seitdem im Laufe der Jahrhunderte stets mehr gebrochen wurde, bis wir endlich zu dem Jammervolke von heute wurden, immer unter dem Einfluss des—Christentums! Über diese harte geschichtliche Tatsache hilft keine dem Christentum noch so freundliche Stellung hinweg. Mit ihr muss erst sich abfinden wer in der Frage 'deutsch oder christlich' mitsprechen will," A.S., Danzig, 1911, p. 196. See also M.V.A.A., 1896, No. 13, p. 100, "Antisemitismus unchristlich"; 1899, No. 12, p. 91, "Antisemitisches antichristliches"; 1902, No. 23, p. 168, "Die Antisemiten und das Christenthum."

The ground was now prepared for the doctrines of Paul de Lagarde, which were to have great vogue in Germany for decades to come. Lagarde's basic doctrine was that Christianity must be swallowed up by Germanism if the extinction of the Germanic race was to be averted. This thesis became an integral part of racial anti-Semitism, especially in the circles of the *Antisemitische Correspondenz,* in the anti-Semitic catechisms published by Theodor Fritsch, in the ideologies of Friedrich Lange and Max Bewer, and, with the advent of the twentieth century, in the pages of the influential periodical *Der Hammer.* Those who adhered to this view looked forward to the day when the church would be superseded by the state, religion by nationality, Christianity by Germanism, and when prayer would be replaced by state legislation, the love of God by the love of the fatherland, fear of divine retribution by the spirit of bold enterprise, and rationalistic man by the noble representative of the superior Aryan race.[80]

The authority for this ideology, in which Christian symbols intermingled with romantic longings and pagan veneration, had its seat in the individual's subjective identification with the gospels and with the traditions related to the life of Jesus. This subjective identification was to serve as the basis for a new nontraditional interpretation of the gospels in the spirit of Germany's heroic past and glorious future. In the modern age of nationalism, Lagarde declared, Christianity had lost its universal ethical significance and should adopt an exclusively national German form. Lagarde set forth his views with convincing power and with a strong assurance that he was witnessing the birth of the new German man, a superior type nourished by a vital vegetative principle that transcended all rational and humanistic credentials. He was persuaded that the liberating concept of the superior Aryan race, as manifested in the German man, would bridge the gap between Christianity and the recrudescent German nationalism. The relation between God and man, as revealed in the person of Jesus, was now revealed in the German. But even though the life of the new German man appeared to be modeled after the life of Jesus as described

80. The principal sources of Paul de Lagarde's doctrines whose influence is clearly apparent in the ideology of racial anti-Semitism are in *Deutsche Schriften von Paul de Lagarde,* 4th ed., Göttingen, 1903: "Über die gegenwärtigen Aufgaben der deutschen Politik" (1853) (1874), p. 24 ff; "Über das Verhältnis des deutschen Staates zu Theologie, Kirche und Religion" (1873), pp. 37 ff, 56 ff; "Die Religion der Zukunft" (1878), p. 217 ff; "Die Stellung der Religionsgesellschaften im Staate" (1881), pp. 248 ff, 256 ff; "Die graue Internationale" (1881), p. 319 ff; "Programme für die konservative Partei Preussens" (1884), pp. 326 ff, 365 ff.

in the gospels, it was, as envisaged by Lagarde, closer to that of Nietzsche's antichrist. In Christianity man strives to reach out to God, the wholly Other, but he is too exhausted to rise to Him, and in the perpetual struggle between feeble man and august God the victory is ceded to the latter. However, as a result of the Incarnation, when the Almighty took on flesh and when the broken body became the way and the truth, a reversal of positions took place. Man put off his finitude and exchanged it for divinity. As the heir of God, he now usurped His wisdom. The barriers were broken down that separated God from man, the spiritual from the corporeal, the ideal from the real, phenomena from the things-in-themselves; and by the same token the boundaries were removed between the church and state, religion and nationality, present and future, moral responsibility and the uninhibited instincts. The millennium was nigh. The only obstacle in the path of this ideal state was Judaism, the archenemy of the Incarnation, the defender of the abstract, the trumpeter of the rational and the intellectual (in the pejorative sense). Lagarde's ideology with its antiecclesiastical formulations and prophetic fervor that spoke of "the final victory . . . of the immortal society of the sons of God" burst the narrow limits of scholastic Catholicism and Lutheranism. The spirit of the times demanded a renewal commensurate with the ancient Germanic virtues and the native vigor of the German soul. Lagarde's new myth gathered its strength from these ancient powers of the Teutonic soul which were not erected on a well-defined ontological or metaphysical basis but which resided in their concrete ideological application and in their influence on society and the state.[81]

In the closing years of the nineteenth and the first decade of the twentieth century these views were consolidated into a relatively unified ideology. The primary concern in this process was to incorporate Jesus and Christianity into a racialist Aryan ideology and at the same time retain non-Christian or even anti-Christian elements. Representatives of various schools of thought took part in this movement: of the exponents of anti-intellectualism and *Kulturpessimismus* there were Julius Langbehn, Max Bewer, Fritz Bley; of the Alldeutsche movement, Friedrich Lange,

---

81. In addition to the above sources, No. 80, for the words of Paul de Lagarde himself, see Fritz Stern, *The Politics of Cultural Despair: A Study in the Rise of the Germanic Ideology,* Berkeley, Los Angeles, 1961, pp. 35 ff, 53 ff; and the testimony of the racial anti-Semites themselves, Theodor Lindström, *Paul de Lagarde, ein Vorkämpfer Deutsch-sozialer Reform, Antisemitisches Jahrbuch,* Berlin, 1898, p. 4 ff; also Müller, p. 25 ff.

Heinrich Class (also known by his pseudonym Daniel Freyman), and a number of influential literary figures, such as Wilhelm Schwaner and Theodor Fritsch (also known as Thomas Frey), whose anti-Semitic catechisms during this period were published in scores of editions and, beginning in the early years of the twentieth century, in the pages of *Der Hammer;* Paul Förster and Hans von Mosch within the framework of the Deutscher Volksbund, as well as the followers of E. Dühring who aired their views in short-lived periodicals.[82] All these representatives of racialist anti-Semitism defined their attitude toward Christianity not as a hostile but as a liberating attitude that was designed to redeem German Christianity from its constant and profitless confrontation with Judaism wherein the Christian German was at a decided disadvantage. Instead of being faithful to his own ideals and returning to the rock whence he was hewn, the Christian accepted the notion of Jewish election and bowed down to arrogant Jewish rationalism which he took as the criterion of his self-evalution. The German children should be taught that the Germans were "a chosen race, a royal priesthood, a holy nation, God's own people, that you may declare the wonderful deeds of him who called you out of darkness into his marvelous light." [83]

This dependence on Judaism from which racial anti-Semitism wished to liberate Christianity was described by Dühring's followers as a double dependence. From the theological point of view Christianity was dependent on the continued existence of the Jews (however lowly and wretched) as the living witness of the truth of its own beliefs, and herein lay the diabolical power of the Jew. Second, the Christians were dependent on the Jews in the empirical realm where the Jews were by no means helpless but rather in a dominant position. Here Germanism should go

82. For references to sources concerning public and ideological activities, see A.S., Danzig, 1892, 1911. See also the following reports and polemics: M.V.A.A., 1896, No. 1, p. 150, "Antisemitismus"; 1898, No. 7, p. 54, "vom 'Arier' Christus"; 1898, No. 9, p. 71, "Christus als 'Arier' "; 1904, No. 4, p. 25, "Die Antisemiten und das Alte Testament"; 1904, No. 12, p. 89, "Das Jesus Christus eyn geborenen Jude sey"; 1904, No. 16, p. 126, "Christus ein Germane (aus der 'Frankfurter Zeitung')"; 1904, No. 38, p. 301, "Christentum und Deutschtum"; 1904, No. 41, p. 322 ff, "Die Neue Heilslehre" (A. Müller, *Jesus ein Arier,* Leipzig, 1904); 1905, No. 11, "Ist es Christlich Antisemit zu sein?"; 1906, No. 29, p. 220, "Antisemiten und Christentum"; 1906, No. 44, p. 344, "Christentum und Judenthum"; 1909, No. 19, p. 166, "Christentum und Antisemitismus."

83. The New Testament source is 1 Peter 2:9; the whole argument presented here is for the most part based on the collection *Reden und Aufsätze,* pub. by D.S.P., Leipzig, 1889, pp. 4, 14, 28, Appendices II, IV.

forth with the ardor of a knight-errant to remold Christianity and redeem it from its subservience to Judaism. Germanism was rooted in the love of nature, in the innocent pastimes of rural life, in the landscape of its native land, and in the recollection of its pristine aboriginal power that rejected all spiritual and cultural phenomena nourished by foreign sources. Germanism was based on the cardinal virtues of self-reliance, probity, valor, and the consciousness of the universal rule of the master race. The time had come for Christianity to free itself completely from the ruinous influences of Judaism and regain its rudimentary Teutonic potencies of racial purity, unadulterated blood, and the love of the native soil. A typical slogan of the racial anti-Semites was that of E. Hasse, the founder of the Alldeutscher Verband (1897): "Our future lies in our blood"; or that of Friedrich Lange, the publisher of the *Neue Deutsche Zeitung* and an active member of the Pan-Germanic movement since the year 1909: "Away with belief." [84] Judaism preached the virtues of pity, forgiveness, humility, moderation, and the superiority of the spirit over the natural rights of Nietzsche's "genius" and Fichte's "total man"—the decadent virtues that had alienated modern man and filled him with feelings of guilt and remorse. In this spirit Friedrich Lange declared that, in contradistinction to Aryan Christianity, Jewish Christianity corrupted the German's original nature and vitiated the exalted qualities that were his birthright. Instead of teaching German children these corrupt Christian doctrines, it would be better to imbue them with the Teutonic virtues and show them "how exemplary men and women practiced German morality that had been instilled in them in childhood and how, even under the oppressive influence of Christianity, adopted what was consistent with their German nature and rejected what was opposed to it . . . these instincts were suppressed so that Christianity might not suffer the slightest harm." [85] A few years later (1896) Lange expressed himself in a similar vein in the pages of the *Deutsche Zeitung:* "For us personally this question is not a question; we are convinced that as long as practical Christianity is capa-

84. Friedrich Lange, *Zur 1900 Gedenkfeier der Schlacht im Teutoburger-Walde, Ansprache an die Mitglieder des Deutschbundes,* Berlin 1909, p. 1. The quotation from Hasse is also quoted by P. Massing, p. 152: "wie . . . vorbildliche Männer und Frauen ihre angeborene deutsche Sittlichkeit darlebten und selbst unter dem erdrückenden Einflusse des Christenthums annahmen was ihrer deutschen Natur gemäss war und ablehnten, was ihr widerstand . . . man unterdrückte diese Instinkte damit ja nicht das Christenthum zu kurz komme."

85. Friedrich Lange, *Reines Deutschtum,* Berlin, 1893, p. 184.

ble of weakening the physical or spiritual energy of our people, we must curb Christianity by means of Germanism and not vice versa.'' [86]

These views of Dühring and his school were shared by some of the active participants of Fritsch's *Der Hammer* with the aim of improving and refining the close connection between the negation of Judaism and Christianity on the one hand and the principles adopted from Social Darwinism on the other. The debilitating morality of Christianity was designed for the benefit of the weak, the oppressed, the embittered, and unsuccessful—all who would endanger the future of the Aryan race and its physical, spiritual, and cultural growth: ''What is Christ to us, whose kingdom is not of this world. . . . Christ consoles the downtrodden, the weak, and the sick; also we pity these unfortunates, and try to alleviate their condition; but they are useless for us and our future. . . . They are only detrimental to what is highest in our eyes: German character [*deutsches Wesen*]. We need the strong, the healthy, and those who are filled with the joy of life. Leave the kingdom of heaven to the lowly, as long as we can keep this world.'' [87]

This anti-Semitic movement that was intent on liberating Christianity from Judaism by crowning it with the racialist principle grew more and more influential. In addition to the sources mentioned above, we find this principle advocated by the writer Wilhelm Schwaner and the members of his circle, the leaders of the *Völkisch* nationalist movement in the early years of the century and in the days of the Weimar Republic. In the Introduction to Schwaner's *Germanenbibel* (1904) Ernst Eberhardt stated that Christianity was not to be repudiated *in toto*. Only those elements within it that were foreign to the German blood and the German spirit (*Christianismus*) should be disavowed, and those elements that were compatible with the Germanic or Aryan nature (*Christenheit*) should be retained. *Christianismus* was a destructive force that sapped the natural vitality of the German by preaching timidity, humility, altruism, and otherworldliness and thus severed him from the life of nature and reality. Insofar as Christianity could be cleansed of its *Christianismus* and reduced to its *Christenheit*—to its pure Aryan sources—it could be enlisted in the service of the strong, the proud, and victorious, of those destined to rule the world:

86. A.S., Danzig, 1900, p. 293.
87. A.S., Danzig, 1911, p. 201 (from the periodical *Der Hammer,* in the issue of October 1908).

The basic thought of *Christianismus* is the redemption of sinful mankind through the self-sacrifice of the innocent One—a Jewish-pagan thought! With its doctrine of grace, that is, the doctrine according to which it is not in man's power to be master of his empirical nature, *Christianismus* has paralyzed the spontaneous power and moral energy of *Christenheit* and thus done incalculable harm to life; and by its doctrine of the hereafter it has taken the solid ground from under the feet of the Christian, diverted his moral impulse to otherworldly matters that cannot be apprehended, and thus removed life's most vital impulse from the real world . . . *Christianismus* strove after a false spiritualization of our nature by its mortification of the flesh.[88]

One of the more popular attempts to incorporate Christianity and the life and teachings of Jesus into the renewed German nationalist mythology was made by Max Bewer, poet, publicist, and active member of the anti-intellectualist Rembrandt movement that had been founded by Julius Langbehn. In his *Gedanken,* which appeared in 1892, a collection of speeches delivered mostly as part of the ideological campaign of the extreme groups of the Antisemitische Volkspartei, and also in his *Der deutsche Christus* (1907), Bewer summed up the basic principles of this Christian-Aryan fusion.[89] Briefly, the antitheses German-Jewish, Aryan-Semitic, Nordic-Oriental were for him synonymous with good-evil, beautiful-repulsive, God-Satan. These contrasts were not temporary or fortuitous but biological, aboriginal, and preordained and could not be altered by legal emancipation, legislative decrees, or baptism. The Jewish character was not only corrupt and evil; it was the essence of corruption and the principle of evil. The Jewish spirit of illicit gain, usury, boasting, self-aggrandizement, ritual murder—these were not only habitual practices, but manifestations of ineradicable turpitude. Conversely, the German character was not only deep, upright, diligent, and enterprising but the essence of profundity, probity, industry, and courage. This mode of thinking hypostasized traits of character and symbols into empirical realities and ontological categories. Jewish blood was defined as the essence

88. Ernst Eberhardt, *Einleitung zu Wilhelm Schwaner, Germanenbibel,* 1904. The source is found in Pross, pp. 69–70.

89. Max Bewer, *Gedanken,* Dresden, 1892 (hereafter, M. Bewer), p. 28 ff, "Christus," p. 46 ff, "Ritualmorde," p. 161 ff, "Rembrandt Gedanken"; *Max Bewer's Reden und Aufsätze . . .* pub. by Kasseler Parteitage der Reform Partei, Dresden, 1906, p. 4 ff. Of the many reactions against Max Bewer, see E. Fuchs, *Max Bewer's Gedanken über eine deutsche Bartholomäusnacht gegen Juden,* pub. by als Sonderausgabe des I.D.R., Berlin, 1898, p. 1. On the Jewish origin of Max Bewer on his maternal side, see F. Stern, p. 111.

of lust, German blood as the essence of purity and nobility. It was therefore obvious that Jesus could not have been of Jewish origin. The forefathers of Jesus, according to Bewer, came from the vicinity of Westphalia
in the Rhineland.[90] Jesus was admittedly born in Galilee, but Galilee did
not have a Semitic or Jewish population for it had been settled by blond,
blue-eyed immigrants fifteen hundred years before the birth of Jesus.
Then again, shortly before the time of Jesus "German blood was once
more operative in Galilee," [91] referring to the Germans from Sleswig-
Holstein who had settled in Upper Italy centuries before the birth of Jesus
and who had come to Galilee as part of the Roman army.

The thesis that Jesus was not of Semitic or Jewish origin but an offspring of the Nordic Germans—although it was not denied that on his
maternal side "a Hebraic turbidity might perhaps have affected his German blood" [92]—occupied an important place in the racial anti-Semitic
ideology and was duly emphasized by Bewer, Fritsch, and the Rembrandt
movement. When Bewer proclaimed "blood is the soul," he meant that
blood was the essence of both body and spirit, so that "everything that
Christ says regarding resurrection in the spiritual sense seems to have
been uttered from out of the blood that was resurrected solely in the bod-
ily sense" [93]—for "in Christ and in the Jews blood against blood rises up
and speaks." [94] In other words, in the struggle that took place within
Jesus between his Aryan and his Semitic blood, between good and evil,
the former emerged victorious: Siegfried conquered Samson in mortal
combat. This victory was made possible through the power of the Incarnation, which was now interpreted not in a spiritual or theological sense,
but as a biological phenomenon whereby the German blood in Jesus overcame his Semitic blood: "God in him had triumphed, German blood over
Jewish blood." [95]

The efficacy of blood in this anti-Semitic racialist ideology was elaborated by Bewer as follows: "Blood, however, has still another effect: to
corroborate antipathy and hostility. . . . A cow that gives milk to a
child, and a Jew who slaughters it are concepts which in the course of
generations have entered the blood of every people as an ineradicable instinct. The child will run to the old cow and stroke it; from an old Jew it
runs away crying. This is the eternal and natural 'fear of the Jew' which

90. M. Bewer, p. 31.     91. Ibid.     92. A.S., Danzig, 1900, pp. 291–292.
93. M. Bewer, p. 31.     94. Ibid., p. 29.     95. Ibid., p. 32.

the Galileans already knew in the days of Christ.'' [96] Blood, then, was an all-comprehensive absolute power: ''In Christ, in the eleven apostles, and in most of the seventy-two disciples their double dose of German blood [*das deutsche Doppelblut*] counteracted their Judaism and produced an intensification of their spiritual powers over and above the normal Germanic measure. German blood in its simple state is always good; when raised to an organic power it becomes divine.'' [97]

The image of Jesus in the eyes of the racialist anti-Semites now became the essence of the Nordic German ideal. The forefathers of Jesus were not the scions of the house of David, but sprang from the loins of Nordics or ancient Germanic heroes. The spiritual and intellectual struggles of Jesus were but the expression of the extraordinary contest between the German blood that flowed in his veins and the Jewish-Semitic blood that was intermingled with it. This struggle was identical with the dramatic struggle between the powers of God and Satan that dwelled within him. The salvation that Jesus brought into the world was not the product of his self-sacrifice, as taught by Christian theology, but the result of his victory over Satan, over Judaism, and over his Semitic blood. Similarly, Bewer, Fritsch, and the circles of *Der Hammer* were convinced that the Maccabees were not Jews but the descendents of the Scythian or Indo-Germanic conquerors since they displayed the Aryan virtue of valor. [98] It was not possible for a member of the Jewish-Semitic race to display valor or any other Aryan characteristic even after conversion to Christianity, any more than it was possible for him to slough off his abhorrent Jewish characteristics. Proof of this was provided by Bewer, who quoted ''scientific'' statistics to show that degenerate or defective children were born of mixed marriages or, as he called them, Jews; and this was also true in the case of parents who became converts. In every case the Semitic-Jewish had the dominant influence. [99] A marked increase in the number of children of converts or of parents of a mixed marriage also had an adverse effect on the German landscape, for the manifestations of nature were only the incarnation of human qualities, for example, the landscape of the Lower Rhine, according to Bewer, was the quintessence of beauty and candor.

The views of the exponents of racial anti-Semitism and their mode of

96. Ibid., pp. 52–53.    97. Ibid., p. 38.    98. Ibid., pp. 28, 32.

99. On intermarriages influenced by Dühring's racial doctrine, see E. Dühring, *Die Natur als Anwalt des Rassenantisemitismus,* Berlin, 1893, p. 47 ff.

expression may seem to us today unreasonable and in many respects even ludicrous. But in their day they had the power to inflame the passions and to influence many strong minds. Bewer's style of writing is typical of the dominant literary manner that was developed in the neoromantic Rembrandt movement and in the racial anti-Semitic propaganda at the end of the nineteenth century and thereafter until the period of the Third Reich. Bewer's writings are replete with noble sentiments, vague feelings, colorful descriptions, and arbitrary associations, dogmatic statements, and illogical sequences. His mystical revelations of racial superiority, his appeal to patriotic sentiments, and his confidence in the potency of blood to unlock all secrets blunt all opposition in the credulous reader. His sentences take the form of sensible stimuli and are designed to create emotional moods and impressions rather than clear rational conceptions, to arouse in the reader a sense of total identification rather than to convince him through logical persuasion. Bewer asserted, for example, that the Oriental complexion was dark, and since Jewish blood was Oriental, *ergo* Jewish blood was dark, black, the color par excellence of the Jew was benighted, gloomy, and pharisaical, the quintessence of "black-souled Judaism" (*das schwarzseelige Judenthum*).[100] Aryan blood, on the other hand, was pure, red, vital, and bright; blue blood was aristocratic; white silvery blood was also pure and precious. Bismarck's colors were red-blue-silvery or blue-white-silvery and represented the bright future of the Christian German Aryan—"the lustrous tints of the resplendent morning."[101] Bismarck, like Jesus before him, meant resurrection, the return to the ancient Aryan source: "Just as Christ returned to his German blood, Christianity returns to her native German soil. . . . Just as a tree is known by its fruits, so is Christ by the Germans."[102]

## Conclusion

At the end of the nineteenth century these various tendencies in modern anti-Semitism were systematically elaborated and consolidated, acquiring

100. M. Bewer, p. 33.    101. Ibid., p. 34.
102. Ibid., pp. 34–35. See Max Bewer, *Rembrandt und Bismarck*, Dresden, 1891, pp. 43 ff, 70–71; also p. 43 for another typical example of the completely illogical arguments used in this ideology: "Bismarck und Rembrandt sind zwei Kreise welche ungleiche Peripherien, aber dasselbe Zentrum haben. Die Peripherie des Einen hat einen ästhetischen, die des Anderen einen politischen Radius. Ihr gemeinsames Zentrum aber ist die Totalität einer volksthümlichen Wesenheit."

immense prestige and influence among growing segments of the population. This increasing interest was for the most part shaped and reinforced by the racial theories of Arthur Gobineau, Richard Wagner, Ernest Renan, and Houston Stewart Chamberlain, the biblical and philological studies of Julius Wellhausen, the theological school of thought known as ''Practical Theology'' which sought to renew Christian life by going back to the historical life of Jesus as recounted in the early gospels and also to Paul's Epistles, and by the popular presentations of Darwinism and materialism in the teachings of Heinrich Czolbe and Ernst Haeckel. These and other currents of thought in the world of science, philosophy, literature, and art all converged in Chamberlain's racial ideology.[103] Chamberlain's principal aim was the exaltation of the German man, the German nation, and the German state as representatives of the superior Aryan race whose mission was to liberate mankind from the corrupt power of the Jewish-Semitic race, a clearly inferior race as was early recognized by Renan: ''I am the first to recognize that the Semitic race compared to the Indo-European race represents in reality an inferior composition of human nature.'' [104]

We now turn to a consideration of the Christian and anti-Christian elements in Chamberlain's anti-Semitism. Chamberlain is an important figure in the history of modern anti-Semitism and merits extensive treatment. He represents a nodal point of forces that had been slowly

103. Houston Stewart Chamberlain, *Die Grundlagen des 19en Jahrhunderts . . . München 1889,* (hereafter, Chamberlain). The following references are taken from the Munich, 1918, edition, which also gives the pagination of the first edition in parentheses This work went through many editions, including a popular edition, Munich, 1912; during the Nazi period the 20th edition was published in Munich, 1938, and the 28th edition in 1942. A detailed and partly annotated bibliography of Chamberlain's many works is in Peter Viereck, *Metapolitics: The Roots of the Nazi Mind,* New York, 1961, pp. 323–326 (hereafter, Viereck). For the place of Richard Wagner in the rise of the national and racial German myth and the rise of anti-Semitism, see Viereck, chap. v, p. 90 ff, chap. vi, p. 126 ff, and bibliography, pp. 330–336. See also Otto Dov Kulka, ''Richard Wagner und die Anfänge des modernen Antisemitismus,'' *Bulletin des Leo Baeck Instituts,* Vol. 4, Dec. 1961, No. 16, p. 281 ff.

104. Chamberlain, p. 324, and E. Renan, *Histoire générale et système comparé des langues sémitiques,* 5th ed., Paris, 1893, p. 4. Another idea from Renan accepted by Chamberlain was ''L'épouvantable simplicité de l'esprit sémitique rétrecit le cerveau humain, le ferme à toute idée délicate, à tout sentiment fin, à toute recherche rationelle, pour le mettre en face d'une eternelle tautologie: Dieu est Dieu,'' from E. Renan, *De la part des peuples sémitiques dans l'histoire de la civilisation,* p. 39, in Chamberlain, p. 324. See also Shmuel Almog, ''The Racial Motif in Renan's Attitude to Judaism and the Jews'' (Hebrew), *Zion,* Vol. 32, Nos. 3–4, 1968, p. 175 ff.

gathering momentum and that culminated in the racial legislation of the Third Reich. His interpretation of World War I as the struggle against Judaism, western culture, and Americanism and the fateful significance of Germany's defeat, as well as his racial and anti-intellectual theories, exerted a deep influence on his contemporaries, including Kaiser Wilhelm II and high government officials, and later in the early twenties on Adolf Hitler, in whom he saw the providential redeemer of the German people, and other leading Nazi ideologists, especially Dietrich Eckart and Alfred Rosenberg. It may be said that he helped pave the way for the Third Reich,[105] with all the consequences this involved for the future of Germany.

The point of departure in Chamberlain's system was the repudiation of reason as the criterion of ethical judgments and of scientific verifiability as the ultimate test in the determination of empirical facts, instead of relying on subjective intuition, direct sensation, unmediated experience, and sound common sense. Science was limited to abstract general laws, thus cutting man off from reality; it must be replaced by life itself "which is more stable, more firmly grounded, more comprehensive, and the quintessence of all reality; whereas even the most precise science describes an attenuated, highly generalized, and no longer unmediated reality. The roots of life . . . nature . . . go down far deeper than could be reached by any knowledge." [106]

Chamberlain presented an apparently easy solution to the problem which, as we have seen, had occupied the neo-Kantians and some of the best minds of the post-Kantian period—the problem of how to separate autonomous cognition from the object of cognition, form from content, spirit from nature, without losing touch with reality; how to find the common root between sense and understanding severed by Kant. The solution proposed by Chamberlain and the members of the Rembrandt movement, as well as many followers of the school of *Kulturpessimismus,* was to deny the existence of a dilemma and to transfer the criteria of cognition from a rational criticism of objective conditions to the subjective realm of instinct and intuition, blind forces beyond the reach of the concept and prior to the understanding and all discursive thought. Rational commit-

---

105. Viereck, pp. 9, 91–92, 113, 115, 137–138, 148–149, 284–285. See also K. Saller, "Die biologisch motivierte Judenfeindschaft," in *Judenfeindschaft-Darstellungen und Analysen,* ed. Karl Thieme, Frankfurt a/M, 1963, p. 181 ff.

106. Chamberlain, p. 217.

ments were dispensed with in the face of the rising tide of subjectivism that now invaded all areas of thought. It was not important, Chamberlain declared, whether or not objective data can be found to verify or disprove what we feel in our hearts. The rules of logic or the rational axioms of science cannot determine the reality or assess the value of phenomena: "I need not bother about definitions; race is in my bosom." [107]

In Chamberlain's system subjective intuition took the place of "teaching" (*Lehre*), nature took the place of "learning" (*Schulweisheit*), and nonrational unmediated experience took the place of critical objective cognition. The objectivity of phenomena and the validity of moral judgments are determined by instinctive feelings. Truth is found in the irrational impulses of our inner life, and beyond that are only the lucubrations of scientists and rationalists. The intuitive experience of the race thus becomes identical with the existence of race itself and the principal criterion in judging Judaism, Christianity, Germanism, religion, nationality, and culture in general. In the spirit of Dilthey's "life-philosophy," although in a simplified and distorted form, the experience of phenomena becomes identical with the existence of the phenomena themselves. Intuition is made the goal of cognition and its method as well. Unlike other anti-Semitic propagandists, Chamberlain did not ignore the difficulties in finding valid criteria for racial investigations, nor did he ignore the scientific findings of prominent writers in this field, such as Rudolf Virchow, Paul Ehrenreich, Friedrich Ratzel, Felix von Luschan, Ernest Renan, Solomon Reinach. By taking words out of context, citing contradictory opinions, and pointing out logical errors, he demonstrated that their scientific conclusions were invalid and that "the more we consult the experts, the less able are we to find our bearings." [108]

Chamberlain's polemical method did not endear him to the anthropologists, ethnologists, and historians of his day,[109] but it increased his pop-

107. Ibid., p. 290.

108. Ibid., p. 268. On the attitude of Chamberlain toward the opposition of other scholars to the concept "Aryan race" (such as Solomon Reinach), and the opposition of anthropologists to the system of skull measurements for the appraisal and classification of races (such as Friedrich Ratzel), see ibid., pp. 121–122; also p. 269, the words of Reinach from *L'origine des Aryans*, Strasbourg 1892, p. 90: "Parler d'une race aryenne d'il y a trois mille ans, c'est émettre une hypothèse gratuite, en parler comme si elle existait encore aujourd'hui, c'est dire tout simplement une absurdité."

109. For a typical example of a long series of criticisms, see Felix von Luschan, *Völker-Rassen-Sprachen*, Berlin, 1922, pp. 25, 93. Clarification of this conception that Jews were not to be defined as a race but as a religious community is in Felix von Luschan, "Offener

ularity among the members of the middle class and the growing number of disillusioned intellectuals. Many prominent persons recognized his increasing influence and, while disassociating themselves from the more violent aspects of his ideology, nevertheless refrained from taking issue with his general position. Werner Sombart, for example, went so far as to declare that Chamberlain's words contained a considerable amount of "genuine lyrical feeling," and that no sensitive person could wholly withstand its strong influence.[110]

The ground was now prepared for dealing with the problems of race, Judaism, and Christianity by using a simple criterion "clearly seen by all and which is adequate, if not for science then at least for life." [111] There was no need for extensive scientific investigations to determine the existence of races, for this obvious fact was determined not by conscious intellectual abstraction but by membership in a "blood community" (*Blutgemeinschaft*). Chamberlain followed Gobineau (with critical reservations) in holding that inequality, physically and hence also morally, was the basis of human existence. This was obvious among animals, such as dogs and horses, in whom "spiritual qualities exist in conjunction with the physical, and this is especially true with respect to moral qualities; it is not rare for a mongrel dog to be very clever, but he is never very reliable and from a moral point of view he is always base." This example from the animal world was cited by Chamberlain to illustrate by analogy the condition in the human world, for "why should mankind be an exception to the rule?" [112]

According to Gobineau pure races existed in the early days of history; in the course of time, however, they lost their purity, so that the superior Nordic race was now faced with extinction. Chamberlain reversed this pessimistic conclusion and, contrary to Wilhelm Marr's ideology,[113] maintained that some races were at the beginning impure but in the course of time became increasingly corrupt and parasitic (like the Jews

---

Brief an Herrn Dr. Elias Auerbach," *Archiv für Rassen und Ges. Biologie,* 1907, No. 4, p. 371.

110. Werner Sombart, *Die Juden und das Wirtschaftsleben,* München, Leipzig (1911), 1918, p. 386.

111. "was klar vor aller Augen liegt, genügt schon, wenn nicht für die Wissenschaft so doch für das Leben," Chamberlain, pp. 269–270.

112. Ibid., p. 265.

113. Ibid., pp. 260 ff, 343 ff. For the pessimistic note in the anti-Semitism of W. Marr, see above, p. 208 ff.

and the Semites), while others (like the Germans or Aryans) became more vital and powerful physically and hence also morally. Inbreeding to produce a select progeny was practiced only among the Greeks, Romans, Franks, Swabians, and Spaniards. The select breeding of generations by carefully removing all inferior qualities and elements (*Zuchtwahl durch sorgfältige Ausscheidung alles Minderwertigen*), such as removing weak children, from the process of race purification, was the only method that could guarantee the cultivation of a superior Aryan race.[114] Miscegenation was permissible to a small degree, depending on the absorption capacity of the race, and then only with racial elements that would improve or refine the race and not with inferior races, particularly the Semitic.

In Chamberlain's opinion no great importance should be attached to the different views of scientists, however eminent—such as Rudolf Virchow, Solomon Reinach, Felix von Luschan—about the existence or nonexistence of an Aryan race or the exact meaning of the term "Aryan." In their scientific systems these "professional anti-Aryan *Konfusionsmacher*" employed vague general concepts, such as "Indo-Germanic," which neither affirmed nor denied the existence of an Aryan racial element. Chamberlain therefore concluded: "Even if it were demonstrated that an Aryan race never existed in the past, we want one to exist in the future; for men of action this is the decisive point of departure." [115] Faith in the existence of a superior Aryan race and its glorious future was at this time a precious possession of the German. He only had to believe in it to be convinced of its power to lift him above the members of all other races, and it filled him with an enthusiasm comparable to the religious fervor and eschatological hope that animated the early Christians. It compensated him for the abasement he suffered at the hands of those who were intellectually and morally superior and endowed him with a uniqueness he could not achieve either through rationality or religion or on any other cultural plane.[116] And then the whole concept of race was sufficiently imprecise and vague to command his general assent and flood his mind with pleasant reveries of superiority.

In addition to the individual, Chamberlain in his polemics with Renan also recognized the importance of nationality as the bearer of race. The Aryan race would not develop its full powers or true genius until it overcame the particularistic states still existing in the empire. To this end the Germans must extirpate all inferior elements in their midst, the mongrel

114. Chamberlain, p. 277 ff.     115. Ibid., pp. 269–270.
116. Ibid., pp. 271–272.

populace of the German Reich, especially the Semitic elements which, more than any other, retarded the purifying process of the Indo-European race and its splendid future in Germany.[117] The full flowering of the German genius then depended on the final liberation of the Aryan race from its tainted Semitic elements and from the inferior Semites or Jews. In the early days, when the Jews were still called Israelites or Hebrews, their degeneracy was not so far advanced. The Hebrews were an amalgam of various nations (here as elsewhere Chamberlain reinterpreted the information provided by Julius Wellhausen)—Ammonites, Moabites, Edomites, Midianites, Ismaelites. Not only the tribes and nations, but also the racial types, were mixed and varied, such as the Semitic Assyrian type which was identical with the Hittite, Indo-European type and also groups with Sumerian-Akkadian blood.[118]

Among this mixed multitude the Jews or Semites still from the period of the Patriarchs, somewhat like the Bedouin or the Arabs of today, were conspicuous as marauding nomads who brought destruction to every culture they inherited. Relying on such scholars as J. Wellhausen, C. Steuernagel, B. Stade, G. C. Maspero, and R. Smith, whose concepts he often distorted because of his racial interpretations and Germanophilia, Chamberlain concluded that the destructive and parasitic characteristics of the Semitic Jews of the Patriarchal period and thereafter were racial. The Hittites were the ones who must be regarded as having constituted the nucleus of the Syrian man, *homo syriacus,* who in turn was the basic element of the Amorites or Canaanites, that is, the uncorrupted vigorous races which subsequently arose not in Judah but in Galilee or in Transjordania. The Amorites were in reality the Canaanites, the tall, fair, blue-eyed ''northerners''—the geographical term being given a racial and hence a moral significance. These racial tribes, together with the Philistines and the various Indo-European groups, gave rise to the type of superior man of whom we read in the Bible and in the mythology of the ancient races—the mighty hero, virile, intrepid, magnanimous, resolute, and enterprising, in short, the Aryan man or *homo europaeus.* The fact that the learned anthropologists, ethnologists, and historians did not accept these racial views was enough to convince Chamberlain and his ''unlearned'' followers (*uns Ungelehrten*) that their feelings of racial superiority were justified.[119]

As the Aryan or *homo europaeus* developed noble virtues, the Semites,

117. Ibid., p. 291 ff.    118. Ibid., pp. 348, 295, 367.
119. Ibid., pp. 366, 378, also above, n. 16.

Bedouins, or Jews became increasingly indolent, dissolute, unproductive, degenerate, and unchivalrous, and these unpleasant traits were expressed in their physical appearance, gestures, gait, intonation, manner of thought, and expression. The Jews continued to live and even prosper only because they could live off the Canaanites, a highly capable people whom the Jews never succeeded in dispossessing altogether. Chamberlain relied on Wellhausen to prove that the Jews were unscrupulous and shiftless and on Renan that they were unable to create a material or spiritual culture. The Semitic or Phoenician alphabet could never have been invented by the Jews or by the Semites in general, including the *homo arabicus,* as they claimed. It was invented by the Hittites and Greeks, racial groups that had been able to liberate themselves from the Semites. The Hebrews, in contradistinction to the Indo-Europeans, were also incapable of sustained thought, for they were "far too subjective to develop pure thought. . . . Objectivity is far removed from the Semites." [120]

Chamberlain's contradictions, illogicalities, and banalities did not escape the notice of his contemporaries, but did not detract from his popularity. Intuitive insight was considered more trustworthy than scientific knowledge. Ideas must be believed, not proved. Life is shaped by the deeds of living men and not by abstractions. Logical thinking deflects us from the life of the spirit, leads us into sophistries and spurious profundities, deprives us of confidence in the conduct of life, and makes us metaphysically uneasy. Nevertheless, this low view of abstract intellectual thought did not prevent Chamberlain from berating the Jews and the Semites in general for their intellectual sterility, their lack of pure thought, lofty ideals, and flights of the spirit. The Semites were too much the slaves of passions to be able to rise from the particular and accidental to the universal and necessary. The Jews, moreover, were afflicted with an inveterate morbidity that stemmed from their excessive preoccupation with the minutia of the law, with ordinances, prescriptions, rites, and commandments, especially since the time of Ezra and Nehemiah. They could not disencumber themselves of this burden, and it filled them with an unrelieved consciousness of guilt and remorse; it not only "tarnishes the individual soul, but it sullies physical purity." [121] In support of these views Chamberlain cited the documentary evidence provided by the liter-

120. Ibid., p. 384.
121. Chamberlain, pp. 374, 372 ff; sin, as a religious and psychological category derived from the same attitude taken toward the system of laws and ordinances was not only "contamination of the individual soul but a contamination of the physical purity." These

ary historian Otto Francke, who showed how the mythical and religious symbols of the Semites, such as the "tree of life," the "deluge," or the various concepts of the Godhead, arose among the Aryans like pure fountains of living water and then degenerated when they were adopted by the inferior Semites.[122] Thereafter, the names of these two races were used to epitomize antithetical moral characteristics. The Semite, the Jew or *homo judaeus,* was the living embodiment of all that was repulsive, self-seeking, artificial, corrupt, and morally blind; the Aryan or *homo europaeus,* like his Ammorite or Indo-Germanic forefathers, was the essence of harmony, beauty, self-reliance, fidelity, valor, moderation, and affability.[123] In one of his typical passages Chamberlain apostrophized the Aryan man and called upon him to resist the peril of Semitic contamination: "O, *homo europeaus,* how could you have strayed and fallen among this company? . . . I call unto you: do not seek counsel from the learned anthropologists, and do not mix with that riff-raff; do not mingle with that Asiatic rabble." [124]

In his attempts to incorporate the founder of Christianity into the Aryan racial world view, Chamberlain employed the same argument as in his defense of race, namely, that the understanding of Jesus and his teachings does not depend on historical verification, scientific corroboration, or theological traditions. Science can apply to the gospels the strong solvent of criticism, but it can neither confirm nor impugn the truthfulness of the synoptic narratives. The gospels were written to establish a faith and not to report biographical or historical details. Science provides us with no criteria for determining the existence of races, which is a living experience based on an inner irrational feeling and a will to believe. Similarly, history, theology, and dogmatic religion give us no certainty about the life of Jesus or the truth of his teachings and are merely a kind of "philo-

words were influenced by the well-known works, Robertson Smith, *The Prophets of Israel and Their Place in History,* London, 1895, p. 247; Julius Wellhausen, *Prolegomena zur Geschichte Israels,* 4th ed., Berlin, 1895, p. 431: "since the exile the consciousness of sin [among the Jews] became to a certain extent permanent"; *idem, Israelitische und jüdische Geschichte,* 3d ed., Berlin, 1894, p. 380. A typical example of the way in which Chamberlain used the authorities he quoted: he took the term "consciousness of sin" (*Sündenbewusstsein*) in Wellhausen's *Prolegomena,* a concept that had a long and varied history among the Jews since the period of the Babylonian exile, and turned it into a "racial consciousness of sin" (*Rassenschuldbewusstsein*), ibid., pp. 372–373.

122. Chamberlain, p. 385. Chamberlain, influenced by Otto Francke, was of the opinion that religious or mythic symbols occupied a central place in Jewish tradition: "They are often brittle and schematic among the Semites, whereas among the Aryans they gush forth like bubbling brooks from the foaming living fountains."

123. Ibid., pp. 386–398.    124. Ibid., p. 378.

sophical delusion'' or an ''ingenious transcendence.'' Just as the certainty of belonging to a race is the proof of its existence, so are the spontaneous feelings of the heart the only pledge of the authenticity of religion in general and of the life of Jesus in particular.[125] Jesus' parables of the kingdom of heaven to explain what is hidden since the foundation of the world (Matthew 13) were interpreted as referring to this world, to a physical and not to a spiritual or transcendent reality. In the present age, Chamberlain assured his disciples, the physical has supplanted the spiritual, and life has replaced abstract speculation. Hence, we must interpret ''the kingdom of heaven'' in the parables of the sower (Matthew 13:19 ff, 24 ff), the mustard seed that was sowed in the field (v. 31), and the leaven that was hidden in three measures of meal (v. 33), as referring to unmediated reality, the reality within man; so that ''the field is the world'' (v. 38) means ''in this world, that is, in this life is the treasure hidden and preserved [v. 44]; the kingdom of God is within ourselves.'' [126]

This psychological interpretation of the gospels gratified the self-esteem of the Germans and helped to recommend ideological principles of race to the public at large, as propounded by Fritsch, Bewer, Langbehn, and Chamberlain. The eternal source of truth was now implanted in the heart of man, not man in general but the Aryan man as a member of the highest race.[127] Every German was assured that the kingdom of heaven was in him and that he merited divine grace not because of the self-sacrifice of Jesus, but because of the pure Aryan blood that flowed in his veins. Just as Jesus was able to overcome his Semitic blood and liberate himself from the human realm, so could the Aryan rise above the inferior races of men. In traditional Christianity the spirit of God rested on Jesus and became flesh; in the new interpretation of the Incarnation this flesh was invested with the incomparable mythical power of race. The message of Jesus was not love, which Chamberlain defined as ''mere passivity to do good, a kind of religion of milk and water,'' [128] but national fervor,

125. Ibid., pp. 193, 222, ''Religion der Erfahrung,'' ''Zustand des Gemütes.''

126. Ibid., pp. 200, 227–228, see also H. S. Chamberlain, *Worte Christi*, München, 1903, p. 260.

127. Chamberlain, p. 201 ff.

128. Chamberlain, chap. iii, ''The Revelation of Jesus,'' p. 189 ff. For the historical and universal significance of national, racial, and totalitarian anti-Semitism, see Jacob Talmon, ''Mission and Testimony: The Universal Significance of Modern Anti-Semitism,'' in *The Unique and the Universal; Some Historical Reflections,* London, 1965, chap. iv, p. 119 ff, and especially p. 156 ff.

devotion to race, an awakening of the slumbering consciousness of the Aryan race whose destiny was to rule the world. This concept of race that was so sedulously preached by Chamberlain proved to be a powerful force in the lives of the Germans—it acknowledged their genius, vivified their spirit, and satisfied the deeper harmonies they craved.

# Conclusion

We began our study with a discussion of the double aspiration of the Jews in the Second Reich to integrate into the dominant society and at the same time retain their Jewish identity. This endeavor on the part of German Jews was part of a larger struggle of men to achieve freedom in modern society without forfeiting individuality. This struggle gave rise to a number of concomitant questions: how was this Jewish aspiration regarded by the German Christian society of that day; how did it affect the relations between Jews and Christians on the one hand and the Jew's conception of his role in the modern world on the other; what can we learn from this historical attempt of German Jewry to become an integral part of German society and still retain its Jewish identity, that is, achieve equality without surrendering its freedom; and, finally, what conclusions can we draw from this study concerning the interrelationship between modern Jewish history and the history of mankind or between Judaism and Christianity in the modern era and between the Second and the Third Reich.

In theory this seemingly contradictory aspiration was based on the two universal principles of modern society—equality and freedom—and was compatible with the basic rational presuppositions that dominated the thought of that period; it was even guaranteed by German legislation of July 3, 1869, which removed all civil disabilities resulting from religious affiliation. In the historical reality of the Second Reich, however, as determined by the political forces and principal intellectual currents of the time, this twofold aspiration of German Jewry did not meet with approval. Integration into the German community and the retention of separate status were held to be mutually exclusive and undesirable because, as Friedrich Paulsen explained in his *System of Ethics,* if one is proud of the fact that he is a Jew and not a German, he has no right to complain that the German people do not accept him as a judge or as a teacher of German children: "To remain a complete Jew and a complete German is impossible." When we recall that Paulsen was a prominent liberal and humanist and an outspoken opponent of anti-Semitism, his words take on added significance as a reflection of Germany's determination not to acknowledge the claims of German Jewry to civil equality while retaining its Jewish identity.[1]

Religion became a central factor in determining the social status and self-identity of the Jews.[2] Paradoxically, this happened at a time when the process of secularization and modernization had reached a high point in Germany, a process to which both Jews and Christians had contributed, thus confirming the thesis put forward by Professor Salo W. Baron in his *Modern Nationalism and Religion* (1947, 1960) that even in modern times the history of nationalism goes hand in hand with the history of religion. Even in the early days of the emancipation and the Reform movement in religion most Jews rejected the national element in their definition of Judaism. Many leaders of the Jewish community even outside of the Reform movement, as well as prominent Jewish scholars, rejected not only the concept of nation but also that of peoplehood. An increasing number of Jews no longer regarded themselves as members of an ethnic community, for this smacked of racialism and was alien to the rationalistic presuppositions of the western Enlightenment. For most Jews, therefore, attachment to the Jewish religion, even though it was in many respects repugnant to the Orthodox community, remained the principal and perhaps the only component of their Jewish self-identity.

In the Second Reich as well, religion, albeit in its secular form, occupied an important place. Contrary to the expectations of the Jews and the liberals, religion had not become a private matter limited to the sphere of the individual, nor was it cleansed of its irrational elements in accordance with the principles of the Enlightenment. On the contrary, as a result of the process of religious secularization, Christian and especially Protestant patterns of thought and behavior were impressed on the cultural, social, and political life of the Second Reich. The national move-

1. See Fritz K. Ringer, *The Decline of the German Mandarins: The German Academic Community, 1890–1933,* Cambridge, Mass., 1969, p. 134 ff.

2. A different aspect of the Jewish self-understanding vis-à-vis the non-Jewish world emerged with, as Ismar Schorsch called it, "the transformation of German Zionism"; see his important study, *Jewish Reactions to German Anti-Semitism, 1870–1914,* New York, London, Philadelphia, 1972, p. 182 ff.

ment, the political parties, the social and economic organizations, and some of the principal scientific societies—all of which were an integral part of Germany's rapid process of industrialization—defined themselves explicitly as Christian in essence. The Conservative Protestants and an increasing number of Catholics wished to establish the Second Reich on the principle of a Christian state as it had been formulated in conservative ideology throughout the greater part of the nineteenth century. The only difference was that now the principle of the Christian state was made to conform to the new conditions and to the realities of the modern state, for most of the conservative Protestant and Catholic leaders recognized that it was impossible to return to a preindustrial society. Nevertheless, they retained their basic political and theological ideology with its romantic nostalgia for an ideal Christian society that excluded all foreign elements, especially those of a rationalistic and Jewish nature. This method of the conservatives thus combined political expediency that advocated economic reforms in keeping with the country's industrial progress with a strong belief in the traditional absolute authority of the political regime.

In the Protestant community this affinity between modernism and conservatism became a fixed cultural and even anthropological pattern. This pattern had its roots in Luther's teaching of the internalization of the law, whereby the citizen assents to obey the law not because of external compulsion (the visible church has no sword to compel obedience) but because of his acceptance of its authority. The individual Protestants, and in the course of time the Germans in general, demanded this self-induced subjection to the law. Civil liberty was interpreted not in terms of the separation of church and state or of religion and society, but as obedience first taught by the Roman Catholic church in the pre-Lutheran days, which was then transferred to the authority of the national church and, finally, to the German state and nation. The more the individual was capable of internalizing the law, that is, regulating his actions by personal insight without external compulsion, the stronger would be his claim to membership in the community of the faithful, with those whose freely chosen allegiance to the political regime was a reflection of spiritual membership in the celestial kingdom. In this ideology the Jew was the symbol par excellence of the loss of grace in both worlds. From the theological point of view Judaism was an anachronism, for the New Dispensation and the Incarnation had rendered it superfluous and deprived it of its *raison d'être*. The blind refusal of the Jews to embrace Christianity and its doctrine of salvation was the sole obstacle in the path of universal salvation. To turn the mind of the Jew from his dead faith to the living truth, therefore, was the hinge, as it were, on which Christian belief depended, the article by which the church must stand or fall, *articulus stantis et cadentis ecclesiae*.

Moreover, the continued existence of Jews in modern times as a separate and singular people in defiance of all reason was preposterous and irritating and not conducive to the growth of brotherly love. This argument was directed not against Orthodox Judaism or Zionist nationalism but against modern Liberal Judaism, the religion of the majority of the German Jews which was regarded by the Conservatives, and after the *Kulturkampf* by an increasing number of Catholics, as a negation of the two basic principles on which they had hoped to build the new society and culture of the Second Reich, namely, religion and nationality. The insistence of the non-Orthodox Jews that they were German citizens of the Mosaic persuasion was taken by the Conservatives as nothing more than a convenient verbal declaration with little substance; by abandoning their traditional religion the Liberal Jews in fact denied the very principle on which not only Judaism but the Christian state as well was based, that is, the religious principle as the highest authority of law and social order that transcended all rational and historical criteria. A similar argument was directed by the Conservatives principally against those Jews who rejected the component of nationality and political Zionism in their definition of Judaism. Here as well their protestations as loyal citizens of the national state met with distrust, for in disavowing their national and historical origin these Jews also denied the principle of national allegiance. In the eyes of the Conservatives, therefore, the Jews came to represent an anachronistic, anti-Christian phenomenon from the religious point of view and an unreliable element from the national point of view. With the growing industrialization of German society, all the ills of modern life were attributed to Jewish greed, commercialism, and rationalism (in the pejorative sense), and the Jews were thus made responsible for the disintegration of the traditional social, religious, and cultural patterns of German life, the decline of good manners, the deterioration of the German language, the breakdown of discipline and order, the increase in fraudulent business practices, the revolt of the younger generation against parents, teachers, church, and state, the resentment of the lower classes, the alienation of the German worker from his environment and the product of his labor.

The attitude of Germany Jewry toward these Christian critics also underwent considerable changes. At first it looked upon the conservative Protestants and Catholics as the natural opponents of its liberal aspirations and its struggle for self-identity since their avowed aim was to establish the institutional and cultural life of the Reich on religious foundations. In practice, however, religion constituted an area of common interests and activities, for the Liberal Jews of the Second Reich also justified their essential existence on the principle of religious affiliation. In its apologetics to the outside world German Jewry rejected the conservative argument that rationalism and liberalism were disintegrating forces inimical to the traditional religious and ethical basis of society. Internally, however, in their efforts to sustain and promote Jewish education, culture, and communal life the leaders of Liberal Judaism were well aware of the difficulty of basing their Judaism and their status in German society on formal rational presuppositions. In the period we are studying the complaint heard among Jews was similar to that of their conservative Christian opponents, namely, that the liberal attitude had deprived religion of its positive content, so that it no longer served as a spiritual or social guide for the youth of the nation which was rapidly succumbing to the philosophies of materialism, anarchism, and cultural pessimism (*Kulturpessimismus*).

At the beginning the Jews in the Second Reich were favorably inclined toward liberalism and were opposed to the policies of the Conservative Protestants and at times also to the policies of the Catholics when they felt that their equal status as citizens was threatened. In the course of time, however, as liberalism became an ally of the regime and advocated spiritual and national uniformity through state intervention and political pressure, the Jews, who were determined to retain their separate status, found that they had much in common with the Christian conservatives who defended regional separatism and the particularistic tradition of the various religious groups and social classes in opposition to the liberal egalitarianism of the modern state. We thus find that as early as 1872 the influential Jewish periodical *Allgemeine Zeitung des Judenthums* (No. 223) sharply criticized the egalitarian tendencies of German liberalism which it contemptuously described as French rationalism and the antidemocratic product of the French Revolution: "French leveling without freedom" (*Französische Gleichmacherei ohne Freiheit*).[3] In contrast to classical liberalism, which left room for the self-determination of social and religious particularistic groups, German liberalism tended to suppress such groups and to create "a political-social porridge from the masses of people." The Jews felt that they had no choice but to oppose these tendencies which the above-mentioned periodical described as "a zeal for leveling down" prompted by "a fear of all strong individuality . . . a suspicion of every religious manifestation." But it was precisely the preservation of individuality or the concrete manifestation of the ideal that the spokesmen of the organized Jewish community considered to be one of the principal tasks of Jewish existence, a view subsequently adopted also by the scholars of the Wissenschaft des Judenthums. In the *Jahrbuch für jüdische Geschichte und Literatur* (Vol. II, 1899) Martin Philippson declared that despite the genuine feeling of national patriotism displayed by German Jewry the Jews must not forget that "the Jewish community which is dispersed throughout the whole world is without doubt . . . a living refutation of the excessively morbid development of the nationalistic principle of our day."

German nationality, contrary to the expectations of the Jews, was not acquired by conscious selection or subjective feelings of the citizen but (according to the romantic school of thought) by belonging to a historic community whose roots went back to ancient tribal and pagan sources or in the more recent past to Lutheran Christian culture or (according to the anthropological school of thought) by belonging to a community whose roots went back to groups of different ethnic, cultural, and even religious origins which, through intermarriage and mutual biological assimilation, had come to constitute the present German nation.

Neither of these two views was favorable to German Jewry in its determined effort to integrate into the dominant society while retaining its identity, the first view because of its exclusive conception of German nationality according to which it was not the conscious acknowledgment of belonging to the nation that determined German nationality, but the objective fact of belonging to an organic ethnic group whose roots went

3. Regarding the factual historical background to this ideology see the two illuminating works that complement each other: Peter Gay, *The Enlightenment: An Interpretation, The Rise of Modern Paganism*, New York, 1966, 1968, Book Two, p. 212 ff; Arthur Hertzberg, *The French Enlightenment and the Jews: The Origins of Modern Anti-Semitism*, New York, 1968, 1970, chap. viii, p. 248 ff, and chap. ix, p. 268 ff.

back to the pagan Germanic tribes and to the Germans who became Christians and lived under a feudal system in principalities, duchies, and other traditional social forms in the historical German states; the second view because of its inclusive conception of German nationality according to which the determining factor in nationality was not membership in the nation, but the religious and biological fusion of the various ethnic components of the nation that left no room for particularistic internal groups. This second view was the one accepted by a considerable number of intellectual liberals, including many of the leading opponents of modern anti-Semitism, such as Rudolf von Gneist and Theodor Mommsen, who urged the complete assimilation of Jews into German society and argued that the addition of the Jewish heritage and the personal talents of the Jews would constitute an immense contribution, culturally and biologically, to the growing German nation and would at the same time strengthen the cause of the liberal intellectuals in their struggle against the irrational and pagan elements in German romanticism, potent ingredients in the anti-Semitic ideology of this movement.

As the nationalistic feeling grew stronger, it became plain to the liberal ideological leaders to what extent the lack of a common tradition among the various German states impeded national unification. In their zeal to achieve national unity they interpreted spiritual equality as cultural uniformity, and civil liberty as national identification. Liberalism thus changed from a reform movement into a conservative, egalitarian movement whose principal aim was to preserve the economic and cultural gains made by the liberals in the last half of the nineteenth century; it therefore was opposed to diversity and pluralism, holding that human nature was everywhere the same and shared by all. The insistence of Germany Jewry on retaining its identity was contrary to the liberal view of material progress, spiritual enlightenment, and the goals of national destiny; the liberals therefore began to regard the Jews, the prototype of particularism, as the chief impediment to national and spiritual unity.

The theoretical basis of the Jewish emancipation from which German Jewry derived its double aim of integration and identity also underwent fundamental changes that were reflected in the mutual relations between Liberal Protestantism and Judaism. At the beginning the relations between the two liberal groups were characterized by mutual respect and salutary interaction for they both shared the general temper and state of mind of the liberals of that period—a strong assurance in man's ability to achieve a rationally ordered society, an aversion to social distinctions, utilitarian motives, and ecclesiasticism, and a determination to resist the invading influences of materialism, atheism, Darwinism, and cynicism, influences that were inimical to the progressive illumination of the spirit. Both groups were governed by the conviction that man could best direct his judgment and support his faith by stressing the zetetic and not the dogmatic aspects of religion. In this spirit they sought to reinterpret their respective religious heritages in the light of modern philological and historical research, submitting them to rational examination as the highest criterion for determining the validity of faith and knowledge. Both groups also took ethics to be the essence of liberal religion, and in the theoretical elements of cognition they saw an analogy to ethical judgment and religious belief. Just as empirical cognition achieved objectivity when liberated from the cognized object, so ethical judgment achieved objectivity by freeing itself of its dependence on the consequences of acts. This view of ethics was regarded, especially by the neo-Kantians, as an expression of human autonomy and of man's freedom as a rational being, for it liberated his ethical judgments from dependence on an irrational and mystical faith.

But at the end of the century severe tensions arose between these two liberal groups, tensions that had their source in the common disappointment in rationalism with its vision of a common human destiny and promise of endless moral progress. This deep disappointment compelled both groups to look more deeply into their own character and the sources of their allegiance. They found that the rational assault on religion had been trivial and barren, for it deprived religion of its unique spiritual quality. Rationalism had attempted to draw every aspect of life, including religion, into the orbit of logical systems, subjecting the religious consciousness to the same kind of investigation as the logical formulations, that is, to methods of abstract speculation on the a priori conditions of cognition. This attempt, especially on the part of the neo-Kantians, was meant to ensure the freedom of cognition, but it was achieved only at the price of reality. Modern man sought in religion not a logical method, but a system of positive values and an answer to the questions of his existence. The very life of religion demanded liberation from this bondage to rationalism.

In their disillusion with abstract rationalism and neo-Kantianism the two liberal religions turned to the historical, philological, and anthropological study of their respective traditions, hoping thereby to regain their sense of direction and lost unity and preserve the continuity of their corporate life in the light of the social reality of their time. But this time they returned not to the rationalistic principle of a common humanity but to their respective religious heritages, to two different sources of religious inspiration, to two different and at times antagonistic conceptions of life. Liberal Protestantism went back to its historical Christian source with renewed faith in Jesus as the Messiah and in his historical life and message as recounted in the three early gospels. It regarded itself as the custodian of authentic Judaism of the prophets and the psalms before the days of Ezra and Nehemiah, before it was corrupted by the Pharisees into a petrified "talmudic, rabbinic Judaism." Liberal Judaism, however, was not disposed to accept this claim of the Protestants. It regarded itself not only as the legitimate heir of the Old Testament but also of the teachers of the Mishnaic period, such as Hillel, and the circle of Pharisees to which Jesus also belonged. The Liberal Protestants argued that modern Liberal Judaism was not justified in preserving its separate existence, for by its rejection of the halacha it acknowledged the basic doctrine of Christianity and by making ethics the central concern of religion it accepted the basic principle of western humanistic culture. The Liberal Jews, on the other hand, contended that Liberal Protestantism was not justified in asserting the superiority of Christianity over Judaism, for with the rejection of the relatively late traditions whose sources were in pagan Christianity it virtually accepted Judaism's basic opposition to Christianity, and by reducing religion to ethics and its theological mysteries to anthropology it denied the dogmatic traditions of the church and acknowledged the prophetic teachings of Jewish ethics. As the two liberal camps became entrenched in their respective theological positions, they began to attach great importance to the merits of their cause—which only served to inflame the growing spirit of dissension.

Against the background of these conflicting ideologies and political parties within the Second Reich the Jews endeavored to achieve their double goal of complete integration into the social environment without surrendering their identity. Political and racial anti-Semitism during this period failed to exert any appreciable public influence, and whatever effectiveness it had was limited to short intervals and restricted regions. The members of this movement were for the most part recruited from the unstable lower middle class, that is, from marginal groups within the liberal professions, workers who had migrated from rural to urban areas where they led a precarious existence, and city dwellers of the proletarian working class. Only a small number among these social classes turned to the racial-political anti-Semitic movement, most of them being represented in Christian or socialist political and economic organizations.

In the early days of this movement in 1878, when the groups of the Christlich-Sozial under Adolf Stöcker still served as its nucleus, it received 2,310 votes or 0.04 percent of the total vote of 5,650,947. Even after Stöcker and the other anti-Semitic propagandists, led by Paul Förster and Ernst Henrici, had made anti-Semitism a central issue in the electoral campaign three years later, after the rise of the movement known as "Berlin Anti-Semitism," which was responsible for the well-known Anti-Semitic Petition presented to the head of the state in March 1881, and after the anti-Semitic incitement fomented in Berlin had reached Cassel, Marburg, Giessen, Stettin, Danzig, and Königsberg—after all this the instigators of the anti-Semitic agitation, the Christlich-Sozial, managed to obtain only 1,692 votes in the Reichstag election of October 1881 or 0.03 percent of the total vote of 5,097,760.

Beginning in the early eighties, and especially after 1887 when Otto Böckel, the leader of the Antisemitische Volkspartei and the owner of the *Reichsherold* published in Marburg, was elected as the first anti-Semitic delegate to the Reichstag, the anti-Semites attempted to give their party the image of a social and economic reform movement that was primarily concerned with protecting the interests of the "small man"—the small artisans and merchants who found it increasingly difficult to earn a livelihood in a highly competitive industrial society of large corporations and commercial enterprises, the impoverished aristocracy, the struggling farmers, the disgruntled teachers, and civil servants who had failed to advance to higher positions. This policy of defending the "small man" was reaffirmed in the regional and national conventions of the anti-Semitic organizations at Bochum in 1889, in Erfurt the following year, and also during the days of the blood libel in Xanten in 1891–1892. During this period serious efforts were made to develop a consistent policy of social reform in the field of agrarian legislation, providing favorable terms of credit for farmers and financial aid to impoverished landowners, and the enactment of laws to protect the small merchants, artisans, unskilled workers, and the indigent classes in the urban areas.

As a result of this policy of social reform, in which anti-Jewish propaganda had little part, the anti-Semites in 1893, the year when they first became politically significant, received 263,861 votes in the Reichstag election or 3.4 percent of the total vote of 7,673,973. In 1898 they reached the high point of their political success when they received 284,250 votes or 3.7 percent of the total vote of 7,752,693. It is therefore obvious that even in the heyday of their political activity the anti-Semites could not muster enough votes to endorse their policy among their own rank-and-file supporters, who voted instead for the Conservative Protestant and Catholic parties on the one hand and the socialists on the other. This trend continued until the election of 1907 which was preceded by an intensive anti-Semitic campaign in which the anti-Semites sought to strengthen their image as the party of the "small man." The resolutions adopted at the conventions held in Erfurt (1895), in Halle (1896), in Cassel (1898), and in Berlin (1903) reiterated this policy of social reform in favor of the lower middle class, the impoverished farmer, the underprivileged economically and socially, and the embittered and frustrated elements in the large urban centers.

A similar and sometimes identical policy of social reform was adopted by the Christian political parties, the agrarian organizations and their affiliated groups of artisans, and also, in conformity with their own ideological goals, the Social Democrats. We find that at the end of the last century and during the first decade of the present century the majority of the electorate supported these political parties and organizations and not the anti-Semitic parties. A considerable number of voters on whose support the anti-Semitic parties had relied—including the Deutsch-Soziale Reformpartei, which at the convention of Eisenach in 1894 had begun to unite the main political groups within the anti-Semitic movement—voted for the Deutsch-Konservative Partei, the Center party, and, after the early nineties, the Bund der Landwirthe. These parties and organizations were also at times anti-Jewish, but they were affiliated with the conservative Protestants or Catholics and not with the racial anti-Semitic movement with its non-Christian and anti-Christian bias. Christian anti-Semitism was decidedly more widespread and effective than non-Christian and anti-Christian anti-Semitism in the nineties, especially in East Prussia, West Prussia, Pomerania, Posen, Silesia, Hanover, Westphalia (where Catholic anti-Semitism was stronger than anti-Christian racial anti-Semitism), Sleswig-Holstein, Hessen, Hessen-Nassau, and also the kingdom of Saxony (where in 1893 six electoral districts were captured by racial anti-Semitic organizations, three of which went to the Social Democrats in 1898). Similarly, urban and semiurban groups, among them small merchants, artisans, shopkeepers, and lower grade civil servants, showed a marked preference, especially in 1907, for the Wirtschaftliche Vereinigung (Economic Association) which included outspoken anti-Semitic organized groups such as factions of the Deutsch-Soziale Partei and which hardly differed from the racial anti-Semitic organizations even in its social and economic policy. But a considerable part of the electorate, including the members of the Christlich-Sozial and the Süddeutsche Bauernbündler, preferred the Christian anti-Semitism of this association to non-Christian or anti-Christian racial anti-Semitism. In their economic and social policies the spokesmen of the anti-Semitic party did not differ from those of the Wirtschaftliche Vereinigung, the Bund der Landwirthe, and the many pressure groups among the Conservative Protestants and the Center party. Nevertheless, in 1907, the year in which anti-Semitism was said to have reached its highest political development, the Wirtschaftliche Vereinigung obtained 17 seats in the Reichstag, the Protestant Conservatives 60, and the anti-Semitic Deutsche Reformpartei only 6.

Our study has made it clear that it was the non-Christian and anti-Christian character of racial-political anti-Semitism that proved to be the greatest obstacle to its development. This factor was all the more significant since from the economic and social point of view the anti-Semites did not differ from the Christian candidates. Moreover, in practice, the anti-Semites cooperated with the Conservatives in the regional elections both from an administrative point of view and in making local agreements concerning surplus votes and factional alliances in conformity with these agreements. The voters were then permitted to choose between two similar or identical platforms, one in which a racial and mythological and to a certain extent anti-Christian anti-Semitism was introduced and one in which the traditional anti-Jewish Christian anti-Semitism was introduced. In the period of the Second Reich, however, the vast majority of voters still disassociated themselves from the non-Christian and anti-Christian attitude of modern anti-Semitism.

After World War I and during the Weimar Republic the mythological, non-Christian, and anti-Christian character of anti-Semitism grew stronger, thus removing one of the main obstacles to the spread of racial anti-Semitism during the Second Reich and its acceptance by growing masses of the population.

Christian anti-Semitism was not as virulent as racial anti-Semitism. It stigmatized Jewish perfidy, but it permitted the Jew to exist (though not flourish) as the living witness to the truth of Christianity. The Jew must remain to act out his preordained ignominious role as villain in the drama of salvation, at the end of which he would be crowned with glory. But he was always free to abrogate his covenant with Jehovah and accept the benevolent efforts of the church to redeem him. According to racial theory, however, baptism could not penetrate the tainted Jewish seed; the deep stain could only be removed by destroying the source of infection and its bearer, the physical Jew. The Jew must not only be excoriated but eliminated. Christianity, insofar as it had succumbed to Jewish influences, was also culpable since Christian agape, love and pity, like Jewish logos, law and reason, had alienated man from nature and weakened him in his struggle for existence. However, the Jewish stain could be removed from the Christian cloth, so to speak, by fumigation without destroying the cloth itself.

In the days of the Second Reich these racial theories were not accepted by the great majority of the German people. After World War I and in the period of the Weimar Republic, however, they became increasingly popular, thus removing one of the chief obstacles in the path of the Nazi rise to power. The source of this ideology at the beginning of the Second Reich could be found in the teachings of Naudh-Nordmann, E. Dühring, C. Radenhausen, A. Wahrmund, F. Lange, and P. Förster, which were then transmitted by Theodor Fritsch, H. S. Chamberlain, and members of the anti-intellectualist Rembrandt movement to the leading Nazi ideologists, to such figures as Alfred Rosenberg on the one hand and to the heads of the Deutsche-Christen movement on the other.[4]

In the period between the end of World War I and the rise of the Nazis to power this new mood became a political factor of great consequence. It had its roots in a long process of secularization, that is, in an effort to construe the world, including man, from the standpoint of materialism. This process began with the negation of the historical revealed religions

---

4. Uriel Tal, Introduction to *The Grey Book, A Collection of Protests against Anti-Semitism and the Persecution of the Jews, Issued by Non-Roman Catholic Churches and Church Leaders during Hitler's Rule,* by Johan M. Snoek, Assen, 1969, pp. i–xxvi.

in the teachings of the deists, the forerunners of the rationalists like Voltaire and the French encyclopedists of the eighteenth century,[5] and culminated in the transformation of religion into anthropology associated with the name of Feuerbach. This affirmation of anthropology as the true theology was continued by the Young Hegelians, such as Max Stirner and Bruno Bauer at the beginning of his career,[6] by those romantics who went back to ancient pagan mythology,[7] by the evolutionary view of nature as developed by such different schools of thought as Schelling and Comte through Darwin to Bergson, and by the phenomenal progress of science throughout the nineteenth century which was recognized as proof positive of a triumphant material civilization. These intellectual and social movements struck a responsive chord in a rebellious generation, altered the traditional views of God, man, and society, and ultimately led to the pseudoreligious, pseudomessianic movement of Nazism.

Animated by this aggressive mood that sought to deprive the Enlightenment of all its gains, the racial anti-Semites put their faith in the efficacy of blood, the mysterious fountain from which all life flows and which determines the hierarchy of powers that shape history. Apriorism, whether in theology or in critical rational thought, was done away with and blood became the epistemological model whose uniqueness, contrary to the logical structure of rational thought, was that it comprehends both form and content, symbol and reality, the concept and that which is expressed by the concept. Blood became an absolute value because it erases the distinction between the symbol and that which is symbolized, between theory and practice; it attempts to create a total identity between the particular and the general, between the individual sphere and the public domain, between society and the state. It was felt that man's life must be rescued from the anemic ideals of Christianity and restored to its root and anchor in blood. Truth is not within reach of the pretentious intellect nor the reward of holiness, for both remove man from the deep sources of life. When the world demands a courageous response and genuine sacrifice, religion covers its face, unable to sustain the bravest ef-

5. Arthur Hertzberg, *The French Enlightenment and the Jews: The Origins of Modern Anti-Semitism,* New York, 1968, chaps. iii, iv.

6. Shmuel Ettinger, "The Criticism of Judaism in the Teachings of the Young Hegelians as One of the Roots of Modern Anti-Semitism" (Hebrew), lecture at the Israeli Academy of Sciences, Jerusalem, 1968; Ettinger, "Judaism and Jews in the Eyes of the English Deists in the 18th Century" (Hebrew), *Zion,* Vol. 29, No. 3–4, 1964, p. 182 ff.

7. George L. Mosse, *Germans and Jews,* New York, 1971, chaps. ii, v.

forts, and the untrustworthy intellect betrays man with its spurious profundities. It is then that blood clamors to be heard, and truth, long repressed, emerges through its cleansing filter. Evangelical Christianity with its morality of humility, selflessness, and excessive self-contempt, reinforced in modern times by democratic social altruism, thus constituted for the racial anti-Semites one of the principal obstructions to man's natural development. By placing spirit above matter, conscience above intuition, and speculative thought above the experience of blood, Christianity poisoned the noblest instincts in man and removed him from his natural roots. The cross is the Christian symbol for the crucifixion of the body and its vital instincts.

It would seem then that racial anti-Semitism and traditional Christianity, although starting from opposite poles and with no discernible principle of reconciliation, were moved by a common impulse directed either to the conversion or to the extermination of Jews.[8] Thus we find that the racial anti-Semites appropriated basic Christian ideas even while reprobating them and adapted them for their own purposes. The Christian doctrine of the Incarnation, for example, whereby God became man, was interpreted by them not in the evangelical sense (John 1:14) nor in the Pauline sense (Colossians 2:9), nor even in Nietzsche's purely mythological sense, but in an empirically political and racial sense. According to the Christian Heilsgeschichte the Jews were the theological means to correct evil by acknowledging the principle (John 1:14): "And the Word became flesh and dwelt among us, full of grace and truth; we have beheld his glory, glory as of the only Son from the Father"; and hence the Jews as the children of promise were eligible for salvation "in order that God's purpose of election might continue" (Romans 9:11). According to the racial anti-Semites, however, the Jews could not be the means to correct evil for they themselves were the essence of evil, evil incarnate, and must therefore be exterminated not only in the spirit (as Christianity) but also in the flesh.

When we recall the traditional Christian bias against the Jews—the collective guilt of deicide and the eternal curse of the world that rests upon them because of their unpardonable defection (Matthew 27:22, 25; I Thessalonians 2:15), the official policy of the church as formulated in such councils as the Synod of Elvira in 306, Clermont in 535, Toledo in

8. See the instructive and stimulating analysis by Saul Friedländer, *L'Antisemitisme Nazi: Histoire d'une psychose collective,* Paris, 1971, p. 13 ff, 53 ff.

681, or the Third Lateran in 1179 and the Fourth Lateran in 1215, the preachments of Martin Luther against the Jews and his incitement to violence, especially after 1543 when he was disillusioned in his efforts to convert them, the blood libels and accusations in which the persecuted wandering Jew became the symbol of sin and abomination—when we recall all this, we see how Christianity created the patterns of prejudice, hatred, and calumny that could readily provide a rationale to justify organized violence. The anti-Christian elements of racial anti-Semitism [9] were interpreted in such a way that the traditional theological concepts of Christianity were not completely rejected; only their meanings were changed by using a pseudoscientific jargon and applied to the historical realities of that day, without the salutary correction of Christian discipline and belief.

Racial anti-Semitism and the subsequent Nazi movement were not the result of mass hysteria or the work of single propagandists. The racial anti-Semites, despite their antagonism toward traditional Christianity, learned much from it, and succeeded in producing a well-prepared, systematic ideology with a logic of its own that reached its culmination in the Third Reich.

9. "Typical for all *völkisch* opponents of Judaism is their radical alienation from Christianity"; see E. L. Ehrlich, in *Judenfeindschaft: Darstellung und Analysen,* ed. Karl Thieme, Frankfurt, Hamburg, 1963, p. 232.

# Appendix

## Facsimiles of Documents

*1a.* Letter of the Deutsch-Israelitischer Gemeindebund (D.I.G.B.), dated November 18, 1879, requesting the prosecuting attorney at the Imperial Court of Justice in Berlin to institute legal proceedings against Wilhelm Marr, who allegedly coined the term "anti Semitism." Among the reasons given for this request were the writings of Marr and the new anti-Jewish periodical *Deutsche Wacht*, which were inciting racial and class hatred. (G.A.J., M 1/16.)

*1b.* The reply of the prosecuting attorney, dated November 26, 1879, wherein he refused to act upon the request of the D.I.G.B. Among the reasons given was lack of legal evidence to prove that Marr's anti-Jewish propaganda was likely to lead to acts of violence. (G.A.J., M 1/16.)

*1c.* The reply of the chief prosecutor at the Imperial Court, dated January 15, 1880, containing his refusal to consider the appeal of the D.I.G.B. and a confirmation of the reply of the lower court as shown in the preceding reproduction. Among the reasons given, the D.I.G.B. was not a legal person and was not authorized to represent German Jewry. (G.A.J., M 1/16.)

# Talmud-Auszug (Schulchan-Aruch.)

(Hauptsächlich entnommen dem Gutachten des gerichtlichen Sachverständigen **Dr. Jakob Ecker in Münster. 1883**)

Enthaltend:

## die wichtigsten bisher übersetzten, noch **heute gültigen, Gesetze der jüdischen Religion.**

Obgleich schon vor nahe 200 Jahren Professor Eisenmenger vieles aus dem Talmud der Juden ans Licht gezogen, auch von vielen anderen gelehrten Männern, in neuerer Zeit besonders auch von Professor **Dr. Rohling** den Christen mehr Aufklärung über die Geheimnisse des Talmud gebracht worden sind, so lassen sich doch die meisten Christen in Deutschland von den Juden und bei in ihrem Dienste stehenden Presse immer noch irreführen und täuschen.

„Die Behandlung der Christen seitens der Juden und die Praktiken und Kniffe, welche den Christen gegenüber sehr häufig anwenden, können nicht hinreichend begriffen werden, wenn man die Gesetze nicht kennt, welche den Juden in dieser Beziehung Form und Richtschnur sein sollen.“ —

Auf Grund des Gutachtens des **gerichtlichen Sachverständigen Dr. Jakob Ecker in Münster** veröffentlichen wir diese Gesetze nachstehend in aller treuer und wörtlicher Uebersetzung aus dem im Jahre 1576 verfaßten Gesetzbuche, betitelt: **Schulchan-Aruch.** — Dieses Gesetzbuch hat damals, wie es begreiflich war, für alle Juden Geltung erlangt und besitzt diese Geltung bis auf den heutigen Tag; die Verfasser desselben waren Joseph Karo, Rabbiner in Palästina und Mojes Usserls, Rabbiner in Krakau.

Daß die Gesetze des **Schulchan-Aruch** für die Juden **noch in Kraft** sind wissen die Rabbiner aller Länder, auch sieht in dem von dem Juden **Heinrich Ellenberger** herausgegebenen und **1883** in Budapest erschienenen Werke, betitelt: „Geschichtliches Handbuch“ auf Seite 47 gedruckt: Der Schulchan-Aruch ist drei Jahrhunderte das einzige theologische Gesetzbuch für die Juden und unser Katechismus! ...

## Gesetze.

1. Der Jude darf kein Kleid, welches Zizis (Quasten an den Zipfeln des Kleides), an die Juden bei ihrem Morgengebete anhaben, 4 B. Mos. 15, 37) hat, einem Akum (Nichtjuden) verkaufen; er darf sogar ein solches Kleid einem Akum (Nichtjuden) nicht einmal als Pfand geben oder ihm zum Zwecke, daß er es behalte. Denn wenn ein Akum (Nichtjude) ein solches Kleid bei sich haben würde, dann ist es denkbar, es könnte einen Juden ermorden, indem er, indem er sagen würde, er sei ein Jude, und man würde ihn Zutrauen schenken und allein in seiner Gesellschaft eine Reise machen würde, würde ihn ein Akum (Nichtjude) töten können. Schulchan Aruch Orach Chajjm § 20. —

2. Akos, nach der Lehre rituell zum Gottesdienste nöthig hat darf kein Akum (Nichtjude) bereiten, sondern nur ein Jude; weil dazu eine fromme Absicht gehört, die der Akum (Nichtjude) nicht besitzt. ...

9. Ein jeder Jude ist verpflichtet, wenn er bei einer Reise die Richtplätze, die zur Hinrichtung vorbereitet wurden, sieht, Gott zu danken ...

*2b.* Statement by Professor Franz Delitzsch, distinguished theologian and one of the leaders of the Mission unter Israel, dated November 7, 1883, to the effect that the term "talmudic idolaters" did not refer to Christians. The Jews had requested Delitzsch to state publicly that prescriptions or halachic traditions not in keeping with modern social morality were not binding on German Jews. (G.A.J., M 1/20.)

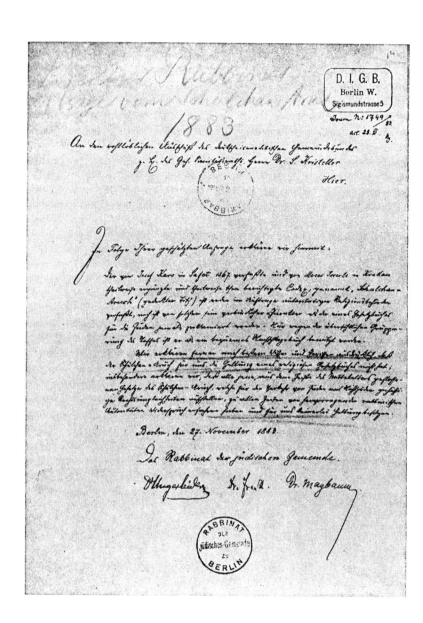

2c. Reply of the non-Orthodox rabbinate of the Berlin community, dated November 27, 1883, regarding the internal questionnaire of the D.I.G.B., stating that the oral law, the Schulchan Aruch, had no binding authority on present-day German Jewry. (G.A.J., M 1/20.)

314

145

3a. Excerpt from a letter by Professor A. Suchsland, the chairman of the Conservative Society in Halle, dated February 15, 1901, to the minister of justice in the kingdom of Prussia, Schönstedt, containing an expression of support in behalf of the society in favor of the minister's decision not to appoint Jews to high government posts in the Department of Justice. Reason given was that the German state and society were Christian. (B.A.K., P135/3259.)

3b. Excerpt from a letter of an ordinary citizen, a member of the conservative Protestant community, addressed to the minister of justice in the kingdom of Prussia supporting the policy of the minister in not appointing Jews to government offices that represent the Christian character of the state. Not the different religion of the Jews but their foreign racial origin was the reason for their exclusion. This letter was also sent as part of the official petition of the Conservatives in the year 1901. (B.A.K., P135/3259.)

# Antisemitisches Christenthum u. christlicher Antisemitismus.

**Motto:** *„Ein Christ, wenn er sich selbst versteht, kann kein ernsthafter Antisemit sein."* Tr. Döllinger.

In dem Artikel des Antisemitenspiegels: **„Die Antisemiten und das Christenthum,"** welcher auch als Flugblatt erschienen ist, ist nachgewiesen, daß das Christenthum geschichtlich auf jüdischem Boden gewachsen, daß deshalb der Haß gegen die Semiten nur zu leicht mit Haß gegen das Christenthum verbunden ist.

Beispiele für diese Abneigung gegen das Christenthum sind auch aus den Schriften von Marr, Rabenhausen, Dühring beigebracht worden, bei Rohling wurde sein Haß gegen den Protestantismus, bei Beta sein Haß gegen den Katholizismus nachgewiesen. Daß man da hineingeleuchtet hat, scheint den Antisemiten recht unbequem zu sein. Dies ist auch begreiflich; es kann ihrer Sache nichts nützen, wenn die Behauptung, daß das Christenthum bisher nur „Früchte des Todes getragen hat" oder daß die Reformatoren „Schurken" gewesen, als Aussprüche berühmter Antisemiten nachgewiesen werden. Die Antisemiten suchen deshalb die Dühring, Rabenhausen u. s. w. von ihren Rockschößen zu schütteln.

So erklärt Liebermann von Sonnenberg bei Gelegenheit der Kasseler Reichstagswahl im „Melsunger Kreisblatt" vom 16. Juli d. J.:

„Es ist unwahr, daß die Schriftsteller Dr. Dühring, Rabenhausen und Marr Mitglieder der deutschsozialen antisemitischen Partei sind. Für ihre Aeußerungen kann uns Niemand verantwortlich machen. Noch weniger kann man uns Aeußerungen anrechnen, deren der katholische Professor Rohling gegen den Protestantismus gethan hat."

Und im „Reichsherold" heißt es:

„Dies Flugblatt wimmelt von Lügen. Die tollste aber ist folgende: „Marr, Rohling, Dühring, Beta sind Hauptautoritäten der Antisemiten." Einfach frech gelogen, denn diese vier Herren gehen die antisemitische Volkspartei gar nichts an." Wer hat denn behauptet, daß die Herren Mitglieder der deutschsozialen oder der antisemitischen Volkspartei sind? Niemand! Es ist nur behauptet, daß diese Herren Hauptautoritäten der Antisemiten sind. Und das ist die Wahrheit! So sagte der Antisemit Dr. Erwin Bauer in einer Versammlung zu Leipzig am 13. August von Rohling: „Er ist für die Judenfrage eine Autorität." Der Deutschsoziale Kalender für 1892 enthält Rohlings Lebensbeschreibung, die antisemitischen Blätter empfehlen seine Werke, Herr Carl Paasch hat eine Rohling'sche Schrift bei Fritsch neu herausgegeben. Ottomar Beta ist Mitarbeiter der „Deutschsozialen Blätter". Die Schriften von Marr, Dühring und Rabenhausen werden von Herrn Fritsch zum Kauf empfohlen. Und jeder, der die Geschichte der antisemitischen Bewegung kennt, weiß, daß neben Stöcker auch Marr, Dühring und Rohling die geistigen Führer der Antisemiten gewesen sind. Ausdrücke von ihnen zur Verbreitung ihrer Gesinnung suchen sie auf. Ausdrücke von ihnen zur Verbreitung ihrer Gesinnung suchen sie auf. Ausdrücke von ihnen zur Verbreitung ihrer Gesinnung suchen sie auf.

Rabenhausen, den sowohl Liebermann von Sonnenberg als Dr. Bödel verleugnen, wird in der letzten Nummer (vom 11. Oktbr. d. J.) der „Antisemitischen Korrespondenz," dem Organ des Herrn Liebermann von Sonnenberg, „der alte, wackere Rabenhausen" genannt, und in der letzten Nummer des „Reichsherold" (vom 9. Oktober d. J.) schreibt Dr. Bödel: „Unser altbewährter, geistiger Vorkämpfer Rabenhausen in Hamburg erfreut uns mit einer dritten vermehrten Auflage seiner trefflichen, hochinteressanten „Esther". Dieses Buch, seither unwiderlegt, ist wie selten eines geeignet, geistig Blinden die Augen über die Gefahr des Judenthums zu öffnen."

Wenn ein Jude irgendwo etwas Böses thut, werden alle Juden verantwortlich gemacht. Für ihre geistigen Führer aber, Leute, die sich durch ihren Antisemitismus in der ganzen Welt bekannt gemacht haben, wollen die Antisemiten nicht einstehen — weil die Herren nicht zu ihrer Partei gehören! Dies ist ein feiges Versteckspielen. Wollt Ihr für Rohling nicht einstehen, so lobt nicht seine Werke. Wollt Ihr, daß Marr nicht zu den Eurigen zähle, so führt seine Aussprüche nicht an! Wollt Ihr nichts mit Rabenhausen zu thun haben, dann nennt ihn nicht mit allen Ehrentiteln.

Uebrigens kommt es nicht so sehr darauf an, ob Herr Liebermann von Sonnenberg oder Herr Bödel für die Herren Marr, Dühring, Rabenhausen haften wollen oder sollen. Worauf es ankommt, war: zu zeigen, daß so oft Haß gegen die Semiten mit Haß gegen das Christenthum sich paart, weil das Christenthum auf „semitischem" Boden erwachsen ist. Wenn man das gerade aus den Schriften der berühmtesten Antisemiten nachweisen konnte, so liegt lieber kein Zufall vor! Ja, ein Mann, den auch die Antisemiten der verschiedensten Richtungen als Autorität preisen, den in ihren Reihen zu haben sie stolz sind, Paul de Lagarde"), sagt (Deutsche Schriften I. S. 238):

„Ein Sohn Gottes, welcher mit der Uhr in der Hand am ersten Januar des Jahres Eins, fünftausend fünfhundert oder vierzehn Jahre nach der Schöpfung in Bethlehem oder Nazareth das Licht der Welt erblickte, hilft Niemanden etwas, der 1878 Jahre nach diesem Zeitpunkt sich mit Gott und der Kreatur abzufinden hat."

Die „Antisemitische Correspondenz" (auch „Deutschsoziale Blätter" genannt), das Organ des Herrn Liebermann v. Sonnenberg, bespricht in Nr. 165 v. 11. Oct. d. J. die „Deutschen Schriften" von **Paul de Lagarde**. Am Schluß der Besprechung heißt es: „Wir schließen mit dem aufrichtigen Wunsche, daß sich die Gemeinde der Lagarde's immer mehr und immer schneller vergrößern möge." Und dabei wimmelt es förmlich in diesen „Deutschen Schriften" von frivolen Bemerkungen über die Religion, über die christliche so gut, wie über die jüdische.

So fragt er S. 2 S. 22, ob irgend welche der in Deutschland thatsächlich bestehenden Religionsgesellschaften zu beschaffen ist, daß wir uns ihrer zu entledigen wünschen müssen. Die Antwort lautet: Heut sind alle mit einander unerwünscht". Und S. 29 heißt es: „Es ist völlig unmöglich, daß der Staat . . . . die drei Religionsgesellschaften (Katholicismus, Protestantismus, Mosaismus) irgend welche Unterstützung werth halte. Der Staat darf dies nicht, weil jene drei einer Unterstützung sich unwerth sind."

Welche Frivolität, die religiösen Gefühle auch des Christen aufs Tiefste verletzend, spricht aus den Worten, welche S. 104, 105 u. a. a. O. zu lesen sind: „Daß der jüdische Stamm nicht der Welt die Verehrung des einzigen Gottes gebracht hat, ist nicht wahr. Einmal weiß die Mehrheit der Bewohner unsrer Erde — Welt sagt man für Erde nur, wenn man nicht nachdenkt — sie weiß von einem einzigen Gotte noch heute nichts, da die Mehrzahl dieser Bewohner, wie der jüdische Ausdruck lautet, heidnisch ist: sodann lehnt auch die christliche Kirche in so gut wie allen ihren Gestalten den Glauben an den einigen Gott ab, da sie an den dreieinigen Gott glaubt und da die bezeichneten, bei diesem ihren Glauben gegenüber vom einigen Gotte redet, als gefälschtungs Feind ihres durch die faselnde Phrase vom frohen Botschaft vom Frieden nicht charakterisirten Wesens ansieht; Drittens haben die Juden den angeblich einigen Gott selbst erst spät entdeckt, da der Dekaloge Jahwe als einen Gott neben allen anderen Göttern kennt, der Vers des Gesetzes V. 6,4 philologisch äußerst schwer zu verdauen ist, und die grobkräftige Leiblichkeit des dem einzig Gott der Juden beigelegten Wesens des ernsten Menschen nach seiner Natur und seinen Außehen knetenden, im Paradiese spazieren gehenden, bei Abraham Kalbsbraten essenden, dem Moses sich von der Rückseite zeigenden Judengottes einem etwa vorhandenen Monotheismus der Juden jeden Werth nimmt . . . ."

**Dr. Dühring,** der für die Beseitigung des Christenthums eintritt, ist nicht nur vom Antisemiten-Katechismus als Autorität genannt; er wird fort und fort von der antisemitischen Presse gelegentlich verherrlicht. So heißt es in der „Westf. Reform" in der Nr. v. 10. Oct. d. J.: „Den Männern aber, welche die Kraft zur eigenen sittlichen Hebung in sich fühlen und noch nicht an der Blasirtheit unserer pessimistisch gesinnten Zeit angekränkelt sind . . . . empfehlen wir auf das Dringlichste, das

---

") Er hieß ursprünglich Paul Bötticher, ein Beweis, daß nicht nur Semiten, sondern auch Antisemiten bisweilen ihren Namen ändern.

---

4a,b,c. Three pamphlets, issued by the Verein zur Abwehr des Antisemitismus (whose leadership consisted mostly of Christian liberals), which state that modern anti-Semitism was incompatible with Christianity. Anti-Semitism that opposed Judaism also opposed Christianity, because Christianity itself had its roots in the Old Testament and also because anti-Semitism, in removing Jews from the influence of Christianity, made the task of Christian salvation more difficult. The racial principle negated Christian ethics; anti-Semitic political propaganda was not in the interest of liberalism. (F.A., No. 2/2.)

# Die Antisemiten und das Christenthum.

Das Christenthum predigt die Liebe, absolut und ohne jede Einschränkung, der Antisemitismus den Haß. Der Antisemitismus wurzelt nimmermehr im Christenthum — und hätte er in seinen Reihen noch so viele Geistliche, wie den früheren protestantischen Hofprediger Stöker und den Professor der katholischen Theologie Rohling in Prag, der sich erboten, den Gebrauch des Christenblutes von Seiten der Juden antisemitisch erhärten zu wollen.

Der Antisemitismus ist unchristlich. Kein guter Christ kann und darf Antisemit sein. Das Christenthum kennt keinen Unterschied der Völker und Racen; der Stifter der christlichen Religion hat die engen Grenzen einer National-Religion durchbrochen, er hat geboten, das Evangelium „aller Creatur" zu predigen. Nicht Land und Stand, nicht Volk und Farbe solle einen Unterschied begründen, sie „sollen allzumal eins sein". Die Hottentotten und Buschmänner sollen also mit eingeschlossen sein, und die Juden nicht, die ja Gott zum Eigenthumsvolk erwählt?! Verdankt denn nicht das Christenthum dem Judenthum seinen Ursprung, ist nicht das Christenthum aus dem Judenthum hervorgegangen, der jüdischen Religion, hat nicht die christliche Religion denselben Stamm, dieselben Wurzeln wie die jüdische? War Christus nicht selbst ein Jude, war nicht seine Mutter eine Jüdin? war also nicht semitisches Blut im Sohne wie in der Mutter? Waren nicht Jesu Jünger, die mit Opferung ihres Leibes und Lebens die Religion ihres Meisters gepredigt, semitischen Geschlechts? War nicht die erste christliche Gemeinde in Jerusalem ein Vorbild aller späteren christlichen Gemeinden, judenchristlich, d. h. hervorgegangen und gesammelt aus jüdischen Männern und Frauen? Darf nun der Christ so sehr die Geschichte seiner Religion und seiner Kirche vergessen, daß er gegen das Nachkommen, gegen das Volk herab wüthet, denen er die Wohlthat seines Glaubens und die Segnungen seiner Religion verdankt? Hat doch gerade der Messiaspropbet dem neuen Bunde dem großen Gedanken des letzten Propheten im alten Bunde reale Gestalt verliehen: „Haben wir nicht alle einen Vater, hat uns nicht Gott geschaffen, warum verachten wir denn einer den andern?" (Maleachi 2 10.)

Dennoch hat man's versucht, den Zusammenhang von Judenthum und Christenthum zu lösen. Historisch freilich geht es nicht, so versuchte man naheliegend, die sowohl der religiöse Inhalt, als auch durch die Religion bedingte Moral der Juden[*], sie und Christenthums völlig verschieden sein.

Hat aber nicht auch das Judenthum und Christenthum, das Alte und das Neue Testament das eine Gebot gemeinsam, dem alle Moral sich aufbaut, das Gebot der Liebe? Gott über Alles lieben und den Nächsten wie sich selbst, das ist nach Christi eigenen Worten der Inhalt des Alten Testaments, das ist auch die Summe des Neuen Testaments. Das ist oft citirte „Auge um Auge, Zahn um Zahn" bezieht sich nicht auf die Moral, sondern auf das Recht. Das Alte Testament gebietet die Liebe gegen Jedermann, auch gegen den Fremdling, denn Israel — so ist das Gebot ausdrücklich begründet — sei auch Fremdling im Aegypten gewesen. Christus wollte nichts Neues bringen, er wollte nur das Alte vollenden. „Ich bin nicht gekommen, Gesetz oder Propheten aufzulösen, sondern zu erfüllen", damit hat er unzweideutig die Einheit des alten und neuen Bundes in Religion und Moral anerkannt. Ja, kein katholischer oder evangelischer Theologe wird es wagen, in Abrede zu stellen, daß das Judenthum das Fundament des Christenthums ist. Die alten Kirchenväter wie Origenes, Irenäus, Tertullian u. A. berufen sich immer gegenüber den judäischen Gegnern auf das Alte Testament. Ein großer Kirchenlehrer des Alterthums, Augustinus, kein Judenchrist, sondern bekanntlich Heidenchrist, hat gesagt: „Das Neue Testament liegt im Alten Testament verborgen" („latet"), „das Alte Testament liegt im Neuen offen" („patet"); und Johannes Damascenus (gest. 780) sagt klar und wahr: „Es ist ein und derselbe Gott, der im Alten und Neuen Testament verehret wird".

Hat nicht das Judenthum den Fortschritt der Sitte und Sittlichkeit dadurch am schönsten bewahrt und bewahrheitet, daß es bin im Gesetz gebotenen Opfer vergeistigt hat zu Opfern der Wohlthätigkeit und Barmberzigkeit? Herr Stöker hat in der 34. Sitzung des Abgeordnetenhauses am 21. März 1890 aus der Offenbarung St. Johannis das Wort citirt: „Sie sagen, sie sind Juden, und sie sind des Teufels Synagoge", um für seine Behauptung über die Juden aus St. Johannes Mund bibliche Belege zu bringen. Er geht davon aus, daß „der Jünger der Liebe", d. i. der Apostel Johannes, die sogenannte Offenbarung geschrieben; es scheint ihm nicht zu wissen, daß der Verfasser ein andrer Johannis ist, den man „der Theologe" führt, daß die Offenbarung für apokryph hielt, wenn er es auch später ein Urtheil gemildert, doch noch erklärte, Christus könne sich in diese teuflische Buch nicht schieben.

*) Der Antisemitenkatechismus sagt, Christus sei kein Semit sondern ein Essäer gewesen. Die Essäer waren aber eine religiöse Secte, keine besondere Race, auch wird Christus als Messias von davidischer d. h. semitischem Stamm gewesen sein.

---

Wenn Stöker's katholischer Gesinnungsgenosse Rohling in seinem Buche „Der Talmud-Jude" das Judenthum mit dem Vorwurfe der niedrigsten Moralität beschmußt, so wird es genügen, darauf hinzuweisen, daß der Professor der evangelischen Theologie Delitzsch, den Rohling selbst einmal eine „geistige Großmacht" genannt, dem Verfasser „Lüge", „tendenziös falsche Uebersetzungen", „Gewissenlosigkeit", „Unkenntniß", „Unwissenheit" u. dergl. nachgewiesen hat. Im Uebrigen erinnern wir an das Zeugniß, welches der Erzbischof von Canterbury 1833 im englischen Oberhause aussprach: „Der Juden Sittengesetz ist aus der reinsten Quelle, aus dem Gesetze Mosis und der Propheten geschöpft, aus der Quelle der Heiligkeit selber! Ungeachtet menschlicher Einwirkungen hat es seinen ursprünglichen Glanz nicht eingebüßt, und es ruht bis auf einen geziesten Grad auf derselben Grundlage mit den Vorschriften des Evangeliums. Was also der Sittlichkeit betrifft, so steht es gut mit den Juden!"

Aber selbst es richtig wäre, daß die Juden schlechter als die Christen seien, was hätte der Antisemit damit gewonnen? Wer trüge die Schuld daran? Wäre es nicht die Behandlung der Christen?

Die russische Fürstin Natalie Gortschakoff hat Recht, wenn Sie sagt: „Ich kenne die Vorwürfe, welche man gegen die Juden erhebt. . . . Viele Handlungen der Juden gegen uns finden eine Entschuldigung darin, daß man ihnen Jahrhunderte lang jeden Zugang zu einem Lebenserwerb gesperrt, daß man sie zur Zielscheibe von Verfolgungen und Erpressungen gemacht hat, daß sie sich oder nur um Goldespreis sich loskaufen konnten, und daß die klingende Münze allein ihnen eine gesicherte, wenn auch nicht ehrenvolle Stellung unter den Söhnen Japhets sicherte". . . .

So eine christliche Fürstin. Aber auch bei denen, welche bei ihrem Antisemitismus noch das Christenthum retten und rechtfertigen wollen, handelt es sich nicht um Religion, um Confession, und nicht um das, was die Menschen mit Gott verbindet, sondern um das, was die Christen von einander trennt; und deshalb verfolgen antisemitische Katholiken den Protestantismus ebenso wie das Judenthum, darum stehen dem antisemitischen Protestantismus und zusammen in dem einen ultramontanen Katholicismus häufig gleich.

Derselbe Rohling, der die Juden mit Schmutz bewirft, nennt in seiner Schrift: „Der Antichrist und das Ende der Welt" die Reformatoren: „Melanchton, Zwingli, Calvin „Schurken, die jeden welche der religiöse Sittlichkeit nicht besaßen". Er sagt in derselben Schrift: „Wohin der Protestantismus seinen Fuß setzt, da verdorrt und verkümmert Alles, ein „entseelt Vandalismus und Anarchie". Die protestantischen Lehren nennt er „Schandlehren" und die „gesammte protestantische Theologie faßt er zusammen in dem einen Satze: „Sündige tapfer und glaube mit größerer Tapferkeit"!

Wohlan, und ist es noch immer nicht einleuchtet, daß bei solchem Christenthum die Frömmigkeit der Deckmantel der Bosheit ist?!

Derselbe Geist, der das Judenthum verhetzt, hetzt auch gegen den Katholicismus! In seiner dem Fürsten Bismarck gewidmeten Schrift: „Juda-Jesuitismus" sagt O. Beta: „Die Unfehlbarkeits-Anmaßung der Judenabkömmlinge in Rom ist nichts als ein ultramontanes Feuerwerf, welches die Augen der germanischen Völker abzieht von dem viel drohenderen capitalistischen Unfehlbarkeit ihrer Stammesgenossen im weltlichen Gewande, welche uns indessen die seidene Cravatte umbinden, um uns damit zu erwürgen wie die Männer von Eisem". . . . Was glauben Sie (die Katholiken) nicht noch? Sie glauben an die Unfehlbarkeit des Papstes Pio aus dem jüdischen (!) Hause Pecci".

Weiter: Der sozialistisch-materialistische Voltairianer Dr. Dühring, selbst unter den Aposteln des Antisemitismus, kämpft offen und frei für die Beseitigung des Christenthums, als der letzten weltgeschichtlichen Schöpfung der verabscheuten, grundsätzlich fremden semitischen Race. Um den semitischen Geist aus dem europäischen Leben zu bannen, will er das Christenthum durch eine höhere Religionsform ersetzen und in seiner Abhandlung „Die Parteien und die Judenfrage", „Das Christenthum hat überhaupt keine praktische Moral, die unzweideutig, brauchbar und gesund wäre. Mit dem semitischen Geist werden dabei die Völker erst fertig werden, wenn sie auch diese zweite jenseitige Gestalt des Hebraismus, der ihre nationale Kindheit durch Unfreiheit anleimichel, wieder aus ihrem heutern Geiste ausgeschieden haben."

Und an einer anderen Stelle:

„Vom Standpunkte des Christenthums, und wäre es auch nur der beßre wahr, heute wegen der Judenstamm auftreten, hat das Schädliche mit einer seiner eigenen Ausländer, also wesentlich durch sich selbst unschädlich machen wollen."

Ein Christ, wenn er sich selbst verachtet, kann kein confessioneller Antisemit sein. Die nordischen Götter und der nordische Gott hat etwas, was einem Naturrecht hat und was von einer tausendjährigen Ableitung aus der Welt geschafft wird

# Katholische Stimmen über die Judenfrage.

## I. Katholische Stimmen über die Juden.

**Papst Paul III.** „Wir fordern unsere theuersten Söhne in Christo auf, daß sie bei ihren Beamten, Dienern und Völkern mit ihrer Autorität eintreten, daß die Juden keine Verfolgungen ungerechter Weise erleiden sollen, damit sie von christlicher Gütigkeit angelockt, und ihre Seelen für Gott zu gewinnen, größere Hoffnung gefaßt werden kann." Gegeben zu Rom, beim heiligen Petrus unter dem Fischerring am 12. Mai 1540, im sechsten Jahr unseres Pontificates.

**Cardinal Manning.** „Seit nahezu vierzig Jahren ist London meine Heimath, und in dieser Zeit sind mir alle Arten des Leidens, der Armuth, aber auch des Lasters vor Augen gekommen. Ich kann deßhalb Zeugniß geben von dem Wohlthätigkeitssinne und der Freigebigkeit meiner jüdischen Landsleute. Ich habe sie bei allen guten Werken in erster Reihe gefunden. In der Sorge für ihre Kinder, ihre Kranken und ihre Armen geben sie uns ein edles Beispiel der hochherzigen Werkthätigkeit . . . . . Es giebt aber noch höhere und zwingendere Motive, die mich zu Aussprüchen und Handlungen bewegen haben, welche von Ihnen in Ihrer Adresse über Verdienst geschätzt werden. Ich wäre meinem eigenen Glauben nicht treu, wenn ich den Ihrigen nicht verehren würde."

**Pater Victor Kolb.** „Es ist Sünde und gegen die Lehren Christi, einen Nebenmenschen zu hassen. Darum ist es auch Unrecht, den Juden zu hassen, weil er ein Jude ist. Christi Gebot heißt: Liebe Deinen Nächsten wie Dich selbst. Christi Gebot gilt für alle Menschen gleich, ob Christ, ob Jude. Selbst dann, wenn ein Mensch in Sünde und Unglauben befangen ist, müßt Ihr ihn lieben als Mitmenschen und dürfet ihn nur bemitleiden ob seiner Fehlerhaftigkeit. Die Fehler, die Sünde darf man tadeln, nicht aber den Menschen. Der Jude ist gleich so nach dem Ebenbilde Gottes geschaffen, wie der Christ, wie alle Menschen. Darum müßt Ihr den Juden lieben nach Christi Gebot als Euren Nächsten und Mitmenschen, wie alle Anderen."

**Windhorst.** „Einer der Hauptpunkte, worüber die Juden sich beklagen können, ist nach meinem Dafürhalten der, daß man, wenn ein einzelner Jude oder eine Mehrzahl von Juden, ein Theil derselben etwas gethan hat, was mit Recht gerügt werden muß, daß man dies verallgemeinert und generell hinstellt, als ob es die ganze Judenschaft träfe. Das ist grundverkehrt und ungerecht. Wenn man Klagen über Einzelne oder über einen Theil hat, so soll man die Einzelnen und diesen Theil concret fassen, aber niemals die Sache generell hinstellen und die ganze Judenschaft verletzen, unter der es die allerehrenwerthesten Menschen giebt."

**Windhorst:** „Daß auch andere Confessionen das Recht hätten," eine Berücksichtigung zu haben, ist unzweifelhaft, und wir haben in den vergangenen Debatten wiederholt unsere Stimmen erhoben, daß den Israeliten ihr Recht werden müsse. Das hat Niemand bestritten."

**Windhorst.** „Ich bin der Ansicht, daß bei dem gegenwärtigen Stande der Verhältnisse in Deutschland es unzulässig ist, daß das religiöse Bekenntniß irgend welchen Einfluß auf die öffentlichen bürgerlichen oder staatsbürgerlichen Verhältnisse hat."

**„Echo der Gegenwart"** (Kathol. Ztg.) „Es ist gewiß eine arge Uebertreibung, wenn die Antisemiten das Anklagen gegen die Juden in Bausch und Bogen erheben, und es ist eine unverantwortliche Hetzerei, wenn sie die Juden sammt und sonders „unschädlich" gemacht wissen wollen, wenn sie aus der Judenfrage eine Rassenfrage machen, wenn sie die Juden-Emanzipation rückgängig gemacht wissen wollen, wenn sie die bürgerliche Gleichberechtigung auf die Juden nicht angewandt wissen wollen oder wenn sie gar aus ihrem innersten Herzenswunsche keinen Hehl machen: daß die Juden je eher je besser mit Sack und Pack über die Grenze gebracht werden sollten. Das wird kein erleuchteter, kein rechtdenkender Christ und am allerwenigsten ein Katholik fordern, welcher den „Culturkampf" mitgemacht und die Ausnahmegesetzgebung auf seinem Rücken verspürt hat. Nein, ein wahrer Christ, ein guter Katholik wird auch den Juden gegenüber die Grundsätze der Gerechtigkeit niemals verleugnen; er wird auch ihnen gegenüber unterscheiden zwischen dem Guten und dem Bösen; kann ihm doch die Thatsache nicht entgehen, daß auch in den christlichen Reihen leider viel Schlimmes vorhanden, sehr viel „Auswuchs" zu finden ist. So wird er denn gottesfürchtige, ehrliche und friedliche Israeliten hochachten und ihnen aller Freiheiten und Rechte des Verfassungslebens in Staat und Gemeinde sich erfreuen lassen. Auf der andern Seite aber wird er im Interesse der Gesammtheit sich eben so energisch gegen die Auswüchse des Judenthums wie gegen unmäßige „christliche" Elemente wenden, welche vom Christenthum nur noch etwas Aeußerliches, einen fast verblaßten Schein sich gerettet haben."

## II. Katholische Stimmen gegen die Antisemiten.

**Hirtenbrief der österreichischen Bischöfe** (Landgraf Fürstenberg, Cardinal von Olmütz, Graf Schönborn, Cardinal u. a. m.) am 15. Februar 1891. „Die katholische Kirche erkennt die einzelnen Völker in ihrem gesonderten Bestehen als eine Einrichtung der göttlichen Vorsehung an und erblickt darin die Berechtigung derselben. Sie befeindet kein Volk und bevorzugt keines; aber die heidnische Absonderung und Trennung der Völker. Die Kirche achtet und ehrt die Liebe und Anhänglichkeit an die Eigenthümlichkeit einer jeden; aber sie muß es entschieden mißbilligen, wenn diese Liebe und Anhänglichkeit ausarten würde zu Ungerechtigkeiten gegen die Rechte Anderer, zur fanatischen Befeindung jeder fremden Volkseigenthümlichkeit. Mit Einem Worte, nach katholischen Grundsätzen darf die Liebe zur eigenen Nation nicht wider das Gesetz der Nächsten- und Bruderliebe sich wenden und zum heidnischen Racenhasse herabsinken. Ja, geliebte Diöcesanen, das ist die bedeutsame Erscheinung unserer Zeit, daß in dem Maße, als die heutige Welt von der christlichen Anschauungen sich entfernt, der heidnische Nationalitätenhaß wächst, und daß diejenigen seine lautesten Prediger sind, welche sich vom christlichen Glauben und Leben am weitesten abgelöst haben. Nein, Geliebte im Herrn, ein treukatholischer Mann wird nicht einstimmen in die Anfeindungen der Völker desselben Reiches."

**Pfarrer Dr. Fr. Frank, bayr. Landtagsabgeordneter.** „Die Antisemiten wollen Aufklärungsschriften über die Gefährlichkeit des Judenvolkes verbreiten. Ja, ist denn das Judenvolk als solches gefährlich? Gewiß nicht! Wir haben gesehen, wie weder in der Thora noch im Talmud, wenn sie nach der gegenwärtig allgemein geltenden Erklärung befolgt werden, eine Gefahr für die Christen liegt; wenn unter dem Judenvolke volksgefährliche Elemente giebt, so bilden dieselben nicht das ganze Volk. Es geht eben bei dem Judenvolke, wie es auch bei den Christen geht. Bei

Dieser Mann ist Herr

## Oberlehrer Professor

# Gustav Hüpeden in Cassel.

In weiten Kreisen ist sein Name als der eines unermüdlichen Vorkämpfers für Volkswohl, Recht und deutsche Sitte längst bekannt und sein bisheriges Eintreten für die idealen und notwhalen Güter unseres Volkes giebt uns die Gewißheit, daß dieser Mann, wenn er gewählt wird, nicht umsonst im Reichstage sitzen und voll und ganz seinen Mann stehen wird. Insonderheit wird er am Platze sein, wenn es gilt, die Interessen des Arbeiterstandes, der Alleingewerbetreibenden, sowie des kleinen Geschäftsmannes und Beamten zu vertreten.

Die Forderungen des Bundes der Landwirthe werden von unserem Kandidaten als eine nothwendige und vollberechtigte Konsequenz der schwerbedrängten Lage der gesammten Landwirthschaft anerkannt, und von demselben mit voller Entschiedenheit unterstützt werden. Besonders wird derselbe einer etwa beabsichtigten Herabsetzung der Getreidezölle gegenüber Rußland und Rumänien entgegentreten.

Die Mitglieder des Bundes der Landwirthe unseres Wahlkreises erkennen daher Herrn Professor Hüpeden auch als ihren Kandidaten an und rathen allen Landwirthen, ihm ihre Stimme zu geben.

Der bisherige Candidat der deutsch-socialen Partei Herr Professor Dr. Paul Förster hat mit großer Selbstlosigkeit zu Gunsten unseres gemeinsamen Kandidaten auf die Wiederannahme einer Kandidatur verzichtet.

Wähler in Stadt und Land! Schließen wir uns deshalb zusammen und treten wir mit der Losung „Einer für Alle und Alle für Einen" ein für Herrn

## Oberlehrer Professor Gustav Hüpeden
### in Cassel,

dessen ganzes Thun und Wesen dafür bürgt, daß er alle Fragen, die an ihn herantreten, unbefangen prüfen und sich stets von dem Grundsatze leiten lassen wird: Der Arbeit ihren Lohn, dem Fleiß sein Recht!

## Und nun vorwärts mit Gott für Kaiser und Reich!

Fehle Keiner am 15. Juni und wähle Jeder den Herrn

## Oberlehrer Professor Gustav Hüpeden
### in Cassel!

Cassel, im Mai 1893.

### Das Wahlkomité der deutsch-konservativen Partei.

### Das Wahlkomité der deutsch-socialen Partei.

### Die Vertreter des Bundes der Landwirthe.

Für Druck und Verlag verantwortlich: L. H. Höhns, Cassel.

5a. Propaganda poster in the election campaign of 1893 testifying to the cooperation between the Christian Conservative candidates (the Conservative Protestants and the Farmers' League) and the racial anti-Semitic candidates, the D.S.P., at the head of which was Professor Paul Förster, one of the leading anti-Semitic critics of Christianity. (S.A.M., B/165.)

# Zur Wahl!

## Mitbürger!

Das Gesetz ruft jeden deutschen Staatsbürger zur Wahlurne. Er soll Männer wählen, die für

### Recht und Gesetz, Freiheit und Wohlstand der Bürger

schaffend und schützend eintreten.

# Gleiches Recht für Alle!

Das ist die erste Forderung, die jeder Abgeordnete zu beachten hat.

**Kein Stand, kein Beruf, keine Konfession oder Religionsgemeinschaft darf in dem Genusse der bürgerlichen Gleichberechtigung beeinträchtigt werden.** Die Antisemiten und die, welche sie unterstützen, wollen aber den Juden Deutschlands ihre bürgerliche Gleichstellung rauben.

### Darum Bürger, wählt nicht den Antisemiten Schriftsteller Leuß.

Mitbürger! Der Antisemitismus ist, wie hervorragende Geistliche beider christlichen Konfessionen wiederholt erklärten, mit dem Geiste des Christenthums unvereinbar; der Antisemitismus ist ein Verbrechen an der Wahrheit, der Sittlichkeit, der Gerechtigkeit, am deutschen Vaterlande.

Seht, welche Schmach ein Ahlwardt, ein Antisemit wie Leuß, ein Paasch und ein Schwindhammer über das Vaterland gebracht haben! Leset, wie in antisemitischen Blättern deutsche Wahrheitsliebe zum Gespötte wird, wie man die Bibel und die Religion in diesen Blättern beschimpft! Seht und hört, wie in antisemitischen Hetzreden die Unzufriedenen zu Lüge und Ungerechtigkeit und Rohheit verleitet werden.

Mitbürger! Die Juden unserer Gegend leben seit Jahren und Jahren mit ihren christlichen Mitbürgern in Frieden. Sie haben für dem Landesherrn zu jeder Zeit Gut und Blut hergegeben. In dem glorreichen Kriege von 1870/71 sind Juden den Heldentod gestorben; nicht wenig Juden wurden mit dem Eisernen Kreuz dekorirt. Wo es gilt, Armen zu helfen, Kranke zu heilen, Kinder zu pflegen, Wissenschaft und Kunst zu fördern, haben auch Juden gern und freudig dazu beigetragen.

Demgegenüber kann die Thatsache nicht ins Gewicht fallen, daß es unter den Juden, ebenso wie in allen anderen Glaubensgemein- schaften, vereinzelte schlechte Elemente giebt. Die Juden sind ja auch nur Menschen. Die Antisemiten benutzen aber diese bedauerlichen, glücklicherweise vereinzelten Erscheinungen zu lügnerischen, tendenziösen Uebertreibungen, zu grundloser Verallgemeinerung, anstatt, wenn sie selbst sich rein und makellos fühlen, uns bei der Besserung dieser Elemente hülfreiche Hand zu bieten.

Mitbürger! Nicht um den Juden Liebe zu erweisen, sondern den deutschen Namen in Ehren zu halten, gebt Eure Stimme keinem antisemitischen Kandidaten.

### Hütet das gleiche Recht für Alle!

Wer Unschuldige ihrer Religion oder Abstammung wegen verfolgt, der legt die Axt an die Wurzeln unseres Rechtsstaates. Darum! Gebt keinem Antisemiten Eure Stimme.

### Schützet die Religion, die Wahrheit, das Recht, den Frieden, die Freiheit im Deutschen Vaterlande!

# Deshalb gebet Eure Stimme
# keinem Antisemiten.

Druck und Verlag von H. S. Hermann in Berlin.

*5b.* Propaganda poster of the electoral campaign of 1893 indicating the competition for votes between the National Liberals and the Conservatives on the one hand and the anti-Semites on the other. The poster urged the voters to support the Liberals and the Conservatives, but under no circumstances to cast their votes for the anti-Semites. Among the reasons given: Christianity could not be reconciled with anti-Semitism and hence anti-Semitism was a grave offense against religion and against the state. (S.A.M., B/165.)

# Ein Wort zum Frieden!

Nur mit tiefer Wehmut beobachtet der Volksfreund, wie seit Wochen infolge
Bestrafung eines israelitischen Metzgers in Haßfurt wegen Unreinlichkeit in seinem
Geschäfte versucht wird, diesen Fall unter dem Hinweis auf Lehren des Talmud
begreiflich zu machen, mit anderen Worten: zu behaupten, in den religiös-sittlichen
Bestimmungen des Judenthums, wie im Talmud, sei befohlen, das Fleisch und die
Fett-Theile, welche die Judenmetzger an Christen verkaufen, vorher zu besudeln.

Urtheilslos sagt einer das dem anderen; von Ort zu Ort dringt diese Ver-
dächtigung und Beschuldigung, und alle trauen nun allen jüdischen Metzgern zu, daß
sie das Fleisch und die Fett-Theile, welche sie an Christen verkaufen, weil die Juden
es nicht essen dürfen, mit ihrem Urin besudeln. Und die israelitischen Metzger ver-
lieren ihre Kundschaft, die Juden insgesammt werden, wo sie sich in Wirthschaften zeigen,
nach der „Geschichte in Haßfurt" befragt in einer Weise, die ihnen zeigt, die Fleischbesudelungs-Beschuldigung wird geglaubt im Volke. Die dümmsten Dinge werden
dann über die Juden kolportiert zum Beweis, daß verständige Ueberlegung brutalem
Fanatismus Platz gemacht hat. Wir brauchen uns wahrlich nichts auf unsere viel-
gerühmte Volksbildung einzubilden; wo derartige Thorheiten noch Boden finden, ar-
beitet die Volksbildung mit traurigem Erfolg.

So wenig man ein Recht hat, von einem christlichen Bäcker, der wegen Unsauber-
keit in seinem Geschäfte einen Strafbefehl vom Amtsanwalt erhielt, zu behaupten, er
habe bei seiner Außerachtlassung der Sauberkeit in seiner Backstube nur nach den Bestimmungen der christlichen Religion gehandelt, so wenig ist das den Juden gegenüber erlaubt. Ihr
lieben Leute, habt acht darauf, was ich euch sage: Im ganzen Talmud steht gerade das Gegentheil von dem, was zur Zeit in eurer Mitte behauptet wird.
Glaubt es nicht, daß die Juden eine so gemeine Sittenlehre haben, wie man euch
verleumderisch sagt.

Die heilige Schrift alten Testaments ist auch die Grundlage für die
Lehre des Judenthums, wie sie bei uns das Wort Gottes des alten Bundes heißt.
Das ist ihre schriftliche Lehre. Daneben hat das Judenthum noch eine
Religionsquelle, den Talmud, der die mündliche Lehre genannt wird.

Du es sich die der Fleischbesudelungs-Beschuldigung nur die Sittenlehre des
Talmud handelt, so will ich euch nur kurz sagen, daß die ganze Sittenlehre des
Talmud nur auf dem alten Testament beruht. Das Gebot der Nächstenliebe, der allgemeinsten, auf alle Menschen, Juden und Nichtjuden sich er-
streckenden Nächstenliebe ist auch jedem Israeliten Gesetz, wie die das Grund-
gesetz des Christenthums ist. Die Sittenlehre des Judenthums erkennt keinen Aus-
spruch und keine Anschauung an, die dem Nichtjuden gegenüber etwas erlaubt, was
dem Juden gegenüber verboten ist. Was sie lehrt in ihren Schulen, von ihren Kan-
zeln ist nirgends — mit dem Maßstab der christlichen Sittenlehre gemessen—
unsittlich!

Das Gebot der Nächstenliebe und Wahrheitsliebe zwingt uns, die gegen das
Judenthum als solches in Franken erhobene Beschuldigung als eine durch nichts zu
begründende Behauptung zurückzuweisen. Haben wir vielleicht im 13. Kapitel
des 1. Korintherbriefs ein Recht, so das 8. Gebot zu halten, wie es in den letzten
Wochen den Juden gegenüber geschehen ist? Steht nicht im Neuen Testament der
große Heidenapostel Paulus ganz auf dem Boden seines herrlichen Lobgesangs über
die Liebe gerade seinen früheren Glaubensgenossen gegenüber? Schreibt er nicht im
11. Kapitel nicht mehr in seinem Brief an die Römer?

So trete denn ab vom Unrecht, wer diese Beschuldigung geglaubt und weiter
getragen — aus Nächstenliebe, um der Wahrheit willen. Die Wahrheit könnt
ihr erfahren aus einem vortrefflichen Buche des Berliner Professors Dr. Strack,
eines der besten christlichen Talmudkenner der Jetztzeit. Er hat eine Einleitung in den Talmud geschrieben, in Leipzig bei J. C. Hinrichs 1894 erschienen ist und 2,50 Mk. kostet. Da habt ihr — die Bessergebildeten, die mit treuem
Urtheil den anderen dienen sollen — eine objektive und wissenschaftliche Belehrung über
das Ganze des Talmud. Ich will für die, welche solche Bücher nicht lesen, im nächsten
Monat eine kleine Schrift über die ganze Angelegenheit veröffentlichen; dann könnt ihr
Letzteren noch mehr beurtheilen, wie unrecht die angegebene Beschuldigung ist.

Solche Gehässigkeit hätte nicht ins neue Jahrhundert mit hinüber genommen werden
sollen. — Vielmehr bleibe das Losungswort:

## Gerechtigkeit und Liebe!

**Ebrach,** 18. Februar 1900.

### Pfr. Dr. Jaeger.

---

6a. A public notice of the year 1900 by a Dr. Jaeger, a clergyman connected with the Mission unter
Israel, urging opposition to racial anti-Semitism. The notice endorsed the words of Professor H. Strack,
an eminent theologian and one of the leaders of the Mission unter Israel, who stated (in his *Introduction
to the Talmud*, 1894) that there was no justifiable ground for attributing an unethical character to the
halacha. (G.A.J., M 1/19.)

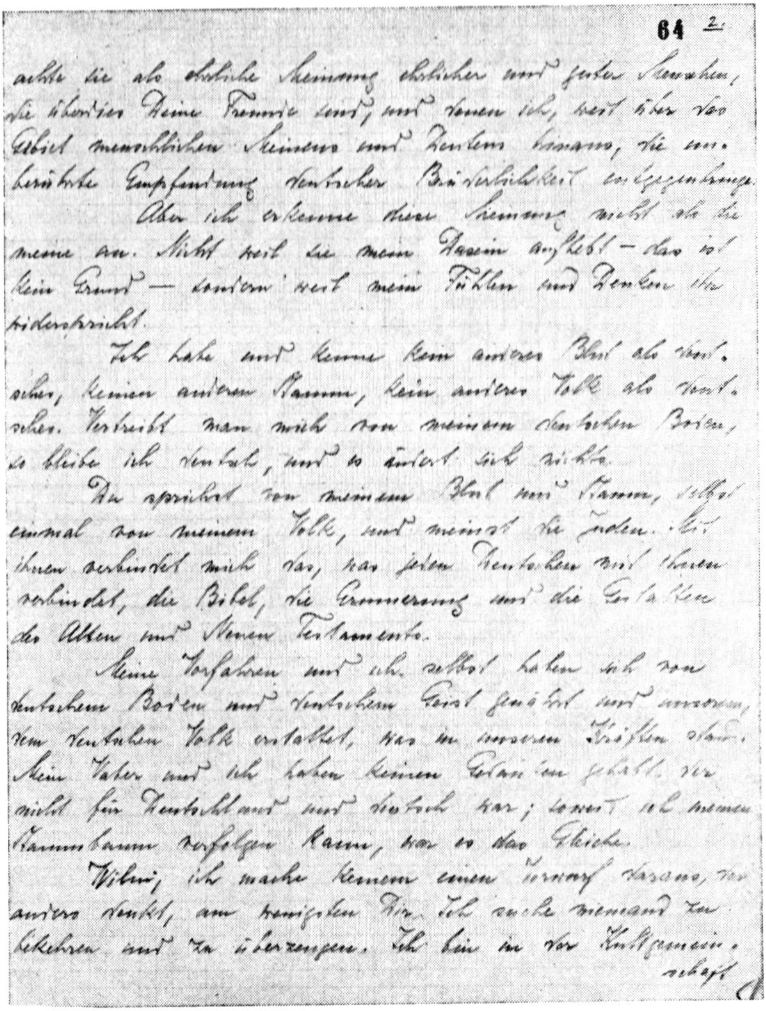

*[handwritten letter in old German cursive script]*

7a. Excerpt from a letter by Walther Rathenau, dated January 23, 1916, to an intimate friend, Wilhelm Schwaner, one of the fathers of German-Christian racial theory. Rathenau emphasized that for him there was no such thing as country, people or, tribe (*Stamm*), but only Germany; nevertheless, he was unable to sever his ties with Judaism. (B.A.K., Nachlass Rathenau, No. 4, 1916–1921 [1927]. Vol. II.)

*7b.* Excerpt from Wilhelm Schwaner's reply to Rathenau, dated January 24, 1916, in which he repeated the basic principle of his doctrine: race and blood were the highest values; men were not equal—those who had noble blood were noble, and those who had inferior blood were inferior.

*7c.* Wilhelm Schwaner's insignia, a mixture of the Christian cross and the swastika, which later became the Nazi symbol. Schwaner wished to fuse the consciousness of the superiority of the pure Aryan race with the ethics of the gospels. (B.A.K., Nachlass Rathenau, Briefwechsel, No. 1, 1913–1921.)

# Bibliographical Essay

## CONTENTS

I. Background
    Preliminary remarks
    Studies and Surveys
II. Areas of Research
    The Christian State and German Jewry
        Primary archival source material
        Primary printed source material
        Additional material from Protestant periodicals
        Historical studies
    German Liberalism, Egalitarianism, and Jewry
        Primary archival source material
        Primary printed source material
        Historical studies
    Intellectual and Religious Tension
        Primary archival source material
        Primary printed source material
        Historical studies
    Anti-intellectualism and the Superior Man
        Primary printed source material
        Historical studies
    The Law and Anti-Semitism
        Primary archival source material
        Historical studies

## I. BACKGROUND

*Preliminary remarks*

The following bibliography consists of selected sources and studies for further reference. In the footnotes to the book the reader will find detailed lists of sources on which each chapter is based. Hence, the following bibliography contains only some of the sources and studies that appear in the footnotes, plus some new bibliographical material.

A complete list of sources and studies would have run into thousands of titles. Whether they deal with theoretical and scientific subjects or with social and political problems, the sources are for the most part of a publicistic nature and are addressed to a definite public, sometimes to a select circle of scientists, teachers, theologians, or prominent figures in the world of art and culture, and sometimes to a wider and more varied public or even to the broad masses. Furthermore, the number of sources required for the study of these problems is greatly increased because of their tendentious character. Since the discussion here revolves around the reciprocal relations of the adherents of different religions, schools of thought, social movements, or political parties, comparative studies are inevitable. This involves the study of historical documents in accordance with their literary forms and in accordance with the various authors who represent different or even contradictory patterns of thought and behavior which by the very nature of our subject take the forms of: Christians and Jews; liberals and conservatives; Protestants and Catholics; observant and nonobservant Jews; high-ranking members of the established church, leaders of the Jewish communities or of political organizations, and those who did not belong to any organized group but who were influential in forming public opinion and in giving expression to the historical reality of the time; members of the well-to-do classes and members of the lower classes; circles close to the ruling class and nonconformists; intellectuals and members of the various professions belonging to different generations.

This abundant source material becomes more complicated in view of the fact that many of the authors, especially among the intellectuals, often changed their opinions in the course of their political careers. Moreover, we frequently find that influential men expressed different and even contradictory views at the same time. The contrast between private opinions and publicly expressed sentiments, especially among intellectuals, is a common phenomenon, for they are accustomed to regard their own views critically and often permit the passion for abstract theoretical criticism to obscure their vital practical interests.

In the face of this abundant source material we selected the various items in the bibliography in accordance with the following criteria: sources that represent and exemplify basic patterns of thought—rational, critical, and scientific, political and ideological, historical, metaphysical, juridical and halachic, romantic, mythical, and irrational ("emotional thinking" also was a common term used in those days)—sources that reflect and articulate the views, intellectual tendencies, and feelings of that period; sources that testify to the social, political, or economic motivations of the people of that era, whether they were aware of them or not.

One of the difficulties of the objective critical investigator is to determine the scientific value of documents. Because of the tendentious ideological character of many of the sources, he must exercise great caution in discriminating between two different functions, two different kinds of information that the document in question may provide: information with regard to the content, and information with regard to the author. Thus, for example, a number of studies or declarations by heads of organizations or by Jewish apologetes give us an objective view of the problem of discrimination against Jews who were eligible for appointments to public posts or concerning the ethical character of religious and halachic traditions. On the other hand, we have a relatively large number of sources that provide information not only about these social disabilities or about the ethical nature of some halachic traditions because, knowingly or unknowingly, the subject is treated from a purely apologetic point of view.[1] This apologetic character, however, does not invalidate a document for critical and historical study; on the contrary, after scientific criticism discovers the contradiction between the objective factual content on which the study or the declaration was based and the views of the apologetes, this contradiction itself becomes a principal source for the understanding of the period in question. The tendentious nature of the documents thus provides a rich source for the understanding of the historical period we are studying by revealing tacit assumptions, latent motivations, economic needs, political aspirations, and even messianic longings for a reformed social order and a better world.

When the Jews complained of official discrimination in appointments to public posts, they often had no interest whatever in obtaining such posts. The complaint itself, however, served to strengthen their Jewish identity; it also served to consolidate their opposition to clerical rule and the principle of the Christian state in their struggle to create a more rational and, in their opinion, a more equitable political system. Similarly, it was plain to the Protestant leaders that their opposition to the dogmatic traditions of the church on the ground that they did not conform to the historical source of Christianity could not always be substantiated historically. The ensuing ideological dispute helped to initiate changes in the church and its dogmatic doctrines and to close the gap between individualism and humanism on the one hand and the historical continuity of the Lutheran legacy on the other.

The original and secondary sources listed throughout the book and in the following bibliography were thus chosen on the basis of their concrete influence on public opinion and also as an expression of public opinion. Works of a purely philosophical or speculative nature therefore find no place in the bibliography; however, all documents, such as symposia, book reviews, and lectures in intellectual circles which obviously reflect contemporary social and political attitudes are carefully noted—and this is in keeping with the discipline that informs this study and on which our researches are based, namely, the social history of ideas.

The archival sources, primary printed sources, and historical studies for every topic are listed in chronological order.

1. This aspect has been treated by Jacob Katz in his article "The Vicissitudes of Three Apologetic Passages" (Hebrew), *Zion,* Vol. 23–24, Nos. 3–4, 1958–1959, p. 174 ff.

*Studies and Surveys*

*Meinecke, Friedrich,* Weltbürgertum und Nationalstaat: Studien zur Genesis des deutschen Nationalstaates (1907), 5th ed. München, Berlin, 1919.

*Niebergall, Friedrich,* Praktische Theologie: Lehre von der kirchlichen Gemeindeerziehung auf religionswissenschaftlicher Grundlage, 2 vols., Tübingen, 1918–1919.

*Bergsträsser, Ludwig,* Geschichte der politischen Parteien, Berlin, 1921.

*Barzun, Jacques,* Darwin, Marx, Wagner, Boston, 1941.

*Leese, Kurt,* Der Protestantismus im Wandel der neueren Zeit: Texte und Charakteristiken zur deutschen Geistes-und Frömmigkeitsgeschichte seit dem 18. Jahrhundert bis zur Gegenwart, 1941.

*Barraclough, G.,* The Origins of Modern Germany, Oxford, 1947.

*Kupisch, Karl,* Von Luther zu Bismarck, Berlin, Bielefeld, 1949.

*Fischer, Fritz,* Der deutsche Protestantismus und die Politik im 19. Jahrhundert, in H.Z., No. 171, 1951.

*Mommsen, W.,* Deutsche Parteiprogramme, München, 1952.

*Buchheim, Karl,* Geschichte der christlichen Parteien in Deutschland, München, 1953.

*Kohn, Hans,* ed., German History: Some New German Views, London, 1954.

*Mommsen, W.,* Stein, Ranke, Bismarck: Ein Beitrag zur Politischen und Sozialen Bewegung des 19. Jahrhundert, München, 1954.

*Bornkamm, Heinrich,* Luther im Spiegel der deutschen Geistesgeschichte, 1955.

*Pinson, Koppel S.,* Modern Germany: Its History and Civilization, New York, 1955.

*Arendt, Hannah,* Elemente und Ursprünge totaler Herrschaft, Frankfurt a/M, 1955.

*Kupisch, Karl,* Zwischen Idealismus und Massendemokratie: Eine Geschichte der evangelischen Kirche in Deutschland 1815–1945, Berlin, 1955.

*Sterling, Eleonore,* Er ist wie Du: Aus der Frühgeschichte des Antisemitismus in Deutschland (1815–1850), München, 1956.

*Krieger, Leonard,* The German Idea of Freedom, Boston, 1957.

*Reichmann, Eva G.,* Flucht in den Hass: Die Ursache der deutschen Judenkatastrophe, Frankfurt a/M [no date].

*Hughes, H. Stuart,* Consciousness and Society, New York, 1958.

*Massing, Paul W.,* Vorgeschichte des Politischen Antisemitismus (trans. Felix J. Weil), Frankfurt a/M, 1959.

*Kohn, Hans,* The Mind of Germany, New York, 1960.

*Kupisch, Karl,* Zwischen Idealismus und Massendemokratie: Eine Geschichte der evangelischen Kirche in Deutschland 1815–1945, Berlin, Stuttgart, 1960.[2]

*Stephan, Horst,* Geschichte der deutschen evangelischen Theologie seit dem deutschen Idealismus, 2d rev. ed. Martin Schmidt, Berlin, 1960.

*Baron, S. W.,* Modern Nationalism and Religion (1947), New York, Philadelphia, 1960.

*Bergsträsser, Ludwig,* Geschichte der politischen Parteien in Deutschland, 10th ed., München, 1960.

*Mosse, George L.,* The Culture of Western Europe, the Nineteenth and Twentieth Centuries: An Introduction, Chicago, 1961.

*Marsch, Wolf-Dieter, and Thieme, Karl,* Christen und Juden: Ihr Gegenüber vom Apostelkonzil bis Heute, Mainz, Göttingen, 1961.

*Thieme, Karl,* ed. Judenfeindschaft: Darstellung und Analysen, Frankfurt a/M, 1963.

*Eckert, W. P., and Ehrlich, E. L.,* Judenhass—Schuld der Christen? Essen, 1964.

*Huss, Hermann, and Schröder, Andreas,* ed., Antisemitismus: Zur Pathologie der bürgerlichen Gesellschaft, Frankfurt a/M, 1966.

*Wilhelm, Kurt,* ed., Wissenschaft des Judentums im deutschen Sprachgebrauch: Ein Querschnitt, 2 Vols., Tübingen, 1967.

*Liebeschütz, Hans,* Das Judentum im Deutschen Geschichtsbild von Hegel bis Max Weber, Tübingen, 1967.

*Mosse, George L.,* Germans and Jews: The Right, the Left and the Search for a "Third Force" in Pre-Nazi Germany, 2d ed., New York, 1970.

*Schleunes, Karl A.,* The Twisted Road to Auschwitz: Nazi Policy toward German Jews, Ch. I, Chicago, London, 1970.

*Emmerich, Wolfgang,* Zur Kritik der Volkstumsideologie, Frankfurt a/M, 1971.

*Hammer, Karl,* Deutsche Kriegstheologie 1870–1918, München, 1971.

*Strunk, Reiner,* Politische Ekklesiologie im Zeitalter der Revolution, München, 1971.

*Stern, Fritz,* The Failure of Illiberalism: Essays in the Political Culture of Modern Germany, Introd., pp. xi–xliv, Part I, pp. 3–75, New York, 1972.

## II. AREAS OF RESEARCH

### The Christian State and German Jewry

The Christian and especially the Protestant character of the state and the monarchal imperial regime. Christian character in the social and political spheres, in labor relations and business ethics, in the social and educational policy of the state and society. The theological and especially the Lutheran elements of the Christian state and their popular public expression in the conservative Christian society. Views of the Christian character of the state and society with respect to the Jewish question and to the civic and social status of Jews. The ambiguous reaction of German Jewry to the Christian state—its opposition to the social conclusions derived from the Christian character of the state on the one hand and its agreement with the basic principle of the Christian state on the other hand, according to which the identity of its citizens is determined on the basis of religious affiliation.

*Primary archival source material*

*G.A.J.* A.F. XVIII, M/23, MSS. Die Idee des Christlichen Staates und die Emancipation der Juden in Preussen.

——, M1/28, Öffentliche Elementarschule, 1886.

——, M1/27, Verhandlungen betreffend: Die Anstellung jüdischer Lehrkräfte an den städtischen Gemeindeschulen zu Berlin, 1896.

*B.A.K.* P. 135/10567, Acta Generalia des Justiz-Ministeriums, betreffend: Die Eidesleistung der Juden, 1861–1913.

——, P. 135/3258, Acta Generalia des Justiz-Ministeriums, betreffend: Konfessions-Verhältnisse der höheren Beamten, 1871 ff.

——, P. 135/1213, Königlicher Gerichtshof für kirchliche Angelegenheiten, 1873–1896.

——, P. 135/1105–09, Die evangelische Kirchenverfassung in den älteren Provinzen (Vol. 2–6), 1874–1920.

——, P. 135/11.949, Generalien Akten des Justiz-Ministeriums, enthaltend: Äusserungen der Presse über die Ausschliessung der Juden vom Staatsdienste, 1878–1900.

——, P. 135/11.944, Acta Generalia des Justiz-Ministeriums, betreffend: Die Konfessions-Verhältnisse der Beamten, 1880–1926.

——, P. 135/11.948, Generalien Akten des Justiz-Ministeriums, betreffend: Die Ausschliessung der Juden vom Staatsdienst, 1866–1921. [G.A.J., H.M., 2495, D.] etc.

——, P. 135/3259, General-Akten des Justiz-Ministeriums, enthaltend: Äusserungen der

Presse und Eingaben, betreffend die Konfessions-Verhältnisse der höheren Beamten, sowie die Judenfrage, 1893–1930.

———, P. 135/3142, General-Akten des Justiz-Ministeriums, betreffend: Das Verhalten der Beamten in politischer Beziehung (Betheiligung an Verbänden, Vereinen, Zeitschriften etc.), 1897–1901; P. 135/3143, ibid. 1902–1909.

———, P. 135/1335, General-Akten des Justiz-Ministeriums, betreffend: Der Entwurf eines Reichsgesetzes betreffend die Freiheit der Religionsübung, 1900–1905.

———, P. 135/4336, General-Akten des Justiz-Ministeriums, betreffend: Die Freiheit der Religionsübung, 1905–1910.

A.E.K.D. A1/331,Acta: Einzelberichte der kirchlichen Statistik, Deutsche-Evangelische Kirchen Conferenz, 1882 ff.

———, A1/349, Übertritte zur Evangelischen Kirche von Juden, Katholiken usw., 1901 ff.

———, A2/597, Acta: betreffend Taufe.

———, A2/617, Gemischte Ehen, 1904 ff. (Schutz des evangelischen Teiles in der Kindererziehung.)


*Primary printed source material*

Richter, F., (Mariendorf), Das christliche Glaubensbekenntniss: Protestantismus gegen Orthodoxismus, Berlin, 1868.

Friedberg, Emil, Die Grenzen zwischen Staat und Kirche und die Garantien gegen deren Verletzung, Tübingen, 1872.

Thiersch, H. W. J., Über den Christlichen Staat, Basel, 1875.

Zorn, Philipp, Über freie Kirche und Gewissensfreiheit, Irrthum und Wahrheit etc. (Buchkritik), P.J., Vol. 39, 1877, p. 184 ff.

Mühlhäusser, Die Christliche Weltanschauung, Vorträge etc., anhängend . . . Über die biblische Lehre vom Reiche Gottes, Winter 1875–1876 in Karlsruhe, in K.Z., 1878, No. 115 (18 May).

Zur Sozialen Frage, in K.Z., 1878, No. 142 (21 June); No. 144 (23 June); No. 149 (29 June); No. 150 (30 June).

Mirbach, Freiherr, von, Preussische Gedanken, in K.Z., 1878, Supplement to No. 179 (3 August); Supplement to No. 187 (13 August).

Erklärung (von Mirbach), in K.Z., 1878, Supplement to No. 179 (3 August).

Unsere Hauptanklagen gegen den Liberalismus, in K.Z., 1878, No. 189 (15 August); No. 190 (16 August); No. 193 (20 August); No. 194 (21 August); No. 195 (22 August).

Wiese, Ludwig, Renaissance und Wiedergeburt: Vortrag . . . im Evangelischen Vereinshaus, Berlin, 5.1.1880, Berlin, 1880.

Eine Vorschule für den Darwinismus, in K.Z., 1881, No. 164 (16 July).

Bausteine für eine allgemeine Rechtswissenschaft, auf vergl. ethnologischer Basis, von Dr. A. H. Post, 2 Vols., Oldenburg 1881, in K.Z., 1881, No. 228 (29 September).

Für die evangelische Volksschule, in K.Z., 1881, No. 171 (24 July).

Christenthum und Politik, Die natürliche Moral, christlich beurteilt und angewendet in Kirche, Schule und innerer Mission, von Detlev Zahn, Pastor, Gotha, 1881, in K.Z., 1881, No. 192 (24 August).

Neue Schriften über Kirche und Staat, in K.Z., 1881, No. 224 (24 September), No. 226 (27 September).

Warneck, F. S., Das Princip der politischen Gleichberechtigung und die modernen Emanzipationsfragen, Hamburg, 1881.

Die Situation nach den Wahlen, in K.Z., 1881, No. 257 (2 November).

Capitalismus, Grundbesitz und das Wahlresultat, in K.Z., 1881, No. 268 (15 November).

*Die Reichstagswahlen und der deutsche Gewerbestand,* in K.Z., 1881, Supplement to No. 177 (31 July).

*Sociale Steuerreform,* in K.Z., 1881, No. 168 (21 July); No. 169 (22 July); No. 170 (23 July).

*Hitze, Franz,* (Member of Parliament), Schutz dem Handwerk, Paderborn, 1883.

*Die Gegensätze in der preussischen Landeskirche* [Jahresversammlung der landeskirchlichen evangelischen Vereinigung, 18.IV.1884, Berlin] in P.J., Vol. 53, 1884, p. 604 ff.

*Die Aufgabe der Kirche und ihrer inneren Mission, gegenüber den wirthschaftlichen und gesellschaftlichen Kämpfen der Gegenwart, eine Denkschrift des Central Ausschusses für die Innere Mission der deutschen evangelischen Kirche,* Berlin, 1884.

*Wiese, Ludwig,* Pädagogische Ideale und Proteste, Berlin, 1884.

*Uhlhorn, Gerhard* (Abbot of Loccum), Der Kampf des Christentums mit dem Heidentum, Bilder aus der Vergangenheit als Spiegelbilder für die Gegenwart, Loccum, 1885 (7th ed., Stuttgart, 1924).

*Martensen, H.* (Bishop), Die christliche Ethik, 3d rev. ed., Karlsruhe, Leipzig, 1886.

*Die Begründung einer christlich sozialen Vereinigung,* in K.Z., 1888, No. 5 (6 January).

*Zur Aufklärung,* in K.Z., 1888, No. 7 (8 January).

*Das Judenthum und die Schule in Österreich,* in K.Z., 1888, No. 34 (9 February).

*Die berechtigten Forderungen der evangelischen Landeskirche und das finanzielle Angebot des Staates, I, II, III,* in K.Z., 1888, No. 35, 36, 37 (10, 11, 12, February).

*Die Schulfrage und die freisinnige Partei,* in K.Z., 1888, No. 56a (16 March), 2d ed.

*Die Schöpfungen des Hofpredigers Stöcker und die "Gebildeten,"* in K.Z., 1888, No. 69a (21 March).

*Die Debatte über den Gesetzentwurf, betreffend die Erleichterungen der Volksschullasten,* in K.Z., 1888, No. 90 (9 April), evening ed.

*Ein Philosophisches Kartell und ein Antisemiten Prozess* (Sitzung des Abgeordnetenhauses, 27.IV.1888), in K.Z., 1888, No. 122 (28 April), evening ed.

*A.Z.d.J.,* 1888, Vol. 52, No. 32, p. 497, Die jüdische confessionelle Schule.

*Röpe, Heinrich,* Rev., Wie haben wir uns zu den Bestrebungen zu stellen die eine grössere Selbstständigkeit der evangelischen Kirche gegenüber dem Staate erringen wollen, in Ch.W., Vol. 3, 1889, col. 672, 694 ff.

*Volkmar, E.,* Die Religion im neuen bürgerlichen Gesetzbuch, in Ch.W., Vol. 4, 1890, Col. 621 ff.

*Konservatives Handbuch,* Berlin, 1892.

*Moeller, L. K.* (Preacher at the Cathedral of Magdeburg), Das Haus in unserer Zeit, seine Bewahrung und seine Erbauung, ethische Zeitbetrachtungen, Hamburg, 1892.

*Riehl, Wilhelm Heinrich,* Religiöse Studien eines Weltkindes, Stuttgart, 1894.

*Walcker, Karl,* Die Judenfrage vom staatswissenschaftlichen Standpunkte aus betrachtet, Sonderhausen, 1894.

*M.V.A.A.,* 1895, No. 39, p. 307, Der christliche Staat, Congress für innere Mission, Dresden 24.9.1895. See ibid., No. 46, p. 367; No. 49, p. 391; No. 52, p. 415.

——, 1897, No. 41, p. 324, Vom christlichen Staat und der christlichen Obrigkeit.

——, 1897, No. 50, p. 399, Ist Deutschland ein christlicher Staat?

*Das Neue Handwerkergesetz,* in K.Z., 1897, No. 381 (16 August), evening ed.

*Zur Lage des Handwerkes,* in K.Z., 1897, No. 399 (27 August). (K.Z., 1895, No. 475/8; 1896, No. 81, 451/2).

*Die Liberalen gegen den Sonntag,* in K.Z., 1897, No. 312, Supplement (10 July).

*Ein Katechismus des Protestanten-Vereins* in K.Z., 1888, No. 19a, 2d ed. (22 January); K.Z., 1897, No. 331 (Supplement); No. 333 (Supplement).

*Die Gesellschaftsordnung und ihre natürlichen Grundlagen,* in K.Z., 1897, No. 521 (6 November).

*Förster, Erich,* Die Möglichkeit des Christenthums in der Modernen Welt, Freiburg, 1898.

*Bünger, Ferdinand,* Entwicklungsgeschichte des Volksschullesebuches, ed. with utilization of official sources, Leipzig, 1898.

*Sorglich, Gustav,* Jesus Christus und das gebildete Haus unserer Tage, Berlin, 1902.

*Sozialismus, Sozialpolitik* etc., in K.Z., 1902, No. 328 (evening ed.); No. 329 (morning ed.).

*Kirchliche Vierteljahres Rundschau (Toleranzantrag),* in K.Z., 1902, No. 341 (24 July). Morning ed., No. 342 (24 July), No. 421 (9 September) Supplement.

*Drews, Paul, ed.,* Evangelische Kirchenkunde: Das kirchliche Leben der deutschen evangelischen Landeskirchen, Vol. 1, Die Evangelisch-Lutherische Landeskirche des Königreichs Sachsen, Tübingen, Leipzig, 1902; Vol. 2, Schian, Martin, Das kirchliche Leben der evangelischen Kirche der Provinz Schlesien, Tübingen, Leipzig, 1903.

*Rade, M.,* Unbewusstes Christenthum, Tübingen, 1905.

*A.Z.d.J.,* 1905, Vol. 69, No. 31, p. 361, Die Rechtsstellung der jüdischen Gemeinden in Preussen.

——, No. 40, p. 472, No. 45, p. 534, Zur Organisation der jüdischen Religionsgemeinden in Preussen.

*Makower, Felix,* Berichte über die Tätigkeit des V.D.J. bei der Vorbereitung des preussischen Volksschulunterhaltungsgesetzes von 1906.

*Förster, Erich,* Die Bewegung gegen das Schulgesetz, in Ch.W., 1906, col. 203 ff.

*Thesen zur Schulfrage, der Herbstversammlung der Freunde der Christlichen Welt in Potsdam vorgelegt,* in Ch. W., 1906, col. 490 ff.

*A.Z.d.J.,* 1906, No. 36, p. 424; No. 40, p. 472; No. 43, p. 520; No. 46, p. 544. Zur Frage der Organisation der Israelitischen Religionsgesellschaft in Preussen.

*Löwinson, M.,* Der Entwurf zum Volkschulunterhaltungsgesetz und die Juden, Vortrag . . . 31. Januar, 1906, in der öffentlichen Versammlung des C.V., Berlin, 1906.

*Classen, W. F.,* Grossstadtheimat: Beobachtungen zur Naturgeschichte des Grossstadtsvolkes, Hamburg, 1906.

*Troeltsch, Ernst,* Die Trennung von Staat und Kirche, Leipzig, 1907.

*Makower, Felix,* Bericht über die Tätigkeit des Verbandes der Deutschen Juden bei der Vorbereitung des preussischen Volksschulunterhaltungsgesetzes von 1906, Berlin, 1907.

*Breslauer, B.,* Die Zurücksetzung der Juden im Justizdienst, Denkschrift des V.D.J., Berlin, 1907.

*Steinmann, Th., ed.,* Religion und Geisteskultur, Zeitschrift für religiöse Vertiefung des modernen Geisteslebens, Vol. 1, Göttingen, 1907.

*Neumann, Sigmund,* Die Stufen des preussischen Konservatismus, in H.S., No. 1910, 1930.

*Handbuch der Deutschkonservativen Partei,* 4th ed., Berlin, 1911.

*Loewenthal, M.,* Das jüdische Bekenntnis als Hinderung bei der Beförderung zum preussischen Reserveoffizier; im Auftrage des V.D.J., Berlin, 1911.

*Breslauer, B.,* Die Zurücksetzung der Juden an den Universitäten Deutschlands, Denkschrift im Auftrage des V.D.J., Berlin, 1911.

*Stahl, Friedrich, Julius,* 50 Todestag, in K.Z., 1911, No. 371 (10 August), morning ed.

*Adler, S.,* Für und wider die jüdische Volksschule in Preussen, ed. Verband der jüdischen Lehrervereine im Deutschen Reiche, Frankfurt a/M, 1913.

*Loeb, M.,* Ein Ausnahmegesetz gegen die jüdischen Handlungsgehilfen, Berlin, 1913 (Special printing of "Soziale Praxis und Archiv für Volkswohlfahrt," Vol. 23, No. 30).

*Lemp, Eleonore, ed.*, Aufsätze zeitgenössischer Schriftsteller, No. 1, Zur Religion und Ethik, Bielefeld, Leipzig, 1914.

*Additional material from Protestant periodicals on the Jewish question and anti-Semitism*

*A.E.L.K.Z.*, 1871, p. 252 ff, p. 837 ff; 1878, p. 195 ff, pp. 348, 377, 406, 416, 448, 466, 494, 513, 540, 567; 1880, p. 83 ff, p. 184 ff, p. 1156 ff, p. 1167, p. 1216 ff, p. 1236 ff; 1893, pp. 209, 235, 412, 680, 726, 749, 794, 814, 836, 862, 885; 1902, p. 676 ff; 1907, p. 1169.
*N.E.K.Z.*, 1871, p. 152 ff, pp. 736, 765, 778; 1880, Ergäbniss der antijüdischen Bewegung, pp. 420, 436, 453.
*D.E.K.Z.*, Vols. 1, 1887; 2, 1888; 3, 1889.

*Historical studies*

*Mannheim, Karl*, Das konservative Denken, A.S.W., 1927, Vol. 57.
*Matthes, K.*, Das Corpus Christianum, 1929 (Literaturverzeichnis, pp. 131–134). (No place.)
*Tiedemann, Helmut*, Staat und Kirche vom Untergang des alten bis zur Gründung des neuen Reiches (1860–1871), Berlin, 1936.
*Bowen, Ralph*, German Theories of the Corporative State, with Special Reference to the Period 1870–1919, New York, 1947.
*Booms, Hans*, Die Deutsch-Konservative Partei: Beiträge zur Geschichte des Parlamentarismus und der politischen Parteien, Düsseldorf, 1954.
*Böld, Willy*, Obrigkeit von Gott? Studien zum staatstheologischen Aspekt des Neuen Testamentes, Hamburg, 1962.
*Stoodt, Dieter*, Wort und Recht: Rudolf Sohm und das theologische Problem des Kirchenrechts, München, 1962.
*Raab, Heribert, ed.*, Kirche und Staat, von der Mitte des 15. Jahrhunderts bis zur Gegenwart, München, 1966.
*Meier, Kurt*, "Zur Interpretation von Luthers Judenschriften" in Kirche und Judentum, Göttingen, 1968, pp. 127–153.
*Tal, Uriel*, Religious and Anti-Religious Roots of Modern Antisemitism, Leo Baeck Memorial Lecture, No. 14, New York, 1971.

German Liberalism, Egalitarianism, and Jewry

The dynamic nature of the history of German Liberalism. The transition from liberalism as a rationalistic force that endeavored to emancipate man from irrational modes of thought and from the antiquated traditions of a preindustrial society to liberalism as a conservative force which sought to enforce its principles by enlisting the power of the regime as, for example, in the days of the *Kulturkampf*. Liberalism as an established force that attempted to consolidate its gains by imposing a uniform character on the state, society, culture, and education.

The transition from the conception of equality of all as men and as citizens with the right of self-determination or the right to be different to the conception of equality in the sense of egalitarianism.

The tendency to minimize or remove the distinction between state and society, society and nationality, nationality and ethnic origin, and hence between a state governed by laws (*Rechtsstaat*) and a state governed by men (*Machtstaat*).

The place of the Jews in this process as a symbol and as a tangible factor which by insisting on its separate existence negates the principle of egalitarianism. The dilemma of German Jewry—its dependence on rationalism and liberalism in theory on the one hand and its fear of the egalitarian tendencies of these movements in practice on the other.

*Primary archival source material*

*G.A.J.* A.F., XXV, St/73, Reichskirchenrecht. Ibid., St/33, Austrittsgemeinden.

——, M/1/21, Laskersches Austrittsgesetz, 1874.

*G.A.J.,* H.M.P. 1, II 38–4, 51 (Collection S. R. Hirsch), betreffend: den Austritt aus den jüdischen Synagogengemeinden. Ibid VI, Handschriftliches, B.

——, A.F., XVIII, M/2, MSS. Rechtsgeschichte der Juden in Preussen, das Austrittsgesetz, 1876.

*B.A.K.,* P. 135/3148. Acta Generalia des Justiz-Ministeriums, betreffend: Das politische Verhalten einzelner Justizbeamten, 1863–1866.

——, P. 135/10.831, Acta Generalia des Justiz-Ministeriums, betreffend: Die Rückwirkung des Dogmas der Infallibilität auf das Verhältniss zwischen Staat und Kirche, 1872–1882.

——, P. 135/8225, Acta Generalia des Justiz-Ministeriums, betreffend: Die Vergehen welche sich auf die Religion beziehen, St.G.B., § 166–168, 1873–1932.

——, P. 135/10.827, Acta Generalia des Justiz-Ministeriums betreffend: Die geistlichen Angelegenheiten in den alten Provinzen, 1875–1921.

——, P. 135/1207, Acta Generalia des Justiz-Ministeriums, betreffend: Den Austritt aus der Kirche und den jüdischen Synagogengemeinden (Vol. 1). Ibid., P. 135/1207 (Vol. 2).

——, P. 135/2982, Acta Generalia des Justiz-Ministeriums, betreffend: Petitionen, 1882–1928.

——, P. 135/3144, General Akten des Justiz-Ministeriums, betreffend: Die Pflichten der Beamten in Bezug auf die Ausübung staatsbürgerlicher Rechte (Meinungsäusserung, Petitionsrecht, Vereinsrecht, Äusserungen der Presse), 1909–1913.

——, KL.E. No. 303 (2, 5, 8, 9, 17), Unterlagen zur Geschichte des Liberalismus.

——, KL.E. No. 303/3, Abschriften, von Prof. Wenzke, aus Nachlässen Nationalliberalismus, 1848–1902.

——, KL.E. No. 159, Urteile bedeutender Persönlichkeiten über Bismarck als Antwort auf eine Umfrage der "Gegenwart," 1881–1898.

*A.E.K.D.,* A2/457, Äusserungen der Presse zum Jesuitengesetz (1872), 1912–1914.

——, A2/441, Kirchenbundesamt, Acta betreffend: Die Freiheit der Religionsübung (Toleranzantrag), 1904–1906. A2/442, ibid., 1906–1921.

*A.E.K.D.,* A2/443, Kirchenbundesamt, Acta betreffend: Die Äusserungen der Presse zu dem Toleranzantrag des Centrums, 1905–1910.

Note: The study of pretotalitarian manifestations during the *Kulturkampf,* including the use of force and violence, government supervision of ideology, the political or religious beliefs of government officials, teachers, educators, scholars, and members of the clergy requires further regional research, especially of the state archives, for example: *Staatsarchiv Koblenz, Oberpräsidium der Rheinprovinz,* Bestand 403:2, Auseinandersetzungen zwischen Kirche und Staat, No. 7558, Die Ausführungen des Reichsgesetzes vom 4. Mai 1874; No. 7560, Die Ausführung des preussischen Gesetzes über die kirchliche Disziplinargewalt und Errichtung des kirchlichen Gerichtshofes vom 12. Mai, 1873. Bestand 403 : 2, No. 8806, Verhalten der Geistlichen, Lehrer, bei den Wahlen. *Staatsarchiv Marburg,* 165/4389, Ausweisung katholischer Geistlichen aus dem preussischen Staatsgebiet, 1874–1875. Ibid.,

165/4226, Spezial Akten, betreffend: Die religiösen Agitationen gegen die Staatsregierung, 1874–1876.

*Primary printed source material*

Hartmann, Eduard, von, Die Philosophie des Unbewussten, Berlin, 1868–1869.

——, Gesammelte philosophische Abhandlungen zur Philosophie des Unbewussten, Berlin, 1871.

*A.Z.d.J.,* 1870, Vol. 34, No. 15, Die Israelitische Welt und die neuen Ideen.

——, 1871, Vol. 35, No. 6, 7, 8, 9, 10, Was haben die Juden vom Staate zu fordern?

Gneist, Rudolf, von, Über das Nationalitätsprinzip in der Staatsbildung, in Hirths Annalen des Deutschen Reichs, 1872, p. 928 ff.

——, Der Rechtsstaat, Berlin, 1872.

*A.Z.d.J.,* 1872, Vol. 36, No. 11, p. 199 ff. Der neu erwachte Rationalismus.

——, 1872, Vol. 36, No. 23, Der Liberalismus und das Judenthum.

Zeller, Eduard, Nationalität und Humanität, Vorträge und Abhandlungen, Berlin, 1873.

——, Staat und Kirche, Vorlesung an der Universität zu Berlin, Leipzig, 1873.

Sohm, Rudolf, Das Verhältniss von Staat und Kirche, Tübingen, 1873.

*A.Z.d.J.,* 1873, Vol. 37, No. 3, p. 33, No. 5, p. 67, No. 7, p. 99: Die öffentliche Meinung und die Juden.

Anon., Die Unterbindung der Meinungsfreiheit: Auf dem Wege zum absolutistischen Polizeistaat in Preussen, Berlin, 1873.

*A.Z.d.J.,* 1873, Vol. 37, No. 6, p. 83, Die neuen preussischen Religionsgesetze und das Judenthum. 1874, Vol. 38, No. 2, p. 17, Was hat die Religion bei der gegenwärtigen Tendenz des Staates zu thun?

*J.W.,* 1874, Vol. 4, No. 8, Parteistellung der Juden.

Schmoller, Gustav, Die Sociale Frage und der preussische Staat, in P.J., Vol. 33, 1874.

Sommer, Hugo, Die Lotzesche Philosophie und ihre Bedeutung für das geistige Leben der Gegenwart, in P.J., Vol. 36, 1875, p. 283 ff; p. 422 ff; p. 469 ff.

*A.Z.d.J.,* 1876, Vol. 40, No. 5, p. 65. Zur welchen Partei steht das Judenthum?

——, 1876, Vol. 40, No. 30, p. 475, Der Pseudo-Liberalismus und das Judenthum.

Parisius, Ludolf, Deutschlands politische Parteien und das Ministerium Bismarck, Berlin, 1878.

*A.Z.d.J.,* 1878, Vol. 42, No. 49, Humanität und Religion.

Eicken, H.v., Die Geschichtsschreiber der Manchesterpartei, in P.J., Vol. 42, 1878, p. 377 ff.

Glass, G., Über Fichtes Rede an die deutsche Nation, in P.J., Vol. 43, 1879, p. 534 ff.

Gneist, Rudolf von, Der Rechtsstaat und die Verwaltungsgeschichte in Deutschland, Berlin, 1879.

Sommer, Hugo, Die Ethik des Pessimismus (Phänomenologie des sittlichen Bewusstseins, Prolegomena zu jeder künftigen Ethik, von E. von Hartmann, Berlin, 1879), in P.J., Vol. 43, 1879, p. 375 ff.

——, Kant als angeblicher Vorfechter des Pessimismus, in P.J., Vol. 44, 1879, p. 602 ff.

Der christliche Glaube und die menschliche Freiheit, Part 1, Gotha, 1880, in P.J., Vol. 45, 1880, p. 661, ff. (Rudolf von Bennigsen?).

Preussisches Abgeordnetenhaus: Die Judenfrage im Preussischen Abgeordnetenhause. Wörtlicher Abdruck der stenographischen Berichte vom 20, 22 November 1880, Breslau, 1880.

Bamberger, Ludwig, Deutschthum und Judenthum, 2d ed., Leipzig, 1880.

Sommer, Hugo, Über das Wesen und die Bedeutung der menschlichen Freiheit und deren modernen Widersacher, P.J., Vol. 48, 1881, No. 6, p. 533 ff.; P.J., Vol. 49, 1882, No. 1, p. 1 ff.

*Philosophie und Naturwissenschaft,* P.J., Vol. 48, 1881, No. 5, p. 449 ff.

*Prutz, H.,* Kant und der preussische Staat (Gedächnissrede, Kantgesellschaft, Königsberg, 22.IV.1882), in P.J., Vol. 49, 1882, p. 537 ff.

*Der Kirchenstreit in Preussen,* in P.J., Vol. 50, 1882, p. 154 ff.

*Sommer, Hugo,* Notizen zur neueren ethischen Literatur, in P.J., Vol. 50, 1882, p. 102 ff.

*Der Eid und das religiöse Gewissen,* in P.J., Vol. 51, 1883, p. 290 ff.

*Treitschke, Heinrich, von,* Luther und die Deutsche Nation, Vortrag, Darmstadt, 7. November 1883, in P.J., Vol. 52, 1883, p. 470.

*Sommer, Hugo,* Positivistische Regungen in Deutschland (Ernst Laas, Idealismus und Positivismus, 2 Vols., Berlin, 1879, 1882), in P.J., Vol. 52, 1883.

Die Reform unserer Gymnasien nach jesuitischer Anschauung: G. M. Pachtler, Die Reform unserer Gymnasien, Paderborn, 1883, in P.J., Vol. 57, 1886, p. 138 ff.

*Gierke, Otto,* Eine Grundlegung für die Geisteswissenschaften: W. Dilthey, Einleitung in die Geisteswissenschaften, Versuch einer Grundlegung für das Studium der Gesellschaft und der Geschichte, Leipzig, Vol. I, 1883, in P.J., Vol. 53, 1884, p. 105 ff.

*Gegen den Staatssozialismus,* in P.J., Vol. 53, 1884, p. 426.

*A.Z.d.J.,* 1884, Vol. 48, No. 41, p. 648, Die Culturkämpfer unserer Zeit.

——, 1884, Vol. 48, No. 47, p. 742, Nationalliberalismus und Judenthum. (see ibid., Die Bewegungen in Deutschland.)

*Lehnhardt, Erich,* Judentum und Antisemitismus, in P.J., Vol. 55, 1885, p. 667 ff.

*A.Z.d.J.,* 1885, Vol. 49, pp. 35, 51, 68, 86, 102, 151, 168, 183, 204, 332, 345. Rückblick auf die Kämpfe des letzten halben Jahrhunderts.

——, 1885, Vol. 49, No. 51, p. 810. Vom Rechtsstaat und den Urrechten.

*Delbrück, Hans,* Bierling, C.R., Die Konfessionelle Schule in Preussen und ihr Recht, Gotha, 1885 in P.J., Vol. 56, 1885, p. 646 ff.

——, Historische und Politische Aufsätze, Berlin, 1887.

*A.Z.d.J..,* 1887, Vol. 51, No. 7, p. 97, Die politischen Ansichten der Juden.

——, 1887, Vol. 51, No. 7, p. 99, Die Trennung von Staat und Kirche.

——, 1887, Vol. 51, No. 11, p. 162, ''An die deutschen Juden'' von M. Lazarus.

*Lazarus, Moritz,* Prof. Dr. M. Lazarus und die öffentliche Meinung (ed., E. Berliner), Berlin, 1887.

*Lazarus, Moritz,* Treu und Frei: Gesammelte Reden und Vorträge, Leipzig, 1887.

*Preuss, Hugo,* Nationalitäts- und Staatsgedanken, in D.N., 1887, No. 18, p. 270 ff.

*A.Z.d.J.,* 1888, Vol. 52, No. 33, p. 513, Das Humanitätsprinzip.

——, 1888, Vol. 52, No. 36, p. 562, Die Politik und das Judenthum.

*Neumann, F.R.J.,* Volk und Nation, 1888.

*Barth, Th.,* Practisches Christenthum, in D.N., 1888–1889, Vol. 6, No. 38.

*Bamberger, Ludwig,* Heinrich von Treitschke: Deutsche Geschichte im 19. Jahrhundert (Vol. IV), in D.N., Vol. VII, 1889–1890, pp. 362–365, 377–380, 396–399.

*A.Z.d.J.,* 1889, Vol. 53, No. 15, p. 221. Die Politik in der A.Z.

*Hessen, Robert,* Unsere Aufgaben gegenüber dem Judenthum: Ein Rückblick auf den Antisemitismus, in P.J., Vol. 64, 1889, p. 560 ff.

*A.Z.d.J.,* 1889, Vol. 53, No. 51, p. 797, Die Preussichen Jahrbücher und der Antisemitismus (R. Hessen).

*Weber, Max,* Was heisst Christlich-Sozial? in Ch.W., 8th year, 1894, Col. 472–477.

*A.Z.d.J.,* 1893, Vol. 57, No. 27, Die jüdischen Parlamentarier.

*Verhandlungen des 5. Evangelisch-Sozialen Kongresses,* 1894.

*A.Z.d.J.,* 1895, Vol. 59, No. 4, p. 39, Das Judenthum und die Sozial-Demokratie.

*Treitschke, Heinrich, von,* Deutsche Kämpfe, Neue Folge: Schriften zur Tagespolitik, ed. Erich Liesegang, Leipzig, 1896.

——, Zehn Jahre Deutscher Kämpfe: Schriften zur Tagespolitik, Berlin, 1897.

*Verhandlungen des 8. Evangelisch-Sozialen Kongresses,* 1897.

*A.Z.d.J.,* 1897, Vol. 61, No. 18, p. 210, Judenthum und Sozialismus.

*Sybel, Heinrich, von,* Vorträge und Abhandlungen, München, Leipzig, 1897.

*A.Z.d.J.,* 1898, Vol. 62, No. 6, p. 61, Jüdische Sonderkandidaturen.

——, 1899, Vol. 63, No. 21, p. 242, Jüdische Sozialisten.

*Treitschke, Heinrich, von,* Historische und Politische Aufsätze, Leipzig, 1897–1903, Vol. I, Vol. IV.

*A.Z.d.J.,* 1900, Vol. 64, No. 21, p. 244, Politische und Soziale Gerechtigkeit.

——, 1900, Vol. 64, No. 43, p. 505, Die Erlösung des Judenthums? (see P.J., October 1900).

*Tönnies, Ferdinand,* Politik und Moral, eine Betrachtung, Frankfurt a/M, 1901.

*A.Z.d.J.,* 1901, Vol. 65, No. 19, p. 217, Die Angabe des Glaubensbekenntnisses.

——, 1901, Vol. 65, No. 31, p. 361. Die Träger der Nationalität.

——, 1904, Vol. 68, No. 9, p. 103, Die Juden in Mommsens Römische Geschichte.

Anon., Das Deutsche Bildungswesen im letzten Wahlkampf, Berlin, 1906.

*Die Hilfe,* 10th year, 1904, No. 2, Klassenpolitik des Liberalismus.

*A.Z.d.J.,* 1906, Vol. 70, No. 47, p. 559, Die Juden und die Politik.

*Weber, Max,* Die sogenannte Lehrfreiheit an den deutschen Universitäten, in Frankfurter Zeitung, 20.9.1908 (3d morning paper).

*D.J.P.,* 1908, Vol. 32, No. 26, Die Juden im Preussischen Abgeordnetenhaus.

*Rade, M.,* Machstaat, Rechtsstaat, Kulturstaat (Rede auf dem deutsch-nationalen Friedenskongress zu Jena, 10.5.1908), in Ch. W., 1908, No. 21, col. 505–506.

*A.Z.d.J.,* 1909, Vol. 73, No. 7, p. 73, An die liberalen Parlamentarier.

*Oncken, Hermann,* Rudolf von Bennigsen: Ein deutscher liberaler Politiker, Stuttgart, Berlin, 1910.

*Treitschke, Heinrich, von,* Politik: Vorlesungen gehalten an der Universität zu Berlin, ed. Max Cornicelius, Leipzig, 1911, Vols. I, II.

*Verhandlungen des 4. Deutschen Hochschullehrertages,* Bericht, erstattet vom engeren Geschäftsführenden Ausschuss, Leipzig, 1912.

*Eucken, Rudolf,* Zur Sammlung der Geister, Leipzig, 1913.

*Delbrück, Hans,* Regierung und Volkswille: Eine akademische Vorlesung, Berlin, 1914.

*Troeltsch, Ernst,* Das Wesen des Deutschen (Rede . . . 6.12.1914), Heidelberg, 1915.

*Troeltsch, Ernst,* Deutscher Geist und Westeuropa: Gesammelte kulturphilosophische Aufsätze und Reden, ed. H. Baron, Tübingen, 1925.

*Historical studies*

*Meinecke, Friedrich,* Weltbürgertum und Nationalstaat, Part I (1907), 5th ed., München, Berlin, 1919.

*Wiese, L., von,* Der Liberalismus in Vergangenheit und Zukunft, Berlin, 1917.

*Löhn, Joseph,* Das preussische Allgemeine Landrecht und die katholischen Kirchengesellschaften, Paderborn, 1917.

*Maenner, Ludwig,* Deutschlands Wirtschaft und Liberalismus in der Krise von 1879, in Archiv für Politik und Geschichte, Vol. 9, 1927.

*Löwith, Karl,* Max Weber und Karl Marx, in Archiv für Sozialwissenschaften und Sozialpolitik, Vol. 67, 1927.

*Meinecke, Friedrich,* Geleitwort zum 150.Bande der *Historischen Zeitschrift* und zum 100.Geburtstage Heinrichs von Treitschke, in H.Z., No. 150, 1934.

——, Leipprand, Ernst, Heinrich von Treitschke im deutschen Geistesleben des 19. Jahrhunderts, Stuttgart, 1935.

*Theune, Brigitte,* Volk und Nation bei Jahn, Rotteck, Welcker und Dahlmann, Berlin, 1937.

*Sell, Friedrich, C.,* Motive, Methoden und Ideen des Bismarckschen Kulturkampfes, in Th.R., Vol. IX, 1937.

*Bussmann, W.,* Treitschke, sein Welt und Geschichtsbild, Göttingen, 1952.

*Holborn, Hajo,* Der deutsche Idealismus in sozialgeschichtlicher Bedeutung, in H.Z., No. 174, 1952, pp. 359–384.

*Stern, Fritz,* The Maturing of the Nation-State, in Chapters in Western Civilization, Vol. II, 3d ed., New York, 1952.

*Dorpalen, Andreas,* The German Historians and Bismarck, in Review of Politics, No. 15, 1953, pp. 53–67.

*Sell, Friedrich C.,* Die Tragödie des deutschen Liberalismus, Stuttgart, 1953.

*Mommsen, Wilhelm,* Stein, Ranke, Bismarck: Ein Beitrag zur politischen und sozialen Bewegung des 19. Jahrhunderts, München, 1954.

*Bussmann, Walter,* Treitschke als Politiker, in H.Z., No. 177, 1954, pp. 249–279.

*Franz, G.,* Kulturkampf, Staat und Katholische Kirche in Mitteleuropa von der Säkularisation bis zum Abschluss des preussischen Kulturkampfes, München, 1956.

*Heuss, Theodor,* Theodor Mommsen und das 19. Jahrhundert, Kiel, 1956.

*Dorpalen, Andreas,* Heinrich von Treitschke, New Haven, 1957.

*Bergsträsser, Arnold,* Max Webers Antrittsvorlesung in Zeitgeschichtlicher Perspective, in Vierteljahreshefte für Zeitgeschichte, 5th year, 1957.

*Mommsen, Wolfgang, J.,* Max Weber und die deutsche Politik (1890–1920), Köln, 1959.

*Stern, Fritz,* The Political Consequences of the Unpolitical German, in History, No. 3, 1960.

*Pfeil, S. Graf von,* Heinrich von Treitschke und das Judentum, in Die Welt als Geschichte, No. 1, 1961.

*Nipperdey, Thomas,* Interessenverbände und Parteien in Deutschland vor dem ersten Weltkrieg, in P.V.J., Vol. 2, 1961, No. 3, p. 262 ff.

*Kupisch, Karl,* Bürgerliche Frömmigkeit im Wilhelminischen Zeitalter, in Z.R.G.G., Vol. 14, 1962, p. 123 ff.

*Schmidt-Volkmar, Erich,* Der Kulturkampf in Deutschland (1871–1890), Göttingen, 1962.

*Buchheim, Karl,* Ultramontanismus und Demokratie: Der Weg der deutschen Katholiken im 19. Jahrhundert, München, 1963.

*Höfele, K. H.,* Sendungsglaube und Epochenbewusstsein in Deutschland (1870–1871), in Z.R.G.G., Vol. 15, 1963, p. 265 ff.

*Lübbe, Hermann,* Politische Philosophie in Deutschland: Studien zu ihrer Geschichte, Basel, Stuttgart, 1963.

*Morsey, Rudolf,* Probleme der Kulturkampfforschung in H.J., Vol. 83, 1964.

*Boehlich, Walter,* ed., Der Berliner Antisemitismusstreit, Frankfurt a/M, 1965.

*Weymar, Ernst,* Die "deutsche Sendung" als Leitgedanke im Geschichtsunterricht in den höheren Schulen, in Tribüne, Vol. 17, 1966.

*Toury, Jacob,* Die politischen Orientierungen der Juden in Deutschland, Tübingen, 1966.

*Liebeschütz, Hans,* Das Judentum im deutschen Geschichtsbild von Hegel bis Max Weber, Tübingen, 1967.

*Kümmel, Werner,* Rudolf Virchow und der Antisemitismus, in Medizinhistorisches Journal, Hildesheim, Vol. 3, 1968, No. 3.

Intellectual and Religious Tension

Changes in the definition of the concepts "essence of Christianity" and "essence of Judaism." Reciprocal relations between the development of the critical disciplines in the social sciences and the self-identity of Christians and Jews. The inner tension between the historical, philological, and theological studies on the one hand and religious faith on the other. The changing position of neo-Kantianism in German culture; a turning to historical consciousness and historical empathy under the influence of Troeltsch and Dilthey on the part of both Christians and Jews, which, however, also created mutual tensions. The dilemma of the non-Orthodox Jews: the desire to abandon the traditional religious way of life on the one hand and the need for self-identification on the basis of religious affiliation on the other.

*Primary archival source material*

*G.A.J.*, M7/1, Protokolle des Vereins Israelitischer Kultusbeamten etc., 1878–1903.
——, M1/23, Historische Commission, 1885 ff.
——, M1/24, Historische Commission, Correspondenz-D.I.G.B.
——, M4/1, Acten des reorganisierten Rabbinerverbandes in Deutschland, 1896–1899.
——, M4/2, Rabbinerverband in Deutschland, Briefwechsel, 1909–1911.

*Primary printed source material*

*Philippson, L.,* Zur Charakteristik der ersten jüdischen Synode, Berlin, 1869.
*Mass, M.,* Die Religion der Juden und die politisch-socialen Principien unseres Jahrhunderts: Zur Kritik der Philippsonischen Resolution auf der ersten Israelitischen Synode zu Leipzig, Leipzig, 1870.
*Erste Israelitische Synode,* Leipzig, 1869, in A.Z.d.J., 1873, Vol. 37, No. 17, p. 273 ff.
*Ritschl, Albrecht,* Unterricht in der christlichen Religion, Bonn, 1875 (1866).
——, Die christliche Lehre von der Rechtfertigung und Versöhnung, 3 Vols., 1870 ff, Bonn, 1900 (1895).
*Philippson, L.,* Haben wirklich die Juden Jesum gekreuzigt, 1876.
*Steinthal, H.,* Die erzählenden Stücke im 5. Buch Mose, in V.V.Ps., 1880, Vol. 12, p. 253 ff, 1890, Vol. 20, p. 47 ff.
*Delitzsch, Franz,* Christentum und jüdische Presse: Selbsterlebtes, Erlangen, 1882.
*Münz, L.* (Rabbi, Kempen, Posen), Die modernen Anklagen gegen das Judentum als falsch nachgewiesen, Frankfurt a/M, 1882.
*A.Z.d.J.,* 1883, Vol. 47, No. 12, p. 121, Die Culturmission des Judenthums und seiner Bekenner.
*Scholz, H.,* Die Gesetzesfragen im Leben Jesu und in der Lehre des Paulus, von J. Ph. Glock, Pastor of Zuzenhausen near Heidelberg, Karlsruhe, Leipzig, 1885, in P.J., Vol. 56, 1885, p. 429 ff.
*Rothe, Richard,* Gesammelte Vorträge und Abhandlungen aus seinen letzten Lebensjahren, ed., Nippold, 1886.
*Müller, Joel* (Reader on Rabbinics at the Lehranstalt für die Wissenschaft des Judentums in Berlin), Die jüdische Moral im ersten nachtalmudischen Zeitalter (separate printing from Dr. A. Brülls "Populärwissenschaftliche Monatsblätter"), Frankfurt a/M., 1886.
*A.Z.d.J.,* 1886, Vol. 50, No. 20, p. 307. Die Protestantisch-Theologischen Facultäten.
*Steinthal, H.,* Die geschichtliche Stellung des mosaischen Gesetzes nach den neueren alttestamentlichen Forschungen, in V.V.Ps., 1886, Vol. 57, p. 339 ff.
*Bornemann, L.,* Die Lotzesche Philosophie innerhalb der modernen Weltanschauung, in Ch. W., Vol. 1, 1887, col. 199, 206, 217, 226.

*Katzer, Dr.* (*Pastor Primarius, Löbau*), Der Geistliche und die moderne Gesellschaft, Vortrag . . . Pastoralkonferenz zu Bautzen, 12.5.1887, in Ch.W., Vol. 1, 1887, col. 265 ff.

*Bürkner, R.*, Rev., Max Nordau und die religiöse Lüge der Kulturmenschheit, gelegentlich der Beratung des Sozialistengesetzes im Reichstage 13.2.1889, in Ch.W., Vol. 2, 1889, col. 145 ff.

*Kaftan, J.*, Der christliche Glaube und das sittliche Leben in Veranlassung von Wundt's Ethik, in Ch.W., Vol. 2, 1889, col. 98, 110, 122.

*Bornemann, W.*, Aus dem Katechismus frommen Darwinisten, in Ch. W., Vol. 2, 1889, col. 217, 287.

*Katzer, Dr.*, Ethische Fragen (Paulsen, Harms, Frank), in Ch.W., Vol. 4, 1890, col. 171 ff.

*Vom Evangelisch-Sozialen Kongress zu Berlin,* in Ch.W., Vol. 4, 1890, col. 604 ff.

*Loofs, Fr.*, Ein jüdischer Rektor der Universität Halle-Wittenberg ("Deutsche Evangelische Kirchenzeitung" 20.6.1890), in Ch.W., Vol. 4, 1890, col. 659 ff.

*Katzer, Dr.*, Schulreform (christliche Charakterbildung), in Ch.W., Vol. 4, 1890, col. 1062 ff.

*Geiger L.*, H. Grätz Volkstümliche Geschichte der Juden, 3 vols. (Vol. 3, 1890), in C.A.J.L., Vol. 1, p. 711 ff.

*Steinthal, H.*, Dr. S. Maybaum, Jüdische Homiletik nebst einer Auswahl von Texten und Themen, Berlin, 1890, in V.V.Ps., 1890, Vol. 20, p. 359 ff.

*Evangelische Gedanken zur Judenfrage,* in Ch.W., Vol. 5, 1891, col. 313 ff, 368 ff, 387 ff.

*Lehmann, E.*, Gesammelte Schriften, 2d ed., Dresden. Die Aufgaben der Deutschen jüdischer Herkunft (1891); Der Deutsche jüdischen Bekenntnisses, Vortrag C.V., 1893.

*Teichmann, M.*, Der Weg zur Verständigung zwischen Judenthum und Christenthum (Johannes Müller, Der Weg etc., Leipzig, 1892), in Ch.W., 1893, col. 396 ff.

*A.Z.d.J.*, 1893, Vol. 57, No. 9, p. 97, Prof. Steinthal über den Talmud (M.V.A.A., 26 February, 1893).

——, 1893, Vol. 57, No. 7, p. 73; No. 8, p. 85, Die Erklärung der Rabbiner.

——, 1894, Vol. 58, No. 50, p. 589, Der Kampf gegen die Bibel.

——, 1897, Vol. 61, No. 27, p. 313, Die Zukunft des Judenthums.

*Lazarus, Moritz,* Die Ethik des Judenthums, Frankfurt a/M. (1898), 1901. (Vol. 2, Nachlass, 1911.)

*Güdemann, M.*, Über die inneren Ursachen der Blüthe und des Verfalls in der Geschichte der Juden, in J.J.G.L., 1898, Vol. 1.

*Schreiner, M.*, Was lehrten die Pharisäer? in J.J.G.L., 1899, Vol. II, p. 55 ff.

*Cohen, H.*, Liebe und Gerechtigkeit in den Begriffen Gott und Mensch, in J.J.G.L., 1900, Vol. 3, p. 75 ff.

*Harnack, Adolf von,* Die Aufgabe der theologischen Facultäten und die allgemeine Religionsgeschichte, Rektorsrede 3.8.1901, 3d ed., Giessen, 1901.

*Weichelt, Hans,* Der moderne Mensch und das Christenthum [Ch.W., No. 47] Tübingen, Leipzig, 1901.

*Troeltsch, Ernst,* Die Absolutheit des Christenthums und die Religionsgeschichte: Vortrag auf der Versammlung der Freunde der Christlichen Welt zu Mühlacker, 3.10.1901, Tübingen, Leipzig, 1902.

*Harnack, Adolf von,* Das Wesen des Christentums: Sechzehn Vorlesungen vor Studierenden aller Facultäten im Wintersemester 1899/1900 an der Universität Berlin gehalten (Akademische Ausgabe, Leipzig, 1902), 18th ed., München, Hamburg, 1964.

*Harnack's* "Wesen des Christentums" und die religiösen Strömungen der Gegenwart (Delbrück, Neumann, Albrecht, Haupt, Bousset, Kähler, Rolffs), in Ch.W., Vol. 15, 1901, col. 931 ff.

*Goldschmidt, J.*, Das Wesen des Judentums, Berlin, 1902.

*Schreiner, Martin*, Die jüngsten Urteile über das Judentum, kritisch untersucht, Berlin, 1902.

*Jelski*, Das Wesen des Judenthums, Berlin, 1902.

*Güdemann, Moritz*, Das Judenthum in seinen Grundzügen und nach seinen geschichtlichen Grundlagen dargestellt, 2d ed., Wien, 1902.

*Karpeles, Gustav*, Wesen des Judenthums, etc., in J.J.G.L., 1902, Vol. 5, p. 20 ff.

*A.Z.d.J.*, 1901, Vol. 65, No. 50, p. 589, Ein Wort über die jüdische Wissenschaft; 1902, Vol. 66, No. 5, p. 49, Für die jüdische Wissenschaft.

*Fiebig, Paul*, Talmud und Theologie, Tübingen, Leipzig, 1903.

*Troeltsch, Ernst*, Politische Ethik und Christenthum: Rede . . . 15. Evangelisch-Sozialer Kongress, Breslau, Göttingen, 1904.

*Joel, M.*, Der Mosaismus und das Heidentum, in J.J.G.L., 1904, Vol. 7, p. 35 ff.

*Bernfeld, S.*, Die jüdische Staatsverfassung, in J.J.G.L., 1904, Vol. 7.

*Fromer, J.* (Elias Jakob), Das Wesen des Judentums, Berlin, Leipzig, Paris, 1905.

*Rade, Martin*, "Unbewusstes Christenthum" [Ch.W., No. 53], Tübingen, 1905.

*Gross, H.*, Hillel und seine Zeit, in J.J.G.L., 1905, Vol. 8, p. 52 ff.

*Beiträge zur Weiterentwicklung der christlichen Religion*, ed. A. Deissmann, A. Dormer, R. Eucken, H. Gunkel, W. Herrmann, G. Wobbermin, etc., München, 1905.

*Baeck, Leo*, Das Wesen des Judenthums, Berlin, 1905 (3d ed., Frankfurt a/M., 1923). (Cf. Ernst Simon, Leo Baeck—Last Representative of German Jewry [Introduction to the Hebrew translation of the above], Jerusalem, 1968, pp. 7–44).

*Eschelbacher, Joseph*, Das Judenthum und das Wesen des Christenthums, ed. Gesellschaft zur Förderung der Wissenschaft des Judentums, Berlin, 1905 (1908).

*Strack, Hermann L.*, Das Wesen des Judentums: Vortrag gehalten auf der Internationalen Konferenz für Judenmission zu Amsterdam (Schriften des Institutum Judaicum in Berlin, No. 36), Leipzig, 1906.

*Steinthal, H.*, Über Juden und Judentum; Vorträge und Aufsätze, ed. Gustav Karpeles, Berlin, 1906.

*Fiebig, Paul*, "Jesu Blut," Tübingen, 1906.

*Köberle, Justus*, Im Kampfe um das Alte Testament: Drei Vorträge, 1906.

——, Heilsgeschichte und religionsgeschichtliche Betrachtungen des Alten Testamentes, in N.K.Z., 1906, p. 200 ff.

*Fiebig, Paul*, Jüdische Gebete und das Vaterunser (Eschelbacher, Das Judentum und das Wesen des Christentums, Berlin, 1905), in Ch.W., 1906, col. 947 ff.

*Christentum und Judentum: Parallelen*, in J.J.G.L., 1906, Vol. 9, p. 59 ff.

*Troeltsch, Ernst*, Die Bedeutung des Protestantismus für die Entstehung der modernen Welt: Vortrag gehalten auf der 9. Versammlung deutscher Historiker, Stuttgart, 21.4.1906, München, Berlin, 1906.

*Weinel, Heinrich*, Lebensfragen: Schriften und Reden, Berlin, 1906 (?).

*Kaftan, J.*, Jesus und Paulus: Eine freundschaftliche Streitschrift gegen die religions-geschichtlichen Volksbücher von Bousset und Wrede, Berlin, 1906.

*Holtzmann, Oscar*, Leben Jesu, Giessen, 1906.

*Eschelbacher, Josef*, Das Judenthum im Urteile der modernen protestantischen Theologie [Schriften, ed. Gesellschaft zur Förderung der Wissenschaft des Judentums, Leipzig, 1907].

*Fiebig, Paul*, Über jüdisches und protestantisches Gelehrtentum [Eschelbacher, Das Judentum im Urteil der modernen protestantischen Theologie, Schriften, ed. Gesellschaft zur Förderung der Wissenschaft des Judentums, Leipzig, 1907], in Ch.W., 1907, col. 631 ff.

*Cohen, Hermann,* Religion und Sittlichkeit, in J.J.G.L., Vol. 10, 1907.

*Bousset, Wilhelm,* Unser Gottesglaube, Tübingen, 1908.

*Natorp, Paul,* Religion innerhalb der Grenzen der Humanität, 2d ed., Tübingen, 1908.

*Niebergall, Friedrich,* Wie predigen wir dem modernen Menschen? 2 Vols., 3d ed., Tübingen, 1909, 1912.

*Kattenbusch, Ferdinand,* Jesus "ein Gott'? [Korrespondenzblatt des Verbandes der deutschen Juden, Apologetische Sondernummer, No. 5, July 1909], in Ch.W., 1909, No. 33.

*Fiebig, Paul,* Moderne Positive Theologie des Judentums, in Ch.W., 1909 col. 779 ff.

*Cahn, M. (Rabbi),* Die Religiösen Strömungen in der Zeitgenössigen Judenheit, Frankfurt a/M, 1912.

*Perles, Felix,* Jüdische Skizzen, Leipzig, 1912.

*Fiebig, Paul,* Die Gleichnissreden Jesu im Lichte der rabbinischen Gleichnisse des neutestamentlichen Zeitalters: Ein Beitrag zum Streit um die "Christusmythe," und eine Widerlegung der Gleichnisstheorie Jülichers, Tübingen, 1912.

*Wernle, Paul,* Die Quellen des Lebens Jesu, Tübingen, 1913.

*Harnack, Adolf von,* Über die Sicherheit und die Grenzen geschichtlicher Erkenntnis: Vortrag gehalten in der Ausschusssitzung des Deutschen Museums, 6.2.1917, München, 1917.

——, Ausgewählte Reden und Aufsätze, new ed. Agnes von Zahn-Harnack und Axel von Harnack, Berlin, 1951.

*Historical studies*

*Seeberg, Reinhold,* Die Kirche Deutschlands im 19. Jahrhundert, Leipzig, 1903.

*Hessen, Johannes,* Die Religionsphilosophie des Neukantianismus, Freiburg i. Br. (1917), 2d ed., 1924.

*Eger, H.,* Der Evangelisch-Soziale Kongress: Ein Beitrag zu seiner Geschichte und Problemeṣtellung, Leipzig, 1931.

*Kattenbusch, Ferdinand,* Die deutsche evangelische Theologie seit Schleiermacher, Part 1, Das Jahrhundert von Schleiermacher bis nach dem Weltkrieg, Giessen, 1934.

*Nigg, Walter,* Geschichte des religiösen Liberalismus, Zürich, Leipzig, 1937.

*Lindeskog, G.,* Die Jesusfrage im neuzeitlichen Judentum: Ein Beitrag zur Geschichte der Leben-Jesu Forschung, Uppsala, 1938.

*Barth, Karl,* Die Protestantische Theologie im 19. Jahrhundert, ihre Vorgeschichte und ihre Geschichte, Zürich, 1947.

*Lindeskog, G.,* Jesu als religionsgeschichtliches und religiöses Problem in der modernen jüdischen Theologie, in Judaica, Vol. 6, 1950, No. 3/4.

*Rathje, Johannes,* Die Welt des freien Protestantismus: Ein Beitrag zur Deutschen Evangelischen Geistesgeschichte, dargestellt am Leben und Werk von Martin Rade, Stuttgart, 1952.

*Ben-Chorin, Schalom,* Das Jesus Bild im modernen Judentum, in Z.R.G.G., Vol. V, 1953, No. 3.

*Huber, Max,* Jesus Christus als Erlöser in der liberalen Theologie, Winterthur, 1956.

*Kraus, Hans Joachim,* Geschichte der Historisch-Kritischen Erforschung des Alten Testamentes von der Reformation bis zur Gegenwart, Neukirchen, 1956.

*Walther, Christian,* Typen des Reich-Gottes Verständnisses: Studien zur Eschatologie und Ethik im 19. Jahrhundert, München, 1961.

*Wrzecionko, Paul,* Die philosophischen Wurzeln der Theologie Albrecht Ritschls: Ein Beitrag zum Problem des Verhältnisses von Theologie und Philosophie im 19. Jahrhundert, Berlin, 1964.

*Bleuel, Hans Peter,* Deutschlands Bekenner, Professoren zwischen Kaiserreich und Diktatur, Bern, München, Wien, 1968.

*Ringer, Fritz K.,* The Decline of the German Mandarins, The German Academic Community 1890–1933, Cambridge, Mass., 1969.

*Veit, Otto,* Christlich-jüdische Koexistenz, 2d rev. ed., Frankfurt a/M, 1971.

*Wagenhammer, Hans,* Das Wesen des Christentums, eine begriffsgeschichtliche Untersuchung, Part III, pp. 169–256, Mainz, 1973.

## Anti-intellectualism and the Superior Man

The growth of irrational, mythological, and anti-intellectual elements in state and society, in the economy, in the church and religion, in culture and education, in private and public life. Human personality, no longer subject to critical and rational criteria, became rooted in nature as an absolute value. The embodiment of this value in the image of the perfect or superior man, either as a Christian German or as a pure Aryan or as a mixture of the two. Feeling is placed above rational thought, emotion above cognition, vital action above contemplation, the obscure longing to be one with cosmic nature above self-restraint by the application of rational and ethical a priori principles. Judaism and Jews as a historical subject of anti-intellectual opposition, as the bearers of rationalism and humanism on the one hand and as the founders of Christianity on the other.

*Primary printed source material*

*Riehl, Wilhelm Heinrich,* Die Bürgerliche Gesellschaft, Stuttgart, Tübingen, 1854 (1851).

——, Die Naturgeschichte des Volkes als Grundlage einer deutschen Sozial-Politik, 1854, Vol. 3, 7th ed., 8th printing, Stuttgart, 1873.

*Goltz, Bogumil,* Exacte Menschenkenntniss, Vol. 1, Die Deutschen, eine ethnographische Studie, Vol. 2, Physiognomie und Characteristik des Volkes, Berlin, 1859–1860.

*Naudh (Nordmann), H.,* Die Juden und der deutsche Staat, 1859 (11th ed., Chemnitz, 1883).

*Wiese, Ludwig,* Die Bildung des Willens, 2d ed., Berlin, 1861.

*Hanne, J. W.,* Die Idee der absoluten Persönlichkeit, oder Gott und Sein Verhältniss zur Welt, insonderheit zur menschlichen Persönlichkeit, Hannover, 1862, 2 vols.

*Marr, Wilhelm,* Der Judenspiegel, Hamburg, 1862 (Selbstverlag), 1863.

Anon., Der arme Jude, wie ihn der grosse Demokrat Herr W. Marr besp . . . (richt), beleuchtet von keinem Juden, Hamburg, Leipzig, 1862.

*Freystadt, Moritz,* Der Christenspiegel von Anti-Marr, eine offenes Sendschreiben an die modernen Judenfeinde, 2d ed., Königsberg, 1863.

*Riehl, Wilhelm Heinrich,* Über die bürgerliche Gesellschaft: Vortrag . . . in der öffentlichen Sitzung der königlichen Akademie der Wissenschaften, 3.3.1864, München, 1864.

*Goltz, Bogumil,* Das Kneipen und die Kneipgenies, Berlin, 1866.

*Wiese, Ludwig,* Von Lebensidealen, Berlin, 1868.

*Marr, Wilhelm,* Streifzüge durch das Koncilium von Trient, Voltaire frei nacherzählt, Hamburg, 1868.

*Riehl, Wilhelm Heinrich,* Wanderbuch, Stuttgart, 1869.

*Goltz, Bogumil,* Die Bildung und die Gebildeten: Eine Beleuchtung der modernen Zustände, 2d ed., Berlin, 1869.

*Wiese, Ludwig,* Deutsche Bildungsfragen aus der Gegenwart, Berlin, 1871.

*Riehl, Wilhelm Heinrich,* Freie Vorträge, 1st Collection, Stuttgart, 1873, 2d Collection, Stuttgart, 1885.

*Hellwald, Friedrich von,* Kulturgeschichte in ihrer natürlichen Entwicklung bis zur Gegenwart, Augsburg, 1875 (see ibid., Zur Charakteristik des jüdischen Volkes, in "Das Ausland," 1872. See Ernst Zeitlman, Der Materialismus in der Geschichtsschreibung, in P.J., Vol. 37, 1876, p. 177).

*Wiese, Ludwig,* Die Macht des Persönlichen im Leben: Vortrag im Saale des älteren evangelischen Vereinshauses Berlin, Berlin, 1876.

*Marr, Wilhelm,* Religiöse Streifzüge eines philosophischen Touristen, Berlin, 1876.

——, Der Sieg des Judenthums über das Germanenthum vom nicht Confessionellen Standpunkt aus betrachtet, 5th ed., Bern, 1879 (11th, 12th ed., Bern, 1879).

*Linden, Gustav von,* Der Sieg des Judenthums über das Germanenthum: Eine Widerlegung der W. Marrschen Polemik in historischer und allgemeiner Beziehung zugleich eine Mahnung an das deutsche Volk, Leipzig, 2d ed., 1879.

*Stern, Ludwig,* Die Lehrsätze des neugermanischen Judenhasses, mit besonderer Rücksicht auf W. Marr's Schriften, historisch und sachlich beleuchtet, Würzburg, 1879.

*Köhler, P.,* Die Verjudung Deutschlands und der Weg zur Rettung, W. Marr—Der Sieg des Judenthums über das Germanenthum, Stettin, 1880.

*Marr, Wilhelm,* Der Weg zum Siege des Germanenthums über das Judenthum [4th ed. from "Wählet keine Juden"], Berlin, 1880.

*Wedell, V.,* Vorurteil oder berechtigter Hass? Berlin, 1880.

*Marr, Wilhelm,* Der Judenkrieg, seine Fehler und wie er zu organisieren ist, Part 2 of "Der Sieg des Judenthums über das Germanenthum," Chemnitz, 1880, 1888.

*Statuten des Verein zum Schutze des Handwerkes,* Breslau, 1880.

*Waldegg, Egon,* Judenfrage gegnüber dem deutschen Handel und Gewerbe, ein Manifest an die deutsche Nation, 5th ed., Dresden, 1880.

——, Judenhetze oder Notwehr (Deutscher Reform Verein), 1881.

*Perrot, Dr.,* An die deutschen Handwerker: Aufruf zur Bildung von Vereinen zum Schutze des Handwerkes, Frankfurt a/M., 1881.

*Fechenbach-Landenbach, Reichsfreiherr von,* Aufruf an die deutschen Handwerksmeister und Arbeiter, Landenbach, 1881.

*Die Fälschung der öffentlichen Meinung nachgewiesen durch den stenographischen Bericht über die erste öffentliche Sitzung des neubegründeten Deutschen Volks-Vereins am 14.3.1881,* ed. Vorstande des D.V.V., Berlin, 1881.

*Dühring, Eugen,* Wert des Lebens, 3d ed., 1881.

*Manifest an die Regierungen und Völker der durch das Judenthum gefährdeten christlichen Staaten,* laut Beschluss des ersten Internationalen Antijüdischen Kongresses zu Dresden, am 11/12 September, 1882, Chemnitz, 1882.

*Ibid.,* Gedrängter Bericht über den ersten Internationalen Antijüdischen Kongress in Dresden, p. 4 ff.

*Dühring, Eugen,* Die Überschätzung Lessings u. dessen Anwaltschaft für die Juden, Karlsruhe, 1881.

——, Die Judenfrage als Frage des Rassencharakters und seiner Schädlichkeit für Existenz und Kultur der Völker (1880), Karlsruhe, 1886, Berlin, 1892 (6th enlarged ed., Leipzig, 1930).

——, Die Judenfrage als Racen, Sitten und Culturfrage, Karlsruhe, 1881.

*Wahrmund, Adolf,* Babylonierthum, Judenthum, Christenthum, Leipzig, 1882.

*Dühring, Eugen,* Die Parteien in der Judenfrage, Separatausgabe von Heft 7/8 des ersten Bandes der Schmeitznerischen internationalen Monatsschrift, Leipzig, 1882.

*Riehl, Wilhelm Heinrich,* Die deutsche Arbeit, 3d ed., Stuttgart, 1883.

*Dühring, Eugen,* Der Ersatz der Religion durch Vollkommeneres und die Abstreifung alles

Asiatismus [alles Judäerthums durch den modernen Völkergeist], Karlsruhe, 1883 (1896), 3d rev. ed., Leipzig, 1906.

*Bötticher, G.*, Die dichterischen Stoffe des deutschen Altertums in ihrer nationalen Bedeutung, in P.J., Vol. 53, 1884, p. 145 ff.

*Jahn, Fr. L.*, Werke, 2 Vols., ed. Carl Euler, Berlin, 1884–1887 ("Deutsches Volksthum," Lübeck, 1810).

*Marr, Wilhelm*, Lessing contra Sem, Allen Rabbinern der Juden und Christenheit . . . gewidmet, 2d ed., Berlin, 1885 ["Antisemitische Flugblätter der Wahrheit"].

*Hartmann, Eduard von*, Das Judentum in Gegenwart und Zukunft, 2d ed., Berlin, 1885.

*Radenhausen, Christian*, Christenthum ist Heidenthum nicht Jesu Lehre, Hamburg, 1886.

*Frey (Fritsch), Th.*, Zur Bekämpfung 2000 jähriger Irrtümer, Leipzig, 1886.

*Wahrmund, Adolf*, Das Gesetz des Nomadenthums und die heutige Judenherrschaft, Karlsruhe, Leipzig, 1887 (Cf. A.C., 1891, No. 148).

*Radenhausen, Christian*, Esther: Die semitische Unmoral im Kampf wider Staat und Kirche, 1887.

*Damaschke, Adolf*, Manchestertum, Antisemitismus oder Bodenbesitz-Reform: Vortrag gehalten am 30.11.1891 in öffentlicher Versammlung des Deutschen Bundes für Bodenbesitz-Reform, Berlin, 1891.

*Langbehn, Julius*, Rembrandt als Erzieher, von einem Deutschen, 33d ed. Leipzig, 1891.

*Bewer, Max*, Rembrandt und Bismarck, 10th ed., Dresden, 1891.

——, Bei Bismarck, Dresden, 1891.

——, Gedanken, Dresden, 1892.

*Verhandlungen des ersten Norddeutschen Antisemitentages*, Berlin, 1892.

*M.V.A.A.*, 1892, No. 41, p. 333, Der Antisemitismus der Kreuzzeitung.

——, 1893, No. 16, p. 179, Paul de Lagarde gegen den "christlichen Staat."

*Fritsch, Th. (Frey)*, Antisemiten-Katechismus, 25th ed., Leipzig, 1893.

*Amon, O.*, Die natürliche Auslese beim Menschen, Jena, 1893.

——, Die Gesellschaftsordnung und ihre natürlichen Grundlagen, Entwurf einer Sozialanthropologie zum Gebrauch für alle Gebildeten die sich mit sozialen Fragen befassen, Jena, 1895.

*Deutsche Antisemiten Chronik*, 1888–1894, Zürich, 1894.

*M.V.A.A.*, 1896, No. 13, p. 100, Antisemitismus: Unchristlich.

——, 1896, No. 19, p. 150, "Asemitismus."

——, 1898, No. 7, p. 54, vom "Arier" Christus; ibid., No. 9, p. 71, Christus als "Arier."

*Bley, Fritz*, Die Weltstellung des Deutschtums, München, 1897.

*M.V.A.A.*, 1899, No. 12, p. 91, Antisemitisches—Antichristliches.

——, 1899, No. 16, p. 121, Vom christlichen Staat zum nationalen Staat.

*Chamberlain, H. S.*, Die Grundlagen des 19. Jahrhunderts, München 1899–1900, 10th ed. (Popular ed.), München, 1912.

*M.V.A.A.*, 1900, No. 1, p. 5, Zu dem Missgebrauch des Namens Christi.

——, 1900, No. 10, p. 73, Der Antisemitismus "Vom kirchlichen Standpunkte aus" gesehen.

*Müller, Johannes*, Judenfrage und Antisemitismus, in S.A.H., Vol. 38, 1901.

*Gobineau, Arthur J. de*, Versuch über die Ungleichheit der Menschenracen: Deutsche Ausgabe von Ludwig Schemann, 4 Vols., 2d ed., Stuttgart, 1902–1904.

*M.V.A.A.*, 1902, No. 23, p. 168, Die Antisemiten und das Christentum.

——, 1902, No. 36, p. 269, Antisemitische Schulweisheit vor dem Richterstuhl der practischen Pädagogik.

*Lagarde, Paul de*, Deutsche Schriften, 4th ed., Gesammtausgabe letzter Hand [1853–1885], Göttingen, 1903 (1885).

*Chamberlain, H. S.*, Worte Christi, München, 1903.

*M.V.A.A.*, 1904, No. 4, p. 25, Die Antisemiten und das alte Testament.

*Müller, Johannes*, Blätter zur Pflege persönlichen Lebens, Vol. 2, 2d ed., Leipzig, 1904. Ibid., Vol. 10, München, 1907.

*M.V.A.A.*, 1904, No. 16, p. 126, "Christus ein Germane" (from the Frankfurter Zeitung).

——, 1904, No. 41, p. 322. Die neue Heilslehre (A. Müller, Jesus ein Arier, Leipzig, 1904).

——, 1905, No. 39, p. 305, Christen und Juden.

——, 1906, No. 29, p. 220, Antisemiten und Christenthum.

——, 1906, No. 44, p. 344, Christenthum und Judenthum.

*Müller, Johannes*, Von den Quellen des Lebens, Sieben Aufsätze (2d ed.), München, 1907.

——, Das Problem des Menschen, Bausteine für Persönliche Kultur, No. 1, München, 1908.

——, Zur Beurteilung der modernen Persönlichkeitskultur: Leitsätze für die Verhandlung der Freunde der Christlichen Welt in Darmstadt, am 24. April 1908, in Ch. W., 1908, No. 16, col. 339 ff. Koch, Georg, Ch.W., 1908, No. 23, col. 554 ff; No. 24, col. 579 ff.

——, Zu dem Aufsatz über Persönlichkeitskultur, in Ch. W., 1908, col. 656 ff.

*Koch, Georg*, Johannes Müllers Pflege persönlichen Lebens, Ch. W., 1908, col. 722 ff, 728 ff.

*Müller, Johannes*, Persönliches Leben, München, 1908; Hemmungen des Lebens, 2d ed., München, 1907 (1908).

*Levenstein, Adolf*, Aus der Tiefe, Arbeiterbriefe, Beiträge zur Seelenanalyse moderner Arbeiter, Berlin, 1909.

*M.V.A.A.*, 1909, No. 19, p. 166, Christenthum und Antisemitismus.

*Sawicki, Fr.*, Das Problem der Persönlichkeit und des Übermenschen, Paderborn, 1909.

*Schemann, Ludwig*, Gobineau und die deutsche Kultur, 7th ed., Leipzig, 1910.

*Müller, Johannes*, Die Entstehung des persönlichen Christentums der Paulinischen Gemeinde, 2d ed., Leipzig, 1911.

*Niebergall, Fr.*, Person und Persönlichkeit, Leipzig, 1911.

*Natorp, Paul*, Volkskultur und Persönlichkeitskultur: Sechs Vorträge, Leipzig, 1911.

*Frymann, Daniel (Class H.)*, Wenn ich Kaiser wäre, 1912 (5th ed., 1914).

*Chamberlain, H. S.*, Deutsches Wesen, 2d ed., München, 1916.

## Historical studies

*Bonhard, Otto*, Geschichte des Alldeutschen Verbandes, Leipzig, Berlin, 1920.

*Lübgert, Wilhelm*, Das Ende des Idealismus im Zeitalter Bismarcks, Gütersloh, 1930.

*Steinhausen, Georg*, Deutsche Geistes-und Kulturgeschichte von 1870 bis zur Gegenwart, Halle, 1931.

*Schmahl, E.*, Entwicklung der völkischen Bewegung: Die antisemitische Bauernbewegung in Hessen von der Böckelzeit bis zum Nationalsozialismus, Giessen, 1933.

*Wermer, Lothan*, Der Alldeutsche Verband, 1890–1918, in H.S., 1935, No. 278.

*Voelske, Arnold*, Die Entwicklung des rassischen Antisemitismus zum Mittelpunkt der Weltanschauung Eugen Dührings, Hamburg, 1936.

*Müller, Josef*, Die Entwicklung des Rassenantisemitismus in den letzten Jahrzehnten des 19. Jahrhundert, dargestellt hauptsächlich auf Grundlage der "Antisemitischen Correspondenz," in H.Z., 1940, No. 372.

*Schulze, R.*, Die Anfänge der Volksglaubensforschung, H.S., 1940, No. 373.

*Blome, H.*, Der Rassengedanke in der Deutschen Romantik und seine Grundlagen im 18. Jahrhundert, München, Berlin, 1943.

*Kruck, Alfred,* Geschichte des Alldeutschen Verbandes, 1890–1939, Wiesbaden, 1954.

*Conrad-Martius, H.,* Utopien der Menschenzüchtung: Der Sozialdarwinismus und seine Folgen, München, 1955.

*Mosse, George L.,* The Image of the Jew in German Popular Culture: Felix Dahn and Gustav Freytag, in L.B.Y., Vol. II, 1957.

*Viereck, Peter,* Metapolitics: The Roots of the Nazi Mind (1941), New York, 1961.

*Stern, Fritz,* The Politics of Cultural Despair: A Study in the Rise of the Germanic Ideology, Berkeley and Los Angeles, 1961.

*Killy, Walther,* Deutscher Kitsch, ein Versuch mit Beispielen, Göttingen, 1962.

*Altner, Günter,* Schöpfungsglaube und Entwicklungsgedanke in der protestantischen Theologie zwischen Ernst Haeckel und Teilhard de Chardin, Zürich, 1965.

*Tilgner, Wolfgang.* Volksnomostheologie und Schöpfungsglaube, Chs. 1–5, Göttingen, 1966.

*Kaltenbrunner, Gerd-Klaus,* "Houston Stewart Chamberlains germanischer Mythos" in Politische Studien, No. 175, 1967, pp. 568–583.

*Kuemmel, Werner,* "Rudolf Virchow und der Antisemitismus" in Medizinhistorisches Journal, Hildesheim, 1968, Vol. 3, No. 3, p. 165 ff.

*Schwedhelm, Karl,* ed., Propheten des Nationalismus, Chs. 2, 3, 5, 6, München, 1969.

*Zmarzlik, Hans-Günter,* "Der Sozialdarwinismus in Deutschland als geschichtliches Problem" in Wieviel Zukunft hat unsere Vergangenheit, p. 56 ff, München, 1970.

*Clemenz, Manfred,* Gesellschaftliche Ursprünge des Faschismus, Chs. 3, 4, Frankfurt a/M, 1972.

## The Law and Anti-Semitism

Juridical and political acts against anti-Semitism as a factor in the struggle of liberalism against conservatism and the Right, and also as a factor in the struggle of the Jews to justify their right of self-determination. This subject requires further study; the sources cited serve only as an introduction to the subject.

### Primary archival source material

*G.A.J.,* M1/35, Briefwechsel mit Reichskanzleramt wegen rumänische Judenverfolgung, 1872 (D.I.G.B., No. 5).

——, M1/13, Strafanträge in Bekämpfung des Antisemitismus, und Verfügungen der Behörden darauf (D.I.G.B., No. 44, Antisemitica).

——, M1/16, Strafanträge in Bekämpfung des Antisemitismus, 1876–1881 (D.I.G.B., No. 15).

——, M1/14, Antisemitismus, Verein gegen Wucher, 1878–1888.

——, M1/38, Antisemitica-Varia, 1880–1884.

——, M1/20, Gutachten über den Schulchan Aruch, 1883 (D.I.G.B., No. 48).

——, M1/17, Antisemitica, Process Contra Justus, Münster, Westf., 1883–1885 (D.I.G.B., No. 45).

——, M1/18, Antisemitismus, Mordaffaire Moses Ritter (Krakau), 1884 (D.I.G.B., No. 51).

——, M4/1, Akten des reorganisierten Rabbinerverband in Deutschland, 1896–1899.

——, K. 20, H.M. 1555, A 33, Emanzipation und Abwehr des Antisemitismus (Regensburg).

——, Litt. A. No. 6, Acta der Synagogengemeinde zu Königsberg in Pr., Comitee zur Abwehr antisemitischer Angriffe; Zur Abwehr des Antisemitismus; Bericht über die Thätigkeit des V.A.A., 1892.

——, H.M. 1112 (124/1ª—1ᵇ), Protokolle, Sitzungen des Vorstandes des C.V., 2 Vols., 1894–1905.

——, M1/19, Antisemitica, 1900 (D.I.G.B., No. 47).

——, M4/2, Vols. 1, 2, Rabbinerverband in Deutschland, Briefwechsel, 1909–1911.

*B.A.K.,* P. 135/8225, Acta Generalia des Justiz-Ministeriums, betreffend: Die Vergehen welche sich auf die Religion beziehen, St.G.B. §§ 166–168, 1873–1932.

——, P. 135/8431, Acta Generalia des Justiz-Ministeriums, betreffend: Brichte über die §§ 110, 111, 130, 131, des St.G.B., 1878.

——, P. 135/8139, General-Akten des Justiz-Ministeriums, betreffend: Beleidigungen; St.G.B. §§ 185–200.

——, P. 135/8142, General-Akten des Justiz-Ministeriums, enthaltend: Äusserungen der Presse betreffend die Beleidigungen, St.G.B., §§ 185–200, 1882–1932.

*Historical studies*

Schorsch, Ismar, Jewish Reactions to German Antisemitism, 1870–1914, New York, London, Philadelphia, 1972. (This outstanding study refers to many additional archival sources.)

# Index

Ackermann, A., 205, 206n, 209
Adler, G., 58n
Agrarians, 88, 141, 233, 235, 242n-243n, 244, 246, 254, 299, 300; see also Farmers' League
Albrecht, Franz, 77
Allgemeine Zeitung des Judenthums, 43, 44, 45, 100, 107, 108, 109, 111, 138, 294
Almog, Shmuel, 201n, 280n
Altmann, Alexander, 80n, 87n, 184n
Anthropocentrism, 69, 125
Anthropology, 161, 183, 262, 282, 303
Anti-intellectualism, 177-178, 179, 272, 276, 281, 302
Anti-Semitism, 91-94, 130, 138, 141, 158, 177, 279-289, 299-300, 309, 317-319, 321; anti-Christian, 120n, 131, 227-229, 246, 252, 259-279, 300, 301, 320; Christian, 16, 131, 180n, 235-259, 300-301, 302; distinctions in, 230-234; economic arguments of, 242-246; history of, 223-228; political, 48-53, 55, 58, 59n, 63-64, 74, 88, 135, 232-233, 249, 252, 298; racial, 55, 56, 74, 88, 89n, 134, 142, 147n, 159, 179, 212, 213, 225-226, 228, 242, 246, 247-251, 260-264, 266-267, 269, 270, 273, 274, 277, 278, 279, 298, 301, 302, 303, 304, 305, 322; *Radauan-tisemitismus*, 129, 133, 134, 230, 232, 259; *see also* Conservatism *and* Discrimination
Arendt, Hannah, 227n
Aristotle, 144n
Arnim, L., 55
Artisans, 124, 240, 241, 243, 245-246, 248, 255, 260, 299, 301
Association of Jewish Teachers, *see* Verband der jüdischen Lehrervereine im Deutschen Reiche
Astruc, Jean, 197
Atheism, 149, 151, 235, 255, 297
Auerbach, Berthold, 213
Auerbach, J., 136n
Auerbach, Leopold, 114n, 156n, 177n, 231, 242n
Augustine, Saint, 147
Authority: principle of, 86, 87, 108, 145; religious, 118, 121, 170, 181, 182, 256; state, 38, 39, 110, 118, 126, 134, 144, 148, 153, 221
Autonomy: of church, 171; individual, 32, 76, 77, 190, 297; moral, 61, 187, 209, 213, 219, 239; political, 95; of reason, 71-72, 73
Avineri, Shlomo, 106n

Baeck, Leo, 166, 188, 190, 205, 206n, 209, 215, 218
Bahrdt, Hans Paul, 34n
Bamberger, Ludwig, 57, 65, 102n
Baptism, 159, 180, 231, 253, 267, 276, 302; *see also* Conversion
Baron, Salo W., 20, 230n, 291
Bartels, Adolf, 230
Barth, Theodor, 57, 102n, 132
Bauer, Bruno, 228n, 263, 303
Baur, Ferdinand Christian, 160, 168, 201
Baumbardt, David, 182n
Baumgarten, Hermann, 35, 36, 42, 67, 232
Bein, Alexander, 158n, 263n
Ben-Horin, Shalom, 209n
Ben-Sasson, Chaim Hillel, *see* Hillel
Bennigsen, Rudolf von, 34, 105, 107, 108, 162, 171

Bergman, Hugo, 267n
Bergson, Henri, 303
Berliner, Abraham A., 213
Bernays, Jacob, 53
Bewer, Max, 271, 272, 276, 277, 278, 279, 288
Biblical interpretation, 163, 191, 192, 195, 197-203, 214, 216, 218, 224, 257-258, 272, 288, 304
Bismarck, 31, 34-35, 37, 41, 47, 57, 82, 83, 87n, 90, 91, 95, 96, 97, 102, 110, 119, 120n, 123, 126, 130, 132-133, 136n, 140, 141n, 236, 254, 264, 279
Bleeck, Friedrich, 200
Bley, Fritz, 178, 272
Bloch, Joseph S., 229n
Blood, 64, 262, 276-279, 303-304, 324; Aryan, 288; blood community, 283; blood libel, 92n, 299; Jewish, 92, 276, 277-278, 279; see also Race theories
Bluntschli, Johann Caspar, 34, 38, 121, 122, 162
Böckel, Otto, 233, 240, 299
Böckler, O. H., 129n
Boehlich, Walter, 49n, 51n, 56n, 60n, 65n, 67n
Booms, Hans, 123n
Bornemann, Wilhelm, 160
Bornkamm, Heinrich, 81, 95n
Bousset, W., 180n, 192, 205n
Breslau, Harry, 54n, 65, 207n
Breslauer, Bernhardt, 138
Briggemann, Geheimrath, 136n
Briman, Aaron (pseud. Justus), 75n, 239n
Bruell, Adolf, 76n
Brunner, Sebastian, 89-90
Büchner, Louis, 69, 107
Budwig, Arnold, 242, 243n
Bülow, Bernhardt von, 138
Bultmann, Rudolf, 205n
Bund der Landwirthe, see Farmers' League
Burckhardt, Jakob, 47, 178, 236
Busch, Moritz, 36
Bussman, W., 106n
Buytendijk, F. J. J., 21

Cahn, Moritz, 166n, 184
Campenhausen, Rudolf, 136n
Capitalism, 93, 241, 243
Caprivi, Leo von, 130, 131
Caro, Ezekiel, 115
Caro, Joseph, 91

Cassel, Paulus, 231
Catholics, 45, 112, 118, 119, 126, 127, 292; attitudes toward Jews, 85-96, 100-103, 319; Center party, 83n, 86, 87, 91, 95, 102, 103, 104, 106, 107, 136, 172, 228, 230, 239, 300, 301; economic policy of, 102-103; ultramontane (ultramontanists), 32, 45, 82, 90, 91, 94, 95, 96, 97, 98, 99, 100-101, 102, 104, 105, 118, 163, 169, 220
Central Verein, 126, 129, 138, 140, 165
Chamberlain, Houston Stewart, 52, 64n, 206n, 280-289, 302
Chosen people, 76, 254
Christian: clergy, 97n, 173, 229, 257; essence, 139, 203, 204, 206, 210; principle, 171-172
Christian state, 121-122, 124, 126-128, 130, 132-133, 135-142, 145, 146, 149, 156, 157, 221, 233n-234n, 239, 241-242, 249, 251, 256, 264n, 293; opposition to, 167-176; principle of, 135, 220, 292
Christianity, 116, 143n, 161n, 217; attacks on, 54n, 180, 208-209, 210-213, 219, 226-228, 234, 238n, 263, 270, 304; concept of Christenheit, 50-51, 272-273, 288, and of Christianismus, 275-276; development of, 160, 168-169, 170, 181, 221-222; doctrines of, 61, 143n, 298; in politics, 167, 170, 172, 173, 174; practical ("practisches Christentum"), 132, 133, 229, 264, 274; relation to Judaism, 16, 60-63, 166, 200, 201, 214, 216, 265, 268, 269, 302; spirit of, 164, 258; as successor to ancient Israel, 192-194, 196, 199, 256, 317-319; see also Pauline Christianity
Christlich-Sozial, 123, 155, 162, 227n, 248, 249, 250, 251, 252, 255, 256, 258n, 259, 299, 301
Christliche Welt, 67, 161, 163, 164, 171, 202, 205n, 210; Hefte zur, 161n
Class, Heinrich (pseud. Daniel Freyman), 273
Cognition, 17, 70, 71, 72, 73, 74, 76, 77, 78, 186, 188, 281
Cohen, Hermann, 60-63, 71, 74, 184-188, 190
Comte, Auguste, 303
Confessio Augustana, 180
Congress: First International Anti-Semitic Congress, 247, 248; First Zionist Con-

Congress (*cont.*)
  gress, 156; *see also* Evangelisch-Sozialer
  Kongress
Conservatism: anti-Semitism of, 129-131,
  134, 140, 141, 142, 253-254; ideology of,
  124, 143-155, 156; political philosophy
  of, 121-122
Conservative parties, Conservatives, 123-
  135, 139, 140, 141, 172, 173, 231-232,
  253, 321; Deutsch-Konservative Partei,
  123, 125, 126, 127, 128, 129, 133, 137,
  228, 300; Free Conservatives (Deutsche
  Reichspartei), 123, 125, 126, 128; *see
  also* Catholics, Farmers' League, *and*
  Protestantism
Conversion, 133, 231, 267, 278, 304
Cornill, C. H., 195, 200, 201n
Cultural state, 82, 84, 114
Culture, 20-21, 62, 282; ancient Israel, 154;
  Christian, 60, 90, 164, 171, 249, 251n;
  German, 170, 191, 251n
Cuvillier, Armand, 182
Czolbe, Heinrich, 280

Dahrendorf, Ralf, 31n
Dalmann, Gustav, 180n, 217
Darwinism, 46, 147, 178, 188, 275, 280,
  297, 303
Daumer, Friedrich, 226, 228n, 260
Deissmann, Adolf, 196, 203
Delbrück, Hans, 64n, 139n, 140n, 205n
Delitzsch, Franz, 207n, 208, 212-213, 313
Deutsch, David, 208
Deutsch-Israelitischer Gemeindebund
  (D.I.G.B.), 53n, 59, 65, 76n, 90, 96-97,
  100n, 101, 103, 104n, 107, 111n, 113n,
  115, 116, 117, 126, 127, 136, 165, 207n,
  236n, 237n, 238n, 239n, 242, 243n,
  247n, 251n, 309, 310, 311, 314
Deutsch-Konservative Partei, *see* Conserva-
  tive parties
Deutsche Reichspartei, *see* Conservative
  parties
*Deutsche Wacht, Die,* 52, 53n, 158, 241,
  309
Deutscher Bauernband, *see* Farmers' League
Deutscher Protestantenverein (D.P.V.),
  105, 161, 162, 171, 174
Deutscher Reform Verein (D.R.V.), 240,
  243, 246, 247
Deutscher Volksverein (D.V.V.), 240-241

Dilthey, Wilhelm, 48, 69, 183, 188, 190,
  282
Discrimination, against Jews, 112, 117,
  135-142, 234n, 252, 315, 316
Dittmar, 139
Döllinger, Ignaz, 89n
Dorpalen, Andreas, 36n
Dove, Alfred, 84
Drews, Paul, 143n
Droysen, Johann Gustav, 36, 38, 41
Dubois-Reymond, Emil, 48
Dühring, Eugen, 159, 228, 229, 234, 235,
  246, 248, 251, 259, 264, 265n, 266, 273,
  275, 278n, 302

Eberhardt, Ernst, 275, 276n
Eckardt, Roy A., 227
Eckart, Dietrich, 281
Ecker, J., 91
Education: Christian, 171-172, 176, 233n;
  Jewish, 39, 50, 170, 294
Ehrenreich, Paul, 282
Ehrlich, Ernst Ludwig, 305n
Eichner, Simon, 92
Elvira, Council of, 94, 304
Emancipation, 17, 39, 40, 45, 56, 57, 58,
  65, 75, 77, 80n, 85, 86, 87-88, 89, 91,
  96, 97, 99, 100, 101, 119, 129, 147, 164,
  254, 276, 296
Encyclicals, 101-102
Engelmann, Hans, 251n
Enlightenment, 16, 48, 80n, 83, 99, 100,
  121, 150, 160, 177, 179, 180, 220, 291,
  303
Equal rights, 89, 90, 111n
Equality, 18, 100, 102, 118, 125, 154
Erler, Ludwig, 92, 94
Eschelbacher, Joseph, 166n, 170, 171n,
  179-180, 195n, 200n, 204n, 205, 206n,
  209, 214, 216, 217, 218
Ethics, 61, 72, 73, 172, 185, 186, 187, 188,
  209, 253, 265
Ettinger, Shmuel, 51n, 54n, 209, 223n, 228,
  303
Eucken, Rudolf, 196
Eulenburg, Friedrich Albert, 113, 147, 148
Evangelisch-Sozialer Kongress (E.S.K.),
  123, 162, 221

Facius, Friedrich, 244n
Falk, Adelbert, 96, 97, 110, 113
Farmers, *see* Agrarians

Farmers' League (Bund der Landwirthe), 123, 128, 129-132, 133, 141, 228, 230, 234, 300, 301, 320

Fechenbach, Friedrich Karl von, 137, 243, 245n, 248

Feuerbach, Ludwig, 69, 226, 260, 262, 263, 264n, 303

Fichte, Johann Gottlieb, 55, 76, 77, 243, 244, 274

Fischer, Alfred, 230n

Fischer, Kuno, 68, 184

Flannery, Edward H., 227

Fleischmann, Jacob, 181n

Fontane, Theodor, 35, 48, 66, 69

Forckenberg, Max von, 49

Förster, Bernhard, 241

Förster, Paul, 100n, 270, 272, 299, 302, 320

Francke, Otto, 287

Frantz, Constantin, 92, 236, 238

Franz, G., 81n, 83n, 103n

Frederick the Great, 99

Freedom, 18 70-71, 118, 124, 188, 190, 297; political, 33, 87, 99, 105, 106; religious, 83, 168; see also Autonomy and Self-determination

Freilich, A., 258n

French Revolution, 85, 100, 294

Freund, A., 111n, 112n

Freystadt, Moritz, 262

Friedländer, Saul, 304n

Friesen, Freiherr von, 134, 232

Fritsch, Theodor (pseud. Thomas Frey), 52, 226, 228, 229, 243, 245, 251, 259, 266, 267, 270, 271, 273, 275, 277, 278, 288, 302

Fromer, Jakob, 206n

Fuchs, Eugen, 126, 129, 138, 276n

Gay, Peter, 295n

Geiger, Abraham, 181, 206-207, 208, 213, 214n, 215, 217

Geiss, Robert R., 184n

Gemeindebund, see Deutsch-Israelitischer Gemeindebund

Gerlach, Ludwig von, 121, 145

Germanism, 130, 148, 178, 237, 241, 271, 273-275, 282; see also Nationalism

Glagau, Otto, 90n, 91n, 243, 259, 260-261

Gneist, Rudolf von, 33n, 34, 37, 41, 46n, 64, 78, 84, 113n, 296

Gobineau, Arthur, 280, 283

Goldschmidt, Israel, 184, 187, 205, 206n, 216

Gompert, Ludwig, 213

Gottschick, Johannes, 160

Gottwohl, Sigmund, 189

Graetz, Heinrich, 53, 54n, 60, 206, 207n, 209, 215, 225n, 270n

Gregorovius, Ferdinand, 46

Gregory XVI, Pope, 101

Greive, Hermann, 120n

Grimm brothers, 55

Grotius, Hugo, 216

Gruber, Pastor, 232

Grünberg, Emil, 250

Gründerkrach, 93, 260

Güdemann, Moritz, 53n, 158n, 192, 205, 211n, 213, 217

Gunkel, Hermann, 192, 196-197, 199

Guttmann, Jakob, 156n

Guttmann, Julius, 182n, 184n

Habermann, G., 139

Haeckel, Ernst Heinrich, 69, 107, 166n, 178, 280

Hahn, Dietrich, 130

Halacha (Jewish law), 75n, 194, 199, 219, 298, 312, 313, 322

Haller, Karl Ludwig von, 145

Hammerstein, Freiherr von, 126, 152, 172, 249

Hänel, Albert, 57, 136, 240n

Hapsburg, House of, 42, 94, 96

Hardenberg, 85

Harms, Claus, 152n

Harnack, Adolf von, 18, 100, 160, 161n, 166n, 175, 183, 187, 190, 194, 195n, 200, 202, 203n, 204-205, 206n, 209n, 210, 214, 215, 216, 217, 219

Hartmann, Eduard von, 69, 70n, 178, 188, 206n, 212, 267

Hasse, Ernst, 274

Hausrath, Adolf, 45, 161, 202, 210, 213, 217, 218

Hegel, Georg Wilhelm Friedrich, 33n, 71, 106n, 122, 168, 186n, 196, 244

Hegelianism, 46, 55, 105, 160, 161, 221; see also Young Hegelians

Heilsgeschichte, see Salvation

Hellenism, 61, 195

Helmholtz, Hermann von, 42, 48

Henrici, Ernst, 240, 241, 299

Hentze, A., 241
Herbart, Johann Friedrich, 68, 70, 182
Herder, Johann Gottfried, 55, 160, 243, 244
Herford, R. Travers, 192n
Herrmann, Wilhelm, 160, 161n, 196, 202, 203n
Hertzberg, Arthur, 295n, 303n
Herwegh, Georg, 47
Herz, Elkan, 179
Herzl, Theodor, 157n, 158n
Hess, Moses, 207n
Hettinger, Franz, 92n, 94
Heym, Dr., 139
Hildesheimer, Israel, 113
Hillebrand, Karl, 37
Hillel, 207, 212, 214, 215, 225n, 298
Hirsch, Samson Raphael, 113, 222
Hirsch, Samuel, 206
Hitler, Adolf, 281
Höfele, K. H., 45n, 46n, 67n, 68n
Hoffmann, Dr. (Rector), 51, 66, 68
Hofstadter, Richard, 22
Hohenzollern, House of, 42
Holborn, Hajo, 58n, 81, 84n, 95n, 163n
Holsten, Walter, 249n, 253n, 257n
Holtzmann, Oskar, 215n, 217
Holzmann, Heinrich, 192
Horovitz, Marcus, 156n
Horowitz, Maximilian, 138
Huber, Victor, 121, 123
Humanism, 61, 62, 66, 74-75, 85, 140, 217
Humboldt, Wilhelm von, 37, 85, 244

Identity (Jewish) and separatism, 18, 40, 58, 61-62, 63-66, 76, 77, 79, 108, 119, 165, 180, 219, 290, 291, 296, 298; see also Emancipation
Incarnation, 61, 208-209, 272, 288, 292, 304
Industrial society, 57, 220, 243-244, 245, 255, 293
Inner Mission, 97n, 123, 174, 175, 250
Integration, 18, 31, 32, 33-34, 50, 53, 63-66, 75n, 119, 133, 224n, 290, 296, 298
Intellectuals, 31-34, 78-80, 83, 166, 176, 180, 198, 220; changing attitudes of, 34-63; conflicting opinions of, 46, 48, 63-78
Intermarriage, 49, 59n, 66, 267, 278, 295
International: Black International (clergy), 229; Gold International (Jews), 229; Red International (Left), 229

Israel, in the flesh and in the spirit, 180n, 252, 253, 255, 257
Istoczy, Victor, 248

Jacobsohn, Bernhard, 53n, 59n, 90n, 104n
Jahn, Friedrich Ludwig, 35, 55
Jellinek, Adolph, 213
Jesus, 88, 93, 101, 105, 162, 169, 170, 171, 172, 191, 194, 195, 268, 269, 272, 287, 288; as Aryan, 259, 269n, 273n, 276, 277, 278-279; life of, 203-204, 271-272, 280; as Messiah, 15, 168, 192, 193, 201, 202, 204n, 209, 210, 219, 225, 257, 298; relation to Judaism, 206-219; as Son of God, 149, 150, 192, 210, 211, 216, 217
Jewish: character, 92-93, 156, 263-264, 276, 286; essence, 212, 214; ethics, 182, 219; communities, 39-40, 59, 65, 110-120, 132, 138, 165, 166; history, 15-17, 166, 193, 194-196; question, 54, 64n, 137, 159, 237, 248, 253, 254, 263, 267; see also Emancipation, Identity, and Integration
Jewish Teachers' Association, see Verband der jüdischen Lehrervereine
Jewry: German, 17, 18, 41, 54n, 56, 57, 58, 59n, 63, 65, 75, 76, 98, 119, 122, 136n, 156, 163, 176, 205, 208, 213, 290, 291, 294, 295, 296, 310, 314; non-Orthodox, 50, 59n, 75n, 97, 114, 115, 293; Orthodox, 113, 116, 147, 155, 163, 165, 184, 206n, 222n, 293
Jews: as a disintegrating force, 51-52, 91, 92, 93, 94, 131, 148, 152, 155, 236, 255, 269, 293; Liberal, 139, 179, 180, 181, 183, 190, 212, 214, 220-221
Jhering, Rudolf von, 41, 42, 64, 244
Joel, Manuel, 65, 97, 101, 207, 213, 214
Judaism, 17, 18, 44, 60-62, 66, 109, 116-117, 122, 164, 182, 186, 187, 190, 203, 206-219, 221, 248-249, 263, 273, 274, 278, 282; deterioration in, 192-197; economic role of, 93-94, 158, 242-243; modern, 41, 75n, 154-155, 212, 255; petrified, 179, 192, 215, 298; polemics against Christianity, 211-213; Reform, 104, 164n; talmudic, 89, 90, 91, 192, 195, 196, 298
—— Liberal Judaism, 59, 181, 187, 204-205, 219-220, 222n, 293, 294, 296-

354    Index

Judaism (*cont.*)
297; definition of, 164-165; organizations of, 165-166
Jülicher, A., 201
Justin, Saint, 93
Justus, *see* Briman, Aron

Kaftan, Julius, 160, 161n
Kaftan, Theodor, 174
Kampmann, Wanda, 249n
Kant, Immanuel, 60, 61, 62, 71-74, 76, 80, 170, 186, 243, 281
Karpeles, Gustav, 75, 76n, 166, 208
Kattenbusch, Ferdinand, 160, 202, 203n
Katz, Jacob, 80n, 86n
Ketteler, W. E. von, 87n, 92, 93, 103
Kingdom: of God, 145, 146, 147, 167, 168, 172, 203, 288; of heaven, 88, 151, 210, 215, 216, 275, 288
Kinkel, Gottfried, 41
Kirschhoff, A., 60
Kleindeutschland, 42
Kleist-Retzow, Hans Hugo von, 126, 152, 172, 234n
Kofler, J. A., 88n, 91n, 92n, 94n
Köhler, Karl, 161n
Kohler, Kaufmann, 161n
Kohn, H., 123
Kohner, Moritz, 39, 90, 104n
Krassow, Count, 152
Kraus, Hans-Joachim, 162n, 197n
*Kreuzzeitung,* 123, 124, 126, 145, 151n, 152, 155, 156, 235, 243, 249
Kristeller, Samuel, 54n, 100n, 138, 207n, 243n
Kulka, Otto Dov, 51n, 237n, 280n
*Kulturkampf,* 19, 44, 56, 81-120, 124, 125, 152, 172, 173, 236, 238n, 239, 260, 293; aims of, 82, 118; concept of, 81-82, 84n; debate over, 104-107; Jewish attitudes toward, 96-109; opposition to, 86, 106-107; period of, 83, 136; results of, 93
*Kulturpessimismus,* 177, 220, 272, 281, 294
*Kulturstaat,* 82, 84, 154
Kupisch, Karl, 124n, 150n, 161n, 169n, 176n, 227n, 249n, 251n

Lagarde, Paul de, 47, 53n, 206, 271-272
*Laissez faire,* 102
Langbehn, Julius, 272, 276, 288

Lange, Friedrich, 68, 228, 229, 271, 272, 274, 302
Lasker, Eduard, 57, 58, 99, 106, 107, 112, 113, 115, 117
Law: divine, 144, 150; natural, 32, 77, 121, 144, 150
Law of Separation, 39, 111, 112-117
Lazarus, Moritz, 56, 60, 63, 65, 98, 99n, 108n, 122, 181-182, 184, 187, 190n, 205, 212
League to Combat Anti-Semitism, *see* Verein zur Abwehr des Antisemitismus
Leese, Kurt, 162n, 167n
Left, leftist movements, 67, 106, 163, 220, 252; *see also* Social Democrats
Lehmann, Emil, 104
Lehnhardt, Erich, 53n
Leibniz, Gottfried Wilhelm, 68, 70, 178
Leimdörfer, David, 219
Leo XIII, Pope, 83, 95
Leonhardt, 113
Lessing, Gotthold Ephraim, 68, 70, 178
Liberal parties, Liberals, 82, 90, 91, 93, 99, 110, 111, 118, 146; National Liberals, 56, 57, 84, 99, 104, 105, 106, 107, 110, 111, 114, 115, 125, 126, 135, 162, 223, 244n, 321; Progressive Liberals, 34, 37, 43, 49, 50, 57, 59n, 66, 75, 82, 83, 100n, 102, 104, 113, 115, 118, 132, 135, 136, 137, 139, 141, 142n, 162, 223, 244n; *see also* Manchesterism *and* Protestantism, Liberal
Liberalism, 34n, 57, 66, 70, 74, 75, 83, 84, 85, 95, 99, 100, 107, 108, 119, 130, 131, 132, 148, 155, 164, 211, 237, 239, 241, 296; philosophy of, 43, 58, 176-185; *see also* Intellectuals, Jews, Judaism, Liberal parties *and* Protestantism
Liebermann von Sonnenberg, Max, 130, 131, 142-143, 234, 241, 267
Liebeschütz, Hans, 47n, 50n, 56n, 184n, 195n, 198n
Liebmann, Otto, 68, 71
Lindeskrog, G., 209
Lindström, Theodor, 272n
Löber, Dr., 174
Löhneysen, Wolfgang von, 68
Loisy, Alfred Firmin, 205
Loofs, Friedrich, 161n, 180, 192, 195, 200, 202
Lotze, Hermann, 70n, 73, 184
Löw, Emmanuel, 207

Luschan, Felix von, 64n, 65, 282, 284
Lütge, Friedrich, 244
Luthardt, Christian Ernst, 90n, 97, 123, 159, 235
Luther, Martin, 20, 58, 61, 121, 122, 150-151, 153, 169, 175, 185n, 186, 202, 224-225, 258, 292, 305
Lutheran Protestantism, 60, 62, 84, 125, 126, 145, 148, 150-153, 161, 169, 170, 173, 186, 202, 220, 239, 272; Lutheran tradition, 46, 83, 99, 100, 105, 143n, 256, 258

*Machtstaat* (power state), 47, 107, 161
Majunke, Paul, 87n
Makower, H., 114n, 115, 117
Mallinckrodt, Hermann von, 83n, 85, 104
Manchesterism, 57, 58n, 83, 84, 99, 102n, 104, 133, 135, 236, 241
Mandel, Simon, 206n
Mann, Thomas, 31
Mannheim, Karl, 143n
Marcion, 205
Marr, Wilhelm, 228, 235, 243, 246, 248, 251, 259, 262-264, 283, 309, 310
Martensen, H., 91n, 145, 153n, 155
Marti, Karl, 192
Martin, Konrad, 89-90, 247n
Marx, Karl, 244
Maspero, G. C., 285
Massing, Paul, 91n, 134n, 224n, 227n, 234n, 238n, 240n, 250, 251n, 252n, 253n, 261n, 274n
Materialism, 57, 67, 68, 69, 85, 107, 189, 235, 255, 280, 297, 302
Matthes, K., 149n
May Laws, 91, 101, 112, 114
Maybaum, Sigmund, 156n, 157n, 191, 211n
Mayer, Reinhold, 206n
Meinecke, Friedrich, 64n, 122n
Meisel, Josef, 54n
Melanchthon, Philip, 144n, 150
Mendelssohn, Moses, 75, 76, 179
Messner, Hermann, 123
Meyer, Eduard, 192, 195, 197, 199, 206n, 214
Michael, Reuben, 50n, 54n
Minnigerode, Wilhelm von, 137
Mirbach, Julius von, 152n
Mission unter Israel (Mission to the Jews), 123, 159, 164n, 206n, 212, 313, 322

Mittelstadt, A., 36
Mixed marriages, *see* Intermarriage
Modernism, 145-147, 152, 153, 155
Moeller, L. K., 145, 154, 236
Molleschott, Jacob, 37, 46
Mommsen, Theodor, 37, 38, 50-54, 56, 58n, 60, 84, 95n, 147n, 231, 296
Mommsen, Wilhelm, 125n, 146n
Mommsen, Wolfgang J., 128n
Monotheism, 60, 61, 62, 63, 94, 200, 209, 210, 227, 264
Mosch, Hans von, 270, 273
Mosse, George, 223n, 303n
Mosse, W. E., 33n
Mossner, A., 251n
Mühlhäusser, Dr., 145n, 146
Müller, Adam, 145, 273n
Müller, Friedrich, 49n, 231
Müller, Johannes, 96n, 164n
Müller, Josef, 89n, 267n, 269n, 272n
Munk, Solomon, 242, 243n
Myth, mythology, 73, 77, 118, 130, 179, 182n, 276, 280n, 301, 303, 304

Nachod, Jacob, 39n, 238n, 247n, 251n
Napoleonic wars, 85, 86
Nathan, Paul, 57
*Nation, Die,* 57, 67, 132
National Liberals, *see* Liberal parties
Nationalism (German), 17, 20, 35-36, 41, 42, 43, 44, 45, 52, 53, 54, 55-57, 58n, 63, 64, 78, 79, 83, 84, 100, 125, 130, 237, 291, 296
Nationality, 105, 157, 158, 274, 284, 295
National state, 84, 255; *see also* Christian state
Natorp, Paul, 71, 74, 188, 189
Naudh-Nordmann, H., 235, 248, 251, 259, 302
Naumann, Friedrich, 136n, 162
Nazis, Nazism, 52, 88n, 89n, 225n, 227n, 230n, 281, 302, 303, 305, 312, 324
Neo-Kantianism, 68, 71-74, 76, 77, 78, 161, 184, 188-190, 219, 220, 221, 281, 297
New Testament, 45, 49, 56, 145n, 147, 149, 172, 197, 199-200, 201, 202, 203, 204, 209, 211, 213, 214, 215, 217, 222, 229, 246, 247, 250-251, 254n, 255, 265; *see also* Biblical interpretation

Nietzsche, Friedrich, 47, 77, 177, 188, 226, 272, 274, 304
Nigg, Walter, 162n, 167n, 201n, 203n
Nihilism, 67, 178, 189
Nobility, 128-129

Old Testament, 62, 155, 166, 192, 196, 197-198, 199, 202, 203, 205n, 217, 229, 231, 250-251, 256, 265, 298, 317; see also Biblical interpretation

Paul, the Apostle, 93, 149, 150, 151, 152n, 191, 200, 201, 207, 218, 219, 224, 225, 253, 268, 280, 304
Pauline Christianity, 187, 203, 210, 218, 219
Paulsen, Friedrich, 32n, 69, 71, 74n, 174, 189, 290
Peltasohn, Martin, 138
Perles, Felix, 195, 198n, 206n, 208, 215n
Perrot, F., 243, 245n
Pfeil, Graf von, 234n
Philippi, E., 244n
Philippson, Ludwig, 39, 113n, 114, 115, 206, 207, 215
Philippson, Martin, 107, 109n, 115, 138, 139n, 166, 208, 211n, 215, 295
Philo of Alexandria, 195, 217
Pickenbach, Wilhelm, 246, 249
Pinkert-Waldegg, Alexander, 240, 241, 247, 248n, 249
Pinson, Koppel S., 43n
Pius IX, Pope, 101
Plessner, Helmut, 21
Plötz, Alfred von, 130, 131
Political parties, see Catholics, Conservative parties, Liberal parties, Manchesterism, and Social Democrats
Preuss, Hugo, 64n, 138
Preussische Jahrbücher, 35, 36, 42, 43, 48, 57, 58, 66-67, 73, 84, 99, 104, 105, 139n, 205n, 212
Progressives, see Liberal parties
Pross, Harry, 68n, 143n, 178, 261n
Protestantism, Protestants, 41, 48, 60, 99, 100, 104-105, 125, 126, 127, 131, 190, 192
—— Conservative Protestants, 90n, 97n, 99, 100, 121, 122, 126, 127, 143, 146, 159, 171, 220, 234, 235, 237, 251, 292, 294, 301, 320; political forces and, 123-125; views on state, 173-176
—— Liberal Protestants, 82, 99-100, 123, 179, 180, 181, 183, 198, 204, 209n, 210, 218, 220-221, 296-297; definition of, 163; expectations of, 164; ideology of, 160-162, 166, 167, 170-171, 176-178, 197, 199, 200-203; views on state, 172-176 see also Deutscher Protestantenverein and Lutheran Protestantism
Prussia, 114, 122, 126, 127, 140, 141, 142n; hegemony of, 36, 42, 46, 47, 66, 121; kingdom of, 19-20, 35, 41, 96, 110, 124, 125, 149, 251; wars of, 34, 35, 36, 37, 41, 44, 45, 46, 54, 55, 68
Prussian Diet, 107, 110, 112, 113, 115, 116, 136, 140, 248, 252
Puchta, Georg Friedrich, 55, 77

Rabbiner-Verband, 65, 156, 157n, 158n, 165
Race theories, 46, 55, 64-65, 77, 92, 178, 226, 234, 240, 246, 249, 251, 253, 262, 266-267, 282, 283-287, 302, 304, 323, 324; Aryan race, 178, 249, 266-267, 268, 271, 272, 275, 282n, 284, 285, 287, 288-289; Christian-Aryan, 259, 260, 269-270, 279; race and nationality, 284-285, 288; see also Anti-Semitism and Blood
Rade, Martin, 160, 163
Radenhausen, Christian, 235, 248, 251, 259, 270, 302
Radowsky, Hundt von, 260
Rahmer, Moritz, 107n
Rationalism, 17, 18, 48, 68, 75, 80n, 83, 100, 121-122, 124, 146, 147, 160, 177, 178, 180, 182, 183, 237, 273, 297
Ratzel, Friedrich, 282
Ratzinger, Georg, 92, 94
Rauchhaupt, Landrath von, 231
Rebbert, Joseph, 90, 91, 120n, 247n
Reichensperger, August, 104
Reichensperger, Peter, 104, 107
Reichert, Dr., 49, 50
Reichstag, 104, 125, 126, 128, 130, 132n, 134, 240, 246, 248, 299, 300, 301
Reinach, Solomon, 282, 284
Reinach, Theodor, 213
Religion, 168, 172, 256, 272, 303-304
Religious affiliation, compulsory, 39, 40, 115

Rembrandt movement, 276-279, 281, 302

Renan, Ernst, 200, 270n, 280, 282, 284, 286

Richter, Eugen, 57, 83

Rickert, Heinrich, 128, 137, 183

Riehl, Wilhelm H., 143n

Ringer, Fritz K., 291n

Rischle, Max, 161

Ritschl, Albrecht, 160, 168-169, 170, 181, 183n, 184

Rohling, August, 89, 91, 120n, 212-213, 238, 239n, 242, 243, 247n, 268n

Romanticism, 76-77, 105, 118, 128, 143, 245, 296

Röpe, D. Heinrich, 173n

Rosen, Zvi, 228n

Rosenberg, Alfred, 281, 302

Rosenberg, Hans, 120n

Rössler, Konstantin, 36, 42, 67

Rost, Hans, 120n

Rotenstreich, Nathan, 85n, 179n, 181n, 182n, 184n, 186n, 187n, 219n, 228n

Roth, Josef, 89n, 94n

Rothe, Richard (pseud. George Taylor), 100, 160, 161, 162, 163, 167, 168

Saller, K., 281n

Salvation (Heilsgeschichte), 86, 89, 159, 181, 194, 196, 225, 231, 253, 257, 293, 304

Salvador, Joseph, 206

Savigny, Friedrich Carl von, 55, 77, 105

Schelling, Friedrich Wilhelm Joseph von, 76, 137, 303

Schenkel, Daniel, 161, 200

Schleiermacher, Friedrich, 160, 168

Schmeitzner, Ernst, 148, 249

Schmidt, Erich, 37

Schmidt, Julian, 67, 73

Schmidt, Martin, 162n, 167n, 183n, 201n

Schmidt-Clausing, Fritz, 87n, 88n, 92n, 93n, 101n

Schmidt-Volkmar, Erich, 82n, 83n, 84n, 102n, 104n, 106n

Schmoller, Gustav, 64

Schoeck, Helmut, 182

Scholem, Gershom G., 18

Schönstedt, Minister of Justice, 138, 140, 141, 142, 315

Schopenhauer, Arthur, 69, 178, 188, 243

Schorsch, Ismar, 291n

Schreiner, Martin, 166, 184, 195n, 205, 206n, 209, 213, 214n, 216

Schröder, Domvikar, 90n, 238, 239n

Schulchan Aruch, 91, 199, 247n, 312, 314

Schulenburg-Beetzendorff, Graf von, 234n

Schulte, Friedrich, 81n

Schürer, Emil, 192, 194, 195n

Schwalbe, Prof., 177n

Schwaner, Wilhelm, 273, 275, 323, 324

Secularism, Secularization, 85, 86, 97n, 100, 107, 108, 223, 291, 302

Seeburg, R., 251n, 253n

Self-determination, 32, 34, 35, 37-38, 73, 118, 180

Sell, Friedrich C., 36n, 58, 67n, 72n, 81, 106n

Semites, 270n, 284, 285, 286, 287

Sieburg, Friedrich, 260n

Siegfried, N., 81n

Siemens, Georg von, 36

Simon, Akiba Ernst, 205n, 206n

Simon, W. H., 133n

Smend, R., 192, 194-195

Smith, Robertson, 285, 287n

Snoek, Johan M., 302n

Social Christian party, see Christlich-Sozial

Social Democrats, 57, 128, 130, 132, 224n, 254, 256, 260, 300, 301

Social Reform movement, 134n, 243, 244, 245, 246, 247, 300, 301

Sohn, Rudolf, 174-175

Sombart, Werner, 65, 283

Sommer, Hugo, 48, 67, 70n, 72n, 73

Stade, Bernhard, 166, 215, 285

Stahl, Friedrich Julius, 121, 145, 146n, 147n

Status (of Jews), 38, 39, 78, 79, 82, 98n, 110-120, 127, 159, 180, 223, 224, 290, 294

Stein, Karl Freiherr vom, 244

Steinheim, Ludwig, 206

Steinschneider, Moritz, 20-21, 213

Steinthal, Heymann, 75, 76, 98, 99, 100-101, 108n, 170n, 182, 190, 198n, 209

Stephan, Horst, 162n, 167n, 183n, 201n

Sterling, Eleonore, 25, 120n, 143n, 223n, 228n

Stern, Fritz, 31n, 47n, 81, 82n, 163n, 272n, 276n

Steuernagel, C., 285

Sticr, Joseph, 212

Stille, G., 53n
Stirner, Max, 303
Stöcker, Adolf, 49, 52, 74, 123, 126, 136, 144n, 203n, 227n, 231, 232, 237, 248-259, 263, 264, 299
Stöhr, Martin, 225n
Stolz, Alban, 91
Stoodt, Dieter, 174n
Strack, Hermann, 206n, 210, 322
Strauss, David Friedrich, 36, 37, 201, 203
Streckfuss, Karl, 145
Suchsland, A., 141, 315
Sybel, Heinrich von, 34, 38, 41, 66, 67, 84, 113n

Tal, Uriel, 31n, 142n, 150n, 166n, 302n
Talmon, Jacob, 77n, 223n
Talmud, 62, 75n, 91, 92, 200, 215, 247n, 312
Taurelius, Nicholas, 150
Teichmann, M., 164n
Tertullian, 93, 210
Thadden, von, 145
Thieme, Karl, 25, 33n, 44, 227n
Thiersch, Heinrich Wilhelm, 121, 154-155
Thron und Altar, 245, 255
Thüngen-Rossbach, Karl von, 248n
Tirrel, S. R., 129n
Tivoli Convention, 134, 135, 137
Todt, Rudolf, 123, 255, 256
Toleration, principle of, 99, 100, 101, 110
Toury, Jacob, 39n, 80n, 87n, 96n
Treitschke, Heinrich von, 36, 38, 50, 54n, 55, 56, 60, 65, 66, 67, 74, 77, 104, 105, 106n, 107, 231, 244, 247n, 270n
Troeltsch, Ernst, 161, 170, 172n, 175, 176n, 183, 184n, 188, 190, 221
Troki, Isaac ben Abraham, 208
Twesten, Karl, 34

Uhlhorn, Gerhardt, 196n
Ultramontanists, see Catholics
Uniqueness (of Jews), 50, 58, 60, 64n, 78-79, 108-109, 166, 186, 268
Unity of the spirit, 32, 66-67, 78

Verband der jüdischen Lehrervereine im Deutschen Reiche, 65, 138n, 165n, 169n, 170, 190n, 208, 219, 230

Verein zur Abwehr des Antisemitismus, 49, 89n, 128, 137, 138, 144n, 153n, 263n, 266, 317
Verjudung, 246
Viereck, Peter, 280n, 281n
Villmar, August, 121
Virchow, Rudolf, 43, 82, 83, 85, 86n, 107, 108n, 282, 284
Vischer, Friedrich Theodor, 47
Vogelstein, Hermann, 53n
Vogt, Karl, 69
Volk, concept of, 54-55, 88, 130, 261, 275; Urvolk, 55, 77; Volkgeist, 54, 55, 105, 182
Völkerpsychologie, 98, 99n, 122, 182, 188, 190
Voltaire, 262, 263, 303

Wachler-Weimar, Ernst, 230
Wackerbarth, von, Deputy, 137n
Wagner, Adolph, 144, 249, 250, 251, 256, 259n
Wagner, Richard, 47, 236, 280
Wahrmund, Adolf, 47, 213, 251, 259, 268, 269, 270, 302
Walcker, Karl, 137
Walther, Christian, 167n, 169
Warburg, Moritz, 113n, 117
Warneck, F. S., 85n
Wawrzinek, Kurt, 240n, 261
Weber, Albrecht, 64
Weber, Beda, 92n
Weber, Ferdinand, 192
Weber, Max, 122n, 128, 188
Wehrpfennig, Wilhelm, 36
Weichelt, Hans, 161n
Weiss, Albert Maria, 92, 120n
Weizsäcker, K. J., 201
Wellhausen, Julius, 180n, 192, 194, 195n, 197, 199, 200n, 204n, 214, 280, 285, 286, 287n
Werkstätter, A., 269n
Werner, Mose C., 156n, 157n
Westphalen, L., Graf von, 237n, 252n, 253n, 258n, 261n
Weymar, Ernst, 68
Wichern, Heinrich, 123, 255
Wiese, L., 123, 150n, 151n
Wilhelm I, 19, 113, 128, 149n
Wilhelm II, 82n, 281

Wilmanns, C., 242, 245n
Windelband, Wilhelm, 183
Windhorst, Ludwig, 83n, 85, 104, 106, 107,
    108n, 136, 239, 240n
Winter, Julius, 44
Winterfeldt, Edmund, 246
Witte, Carl, 255
Wobbermin, Georg, 196
Wolff, Christian, 68, 70
Wollmann, Dr., 97
Wrede, William, 201
Wrzecionko, Paul, 169n

Wundt, Wilhelm, 182, 188
Wünsche, K. A., 180

Young Hegelians, 228n, 303

Zahn, Theodor, 174
Zedlitz, Frieherr von, 159
Zeller, Eduard, 37, 67, 68, 69n, 71, 184
Zimmermann, Oswald, 134, 270
Zionism, political, 156, 157, 158, 159, 163,
    164n, 220, 291n, 293
Zorn, Philip, 84n

CHRISTIANS AND JEWS
IN GERMANY

Designed by R. E. Rosenbaum.
Composed by Vail-Ballou Press, Inc.,
in 10 point linofilm Times Roman, 2 points leaded,
with display lines in Melior.
Printed offset by Vail-Ballou Press
on Warren's Number 66 text, 50 pound basis,
with the Cornell University Press watermark.
Bound by Vail-Ballou Press
in Columbia book cloth
and stamped in All Purpose foil.